The Sociology of Deviance

AN INTRODUCTION

Jack D. Douglas
University of California
San Diego

Frances Chaput Waksler
Wheelock College

LITTLE, BROWN AND COMPANY
Boston   Toronto

Library of Congress Catalog Card No. 80-85440

ISBN 0-316-191116

9 8 7 6 5 4 3 2 1

ALP
Published simultaneously in Canada
by Little, Brown & Company (Canada) Limited

Printed in the United States of America

ACKNOWLEDGMENTS

Page 2: From the film *Hara-kiri (Seppuku)*, Toho Motion Picture Co., Ltd. The Museum of Modern Art/Film Stills Archives. *Page 26:* Photograph by Tony Korody/Sigma. *Page 60:* Photograph by Marjorie Chaset. *Page 92:* © Photograph by Stewart Woodward Skitz-o-graphic Assoc., 1980. *Page 124:* © 1981 Samantha Curtis (a posed photograph). *Page 160:* Photograph by Marjorie Chaset. *Page 196:* Photograph by Marjorie Chaset. *Page 228:* © 1980 Samantha Curtis; also by permission of *Equal Times. Page 264:* Stock, Boston photograph by Jack Prelutsky. *Page 298:* Photograph by Marjorie Chaset; tools provided by Commonwealth Lock Co. *Page 330:* Stock, Boston Inc. photograph © Donald Dietz. *Page 362:* Photograph by Marjorie Chaset. *Page 368:* United Press International photograph.

Preface

Immorality, evil, sin, crime — indeed all the things that sociologists call deviance — hold a special fascination. Crime in the streets, crime in business suites, illicit sex, drugs, political corruption — such topics fill our movie and television screens, newspapers, magazines, paperbacks, and even our everyday conversations. Their allure is partly that of evil, of things both tempting and forbidden, and partly that of the unusual and different, things that pique our curiosity.

Deviance, however, is also a practical matter in our everyday lives, for we are repeatedly called upon to understand and deal with it. We encounter rule-breaking in many ways every day: making new rules and unmaking old ones; interpreting rules; using them to get what we want and stop what we don't want; breaking them; hiding our violations and undoing the messes they have brought about; wrestling with the guilt of violating rules we believe in; overcoming the crises of getting caught; trying to understand why others violate rules; responding to rule-breakers in ways that range from condemnation to forgiveness. Although the sociological study of deviance includes more than rule-breaking, we must study rules if we are to understand deviance. When we consider both laws and the less formal everyday prescriptions covering such behavior as honesty and truth in interpersonal relations, we see how extensive and complex rules are.

The authors of this book, like others, are fascinated with deviance. Even if we were not sociologists, we would be highly motivated to understand it. Because our students share this motivation, we have found deviance fascinating and rewarding to teach. Our aims as sociologists have further enhanced our interest, for sociological understanding requires knowledge of rules — how they are made, interpreted, used, and broken. All societies and social groups make use of rules; indeed they are essential to social order and social existence. In studying deviance, we gain insight into rule-making and rules in general. Deviance reveals what is taken for granted when all is running smoothly.

The sociology of deviance is one of the most creative fields of sociological study today and a major source of a new perspective on the social world. In this book we demonstrate just what this new perspective is, how it is related to earlier perspectives, why it has been developed, and the contribution it can make to understanding human beings and the social worlds in which they live.

In Part I we consider a broad range of sociological theories that have been developed to explain deviance. Instead of abstract and arid chronological exposition, we present concrete instances of deviance and move from them to more general ideas. From two opening examples of suicide, for example, we turn to general ideas about suicide as deviance. Continual movement between concrete realities and general ideas enhances both understanding and interest, using the fascination that deviance arouses as motivation for grappling with its complex issues.

In Part II we draw on the general sociological theory of deviance developed in Part I to understand the many forms in which deviance can appear. Many kinds of activities can in some way be defined as deviant. Readers may find their passions rising as they encounter activities that they feel are obviously deviant and others they think ought not to be called deviant at all. We hope that as readers examine the many issues we raise, they will become actively engaged in trying to understand the social world for themselves.

In writing this book we have received generous assistance from a number of people. Douglas would like particularly to thank Levi Kamel and Beverly Douglas for extensive bibliographic and library work. Kamel also prepared the material for the test bank. Jacque Lynn Foltyn, University of California at San Diego, gathered the data for Chapter 12, wrote drafts of that material, and collaborated with the authors in the development of theories and ideas. John Johnson, H. C. Greisman, and Kenneth Levi provided thoughtful and useful commentary on early drafts of the manuscript. Waksler would like particularly to thank Norman H. Waksler for his careful reading of many chapters and his insightful, if painful, suggestions about both content and style. Nora Lerdau read a number of chapters and contributed to the refinement of some of our ideas; she also prepared the index. Others who read various chapters and provided useful commentary and information include Janet Cooney, Jill Flynn, Evan Greenland, David Halprin, Esq., Ann Herrick, Julia Moore, Kathleen Thompson, Dr. Joan Timm, Pam Wilk, and Mary Wilkes. Jean Finn, Wheelock College reference librarian, gave help at crucial moments.

We would both like to thank Professor Robert Scott, Princeton University, who carefully read the manuscript in a variety of stages and provided criticisms that we found both just and readily assimilable. Charles Frazier, University of Florida, supplied useful commentary and enthusiastic support. Little, Brown and Company gave us generous assistance. The scrupulous copyediting of Robert L. Lentz and the detailed attention and care of David W. Lynch are greatly appreciated. Sheryl Gipstein and Viki Merrick, editorial assistants, kept track of day-to-day details unflaggingly and admirably. We want to extend our special gratitude to Katherine Carlone, sociology editor, for her help, kindness, patience, strength, and indomitability. Finally, we want to thank all the "deviants" who revealed their lives to us.

We are deeply appreciative of the assistance provided by the many people who helped to make this book possible and hope it displays to them the strengths of their contributions.

Contents

The Sociology of Deviance

EXPLAINING DEVIANCE

One of the tragedies of life is the murder of a beautiful theory by a brutal gang of facts.
— La Rochefoucauld

Our goal in this book is to develop an understanding of *the nature of deviance*. In Part I we will look at some of the major issues that arise in studying deviance and the varied theories that have been offered to explain it.

Our emphasis, explicitly in Part I and implicitly in Part II, is on the work that *sociologists* have done to make sense out of deviance: what it is, where it comes from, and what factors affect it. We view deviance *as an element in the social world.* As we discuss the nature of deviance, we will devote attention to the practice of sociology itself and the ways in which sociologists, historically and currently, have sought to understand deviance. We will consider both theories of deviance and the ways in which those theories have been developed. We will also draw upon knowledge from other social sciences wherever it can contribute to our understanding. Finally, we include discussions of common-sense perspectives on deviance in order to compare and contrast them with the findings of sociology.

In Chapter 1 we will look at some problems that arise in thinking about deviance — problems for people in general and problems specific to sociologists. In Chapters 2, 3, and 4 we will explore some social science theories, focusing on what they contribute to our understanding and how they have resolved or failed to resolve the problems presented in Chapter 1. In Chapter 5 we will look in detail at a new sociological perspective on deviance, which we will draw upon in analyzing the topics in Part II.

1

Major Issues in the Sociology of Deviance

The word *deviance* means different things to different people. It may be thought to refer to something bad or wrong, or strange, or illegal, or unusual, and may bring up many kinds of images and responses. We begin this chapter with two examples of suicide and then look at some of the issues that might arise in calling suicide *a deviant act*. Is suicide deviant?

Case Study 1: Karen Kenyon

On the second of November my husband did not come home from work. He was not one for dramatics, not an unpredictable or violent man. He seemed to be a good-humored, sensitive, intelligent and utterly reliable person, until that night.

Dick, the man I had lived with, loved and been married to for sixteen years, the father of our 12-year-old son, had chosen to end his life. He told no one of his decision but left behind two suicide notes which we discovered by 10 that night. Though the campus police at the university where he worked looked for him, they found him too late. Dick had jumped from an eleven-story building. It was not the act of a madman, but the act of someone scrunched in, crumpled, thwarted by his job, and by life. It was the act of a man who just didn't fight back, who just didn't, couldn't talk about what troubled him.

Dick's suicide casts a horrible shadow on those who knew and loved him. The shock and sorrow were, and are, insurmountable. We had, it seemed, a good life, a normal life. To me the idea of suicide was remote, abstract and frightening.

The questions: The question that incessantly arises is *why?* Could we, could I, have prevented it from happening? Those questions go on and on, but there is another question: how do we the survivors go on? How do we live beyond that death which looms so large in our lives?

Last week, I received news that a writer friend, a very successful, intelligent woman, the mother of four, had also taken her life. She took an overdose of pills. I knew she had been seeing a psychiatrist for a year, but she appeared to be progressing. Her condolence note to me still sat propped on the shelf by the phone, offering its strength and caring, the day her husband called to give me his tragic news.

I ask again — for me, for my son, for my friend's family and for the family of man — how do we survive and go on? How do we assimilate this dark legacy into our lives?

I have searched for an answer since that long night when I waited, praying they would find Dick safe. While they looked for him I felt a horrible panic, an unbearable fear that ate at me. All night I sat by the phone in the living room with my neighbor. In the morning, as I was calling the missing persons bureau, three of Dick's co-workers came to the door. I looked at their faces and all I said was, "I don't have to call missing persons, do I?"

I sat down numbly on the couch and held my own two hands together. Our child, Richard, came home from school in a little while. He was too worried to stay there, and had been given permission to come home. "Richard," I said, as we sat down together, "the thing we feared the most has happened. Dad is gone." Richard asked, "Did he do it to himself?" When I nodded, his eyes quickly looked down. I put my arms around him and held him.

For me the days that followed were full of pain. The questions pounded at me. Why? Why? But shock numbs; somehow I could cope with memorial-service plans. Like a robot, I did what I had to do. People came and went, and I sat for hours without moving much. I remember not taking my clothes off for two days. I didn't want to move or change anything. Talking was an effort. Eating was an effort.

At the end of a week, after the service was over and the relatives had left, the real loneliness set in, and the guilt. Each night I dreamed that I was soothing Dick, telling him how much I loved him and still love him, feeling in my dreams that if only he knew, then he would be back and safe.

I, who could always write my feelings, couldn't find words. It was an effort to think. An entry in my journal written Nov. 6, in very small handwriting, simply says:

"I can barely write it. Dick is no longer here. He has died. He is gone. He took his own life. Half my life is gone."

On the 15th of November, I wrote, as a tribute to him, and out of my desire to think that spiritually I could save him:

You fell
  into the air

Sailed for a moment,
a raven-haired bird.
I caught you
in my heart.

On the plane as we came home from a Christmas trip to visit Dick's family, Richard said, "I feel like I really miss somebody and I don't even know who." I said, "Don't you think it's Dad?" and the only tears I saw him cry came then. We talk often and he tells me that now he mostly feels mad. "When I start to feel angry or sad," he says, "I try to concentrate really hard on whatever I happen to be doing at the time, like playing ball or riding my bike."

I've found it difficult to be that sensible, to avoid guilt and constant questioning. The notes Dick left said it was his job, that I had nothing to do with what he did. Still, why couldn't I have seen what was happening? Why couldn't I have saved him? He had been the best friend I ever had. I must not have been a good enough friend to him. I wanted to piece it together; I relived every conversation. But there were no answers, and it didn't fit together.

I visited the spot where it happened. I felt that I needed to go that far with him. I had also sent for the autopsy report, but when it came, I sent it to my doctor. I realized I could not bear to read it. I knew I could only go so far into this journey of death, if I wanted to live. And I decided I *do* want to live. I want Richard to live too, and I want Dick's death *not* to be bigger than his life. Most of all I don't want his death to be worthless or in vain. If he felt his life was meaningless, I will give his death meaning. I will learn from it, grow from it, use it to nourish my life and my son's.

The choices: There are no good answers to the question of why someone takes his or her own life. All we can do is to pose for ourselves the question of our own being or nonbeing. The question of existence every day is a real one. Life need not just happen to us. We can choose. We are choosing every moment which direction to turn — toward the light, or toward the dark.

To write about coping with the fact of suicide is to me a turning toward the light. Our feelings about it are usually hidden. They are too dark, too painful to explore. We fear we will be submerged in that darkness. Something in me wants to say, "No, I will not be pulled down."

We as human beings are capable of dark choices, but we are also continually and everlastingly capable of choices in favor of life and light.*

Case Study 2: Taki Zenzaburo

Mitford, in his *Tales of Old Japan*, describes a Japanese suicide ceremony (*seppuku*, popularly known by Westerners as *hara kiri*) at which he was an eyewitness, along with thirteen other observers and three officials. The ceremony was performed in the main hall of a temple.

* From *Newsweek*, April 30, 1979. Copyright © 1979, by Newsweek, Inc. All rights reserved. Reprinted by permission. This example was brought to our attention by Mary Wilkes.

After the interval of a few minutes of anxious suspense, Taki Zenzaburo, a stalwart man thirty-two years of age, with a noble air, walked into the hall attired in his dress of ceremony. . . .

He was accompanied by a student of his, a skilled swordsman, whose role was that of *kaishaku*. (English has no equivalent for the word or the role *kaishaku*, but its meaning becomes apparent in the following description.)

With the *kaishaku* on his left hand, Taki Zenzaburo advanced slowly toward the Japanese witnesses, and the two bowed before them, then drawing near to the foreigners they saluted us in the same way, perhaps even with more deference; in each case the salutation was ceremoniously returned. Slowly and with great dignity the condemned man mounted on to the raised floor, prostrated himself before the high altar twice, and seated himself on the felt carpet with his back to the high altar, the *kaishaku* crouching on his left-hand side. One of the three attendant officers then came forward, bearing a stand of the kind used in the temple for offerings, on which, wrapped in paper, lay the *wakizashi*, the short sword or dirk of the Japanese, nine inches and a half in length, with a point and an edge as sharp as a razor's. This he handed, prostrating himself, to the condemned man, who received it reverently, raising it to his head with both hands, and placed it in front of himself.

After another profound obeisance, Taki Zenzaburo, in a voice which betrayed just so much emotion and hesitation as might be expected from a man who is making a painful confession, but with no sign of either in his face or manner, spoke as follows: —

"I, and I alone, unwarrantably gave the order to fire on the foreigners at Kobe, and again as they tried to escape. For this crime I disembowel myself, and I beg you who are present to do me the honour of witnessing the act."

Bowing once more, the speaker allowed his upper garments to slip down to his girdle, and remained naked to the waist. Carefully, according to custom, he tucked his sleeves under his knees to prevent himself from falling backward; for a noble Japanese gentleman should die falling forwards. Deliberately, with a steady hand, he took the dirk that lay before him; he looked at it wistfully, almost affectionately; for a moment he seemed to collect his thoughts for the last time, and then stabbing himself deeply below the waist in the left-hand side, he drew the dirk slowly across to his right side, and turning it in the wound, gave a slight cut upwards. During this sickeningly painful operation he never moved a muscle of his face. When he drew out the dirk, he leaned forward and stretched out his neck; an expression of pain for the first time crossed his face, but he uttered no sound. At that moment the *kaishaku*, who, still crouching by his side, had been keenly watching his every movement, sprang to his feet, poised his sword for a second in the air; there was a flash, a heavy, ugly thud, a crashing fall; with one blow the head had been severed from the body.

A dead silence followed. . . .

The two representatives of the Mikado then left their places, and crossing over to where the foreign witnesses sat, called to us to witness that the sentence of death upon Taki Zenzaburo had been faithfully carried out. The ceremony being at an end, we left the temple (Nitobe, 1969, pp. 117–120).*

Discussion

For Karen Kenyon and her child, Dick Kenyon's suicide was *problematic*, by which we mean that it was puzzling, ambiguous, confusing, and open to repeated questioning. No explanation appeared sufficient to account for it. Karen and her child seemed to agree that Dick's suicide was not a normal, expected act; we as sociologists might argue that it was deviant for the very reason that it *deviated* from what was expected. But what precisely *was* expected? What rule had been broken? Who was the actual rule-breaker — Dick in committing suicide or Karen in somehow "failing" him? What *caused* the deviance? Was it actually Dick's job or was Karen herself somehow responsible? Did Dick himself view his act as deviant or as merely necessary? We can see that Karen and her child were struggling to determine simultaneously the social rules governing suicide and which of those rules had come to supersede those of everyday life.

For Taki Zenzaburo and those who observed his suicide, his act was in no way problematic. He offered a reason for his suicide that made sense to him and to his associates. Only Western readers find his suicide problematic. We want to ask: How could he do it? Why would he do it? Why wouldn't someone stop him? The Japanese example suggests that Taki Zenzaburo's suicide was not deviant in the context in which it took place; social rules prescribed when and how it ought to be done and he followed those rules.

These two case studies illustrate a basic idea in the sociological study of deviance: *knowledge of the social context in which deviance takes place is crucial to understanding that deviance.* In both of these cases, those involved compared the suicide they confronted with the social context in which it took place and the social rules known to the participants. They sought explanations based on the common-sense knowledge available to them as members of society. They used their social knowledge to judge the act deviant or nondeviant. For Karen Kenyon, understanding was problematic and difficult. In her social context her husband's suicide was considered deviant because it did not follow the rules of acceptable and expected behavior. In the context of Japanese society, on the other hand, Taki Zenzaburo's suicide was nondeviant because it

---

* Quotations from *Tales of Old Japan*, by A. B. Mitford, and *Bushido: The Soul of Japan*, by Inazo Nitobe, both reprinted by permission of the publisher, Charles E. Tuttle Co., Inc. of Tokyo, Japan.

followed the rules and occurred in a manner and for reasons that were understandable and morally acceptable to members of that society.

These two cases provide us with data to use in developing a general understanding of what deviance is, the different forms in which it appears, and how it can be studied. The issues raised for participants in the two instances have many similarities with the interests of sociologists studying deviance. Sociologists want to discover the social rules that guide behavior, the ways in which these rules develop and change, the ways in which they differ, and the ways in which they are used in everyday life. Sociologists are particularly interested in cases where rules are broken, and they ask: by whom? how? when? under what circumstances? for what reasons? They are also concerned with the social effects of deviance on individuals and on the social structure as a whole. How are rules created? by whom? why? with what results? They want to know, too, how deviance and social order are related.

Although everyday concerns about deviance and sociological interests do indeed overlap, some major differences separate the two points of view. These differences will become clear in this chapter.

Defining Deviance

The sociology of deviance is the scientific study of social deviance — of why deviance occurs in society, how it occurs, and what its social effects are. The obvious question to ask now is: What *is* deviance? Unfortunately, we have no simple answer.

The term *deviance* is now widely used in sociology. In the past, however, many other words were used to describe the behavior we now call deviance. Analysts used such terms as *social pathology, social disorganization, personal disorganization,* and *social disintegration.* Often analysts focused on acts which were publicly identified as illegal and immoral. The term deviance has now almost entirely replaced these others. Do, however, become familiar with them because they frequently occur in our presentation of early studies in the sociology of deviance.

Deviance is a difficult idea to define. To cope with the difficulty, sociologists may paint an impressionistic picture of the spectrum of things that might be considered deviant in everyday life. Albert Cohen constructs a dazzling image of the kaleidoscopic reality of deviance in United States society today. He describes the subject of his book on deviance as "knavery, skullduggery, cheating, unfairness, crime, sneakiness, malingering, cutting corners, immorality, dishonesty, betrayal, graft, corruption, wickedness, and sin — in short, deviance" (Cohen, 1955: 1).

It is common to find scientists encountering severe problems in specifically defining their basic subject matter. We have no simple definition of "deviance" any more than biologists have a simple answer to the question "What is life?" Biologists may fall back on rough approximations, such as "Life is all self-reproducing things." In the same way, sociologists rely on a rough approximation: "Deviance is all those actions considered immoral or bad in a society." Neither approximation is entirely satisfactory. Many things in the world, from simple processes in organic chemistry to complex automatic machines, can be self-reproducing without being organisms that we would describe as alive. Similarly, sociologists have found that some things they want to include in the term deviance are not exactly "evil" or "immoral." They may, for example, want to include stigmas such as physical handicaps (see Goffman, 1963B, especially his final chapter on "Deviations and Deviance"), even though today stigmas are not commonly considered immoral and their sufferers are deemed unfortunate, not evil. Biologists have found that their rough definitions sometimes include topics they want to exclude. Sociologists have encountered the same problem and have also found that their definitions may exclude material they want to include. Against this background, it seems advisable to leave partially open a definition of what we are studying. Giving an absolute definition from the beginning could unintentionally rule out the most important elements in what we are studying or, conversely, force us to deal with unimportant or irrelevant ones.

Nevertheless, we do need some partial and intuitively sound definition to guide us to phenomena* that seem reasonable to consider in our studies of deviance. Social scientists have created a huge literature defining what is meant by deviance. Excellent and extensive treatments of these many definitions can be found, for example, in Becker (1973) and in Sagarin (1975, especially pp. 1–66). The subject of a definition for deviance is itself so broad and so complex, involving as it does all the basic questions of the theory of deviance, that it would only be confusing to provide details now. Major aspects of the question will arise throughout our work on deviance, as they did in the two examples with which this chapter began. For now we shall make use of an open-ended definition that is helpful in showing what we are studying in the real social world and is quite inclusive in comparison with others. In this way we will not impose an arbitrary theoretical position on the way we

---

* We use *phenomenon* (plural, *phenomena*) to refer to "a fact or event of scientific interest susceptible of scientific description and explanation." Definition by permission from *Webster's New Collegiate Dictionary* © 1980 by G. & C. Merriam Co., publishers of the Merriam-Webster Dictionaries.

study deviance. Our open-ended definition is an *ostensive definition;* it *points* to the types of phenomena we want to study but imposes a minimum of preconceptions upon our observations of the social world. We are thus able to get on with the study of deviance without unduly biasing our eventual findings. We have a place to begin and an idea that can be modified and revised as we learn more.

Our ostensive definition, then, describes *deviance* as *any thought, feeling, or action that members of a social group judge to be a violation of their values or rules.* By leaving the definition open in this way, we avoid excluding phenomena that might prove important. At the same time, we give up some precision. Because the scientific study of deviance is still young, many basic questions remain to be answered. It seems better, then, to err on the side of overinclusiveness than on that of false precision. Rather than begin with a precise statement and then look for proof in the real world, we start with a broad, abstract statement that directs us to the real world, where we will find *empirical* answers to our questions — answers based on observation and experience.

To understand why we have selected our definition of deviance, it helps to imagine a funnel filled with all possible definitions of deviance, as in Figure 1.1. Level I allows for an extremely broad definition, which would label deviant anything that anyone found odd. Clearly, if sociologists defined deviance at this level, they would have to study so many kinds of things that it would be impossible to identify common factors or isolate basic variables of the social world for use in scientific theories.

Level X, the least inclusive in the funnel, is the realm of ultimate "Evil," of the doings of *The Powers of Evil* (Cavendish, 1975). All societies have such ideas and feelings, whether they focus on witches, the Mafia, Satan, or the personified evil in the film *The Exorcist.* People consider such evil to be extremely important, but occurrences are rare; most people never encounter such evil except in imagination or in talk. Many studies, of course, have been done of such phenomena, more often by historians and theologians than by sociologists. Sociologists find it very hard to study such evil scientifically because of its rarity: How can we find enough instances to observe? Moreover, if we define deviance so exclusively, we leave out almost everything of day-to-day importance in the lives of ordinary people.

Level IX has been studied by some social scientists as well as by philosophers and religious thinkers. Because this level focuses on whatever is common to all human beings, it does not allow us to call anything deviant that is not universal. Earlier sociologists attempted to look at deviance in this way, but they encountered serious problems, which we will detail in Chapter 2. Level IX would limit too narrowly the subjects we could treat as deviant.

Figure 1.1
The funnel of possible definitions of deviance

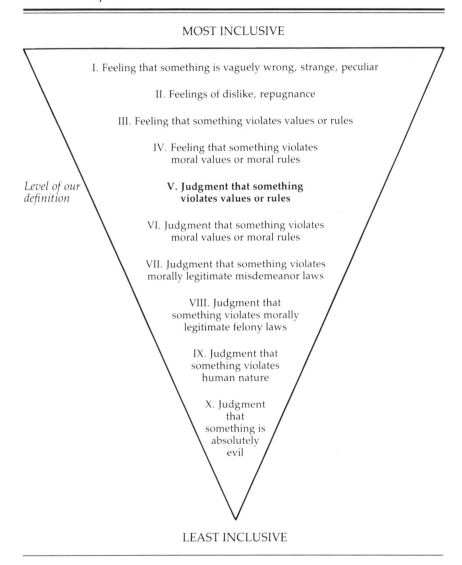

MOST INCLUSIVE

I. Feeling that something is vaguely wrong, strange, peculiar

II. Feelings of dislike, repugnance

III. Feeling that something violates values or rules

IV. Feeling that something violates moral values or moral rules

Level of our definition

V. Judgment that something violates values or rules

VI. Judgment that something violates moral values or moral rules

VII. Judgment that something violates morally legitimate misdemeanor laws

VIII. Judgment that something violates morally legitimate felony laws

IX. Judgment that something violates human nature

X. Judgment that something is absolutely evil

LEAST INCLUSIVE

Levels VII and VIII have been used by criminologists in their studies of deviance, and we will draw on their findings in later chapters. Criminologists, however, limit themselves mainly to legal issues and seldom deal with forms of deviance that have not been formalized into law. We need a more inclusive definition that will allow us to look at a broader variety of behaviors. Level VI more closely approaches that breadth, but its restriction to morality excludes behaviors that might be forbidden for more practical reasons. We might, for instance, want to view celibacy as deviant though not morally wrong.

Thus we arrive at Level V, the definition we have chosen for deviance. This level includes those acts which are judged to violate certain values or rules, without specifying *whose* values or rules they are or whether such values are right or wrong. We have chosen to be inclusive in a modest way. We have determined that Levels I through IV, focusing as they do on feelings, are perhaps best treated through psychological analysis. Although we will certainly consider such data, our focus will be at a level more suitable to sociological analysis. Level V includes material open to sociological study and is sufficiently broad to permit a great variety of comparative data.

Our decision to define deviance at Level V raises some problems in studying and explaining deviance. We will be looking at many kinds of deviant activities; some will make sense to us through our common-sense knowledge, and others we may find abhorrent. It is likely, for instance, that some of us have more sympathy or understanding for Dick Kenyon's suicide than for that of Taki Zenzaburo. We will also encounter groups whose view of their activities is very different from ours. Further, some of these groups will believe their views are the only right ones and all others are wrong. For sociologists to study deviant activities regardless of whether they sympathize with them, they need to strive toward *value neutrality.* And to study groups who believe their own views to be uniquely valid, sociologists need to develop ways of understanding such *absolutism* without adopting such views.

It is important for us to study *value neutrality* and *absolutism* in some detail, but first we need to look at the distinction between common-sense knowledge and scientific knowledge so that we understand the need for value neutrality and the problems of absolutism.

Common Sense and the Study of Deviance

One of the difficulties in presenting sociological findings about deviance is that readers — sociologists and nonsociologists alike — generally expect to find them very much in line with everyday, common-sense beliefs about "bad" or "wicked" or even "evil" things. And, in fact, until the 1960s the sociology of deviance did *not* present a view very different from that of common sense. The past two decades, however, have seen the sociology of deviance become a complex and theoretical field with findings sometimes quite the opposite of what common sense would predict. In order to show how such a state of affairs is possible, we will have to describe some of the varied relationships between sociological findings and common sense.

Members of society have a vast practical knowledge of the physical world in which they live — knowledge that they need simply to make their way around in the everyday world. For example, people begin to learn about falling objects from the time they take their first steps, and they go on to learn a great deal about falling that even the most complex formulas of modern physics could not express. No physicist, for example, can tell a surfer anything of practical value about keeping balance on a surfboard; any surfer can teach a physicist a vast amount about the sport, though putting such knowledge into words may be difficult. The scientist, however, wants to establish general laws. For the physicist, the point of Newton's discovery of gravity is not that objects fall; physicists have always taken such common-sense knowledge for granted and indeed have built their theories upon it. Newton discovered that gravity is a universal force of attraction between physical bodies that follows specific mathematical relations.

Implicit in scientific research is the view that science adds to or is "better than" common-sense ideas about the world. This view has always been a primary justification for scientific work, but it has also set the stage for conflict between scientists and nonscientists, each questioning the knowledge of the other.

Many earlier scientists attacked common-sense ideas about the physical world, even though they themselves relied upon such ideas in their work. They *assumed*, for example, that they could use their ordinary physical senses to make their measurements of the world. Early social scientists took for granted many general common-sense assumptions of their own age in their research and theories. Nineteenth-century sociological research and theory about deviance and social order were based upon assumptions very similar to those lying behind common-sense ideas expressed in novels, magazines, and public speeches of that time. Much of the recent progress in sociology has consisted of bringing common-sense assumptions to light, critically assessing them, and replacing them where necessary with ideas that better stand the test of scientific evidence.

Most social scientists today find themselves in roughly the same position as natural scientists did a few centuries ago — criticized as impractical, lacking common sense, dreamers, biased, and so on — because they purport to understand everyday experience in ways different from (and superior to) those of people who rely upon common sense. Such people may see the sociological viewpoint as a threat to their own beliefs, expertise, and authority.

Like natural scientists, we have come increasingly to recognize that our sociological understandings of society do ultimately draw on everyday experiences and understandings. Indeed, precisely because the goal of sociology is to understand everyday experiences in society, it is more firmly grounded in common sense than any of the natural sciences (Douglas, 1970B). Earlier sociologists, because they saw themselves as openly in conflict with common-sense theories, rarely recognized their dependence on them, although in fact all earlier sociological theories of deviance were shaped by such assumptions about deviance. These ideas will appear as we study how the sociology of deviance developed.

Any reasonably organized and stable human social activity generally leads to the development of shared ideas, beliefs, values, and feelings that come to be taken for granted by the people involved — so much so that pointing them out may seem absurd. For example, while walking in a park with some other sociologists, Peter Manning pointed to a sign that said: "City ordinance forbids dogs and fires in this park" and remarked, "It's interesting they don't forbid murder, rape, fornication, and nudity in this park." Clearly these acts are forbidden, even though they are not mentioned. Meanings that are taken for granted in this way are called *background meanings* or *background understandings* because they are in the background of our interactions with other people. These understandings are generally not expressed in words; everyone involved implicitly understands them. Indeed, such knowledge is a necessary part of membership; anyone without it will be immediately spotted as a nonmember. Moreover, anyone who questions these understandings may be judged to be doing something wrong or even crazy. Harold Garfinkel (1967), for example, had his students raise questions at home about background meanings, such as asking parents if it would be all right to get a glass of milk from the refrigerator. Asking such questions about simple, seemingly unimportant matters that had always been taken for granted was often met with suspiciousness and questioning of the appropriateness of such a request.

In addition to these background meanings, people have a vast number of more explicit common-sense ideas about everyday experience. When these ideas express a belief about systematic relations between some parts of that social experience, we will call them *common-sense social theories;* others have called them *folk theories* or *ethnotheories*. We find such common-sense social theories embodied in some of the stereotypes people hold about deviance and crime. One such theory that has had a great effect on public policy for decades is that the use of "soft" drugs such as marijuana generally leads to the use of "hard" drugs. For many years the causal link between soft and hard drug use was simply taken for granted. (We will consider this idea further when we discuss drugs in Chapter 7.) As many sociologists can attest from personal experience, those who challenged this idea were apt to be met with disbelief and suspicion. These common-sense theories are rarely as clearly and systematically developed as the theoretical ideas of social scientists, nor are they as well supported by evidence. And although common-sense and scientific theories about society share some basic and necessary similarities in both form and content, they are separated by some fundamental differences. (For a detailed comparison, see Schutz, 1967A.)

One basic distinction between common-sense and scientific knowledge lies in their goals. Common-sense knowledge is concerned with practical activities and how to carry them out in a predictable and meaningful way. A basic goal of scientific knowledge, on the other hand, is the pursuit of knowledge for its own sake. When scientists strive to "prove" a theory for personal reasons, they are being guided by common sense, not science.

A second distinction between these two types of knowledge is in the kind of evidence each uses to support theories. Common-sense knowledge is built upon what works. Science requires more extensive evidence that is gathered according to explicit rules. In gathering knowledge, scientists will even seek to *disprove* their theories; such behavior on the part of people in general would seem rather foolish. Scientists are thus able to offer convincing systematic evidence for their theories to anyone who accepts the rules of evidence being used. Sociologists are particularly offended when their findings are belittled as "just your opinion," because such a statement equates common sense with scientific knowledge. Scientists may in fact produce findings that contradict their own previously held common-sense opinions.

A third distinction is that scientific theories are by their very nature explicit and formulated in statements, whereas common-sense theories may be taken for granted and (as in the case of surfing mentioned earlier) may not easily be verbalized.

For sociologists, common sense is a *topic* for study, not a source of sociological theories. Because, however, sociologists also live in the world of common sense, they must constantly be aware of their use of it so that in their sociological endeavors they do not present common sense as sociology.

Value Neutrality

It is very important to be aware that in our definition of deviance it is value or rule violations *perceived by members of a social group* that determine what constitutes deviance. Whether or not we ourselves view such acts as deviant is irrelevant to our sociological purpose. But how is it possible for sociologists to study others without letting their own values distort their findings? Can they really eliminate biases of personal involvement, feelings, and values, and thus achieve value neutrality in their studies and analyses of deviance?*

---

* The term *value neutrality* or *ethical neutrality* was developed by the sociologist Max Weber. See *From Max Weber: Essays in Sociology,* 1958.

The values of sociologists are most likely to be introduced into a study as they go about (1) selecting a topic for study, (2) gathering and analyzing data, and (3) providing a broad theoretical explanation for what is going on. We will deal with each of these in turn.

SELECTING A TOPIC

Clearly, the selection of topics for sociological study is influenced by the values and interests of the sociologists involved. Today, sociologists who study deviance are increasingly aware of this bias and are attempting to study a broad range of types of deviance in order to cover the subject completely. Historically, sociologists devoted far more time to studying lower-class forms of deviance than to studying upper-class forms, such as official corruption and multinational corporate offenses. In many ways street deviance is easier to study than board-room deviance. Nonetheless, sociologists are increasingly aware of this bias and are moving to study more types of deviance and to develop methods that will make such study possible. Although the choice of topic to be studied will always be an individual one, sociologists today are consciously trying to minimize bias of this kind. Part II of this book provides evidence of decreasing bias in the selection of topics for study.

GATHERING AND ANALYZING DATA

A great deal of evidence suggests that personal biases have relatively little effect on the actual descriptions provided by sociologists. For example, regardless of how their political values or personal feelings differ, few researchers disagree over the basic facts of police work. Major disagreements do emerge, however, at the level of analysis, where personal factors are more likely to influence interpretation. One major question over which sociologists of deviance disagree is that of how important police and other control agents are in producing the very deviance they are supposed to be stopping. Various personal characteristics of individual sociologists, such as "sympathy for the underdog" or "personal history" or "identification with the repressor," could certainly affect their answers to analytic questions. Sociologists have more problems with this type of bias than do some other types of scientists; a physicist can be relatively impartial when analyzing electrons because such a topic elicits few deep emotions or value commitments.

Today, sociologists of deviance generally strive to eliminate the most intrusive biases in their analyses and to achieve value neutrality by studying different forms of deviance from as many perspectives as possible. In almost every instance deviance is found to involve *conflicts* over what is right and wrong, good and bad, and so on. Sociologists therefore try to study deviance *multiperspectively* — from the different standpoints of those involved. They study deviants from the perspective of the deviants themselves (do they see themselves as deviants or as the only sane people around?); from the standpoint of their relatives; from the standpoint of other groups or individuals involved; and from any other perspective that seems fruitful.

A good example of this multiperspective approach is Jacqueline Wiseman's study of the social world of "skidrow drunks" in *Stations of the Lost* (1970). She studied alcoholics, the police who dealt with them, the judges, the people who ran the institutions to which they were often committed, and many other of the "multiple realities" (see the article "On Multiple Realities" in Schutz, 1967A) involved in this form of "deviance." The groups involved were found to differ in their identification of the behavior — some found it deviant, others did not. Sometimes these conflicting feelings, values, and ideas about deviance are a source of major disagreement, which the participants must negotiate among themselves.

Although the complex feelings, ideas, values, and actions associated with every point of view are necessary to a complete understanding, it is unlikely that any group of researchers, far less a lone researcher, could gather such extensive data. Practical constraints force compromises, but our ideal today is reasonably clear and generally shared: an increasing commitment to value neutrality on the part of researchers. Multiperspective study contributes to such an ideal.

Another way in which sociologists try to achieve value neutrality is by giving detailed accounts of their personal involvement with the group being studied. (See, for example, Hammond, *Sociologists at Work,* 1967.) Some sociologists even advocate taking explicit value positions toward the subjects of study before proceeding with analysis. Their purpose is not to allow personal values to *determine* observations, reporting, or analysis, but to enable readers to evaluate how these values have affected the work and thus to distinguish between researchers' values and subjects' values.

PROVIDING A BROAD THEORETICAL EXPLANATION

Theoretical explanations may be of many types and may cover phenomena that range from the small and carefully specified to the broad and varied. Broad theoretical explanations are called *theoretical perspectives*. A theoretical perspective provides a general way of looking at things, a lens that allows us to see reality in a different way. It consists of a general set of ideas that together provide the foundation for more specific ideas.

Generally scientists become committed to one of the competing perspectives in their field of study. How they arrive at such a commitment is not clear, but we can speculate that the process involves both scientific understanding and common-sense knowledge. In any case, it is not unusual to find scientists remaining committed to their theoretical perspectives even in the face of strong contradictory evidence. Einstein, for example, refused to accept the uncertainty principle* that underlies so much of the modern physics of elementary particles, not because he had a personal bias against uncertainty or its creator, but because he was deeply committed to an earlier and different theoretical perspective on the universe.

Among sociologists, too, commitments to a theory are potentially a source of far greater bias than personal values, feelings, or political commitments. Major disputes among sociologists of deviance spring far more from commitments to general social theories than from personal biases or political involvements. Once a commitment is made to a theoretical perspective, a series of professional ties and alignments are created that are extremely important and difficult to change. Theoretical and professional commitments may be an inevitable source of bias in the structure of science itself and may even be of positive value in the development of science. As Mitroff argues in his study of geologists, *The Subjective Side of Science* (1974), passionate commitment to a theory may be crucial in motivating the work of the greatest scientists.

Later in this chapter and in Chapter 5 we will look at a new theoretical perspective on deviance, and in Chapters 2, 3, and 4 we will consider earlier theoretical perspectives and the explanations they provide. Readers might find it interesting to examine their own responses to all these theories and the ways in which they come to accept some and reject others.

When sociologists of deviance speak of value neutrality, they are not referring primarily to the elimination of bias, passion, and feeling in either the choice of topic or the theoretical perspective espoused, for in those areas passion, commitment, and interest serve positive functions. Sociologists' particular concern is with value neutrality in the gathering and analyzing of data. Their goal is to allow subjects to speak for themselves from their own perspective. Perhaps the easiest test of value neutrality is to ask of the research report: Can we determine from the data alone whether the researcher is "for" or "against" the subjects' point of view? If we cannot — if the subjects appear both good and bad, strong and weak, smart and stupid — then it would seem that the researcher has achieved value neutrality.

Nature and Uses of Absolutism

If we return for a moment to Figure 1.1, we can see that Levels I through IV relate to feelings and Levels V through X involve judgments. When judgments are made in terms of standards, principles, or values that

* The *uncertainty principle* states that knowledge of the physical world can never be complete, that our knowledge will always necessarily contain an irreducible factor of uncertainty.

are without restriction, exception, or qualification, we speak of *absolutism* or of *absolute* judgments. The gun law in effect in some states is an example of an absolute rule: if a person is apprehended in the state with an unlicensed gun, that person is supposed to be automatically sentenced to one year in prison *no matter what the reason was.* In actual practice such absolute laws are never enforced absolutely. Absolutism is more likely to occur at the less inclusive levels of deviance because judgments at those levels involve broad, basic, and important ideas.

For many centuries members of Western societies assumed an absolutist view of morality — what was right and wrong, good and bad, and so on was seen as a basic and necessary part of reality. As such, morality and immorality were thought to be *universal,* the same for everyone in all societies, regardless of personal situations, desires, or choices. Morality and immorality were also seen as obvious and unproblematic, readily determinable by any ordinary human being. Suicide, for example, was considered wrong; against such a background, Dick Kenyon's suicide and that of Taki Zenzaburo would be viewed as equally and unquestionably wrong. This absolutist view of morality has long been tempered in Western societies by various countervailing ideas, but it can still be found undiluted in some members of these societies and has formed the foundation for extremely repressive measures against "immorality."

Absolutist morality is seen in its purest form in the idea of *taboo.* Taboos are absolute prohibitions against specific kinds of actions. Violations of taboos are regarded as totally evil, almost unthinkable. Those who are discovered violating such taboos are commonly stigmatized for life, ostracized from society, or executed. There is a striking similarity between the sense of horror and the ideas of ritual impurity associated with taboos in tribal societies and those associated in United States society with some sex acts. Incest is the most obvious example; it is considered so horrible as to be all but unthinkable and certainly unspeakable. In fact, such considerations probably explain why it is seldom reported. Yet certainly some members of United States society do think of it, for researchers indeed have found people who do admit to at least some incestuous experience. The absolutist social view of sex acts is apparent in their legal definition as "unnatural acts" or "crimes against nature." This definition clearly locates them at Level II of the "funnel," where absolutist responses are most likely.

In Western societies most of the absolutist ideas about morality and immorality have been associated with Judeo-Christian religious ideas, which were themselves absolute; they were believed to be universal, necessary, a part of the very nature of being, and obviously true and unquestionable. In fact, however, in the early days of Christianity, most moral rules were not commonly expressed in such absolutist terms. Christian theologians compromised with the values of Roman society in an effort to win converts. Various forms of sexual behavior that were seen as deviant, such as prostitution, were not regarded with horror. Even suicide — in some situations, as when committed by a woman to avoid the dishonor of being raped — was considered honorable. (See Lecky, 1955.) In time, however, absolutist religious ideas increasingly came to be applied to morality and immorality, especially to sex. All suicidal acts were condemned. A woman threatened with rape was no longer granted the option of taking her own life; she was damned if she did and damned if she didn't. Theologians and moralists recognized the problems associated with such absolutist ideas of morality, and intellectuals debated over them for centuries. Nonetheless, absolutist ideas prevailed among intellectuals and nonintellectuals alike and were commonly taken for granted. Immoral actions were often looked upon as the work of the devil and as acts against the absolute will and word of God. They demanded absolute condemnation and punishment, both in this world and in the next.

Throughout the Christian era, the absolutist perspective in European societies did in fact vary from one group to another, as well as in the areas of life to which it was applied. Southern or Mediterranean societies, for example, were commonly less absolutist than Northern in their attitudes toward sexual acts (at least when committed by men), while Northern societies appear to have been less absolutist toward suicide. Some degree of *pluralism** appears always to have existed in Western societies in views of morality; public pronouncements of moral outrage over the acts of others have often been combined with cynical tolerance for one's own acts. Nevertheless, the absolutist perspective — at least in public statements — dominated questions of morality and immorality throughout European societies during the Christian period. This perspective was greatly accentuated by the Protestant Reformation and the subsequent tightening up within the Catholic Church. Those societies most affected by the Reformation became the most absolutist in their attitudes toward matters of morality, especially matters of sexual morality. In fact, "Puritanism" became a common word to refer to moral absolutism.

However, even such moral absolutists could and did take a relativistic and tolerant attitude toward violations of rules that were not viewed as moral matters. The most obvious case of such relativism and tolerance is that of "rules of good taste." Such rules were commonly understood to be restricted largely to one's own group, to be the creation of humans rather than of God, and to be subject to change. One might be ostra-

---

* *Pluralism* refers to plural or multiple parts. A pluralistic society is one made up of multiple parts rather than being homogeneous. Switzerland is linguistically pluralistic because it has four official languages. Pluralistic societies are also called heterogeneous societies.

cized as a "boob" for violating them, but very few believed that they were a necessary part of being or that violators should lose their heads.

Rules of taste are an example of what William Graham Sumner called *folkways,* the topic of his famous work by that name published in 1906. Folkways are "customary acts" of a social group. Their violation earns nothing more extreme than disapproval. They are distinguished from *mores,* which are more important — even compulsory — rules of behavior. Taboos are mores. Obedience to mores is believed to be a matter of *social* rather than simply *individual* interests, and disobedience is punished more harshly. Mores that are supported by the formalized, institutionalized punishments of the political system are *laws.*

In the past, those studying deviance directed much of their study to mores and their violations. In doing so, they quite uncritically adopted the absolutism of their own society. Early studies of deviance are almost uniformly absolutist, not because theorists *chose* absolutism but because they *assumed* it. It was something they took for granted. More recently social scientists — and sociologists in particular — have moved away from absolutism and toward a new perspective that recognizes the legitimacy of diverse practices *for those who follow them.* In this process, sociologists have come increasingly to focus on folkways, for they display even more diversity than mores. Sociologists have moved from a condemnation to an appreciation of diversity. (See Matza, 1969, for a fuller account of this appreciation.)

Alternatives to Absolutism: A New Theoretical Perspective

In the past, sociologists assumed that society possessed a set of universally shared values or morals such that deviance could be defined simply as *the violation of social values.* Now, however, an increasingly strong movement in sociology rejects this assumption. On the contrary, these sociologists regard many, though not all, of society's rules as highly problematic and controversial; they believe people often differ over questions of right and wrong.

An obvious example is the issue of premarital sex in the United States. Some people believe premarital sex is absolutely evil, damned in the eyes of God. Others leave it up to individual choice: "Do your own thing." Still others argue that it depends on the situation; generally they see it as justified if the couple are in love, unjustified if they are not. And some people simply throw up their hands over deciding such an issue. In the past, the sociology of deviance simply assumed that premarital sex was considered immoral in our society and readily defined it as a form of deviance. In fact, earlier sociologists saw a virtual identity among the illegal, the immoral, and the deviant. They further assumed that any disagreement among members of society — if such disagreement was perceived at all — was irrelevant to sociology and, presumably, to society itself.

The first real challenges to the earlier, absolutist perspective in the sociology of deviance came with the introduction of conflict theory and interactionist-labeling theory. Although labeling theory did have an impact on general sociological theory at an earlier date, it was only with the publication of works by Tannenbaum (1938), Lemert (1951), Becker (1963), and others, that it challenged absolutism in the sociology of deviance. This challenge was not fully faced, however, until the explosion of social conflicts in the 1960s made the weaknesses of the earlier model obvious. The field of deviance quickly became the most theoretically creative of sociology and played a major part in forging a new theoretical perspective on society and social life. In recent years the number of empirical studies done from this emerging perspective has steadily accelerated, and these in turn have contributed a growing number of basic theoretical ideas to sociology. Although we will learn about many of these ideas in detail in Chapter 5, we will briefly describe some of them now.

Although these new theoretical perspectives on deviance differ from one another in many respects, they also share some basic ideas that can be said to constitute a *new* perspective. This new perspective has emerged through the work of a number of theorists and has been given a number of names: new symbolic interactionism, labeling theory, dramaturgy, phenomenology, ethnomethodology, and existential sociology. The differences of names and of specific theories must not, however, obscure for us the fundamental similarities in their views of the sociology of deviance and their fundamental dissimilarities from earlier absolutist theories of deviance. These similarities constitute the new theoretical perspective and distinguish all these theories from earlier perspectives on deviance.

CHARACTERISTICS OF THE NEW PERSPECTIVE

According to the new sociological perspective, research and analysis must recognize that members of society often disagree — sometimes violently — over a multitude of issues, and these conflicts are of tremendous importance to them. Such conflicts are of equal importance to any sociological theory that purports to deal with the real social world in which we live. Therefore, disagreements among people over the meanings of right and wrong, good and bad, deviance and conformity, are of fundamental importance to the sociology of deviance.

Proponents of the new perspective do not use the term "deviance" as if there were some obvious, definite, absolute set of good and bad activities. Rather they see the sociology of deviance as the study of the diverse views held by members of a society or social group on the questions of defining right and wrong, deviant and conformist. They do not, for example, assume that premarital sex or marijuana smoking is good or bad. Instead they seek to *determine what people feel and think about such activities.* They do not simply classify pot smokers as deviants; rather they try to show how some groups, such as the police, may see pot smoking as deviant, while other groups, such as college students, may see it as nondeviant. Sociologists now ask such questions as: How exactly do legislators come to define marijuana smoking as an illegal activity? How do marijuana smokers justify or, in sociological terminology, *legitimate* their activities? In struggles between the two, what values are invoked? Is marijuana smoking seen as a moral right? Are there social advantages to "decriminalizing" marijuana use because so many people use it anyway? Sociologists now try both to recognize the many moral and legal definitions of specific activities and to determine why and how different individuals and groups arrive at them. They are also interested in knowing how these different definitions affect the activities and those involved in them.

Simply stated, the new sociological perspective on deviance is concerned with looking at deviance and conformity *from the standpoints of all members of society.* Although the goal of adopting *all* perspectives may be practically unrealizable, it directs us toward asking: *What* do different members of society see as right and wrong, good and evil, legal and illegal? *How* do they see these things? *When* do these definitions apply — all the time or only in some situations? *Why* do people define things in the ways that they do? *What* do they do about such definitions? *What happens* as a result — more social order, more disorder, more justice, less? Once these questions are answered, sociologists can examine the practical implications of this greater sociological understanding and ask themselves such questions as: What can we propose that would lead to more feelings of justice in society? How can we create more order or, if that is our goal, less? If the knowledge of how and why people come into moral conflicts were made available to members of society, they could use it to deal with their conflicts and resolve them in ways they saw as more satisfactory.

ASSUMPTIONS UNDERLYING THE NEW PERSPECTIVE

Sociologists now recognize that different social groups look at the world in different ways. The newly emerging sociological perspective on deviance entails recognizing and studying various views on deviance without espousing any one. Three major assumptions underly the new perspective, guiding both research and theory:

1. *Deviance is a construction of social actors.* The concept of deviance is not a natural or absolute part of the world; rather it is something we ourselves construct. No action is inherently deviant. Whether it is labeled as such depends upon human interpretation. Consider the ex-

ample provided by the sociologist Pitirim A. Sorokin: members of our society may describe a couple engaged in sexual relations as "making love," involved in "rape," committing "adultery," "playing around," or any number of other things. Whether this act is considered deviant depends on what rules are considered relevant and the meanings and intentions attributed to the act and the actors. Meaning is not inherent in the act; it must be constructed.

2. *Constructions of meanings can be problematic for members of society.* Earlier sociologists assumed that meanings were inherent in situations and were self-evident, at least to careful observers. Although any society or social group certainly shares some meanings, we now understand that other meanings are not shared and are differently constructed by different people. The immense, tangled, conflicting testimony over the Watergate break-in and cover-up in 1972 exemplifies that not only interpretations but even the facts themselves can be problematic. Problems of meaning can arise between groups, between individuals, or even within an individual. What is happening and what it means is frequently open to question: "Did she really say that?" "Does he really mean that?" What is commonly called gossip may well be a search for meaning in a problematic situation; seldom does gossip involve an issue that everyone understands. That meanings are problematic at the level of an individual and of two interacting people suggests the fundamentally problematic nature of meanings.

3. *Sociologists' constructions of meanings are even more problematic than members' constructions.* Earlier sociologists assumed that they were much better than other people at perceiving the "true" meanings of actions. For example, sociologists took for granted that they could tell whether a death was caused by suicide or accident even when other people could not. This privileged position was attributed to sociologists' aloofness — their lack of direct involvement in the topics they were studying. The new perspective, on the other hand, requires that sociologists take into account the knowledge of those they are studying while going beyond it to construct a more comprehensive understanding. Earlier sociologists ignored the thoughts and feelings of their respondents in a way that is impossible within the new perspective. In the latter, respondents' knowledge provides the building blocks of theoretical knowledge. Direct involvement in group activities is seen as crucial to a sociological understanding of that group's beliefs and activities. Sociologists who remain aloof lose understanding by missing what is really felt, thought, and done by group members. The new perspective sees sociologists' constructions as particularly problematic because they both include and go beyond those of the people being studied. The new perspective demands that sociologists strive for an understanding that gives full respect to people's lives in their social worlds.

The emerging perspective, then, regards the meanings attributed to actions and the judgments made about them as heterogeneous and as a source of conflict rather than as homogeneous and universally shared. It regards the immense and continual arguments and struggles within individuals, between individuals, and between groups as fundamentally important, both to group members and to sociology. It renounces absolutism as a sociological position and, in doing so, sets itself the complex task of understanding the myriad ways in which deviance appears in and to society.

Concluding Remarks

In this chapter we have presented some of the major issues that arise in studying deviance sociologically. This background will be helpful when we look at how deviance has been studied historically and when, in Part II, we examine various types of deviance.

We have described difficulties encountered in defining deviance and the problematic nature of the sociological study of deviance. We have seen how sociologists' values can be both help and hindrance to sociological research and analysis — hindrance when they introduce bias, help when they provide the underlying motivation for undertaking sociological studies. The dangers of absolutism as a sociological perspective should be clear and the strengths of the new perspective evident.

In the next three chapters we will look in detail at numerous explanations that have been offered for deviance. Our goal is twofold: (1) to gather and preserve the insights of the past, and (2) to recognize the unresolved problems and their implications so that we will not fall victim to them in our own analysis.

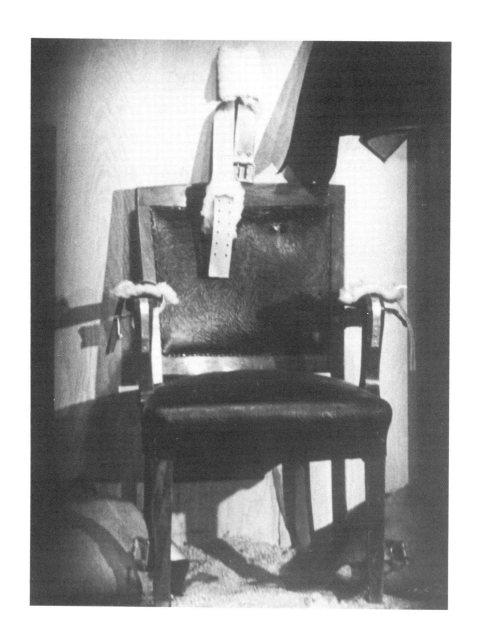

2

General Explanations of Deviance

In this chapter we begin to survey examples of a wide range of explanations that have been proposed to explain deviance. We first look at theories that are most general and attempt to explain all deviance in terms of the operation of a few broad and fundamental factors or variables. Less general theories are covered in Chapters 3 and 4.

Before we proceed, let us be clear about the nature of explanation — what it seeks and how it goes about achieving its goals. We must particularly understand the distinction between common-sense and scientific explanations made in the last chapter. We begin, therefore, with an example that will clarify some of the dilemmas in explanation and the paths to resolution. In this example, look for the variety of sources to which one might turn in the search for an explanation. When we as members of society are faced with a problematic situation, we may seek and be satisfied with one or more explanations selected from a wide variety of sources — whatever makes practical sense to us. As sociologists, faced with a variety of possible explanations for deviant behavior, we are looking for the "true" explanation, regardless of its practical implications. All these opportunities arise in the example that follows.

The Car Accident

A businessman was driving at high speed on a highway when the car ahead of him stopped for a red light. His car, though far behind, continued on and rammed into the rear of the stopped car. Two occupants of the stopped car were killed. Police, arriving on the scene, suspected that the driver of the second car was intoxicated. They had his blood tested for alcohol level, as required by state law, and discovered that it exceeded the legally defined alcohol level above which one may be charged under the felony drunk driving law. He was arrested and charged with manslaughter.

A search of police records revealed that he had been previously arrested and convicted of drunken driving. At his trial the businessman revealed that he had experienced "personal problems" the night before the accident and had drunk almost an entire fifth of liquor before driving. He pled guilty to the charges, but he also argued that his long-standing alcoholic problem and his intoxicated state at the time of the accident were extenuating circumstances that reduced his guilt for the accident, though he expressed great remorse over it and the resulting deaths. The prosecutor argued that he was fully responsible because he had known before drinking that his drinking might lead to such driving behavior. The judge finally decided that there were some extenuating circumstances and gave him a sentence allowing him to go free if he would voluntarily give lectures in the community exposing the dangers of drunken driving. The convicted man accepted this judgment and went free.*

How can we *explain* what happened? What *caused* the accident and the deaths? As members of society we seek common-sense explanations; as sociologists we seek scientific explanations. In either case we may choose very general or very specific theories that apply to the situation. And in either our choice will be strongly influenced by the source to which we turn for our explanation, whether that source is religion, human nature, or the nature of the social world.

Common-Sense Explanations

In using common sense to explain the car accident, we may look to general or specific forms of explanation. Our choice will depend heavily upon the practical purpose to be served by the explanation. Some religious groups, such as the Jehovah's Witnesses, might explain the car accident as one more example of what they refer to as "this wicked old world of ours," seeing the accident as an instance of the sinful nature of the world today. Others might insist that the "irresponsibility characteristic of U.S. culture" was the cause; yet others might attribute it to the pace and character of urban life. Those with more psychological or psychoanalytic interests might focus on the personal problems of the

---

* This incident was reported from court proceedings in many newspapers.

businessman as an explanation, suggesting that alcoholic problems are ultimately caused by childhood experiences that make individuals highly passive and dependent. Those interested in automobile safety might suggest that a specific combination of poor lighting and inadequate signs were the "real" cause of the accident. *The explanation chosen within the common-sense perspective will be related to the practical purposes of those doing the explaining and to the point they are trying to make.*

Sociological Explanations

The ideal of sociology is to arrive at a "true" explanation of what is studied — that is, an explanation oriented not to practical purposes but to *understanding* in its most general sense. Sociologists of deviance have increasingly come to recognize that many variables and a number of levels of analysis are involved in understanding such events as the car accident. Because the explanation of such events and their outcomes is so complex, many social scientists prefer not to use the terms *causation* or *causal* to talk about them. Causation implies a simple, monocausal (single-cause) process such as that of a rock *causing* a window to break or an icy road *causing* tires to skid when the brakes are applied. Social actions and their outcomes are almost never monocausal but instead depend on many individual and social variables. More and more, sociologists are devoting their energies to identifying and understanding these many variables and are setting aside the issue of causation. *What* and *how* are seen as questions prior to *why*. Before we can consider why, we must establish what is going on and how; and what and how in the social realm are exceedingly difficult questions to answer.

Social scientists have confronted immense problems in determining just what variables are most important in understanding different forms of deviance and which level of analysis is most appropriate for the type of explanation sought. In recent years sociologists of deviance have come to see the more situational variables and more specific levels of analysis as explaining more deviance than the more general ones. This is not to say that such general variables or levels of analysis may not be crucial for explaining some forms of deviance; however, their explanatory power is now seen as limited.

General considerations about deviance illustrated by the car accident:

1. A number of variables* are involved in explaining any event and its outcomes.
2. The pertinent variables are sometimes to be found on the same level of analysis and at other times at different levels of analysis.

---

* A variable is any factor or element that can have two or more values — for example, sex (male/female), crime rate (high/medium/low).

3. Different forms of deviance and different concrete acts can best be explained by different sets of variables and different levels.
4. Different variables and levels may come into play during the deviant event.
5. Any complete explanation of deviance in society would require some integration of all levels and variables found to be significant in each type or act of deviance.

All too often social scientists have sought explanations based on only one variable or one level of analysis. *The failure to distinguish different levels of analysis and to recognize the many variables involved in most forms of deviant activity have been continual problems in sociology as a whole and especially in the sociology of deviance.*

One of the best books on methods of analyzing causes of deviance, *The Causes of Delinquency* by Travis Hirschi and Hannan Selvin (1969), shows that social scientists studying delinquency have persistently refused to accept any variable as a causal factor in delinquency unless it explains almost *all* instances of delinquency. For example, early studies found various family factors statistically associated with delinquency, but no factor was found in *all* cases of delinquency and most factors occurred only in a minority (one-fifth to one-fourth) of cases. Early analysts concluded that those factors, such as broken homes or working mothers, were not causes of delinquency. Hirschi and Selvin show over and over again that such a conclusion is not justified by the data and by valid methods of analysis. Earlier analysts should have concluded from their evidence that *no single factor is a universal or monocausal explanation of delinquency.* Many of the factors they studied are now viewed as important variables. Delinquency, like almost all other forms of deviance and like all social behavior, is the outcome of a variety of processes that involve multiple variables, both at any one level of analysis and at different levels of analysis. The problem for sociologists is to determine which variables and which levels of analysis explain particular forms of deviance.

An Overview of Sociological Theories of Deviance

In the past sociologists have considered a wide variety of sources as potential explanations of deviance, from astronomical and geographical conditions to the inner workings of the mind. Figure 2.1 presents the kinds of explanations that have been developed historically by social scientists and upon which they have drawn in trying to understand deviance. A similar figure could be compiled for the common-sense explanations we have just presented; readers might find it useful to imagine one based on the foregoing example of the car accident and their own experience.

In the remainder of Chapter 2 and in Chapters 3 and 4 we will look at examples of social science explanations for deviance following the order of Figure 2.1. We will begin with those which have sought answers on a very general level. The goal of such theories has been to explain *all instances of deviance* or *deviance in general.* We will look at theories as they have appeared historically and as they are currently presented by social scientists. The examples we select will be mainly *sociological,* because that is our perspective in this book, but we will also consider material from other social sciences that were involved in various ways in the development of many sociological theories. We will, of course, present only a limited number of examples for each level. The examples we have chosen are intended to make clear the nature of each level discussed so that readers will be able to characterize other theories when they encounter them elsewhere.

We are presenting many theories in detail so that readers will be aware of the many kinds of explanations that have been offered, the many sources turned to, and the strengths and weaknesses of different attempts at explanation. We will find that many plausible or seemingly true theories cannot withstand close analysis or do not fit more recent empirical evidence. Against the background of this material we will be able to see the reasons for the development of a new perspective and understand the problems it is designed to resolve.

Level I. The Physical Environment and the Physical Organism as Sources of Explanation

Level I explanations are the most general of those used in sociology. Characteristically such explanations of deviance have been sought in the nonsocial realm — either in the physical environment lying outside the individual or within the physical organism itself. For both the goal has been to explain all deviance in terms that go beyond the social world.

THE PHYSICAL ENVIRONMENT

Throughout the history of sociological thought we can find examples of extremely general theories that view the physical environment as the cause of human behavior. For centuries the heavenly bodies, geography, and climate were seen as particularly important environmental determinants of human actions.

Theories involving the heavenly bodies are evident in the work of Morselli (1882), an important nineteenth-century social scientist. Although he did not deny that social factors are important in explaining deviance, he argued that correlations between phases of the moon and suicide were so strong that they could not be ignored in any theoretical

Figure 2.1
Types of explanations offered by social scientists to account for deviance

Level of analysis and source of explanation	Representatives	Example of deviance theory (these are not offered as true statements)	Page on which theory is discussed
SCIENTIFIC EXPLANATIONS			
I Physical environment and physical organism	Morselli, Lombroso, Hooton, S. Glueck, E. Glueck, Dobzhansky, Rosenthal, Lorenz, Ardrey, Wilson	Male aggression is a biologically inherited characteristic. (Lorenz)	31
II Society, social structure, and social conflict	Durkheim, Merton, Parsons, Bell, Davis, Erikson, Marx, Quinney	An increase in social integration will produce a decrease in deviance; an increase in social disintegration will produce an increase in deviance. (Durkheim)	41
III Specific social structural variables	Park, Burgess, Wirth, Faris, Thomas, Znaniecki, Cressey, Frank, Clinard, Shaw, McKay, Cavan, Dunham, Hollingshead, Redlich, Srole, Eaton, Weil	Increased urbanization (increasing size, density, and heterogeneity of a community) causes social disorganization and thus deviance. (Wirth)	64
IV Subcultures	Lind, Sutherland, Sellin, Whyte, Jacobs, Gans, Gordon, Thrasher, Cohen, Kobrin, Cloward, Ohlin, Miller, Spengel	Conformity to subgroup rules can produce deviance from the rules of the larger society. (Lind)	75
V Social Interaction	Simmel, Mead, Cooley, Blumer, Hughes, Lindesmith, Ray, Lemert, Cameron, Zola, Davis, Weinberg, Dexter, Humphreys, Anderson, Wallace, Shibutani	Deviance can be learned through interaction with others and through the development of shared symbolic meanings with them. (Lindesmith)	94
VI Individual psychology	Esquirol, de Boismont, Schneidman, Faberow, Freud, Rabin, Yablonsky, Alexander, Staub, Johnson, Reik, Greenwald, Bieber, McCord,	Deviant acts may be committed in order to relieve unconscious guilt feelings. (Alexander and Staub)	103

McDougall, Hartshorne, May, Piaget,
Allport, Sullivan, Sherif, Asch, Kohlberg

UNSCIENTIFIC EXPLANATIONS

VII Concrete interaction processes	Media presentations and personal, common-sense accounts	Deviance occurs as a specific response to others.	121
VIII Unique properties of given situations and actions	Media presentations and personal, common-sense accounts	Rising murder rates are caused by increased availability of guns.	121
IX Concrete actions and events	Media presentations and personal, common-sense accounts	Any deviant act is the result of inevitable forces.	122

THE NEW PERSPECTIVE: A MULTI-LEVEL THEORY

Labeling theory	Tannenbaum, Becker, Dickson, Currie, Emerson, Henry	"Social groups create deviance by making the rules whose infraction constitutes deviance." (Becker)	127
Dramaturgical theory	Goffman, Lyman, Scott, Manning	Individuals *manage* the impressions they give of themselves to others and thus may *present themselves* as either deviant or nondeviant. (Goffman)	135
Phenomenology and ethnomethodology	Cicourel, Garfinkel, Wieder, Zimmerman, Bittner, Stoddart, McHugh, Daniels, Waksler	Behavior that outsiders view as "deviance" insiders may view as "rule reinterpretation." (Zimmerman)	140
Existential sociology	Tiryakian, Douglas, Johnson, Rasmussen, Flanagan	Feelings, particularly of shame, are significant in producing or preventing deviant behavior. (Rasmussen)	146

* Though theories that form a part of the new perspective do not fall at any one level of explanation (see Chapter 5), these are some major representatives and examples of such theories for comparison.

* Theories at Level I are the most *general* sociological theories available; those at Level IX, the least general (most *specific*).

Figure 2.2
Example of a Daily Horoscope. The underlined phrases are those which seem
to warn against potential deviance. If such deviance does occur, causes might
be sought in astrological conditions.

GENERAL TENDENCIES: Despite some early morning frustrations, in the afternoon you are able to accomplish a great deal by attending to, duties. Repaying favors brings fine results.

ARIES (Mar. 21 to Apr. 19) Go straight to those who have power over your affairs and gain their support where your career is concerned.

TAURUS (Apr. 20 to May 20) Put those new and practical ideas to work so you can advance in life. Get rid of the unwanted and obsolete.

GEMINI (May 21 to June 21) Follow your intuition and handle present situations in a practical way and get excellent results. Use care in motion.

MOON CHILDREN (June 22 to July 21) Take steps to cooperate more with associates and understand their ideas better. Engage in civic work.

LEO (July 22 to Aug. 21) Attend to regular chores early in the day so you'll have more time for social activities later. Be more thoughtful of others.

VIRGO (Aug. 22 to Sept. 22) Be careful of one who likes to downgrade you and others. Take time for amusements during spare time. Be happy.

LIBRA (Sept. 23 to Oct. 22) Make sure home affairs are handled wisely. Be more cooperative with others. Avoid a temptation to spend too much money.

SCORPIO (Oct. 23 to Nov. 21) Good day to discuss business matters with associates and cement better relations. Keep active and free of boredom.

SAGITTARIUS (Nov. 22 to Dec. 21) Analyze your true financial position and you find you are better off than you think. Establish more order around you.

CAPRICORN (Dec. 22 to Jan. 20) Personal aims are difficult to gain in the morning but later they become easy for you. Attend group affair tonight.

AQUARIUS (Jan. 21 to Feb. 19) Make sure you don't react bitterly to conditions you cannot change. Make new acquaintances of worth.

PISCES (Feb. 20 to Mar. 20) Look to an older and serious friend for the backing you need at this time, but be diplomatic in asking for it.

IF YOUR CHILD IS BORN TODAY . . . he or she will be able to comprehend work and career matters well, so be sure to send to college. There is much ability and desire for organizational work. A good background in religion is important here. Sports are a must.

"The Stars impel, they do not compel." What you make of your life is largely up to you!

Source: Reprinted with permission of McNaught Syndicate.

formulation. Astrology,* which explains and predicts human actions in terms of the *movement* of heavenly bodies, is an ancient and widespread example of a theory that links the environment and human behavior. Although astrology is designed to explain behavior in general, it has also been used as an explanation of deviant behavior. Figure 2.2 is an example of a daily horoscope based on astrology; in it one can see the possibility of explaining deviant acts in terms of astrological conditions. The car accident described at the beginning of this chapter might be explained in astrological terms, particularly if the businessman were a Gemini. Nowadays astrology does not play an important part in social science explanations of deviant behavior, though some people still use it as a part of their common-sense explanations.

The influence of the moon on human behavior continues to arise as a topic of serious scientific consideration. In an article entitled "The Moon and the Maternity Ward" (1979), Abell and Greenspan cite a number of

* The social controversies over astrology will be examined in some detail in Chapter 12.

studies that explore the relation between the moon and madness, human birth, postoperative hemorrhage, suicide, homicide, and mental hospital admissions (p. 25). They chose to study the relation between the moon and birth because of the belief, prevalent among the general public and particularly among some nurses in maternity wards and some gynecologists, that more births take place during the full moon. They also located published scientific studies that supported such an idea. In their conclusion they state:

> Our analysis of the nearly 12,000 live and dead births occurring at the UCLA Hospital maternity ward in an interval of 51 lunar months from 1974 to 1978 reveals no correlation between the numbers of births and full moon or any other phase of the moon. This negative result occurs whether we consider all live births, just those that are completely uninduced (that is, natural), incidence of twinning or other multiplicity, or even stillbirths (p. 24).

They recognize that their findings disagree with those of others and suggest continued study.

The idea that geography and climate are major determinants of human behavior was popular among scientists for many centuries. Those studying deviance were struck by such findings as that suicide was more common in temperate northern European societies than in more equatorial southern European ones. To a lesser degree, homicide was found to be more common in southern European societies. Such correlations became the basis for extremely complex theories attempting to show that geography, climate, and other environmental factors were the causes of variations in social rates of deviance.

Surveying climatic theories, the sociologist Pitirim Sorokin concluded less than sympathetically:

> if we try to find out why, how, and in what way climatic agencies condition crimes our results are practically nothing but indefinite dogmatic repetitions of contradictory allusions to the "weakening" or "irritating" influence of temperature or air or humidity or wind and so on. And often the same author on one page ascribes an "irritating" character to one climatic condition, while on another page of the work he lays it to quite different climatic agencies (because there the movement of crime is different and cannot be explained by the first reason). The corresponding "explanations" are so vague that we do not know, of temperature or humidity or barometric pressure, which facilitates and which hinders crime. The situation remains almost mysterious and hopeless. These remarks are enough to show that if there exists any correlation between climatic agencies and crime it is of secondary importance and still needs to be tested. Some indirect influence of these factors appears probable but it is somewhat intangible. At any rate the principal fluctuations of crime in space and time are not due to climatic factors (1928: 166).

Environmental theories are not now widely used in sociology for a number of reasons. First, many correlations that initially appeared important have been found through statistical analysis to be of little significance. Second, many significant correlations have proved to be *spurious* — that is, superficially important but basically unrelated. For example, social scientists for a time were puzzled by the low rate of urban muggings on Monday nights. Some sort of environmental process seemed to be at work, but what could it be? Turning attention to the social realm revealed that the correlation between Monday nights and muggings was spurious: the important factor turned out to be that on Monday nights football games were being televised. Potential muggers and potential victims were watching television and thus muggings were reduced. Once the football season was over, muggings returned to their preseason rate.

A final reason for not adopting environmental explanations is that theorists have never been able to explain satisfactorily the ways in which such forces operate. They have focused on correlations without being able to detail the mechanisms that create them. Referring again to Figure 2.2, what is it about heavenly bodies that causes a Capricorn to have difficulty in gaining personal aims in the morning? How do heavenly bodies achieve such an effect?

Unexamined environmental theories can appear very persuasive, but so far none has survived scientific examination. They do not now serve as satisfactory scientific explanations of the social phenomena of deviance, though they do continue to appear from time to time.

THE PHYSICAL ORGANISM

Theories focusing on human beings as physical organisms gradually gained ground over environmental theories in explaining deviance. Cassius voices this change in Shakespeare's play *Julius Caesar:* "The fault, dear Brutus, is not in our stars,/ But in ourselves, that we are underlings" (Act 1, Scene 2). Theories about the physical organism claimed that they, unlike environmental theories, were able to demonstrate *a direct physical cause* of *any deviant act* committed by *any particular individual.* Although environmental theories based on climate could not demonstrate how or why climate caused one particular individual to commit a deviant act such as suicide or homicide and did not cause such deviance in someone else subject to the same climatic forces, theories based on the physical organism claimed to explain just such differences.

Theories of this kind include those derived from the study of head shapes (phrenology), racial types, body types (somatotypes), intelligence, and genetics. Theorists in each of these areas saw correlations between specific characteristics of the physical organism and deviant behavior and, on the basis of such correlations, claimed that those characteristics *caused* deviant behavior.

One of the best-known theorists who linked characteristics of the physical organism with deviance was Cesare Lombroso (1911), one of the founders of criminology. Initially he believed that all crime could be explained by the inheritance of "biologically inferior," "savage" physical characteristics; after completing a number of studies he claimed that only about 30 percent could be so explained; nonetheless, he argued for the importance of the physical organism in the causation of deviance. The remarks by Lombroso quoted below typify the thinking of early students of the sociology of deviance. Although Lombroso's statements now seem old-fashioned, biased, and perhaps "obviously" wrong, his careful, detailed analysis is impressive:

> The born criminal shows in a proportion reaching 33% numerous specific characteristics that are almost always atavistic.* Those who have followed us thus far have seen that many of the characteristics presented by savage races are very often found among born criminals. Such, for example, are: the slight development of the pilar system; low cranial capacity; retreating forehead; highly developed frontal sinuses; great frequency of Wormian bones; early closing of the cranial sutures; the simplicity of the sutures; the thickness of the bones of the skull; enormous development of the maxillaries and the zygomata; prognathism; obliquity of the orbits; greater pigmentation of the skin; tufted and crispy hair; and large ears. To these we may add the lemurine appendix; anomalies of the ear; dental diastemata; great agility; relative insensibility to pain, dullness of the sense of touch; great visual acuteness; ability to recover quickly from wounds; blunted affections; precocity as to sensual pleasures; greater resemblance between the sexes; greater incorrigibility of the woman (Spencer); laziness; absence of remorse; impulsiveness; physiopsychic excitability; and especially improvidence, which sometimes appears as courage and again as recklessness changing to cowardice. Besides these there is great vanity; a passion for gambling and alcoholic drinks; violent but fleeting passions; superstition; extraordinary sensitiveness with regard to one's own personality; and a special conception of God and morality (Lombroso, in Sykes and Drabek, 1969: 133).

An immense amount of research in the nineteenth and early twentieth centuries led to the conclusion that the explanatory power of such theories was largely illusory. Regardless of the physical factors chosen by researchers, no one of them or even any set of them was found to be universally associated with deviant behavior. Theorists were forced to accept that characteristics of the physical organism could comprise at best only one significant factor in explaining human behavior in general and deviance in particular.

---

* Atavistic: relating to an earlier evolutionary form of an organism or its parts.

When the search for an explanation of deviance in terms of the physical organism proved futile, social scientists turned their attention to the *interaction* between the physical environment and the physical organism. They also began to expand their notion of environment to include not only the physical but also the social environment, though for many years the social environment remained a relatively minor element in theories about deviance.

Biologists, physical anthropologists, physiological psychologists, and medical researchers continue to argue that deviant actions, ranging from crime to war to sexual aberrations, are "antisocial" forms of behavior resulting from complex interactions between environment and "inferior" biological characteristics. Research carried out to confirm such theories has generated an immense literature. Probably the most famous work in this area is the monumental study by Earnest Albert Hooton, *The American Criminal* (1939), an investigation of 4,212 prisoners in nine states and 313 noncriminals (146 Nashville firemen plus 167 Massachusetts militiamen). Hooton used sixty-six biological measurements and ten social measurements of each individual, then correlated the various categories with crime and noncrime. He concluded that both "biological deterioration" and social environment were causes of crime, but that biological factors were the most important causes:

> Criminals are organically inferior. Crime is the resultant of the impact of the environment upon low grade human organisms. It follows that the elimination of crime can be effected only by the extirpation of the physically, mentally and morally unfit, or by their complete segregation in a socially aseptic environment (1939b: 309). . . .
>
> I deem human (biological) deterioration to be ultimately responsible not only for crime, but for the evils of war, the oppression of the populace by totalitarian states, and for all of the social cataclysms which are rocking the world and under which civilization is tottering (1939: 393).

A similar and even more massive series of studies of body types (somatotypes) by Sheldon and Eleanor Glueck (1950, 1952) led to similar, but more specific conclusions about delinquents in Massachusetts.

A closely related but far more sophisticated and unimpassioned line of argument has been followed by geneticists. Dunn and Dobzhansky and others have argued on the basis of studies of twins that heredity does produce a "predisposition" to react to certain environmental situations in such a way that there is a higher probability of committing crimes:

> Several investigators in different countries (United States, Holland, Germany) combed prisons for members of twin pairs among the inmates. When a twin was found efforts were made to locate his co-twin brother and to determine whether the latter did or did not have a criminal record. A total of 111 pairs of identical twins were investigated, and in 80 cases both co-twins were found to have had criminal records of various kinds. Among the same

number (111 pairs) of two-egg twins,* only 38 pairs consisted of co-twins both of whom had criminal records, while in the remaining 73 pairs one of the twins was convicted for some crime while his co-twin was not known to have broken any law. Clearly, then, one-egg twins are more often similar in having criminal records than are two-egg twins (Dunn and Dobzhansky, in Sykes and Drabek, 1969: 135).

This evidence seems to some researchers to mean that heredity necessarily causes crime, but Dunn and Dobzhansky have cautioned that the evidence is not unequivocal: "Even in the environments in which they actually lived, some identical twin brothers of the criminals appeared to be law-abiding citizens." In general, researchers have argued that heredity only *predisposes* to certain responses to environment, and other factors, probably cultural and situational ones, are dominant in determining anything as complex as crime.

Research into the relation between the physical organism and deviance continues. Geneticists now believe that studies of single-egg twins have shown conclusively that some forms of mental illness are inherited. Evidence has been accumulating that there is a very high involvement of hereditary factors in severe depression and in most forms of extreme schizophrenia, such as catatonia, an almost total withdrawal from the world. Such findings have encouraged others to argue once again that certain forms of crime are highly dependent on inherited factors. Research on this subject especially focused on violent or aggressive acts of crime, presumably because such acts are more clearly "antisocial" and seem more likely to be tied to bodily states than are other forms of deviance such as nude bathing or draft-card burning.

Some researchers have tried to show that criminal behavior is associated with a different chromosomal arrangement in criminals. Typically females possess two X chromosomes (XX) and males possess one X and one Y chromosome (XY). Some researchers found that violent male criminals possessed a double Y chromosome (XYY) and suggested that the "additional male" chromosome might somehow be responsible for violent crimes among males. Research has not, however, been able to provide any conclusive findings. Major problems arise for such a theory: that the double Y chromosome does not appear in all violent criminals, its distribution among unapprehended violent criminals is not known, it does not explain violent crimes among women, and the process by which it might work remains unknown.

---

* Twins can be produced in human beings in two ways: by the fertilization of a single egg that later divides (one-egg or identical twins) and by fertilization of two eggs (two-egg or fraternal twins). The former share the same genetic structure; the latter are no more genetically alike than any siblings. Research on the genetic bases of behavior is particularly concerned with one-egg twins.

Current work in *ethology,* the science of animal behavior in natural settings, is also developing explanations of deviant behavior based on the nature of the physical organism. Studies of primates (particularly chimpanzees and baboons), those mammals closest to human beings in physical nature, have been used as a way of discovering what behavior is innate in such animals and, by inference, in human beings. Although there are now many such studies, the most sophisticated is probably that of Lorenz (1966). He argues that males are *necessarily* both aggressive and cooperative, that such motivations are biologically inherited, and that the social and cultural environment can encourage either, so that individuals or whole groups can become violently aggressive and thus criminal.

Ethological studies gave rise to what Donald Ball (in Douglas, 1973: 120–121) has called "pop ethology": popularized and oversimplified ideas about ethology. Works in this vein, such as Ardrey's *African Genesis* (1961), argue that by genetic inheritance males are basically aggressive. Such ideas have been severely criticized by ethologists, neurophysiologists, and other specialists studying human nature. The simplistic theories of "pop ethology" have been largely rejected by scientists and have given way to much more complex theories of behavioral biology and social biology.

The most prominent current example of theories based on the nature of the physical organism are those of *sociobiology,* the study of the biological bases of social behavior. Sociobiology has grown out of biology and uses biological knowledge in attempting to understand the social world of both nonhumans and humans. Edward O. Wilson, winner of the Pulitzer Prize in 1979, is a foremost representative. In presenting his view of human social behavior, Wilson states:

> Let us now consider man in the free spirit of natural history, as though we were zoologists from another planet contemplating a catalog of social species on Earth. In this macroscopic view the humanities and social sciences shrink to specialized branches of biology; history, biography, and fiction are the research protocols of human ethology, and anthropology and sociology together constitute the sociobiology of a single primate species (1975: 547).

Wilson expects that all social behavior eventually will be understood on the basis of knowledge of the brain; all that is needed is continued research.

Again and again in social science we return to the *nature versus nurture argument:* Is human social behavior determined by the nature of the physical organism or by the social world in which humans live or by a combination of the two? There is no agreed-upon answer for social scientists, sociologists, or sociologists of deviance. In this section we have explored the problems that arise when theorists view nature alone as the determinant of human behavior.

Sociologists in general do agree that certain very general inherited human characteristics may be related to various forms of deviance. They agree also that certain forms of behavior called deviant in United States society probably are caused by some organic abnormalities. However, the multitude of activities that in some place at some time are called deviant, the variation among societies and social groups in what is viewed as deviant, and the ever-changing views of what is deviant all suggest to sociologists that social factors transcend those of the physical organism.

The problems that arise in explaining deviant behavior in terms of the physical organism revolve around the nature of the social world. First, such theories are *reductionist,* for they seek to *reduce* the social world to the physical world and all social science to physical science. In so doing, such theories deny all independence to human feelings, thoughts, ideas, beliefs, reasons, and meanings, seeing such phenomena as effects, not causes. Further, such theories either neglect or minimize the variety of the social world, even though known social variations seem to exceed by far known human physical variations. Finally, such theories assume that animal behavior, including human behavior, can be determined by the physical organism without considering the possibility that neither human nor nonhuman behavior is so determined but that all animal behavior has its social dimension as well. Almost all biologists who devote serious study to the relations between the organism, and in particular the brain, and behavior agree that human behavior is greatly affected by the social situations that individuals face.

Level II. Society, Social Structure, and Social Conflict as Sources of Explanation

Level I explanations are attempts to understand the social world in terms of the nonsocial; we as sociologists view such theories as general because they transcend the social altogether. Level II provides the most general of those explanations that remain within the social realm. At Level II deviant behavior is explained in terms of broad features of society, social structure, and social conflict.

STRUCTURAL THEORIES

Structural theories dominated sociological thought about deviance from the 1800s until the 1960s. Rightly seen as "classical" sociological theories of deviance, they made the first important contributions to our understanding of deviance as a *social* phenomenon. Aspects of these theories have been integrated into more recent theories, though generally in somewhat modified form. Many sociologists continue to develop structural theories and to add to the already vast literature. We will now consider a famous example of an early structural theory and then turn to more recent examples.

A Classic Level II Theory: Durkheim's Theory of Social Integration. During the nineteenth century, almost all French sociological thought, and much sociological thought everywhere, was profoundly concerned with the issues of the French Revolution and especially with the crucial questions of the relations of traditional social authority to deviance (sinfulness). With but modest oversimplification we can say that nineteenth-century French sociological thought, especially on deviance and social order, looked at the Revolution as illustrating the truth of the conservative argument: *Social constraint is necessary to prevent deviance because human nature, whatever it is specifically, will lead to deviance when unconstrained. Furthermore, the source of such constraint is society itself.*

Clearly evident in Emile Durkheim's thought are the concerns, assumptions, and taken-for-granted beliefs of his day. Durkheim intended his most famous work, *Suicide* (1951, first published in 1897), as a demonstration of the power of sociological methods he had earlier proposed in *The Rules of Sociological Method* (1964, first published in 1895) and of the validity of the general theory of society and deviance he had begun developing in that and other earlier works, especially in *The Division of Labor in Society* (1964). He argued that *society is a moral phenomenon,* by which he meant that society in its most fundamental and important aspect is a set of morals (values and laws) that individuals are taught as children to accept and that they then use throughout their lives to determine what is right and wrong, what they should and should not do in concrete situations. In a somewhat oversimplified but revealing way we could say that Durkheim looked at society in the way traditional Jews and Christians had looked at God: *God* gave the laws and conscience and these served as the constraints to produce social order. If in this sentence we substitute *Society* for *God,* we come close to Durkheim's idea. Society as a moral phenomenon provided social constraint, in part by producing religious beliefs and rituals. Durkheim did not, however, view these constraints as necessarily external to the individual; morals become part of individuals' ways of thinking and feeling and thus part of what individuals *want* and what they *are.*

Durkheim argued that moral meanings will be more intensely felt and more constraining the more they are communicated and imposed by individuals on each other. This communication and involvement of individuals with each other is what he called *social integration;* lack of communication and involvement he called *social disintegration*. His basic general idea is relatively simple: *The more socially integrated a society is (that is, the more individuals communicate with and are involved with other individuals), the greater are social constraints against suicide and, thus, the lower the suicide rate.* It is important to see that Durkheim was trying to explain differing *suicide rates*, not individual cases of suicide. His argument was that different social arrangements prevent or fail to prevent suicide and such prevention or nonprevention is reflected in suicide rates. He was not arguing that society *causes* individual suicides but that social arrangements *cause* suicide rates. It was his view that individuals who are highly integrated in society will be highly constrained by other people not to commit suicide. Conversely, *the more social disintegration there is, the more suicide there will be.* All of Durkheim's complex statistical arguments are intended to show the truth of his theory of social integration and disintegration. While Durkheim did not do any significant research on other forms of deviance, later sociologists saw a broader applicability of his theory and extended it to deviance in general. In its generalized form the theory states that an increase in social integration will produce a decrease in deviance and, conversely, an increase in social disintegration will produce an increase in deviance.

Durkheim believed in general that lying behind social disintegration was the great transformation from traditional society to modern industrial urban society. He identified two ways in which social disintegration might be manifested and two forms of suicide resulting from such disintegration. *Anomic suicide* results from a situation in which social norms are absent, vague, or so varied as to fail to provide direction for society's members. This idea of *anomie* or normlessness has become an important concept in sociology. Anomic suicide occurs when a society does not possess norms, expectations, or rules upon which societal members can draw for direction; it is characteristic of times of crisis. *Egoistic suicide* results from a situation in which the mechanisms by which social norms are internalized by individuals are absent or inadequate. The norms may well exist on the societal level, but they do not become a part of individuals. Durkheim also recognized two other forms of suicide characteristic of situations of social integration (not social disintegration), but he minimized these two forms, and they were not adopted by later thinkers. They are *altruistic suicide*, occurring in highly integrated societies that ask suicide of their members for the good of the society, and *fatalistic suicide*, which occurs when individuals succumb to the overwhelming weight of the constraints associated with strong social integration. Later sociologists have focused on anomic and egoistic suicide and the social conditions related to them.

What Durkheim was actually arguing, though it is sometimes hard to recognize (see Douglas, 1967, and Pope, 1976, for details of this problem), is that all societies must have both individuality (individual creativity) and social integration (or social constraint) in order to function and continue through time. If a society has a perfect balance of these, then there will presumably be no patterned suicide rate, though there might well still be random instances of suicide. In fact, no society ever seems to achieve such a perfect balance.

Because Durkheim believed that the overall *structure* of society caused differential rates of suicide and of other deviant activities, we speak of his *structural theory of deviance.* It is the best-known part of his theory of deviance but is not the whole theory. He also believed that deviance not only has causes but also serves *functions* for society. One very interesting but little-noticed part of his theory, which is very much in line with social conflict theories, considers deviance as *creative.* Any ideas or acts that are highly creative are apt to be deviant in some way, to violate some earlier moral rules, even if in the name of higher rules. A religious leader, such as Christ, often violates secular laws in the name of a higher morality. Durkheim clearly recognized this form of *creative deviance* as vital to the progressive change of society, but he was at the same time anxious to distinguish between such creative deviance and what he saw as socially destructive deviance. He seems in general to have argued that creative deviance is aimed at improving the life of the society whereas criminal deviance is antisocial or selfish. From this position he must have realized that there are vast problems in deciding just what is good for society and what is not, since it is obvious that deviants such as terrorists define their actions as being for the betterment of society whereas other members of society believe otherwise. Unfortunately, he did not examine these difficulties systematically, perhaps because of the absolutist tenor of the times in which he lived and thought.

The major part of his *functional theory of deviance* (his theory of the functions of deviance for a society) was about the effects that *social response to deviance* had on society. Durkheim believed that morality was important to society not only as a practical way of creating patterns of actions (social order) that individuals could use to order their lives, but also as a major way in which society was defined for its members. He thought that society is in a literal sense morality, that there cannot be society without morality, and that the members of society feel fulfilled by invoking the moral rules. Thus, if society were ever able to eliminate a specific kind of immorality so that the moral rule against it became superfluous, then society would shift its emphasis to other moral rules. For example, if all forms of theft that are currently considered severe moral violations, such as armed robbery, were eliminated, then society might deal more severely with what today are lesser forms of theft, and perhaps shoplifting might be seen as a terrible crime. By maintaining a high level of concern with morality, society is maintaining a high level of concern with itself, with what it as a particular kind of society *is*. Morality *is* the social structure, the social system, the society.

Thus, Durkheim argues, society actually benefits in the long run even from antisocial crimes, *as long as there is an effective social response to the crime*. For example, when society invokes terrible punishment against a murderer, it is reinforcing in the minds of all its members the definition of itself as a society in which murder is intolerable and in addition it is teaching its members by example that murder is a terribly immoral action with terrible consequences. For this reason, society dramatizes its most severe invocations of rules, as in murder trials and executions, which until recently were public events and are still considered front-page news events. It is still common to hear people support such dramatization of punishments because they believe it will help to deter others from doing the same thing. In the famous 1976 controversy over the execution of convicted Utah murderer Gary Mark Gilmore, former Texas governor John Connally argued in a radio interview that the execution by firing squad should be televised: "I just happen to believe the death penalty is a deterrent and the more dramatically it can be demonstrated, the more dramatic is the deterrent." The judges turned down Gilmore's request for such television coverage of his own execution. In some societies it is not uncommon to use television as well as all the more ancient forms of public presentations to dramatize the punishment of "enemies of society." In 1976 when a small group of Palestinian terrorists were captured after they seized hostages in a hotel in Jordan, they were tried, sentenced to death, and hanged before a nationwide television audience within twenty-four hours. These films were shown on television news programs around much of the world.

Durkheim's ideas have profoundly influenced sociological thought about deviance. We will see his influence in the more recent structural theories of deviance and also in conflict theories of deviance, which are in many ways a response to Durkheim's ideas. Even in the Level III theories of social disorganization we will see his influence. Much sociological theorizing about deviance is either an elaboration of or a response to the ideas and insights of Durkheim.

Merton's Theory of Social Structure, Anomie, and Deviance. Merton's influential structural theory of deviance was explicitly intended to be an extension of Durkheim's earlier argument. Merton's presentation of his theory in "Social Structure and Anomie" (1949) and "Continuities in the Theory of Social Structure and Anomie" (1957) begins with a critique of psychological theories of deviance, particularly those which are biologically based. He argues that deviance and nonconformity in general are still commonly viewed, even in the social sciences, as a simple working out of natural biological impulses in situations where sufficient social control is absent. He intended, on the contrary, to show that important forms of deviance, such as juvenile delinquency, were caused by the normal functioning of society itself, by social structure and the way it functions, and not by biological drives. Just as Durkheim had argued earlier — and here Merton refers specifically to Durkheim — deviance is a "normal" human response to abnormal social structures.

Merton argues that two elements are crucial to the understanding of deviance: (1) *the normatively or culturally prescribed goals,* and (2) *the structurally prescribed means of achieving those goals.* A state of equilibrium between legitimate goals and legitimate means exists when members of society are socialized to desire the things that society provides the legitimate means of achieving (legitimate goals) *and* members have access to those legitimate means. However, when members are socialized to want something legitimate but legitimate social means are denied them, or when they are socialized to value the means but not the goals, or when they value neither the legitimate means nor goals, then there is an imbalance between ends and means, or disequilibrium. Merton calls such imbalance or disequilibrium social *anomie,* and the crux of his deviance theory is his interpretation of Durkheim's theory of anomie.

Anomie, as conceptualized by Durkheim, is a state of normlessness or an absence or ambiguity of social rules. Merton explains anomie as follows:

> Cultural structure may be defined as that organized set of normative values governing behavior which is common to members of a designated society or group. And by social structure is meant that organized set of social relationships in which members of the society or group are variously implicated. Anomie is then conceived as a breakdown in the cultural structure, occurring particularly when there is an acute disjunction between the cultural norms and goals and the socially structured capacities of members of the group to act in accord with them. In this conception, cultural values may help to produce behavior which is at odds with the mandates of the values themselves (1957: 162).

In Merton's view, individuals experience such anomie as pressure or anomic *strain.* They seek to relieve this anomic strain in four ways; these alternatives produce four major forms of social deviance. Merton presented this theory in what became a famous diagram of individual orientations to means and ends, as shown in Figure 2.3.

Merton believed that in most societies most of the time individuals are socialized to want what society presents as goals and to accept the means society provides to achieve such goals, and thus there is *conformity.* When however individuals are not so socialized *or* when society does not deliver what it promises, deviance occurs as a response to such anomie.

Figure 2.3.
A typology of modes of individual adaptation[a]

Modes of adaptation	Cultural goals[b]	Institutionalized means[b]
I. Conformity	+	+
II. Innovation	+	−
III. Ritualism	−	+
IV. Retreatism	−	−
V. Rebellion	±	±

[a] This typology was first published in 1937.
[b] Plus sign indicates acceptance; minus sign, rejection.
Source: Reprinted with permission of Macmillan Publishing Co., Inc. from *Social Theory and Social Structure* by Robert K. Merton. Copyright © 1963 by The Free Press, a Corporation.

Merton saw *innovation* as the most common and important type of individual reaction to structurally induced anomic strains in the United States, and thus the most common form of deviance. He saw the high value of the goal of success and the combination of lesser value and lesser availability of legitimate means to that success as fundamental to an understanding of innovative deviance in the United States. Those who are without access to legitimate means and who are highly desirous of success will innovate or create and use illegitimate means to achieve their goals. Merton's famous essays emphasize this type of deviance. What he had in mind here was very much like the common-sense idea that the "have-nots" are more apt to use illegal means to reach their goals than the "haves." More specifically, he argued that the poor in United States society are socialized, particularly by middle-class teachers in schools, to want the same kind of social and monetary success as the middle and upper classes, but the poor, in fact, have far fewer legitimate opportunities to achieve that goal of success. Under anomic stress, they are pressured socially to use illegitimate means to achieve success and reduce anomic strain.

Influenced both by Durkheim and by earlier work by Chicago sociologists, Merton applied his idea of innovative deviance to what had commonly been found about the poor in the urban slums. Others had argued that the slum dwellers of Chicago used forms of vice to achieve the normal success goals of United States society, mainly money, in a situation where only such abnormal (deviant) means would allow them to be successful. Merton argued that such an adaptation was generally true of the poor, especially of juveniles who became juvenile delinquents, and of people such as Al Capone who became mobsters:

Within this context, Capone represents the triumph of amoral intelligence over morally prescribed "failure," when the channels of vertical mobility are closed or narrowed in a society which places a high premium on economic affluence and social ascent for all its members (1957).

Merton did not give much attention to the other three forms of deviance — ritualism, retreatism, and rebellion. We shall consider them briefly here for what they may suggest about other possible causes of deviant behavior. *Ritualism* occurs in situations where individuals accept legitimate means but through socialization or lack of social access do not accept legitimate goals. Such individuals are not likely to be publicly recognized as deviant, because "failure to reach a goal" is less socially noticeable or problematic than "failure to follow legitimate means." An example of ritualistic deviance can be provided by those teachers who, under the stresses of the school system, renounce the goal of educating the children but remain "teachers," ritually following the rules. (See Levy, *Ghetto School*: 1970.) *Retreatism* involves a rejection of both means and goals. Retreatists were seen by Merton as true "aliens" in society. This category includes "some of the activities of psychotics, psychoneurotics, chronic autists, pariahs, outcasts, vagrants, vagabonds, tramps, chronic drunkards, and drug addicts."

The final type of deviance identified by Merton is *rebellion* (or revolution). Merton saw this type as totally different from the others and important in its own right, but he considered it only briefly. This adaptation involves an ambivalent reaction to both goals and means. It involves seeking similar but modified goals in similar but modified ways by "efforts to change the existing structure rather than to perform accommodative actions within this structure." A frequent criticism of structural analysis is its failure to deal with social conflict; Merton's failure to develop the concept of rebellious deviance would seem to support such a criticism.

Merton's theory of social structure, anomie, and deviance has been analyzed, extended, modified, tested, criticized, and rejected by hundreds of social scientists, both in its 1949 version and its 1957 revision. (For a good brief overview of these derivative theories, see Clinard, 1964: 1–64.) Major theorists such as Talcott Parsons (1951) have accepted the basic idea of the theory and merely extended it to other forms of behavior in which there supposedly exists some strain between social learning or expectations (what individuals want) and what they get. Sociologists have now applied Merton's basic theory to almost all conceivable forms of deviant behavior, from deliquency (Lander, 1954) to mental disorders (Srole, 1962), to political behavior (de Grazia, 1948). As Clinard and others have shown, these extensions contain many different interpretations of the concept of anomie, but all of them seem to be concerned in some way with the basic idea that *the normal operations of complex societies such as the United States produce dislocations between desires, values, laws, beliefs, expectations, actions, and outcomes that in some way lead to or encourage individuals to commit actions that are socially defined as violations of social rules.* These dislocations are the very thing Durkheim intended to describe when he developed the concept of anomie.

Merton's theory of deviance and anomie and its later extension by other sociologists is, like Durkheim's theory of integration, a Level II theory. While Merton extends Durkheim's ideas, his analysis remains on the societal level. His concern is with what it is about the structure of society that explains deviance.

Later Theories of Deviance Based on Durkheim's Thought. We have seen that Durkheim really had two closely related theories about deviance. Most of his work, especially *Suicide*, was an attempt to show that *social disintegration* causes deviance. But he was also concerned, especially in his work on *The Rules of Sociological Method*, with a *functional explanation* of deviance, showing that deviance caused by the structural factor of social disintegration has certain *functions* for society. He argued that the social response to deviance of dramatically punishing the deviants reinforces the very rules the deviants have broken. He also argued that those forms of unselfish deviance that prove successful, such as a new form of religion, function to produce valuable social change. Merton, as well as other sociologists, greatly expanded Durkheim's functional explanation and applied it to many other forms of behavior.

Like Durkheim, Merton believed that social structure causes deviance and that this deviance has positive functions in society. Specifically, Merton argued that the "corrupt" political machines of so many big cities in the United States of the late nineteenth and early twentieth centuries, though caused by anomic strains, functioned to allow the lower classes to be upwardly mobile, which was normatively prescribed by society. In a famous essay, "Crime as an American Way of Life," Daniel Bell (1953) took this basic idea and applied it to the historical patterns of deviance among immigrant groups in the United States. He tried to show that each new major group of immigrant poor in the big cities of the Northeast and Midwest found that earlier groups had possession of major forms of deviance that gave them the capital needed to get ahead in respectable society, so that the new group created new forms of deviance for the same purpose. The Irish, the first really big immigrant group into these cities, early created the political machines that allowed them to use various forms of political corruption to advance themselves financially and, eventually, socially. The Italians, the next big group, found it difficult at first to get control of the political power of the Irish. Therefore the Italians created the underworld machines of gambling enterprises and later became the core of the rum-running rackets when Prohibition unintentionally created that criminal opportunity. In general, Bell argued:

> The desires satisfied in extra-legal fashion were more than a hunger for the "forbidden fruits" of conventional morality. They also involved, in the complex and ever shifting structure of group, class and ethnic stratification, which is the warp and woof of America's "open" society, such "normal" goals as independence through a business of one's own, and such "moral" aspirations as the desire for social advancement and social prestige. For crime, in the language of the sociologists, has a "functional" role in the society, and the urban rackets — the illicit activity organized for continuing profit rather than individual illegal acts — is one of the queer ladders of social mobility in American life. Indeed, it is not too much to say that the whole question of organized crime in America cannot be understood unless one appreciates (1) the distinctive role of organized gambling as a function of a mass consumption economy; (2) the specific role of various immigrant groups as they one after another became involved in marginal business and crime; and (3) the relation of crime to the changing character of the urban political machines (1953).

Functional explanations have been developed for many other forms of deviant behavior. Kingsley Davis (1939) explained prostitution in terms of its positive functions for society. He argued that the stable family is of fundamental importance in society and the disorganized family is very disorganizing for society in general. At the same time, the monogamous nature of marital sex sometimes produces a conflict between biological drives and the requirements of social structure for a stable family. Sometimes marriages prove sexually unsatisfying. Davis viewed prostitution as functioning to satisfy male sexual needs in a way that would not undermine the stability of the family. The threat of unsatisfied female needs to the stability of the family is an issue that does not arise in Davis's discussion. In our consideration of prostitution in Chapter 6 we will present and criticize Davis's theory.

Kai Erikson has presented probably the most general functional theory of deviance in his work on *Wayward Puritans* (1966). He studied three great waves of deviance among Puritans in the seventeenth-century United States and was struck by the fact that the *numbers* of deviants at any given time in Puritan society (the *deviance rate*) tended to be very much the same. He concluded that deviants were created by society, almost pushed into deviance, because of needs of the general nondeviant members of that society. Erikson's work has been seen by some sociologists as a key link between earlier functional theories of deviance and later labeling theories. (See Scott, 1972.) His theorizing clearly is at Level II, emphasizing society and social structure as the source of explanation.

Structural and functional theories remain important in current sociology. Increasingly, however, they have been subjected to a variety of criticisms. Older structural theories have been criticized for their problem orientation, not because they sought to remedy problems but because they uncritically accepted problems as defined by society. Durkheim, for example, accepted the societal definition of suicide as wrong, bad, and self-evidently to be avoided. Although any society may be expected to take its own fundamental beliefs for granted, critics suggest that sociologists should not do so.

More recent criticisms of structural and functional theory have elaborated on this point, suggesting that many studies of deviance have taken uncritically the view of the broader society. The actions that are criminal within the United States legal system have been simply *assumed* to be deviant. Critics suggest that deviance is a far more complex and problematic process that can be viewed from a variety of perspectives, of which that of the broader society is but one. Specifically, as we shall soon see in detail, they argue that many groups in United States society have values that are in conflict with the laws. A third criticism has argued that such theories view the individual as merely a pawn of society, totally moved by outside forces. (See in this regard Dennis Wrong's essay, "The Oversocialized Conception of Man" 1961.)

Those who offer these three kinds of criticism have themselves constructed theories at lower levels of generalization, particularly at Levels III through VII, but one final set of critics have constructed theories that remain at Level II. We turn next to those theorists. Their major criticism of structural and functional theories is that they assume social equilibrium to be identified with nonconflict, social disequilibrium with conflict. Social conflict theorists, on the other hand, argue that conflict is a normal and necessary part of social life and should be so recognized.

SOCIAL CONFLICT THEORIES

Early sociologists, drawing on the common-sense knowledge of the societies in which they lived, were certainly aware of the existence of social conflict in society. Surely, too, they recognized the importance of such conflict as a factor in social deviance. What they did not recognize, according to social conflict theorists, was the pervasive and varied nature of social conflict.

Durkheim, for example, had a somewhat positive, largely undeveloped, and narrow view of social conflict. He saw social conflict as consisting of two dimensions. First, he saw some individuals in conflict with society. He believed that "unselfish" or "creative" violations of rules by such individuals was one way in which social progress could be made — somebody must first challenge the rules before something better could be created. Second, he believed that all societies include conflict between basic social forces, especially between the opposing forces of altruism and egoism. These, however, were abstract forces. Durkheim saw both individual and abstract conflict with society as special occurrences; he did not seem to believe that conflict between each individual and society was a normal outcome of the abstract conflict of social forces, nor did he focus at all on conflict between individuals or between social groups.

Like Durkheim, social analysts of deviance before the 1930s tended to look at social conflict as being primarily between individuals on the one hand and society as a unit on the other; they were concerned with each individual's conflict with the whole moral universe of society. Seldom did they consider the possibility that these persons might be in conflict with society not as individuals but as members of organized subgroups or subcultures of society that had values and patterns of action in conflict with those of the larger society. They assumed that the individual faced a social *uni*verse rather than what William James would have called a social *plura*verse.

Social conflict theory as an explanation of deviance has been growing steadily for the past few decades, and its use may increase. (See, for example, Taylor, Walton, and Young, 1973.) Its use in other areas of sociology is currently more widespread than its use in the study of deviance. Recent conflict theorists in the sociology of deviance differ from earlier ones primarily in the degree to which they see conflict as both necessary and important. These recent theorists argue that there are *necessarily* basic conflicts among all individuals in a society, and among social groups, as well as between each individual and the rest of society. Conflict is viewed as a "natural" or "normal" social process, far more pervasive than earlier theorists recognized. Social conflict is viewed as a basic variable involved in the creation of social rules and in their uses, enforcement, and effects.

Social conflict theorists propose two major theories to explain why social conflict is basic, necessary, and important: (1) Conflict is inherent in human nature; (2) Conflict is an inevitable process in complex societies. The first is a Level I theory and will be discussed briefly here. Theory 2 is a Level II theory and will command the greatest amount of our attention.

1. *Conflict is inherent in human nature.* As we saw earlier, some social biologists in recent years have been arguing for the *genetic* basis of conflict. Some sociologists have related this basic variable of genetically based conflict to the analysis of society. Other sociologists have drawn on biological and ethological studies of dominance patterns. In both instances, sociologists have invoked biological theories to support the

argument that conflict is basic to all social action, a position they have generally already arrived at by means of the following argument.

2. *Conflict is an inevitable process in complex societies.* Some social conflict theorists have argued that conflict is general and basic in complex societies because of their very complexity. In simple societies, which are small and *homogeneous* (uniform in structure and composition), conflict may not arise because general values and rules are shared, but in complex societies their *heterogeneous* (dissimilar in ingredients or parts) nature provides for potential conflict between different groups. This idea was partially developed by Freud (in *Civilization and its Discontents*, 1930) and pervades the works of Marx (1848, 1867).

Recent social conflict theorists have elaborated on both Freud's and Marx's theories, arguing that complex societies involve the use of repressive force by state powers to hold society together, to maintain social order, and to prevent heterogeneity from resulting in the war of each against the others. Governments have used police powers to prevent some members of society from doing things they want to do that the state powers don't want them to do. The history of complex societies lends some obvious support to such an argument. All complex societies were partly created by warriors who used their military powers to suppress opposing groups and to force them to submit to the new state powers. Sociologists have argued that almost all complex societies have centralized state bureaucracies that function in accord with formalistic rules that are in *partial* conflict with the rules and feelings of some or all of the subcultures making up the society. Such imposition of rules inevitably leads to conflict with state powers. Other analysts have emphasized other sources of *alienation* of members of society from the state powers. Alienation is defined at the most general level as the feeling of *difference and distance* between the individual and other individuals, groups, the whole society, or, especially, the state. These feelings of difference and distance almost always involve feelings and values *directed against others.* Among the most important of such feelings and values are those directed against state powers.

To minimize alienation, as well as to establish their authority, rulers try to *legitimate* (to give moral authority to) their powers in varied ways: by presenting themselves to the people as gods, the anointed of heaven, the grand leaders of destiny who will bring glory to all the people, the givers of all social welfare and justice, the givers of laws, and so on. These self-dramatizations have worked to varying degrees. Forms of legitimation wax and wane, yet it does appear that today there is generally a great deal of alienation from state powers. Probably social researchers would agree that this alienation is growing rapidly. Even during periods of frenzied nationalism, a very modern set of feelings and ideas that lend legitimacy to some rulers, there is a great deal of conflicting feeling and thinking. One almost never finds a majority of the citizens rushing off to volunteer for military service, and there are always those who take part in black-market operations during nationalistic wars, in clear violation of laws passed "for the good of the nation." (See Clinard, 1952, on the massive black market in the United States during World War II.)

Some theorists have been very concerned with what factors in society increase and decrease the amount of conflict, especially conflict with state powers. In general, the more complex and heterogeneous a society is, the more conflict it experiences. This kind of analysis has been especially important for understanding United States society. All Western nations have important national subcultures that differ from the majority culture; in fact, most Western nations have "separatist movements" of some sort by which subcultures are trying to achieve some form of independence. Many African nations have important tribal units which differ from the majority culture and which are engaged in separatist movements. But United States society is vastly more pluralistic than most other societies. No other nation approaches the degree of ethnic, racial, and regional heterogeneity of the United States. Regional differences alone little more than a century ago produced one of the most destructive civil wars in the history of Western nations. Regional conflicts are apparent today in struggles over federal regulation of energy, efforts of eastern states to prevent industries from moving south, and a variety of other struggles. The most conflictful situations in the United States today are based on ethnic, racial, and economic differences. Many analysts believe that economic conflicts among interest groups, each trying to get more from the state, are increasing racial and ethnic conflicts.

The theory based on heterogeneity as a source of social conflict is rejected by those who believe that United States institutions act as a great "melting pot" in which all the different ethnic and racial groups come to hold the same values and want the same things, such as success in Merton's theory. The "American myth," an ideology weakened by the explosion of conflicts in the 1960s, includes the melting-pot theory, to which there has always been an appearance of truth. As almost anyone knows from personal experience, second- and third-generation Poles, Jews, Italians, and so on speak the same English language that other United States citizens do and express very much the same values. In fact, in questionnaire studies of expressed values Short (1965) and others have found that even juvenile delinquents seem to share most of the same *expressed* values as middle-class suburbanites.

Some of the social conflict theories (especially those of Douglas,

1971B, and Suttles, 1968) have argued that there is a certain element of truth in the melting-pot theory — that the perceived consensus actually exists, but it is only a *public consensus* over a *public morality.* It is prevalent in public settings, such as on network television shows, but most people, including those most adept at presenting and using the public morality in public settings, also have *private moralities* and ideas that differ in important ways from what they say and do in public settings. At the extreme, some people are consciously hypocritical, saying one thing in public settings and doing things they know to be the opposite in their private lives. *Moralistic hypocrisy,* or the expression of moralistic opposition to the very thing one knows one is doing in private, does exist. At the other extreme are those whose public and private moralities are the same. Most people live in the range between these two extremes. We should recognize that the greater the discrepancy between public and private morality, the more likely it is that moralistic hypocrisy will be adopted *if social conflict is to be avoided.*

Public consensus obscures the amount of social disagreement over social rules and values and thus obscures, both for individuals in society and for sociologists, the potential sources of social conflict. The recognition by sociologists of the discrepancy between public and private morality lends support to the argument that complex societies provide particularly strong conditions for social conflict.

Marxist Theory.   More commonly adopted in the sociology of deviance than other forms of conflict theory has been Marxist theory, derived from the writings of Karl Marx. (In addition to Marx's works, see Lichtheim, *Marxism,* 1965.) Marx saw conflict as inevitable in complex societies and was particularly concerned with class structure as a source of conflict.

In his study of Marxist theory, Lichtheim mentions characteristics that allow us readily to identify it at Level II. In Marx's theory:

> society must be viewed historically, and it must be viewed as a whole. To do so is to realise that the social system is propelled by internal contradictions which are essential to its functioning and cannot be legislated out of existence, though they can be overcome "at a higher level," i.e., after history has reached the stage of the classless society. For the time being, class antagonisms are the motor of historical (social) development (1965: 45–46).

According to Marx, conflict is a necessary dimension to societies *as they are currently constituted;* conflict can be overcome only after massive social change. The conflict Marx focused on was that between classes — between those who controlled the means of production and those who did not. Since Marx saw *labor,* in the broad sense of activity in the world, as fundamental to human identity, those who were alienated from their labor (the proletariat, who did not control the means of production) were in conflict with the bourgeoisie (those who did control those means). Marx saw conflict between the proletariat and the bourgeoisie as inevitable because each class was fighting for its identity, for its relation to its own labor.

Since Marx viewed labor and the distribution of products of labor as fundamental to social relations, he is called an *economic determinist*, from his theoretical position that *economic relations determine or cause social relations*. He was both social analyst and social critic. Lichtheim says:

> Even where Marx theorises about the given social structure, as in his later writings, the theory of society is always integrated with a radical critique of the existing order. This is not to say that a politically neutral and "value-free" sociology cannot be deduced from Marx's utterances, but he himself clearly did not believe that this could be done . . . (1965: 46).

In our treatment here of Marxist theory, we must recognize that there is a difference between Marx's writings and the formulations that later thinkers based on his ideas. At the end of his life, Marx himself said: "I am not a Marxist." Marx directly influenced many thinkers in history, politics, philosophy, and sociology. A Marxist stream of sociological theory has continued since his own day and at present is strong if not broad. Marx himself did not directly address the topic of deviance, and later Marxists have not been particularly concerned with it. There has been, however, some Marxist theorizing about crime.

Current Marxist theorists agree that those who control the means of production, the major example being capitalists in Western societies, control the power of the state and use that state power to enact and enforce laws that support their economic interests and necessarily repress the interests of the lower classes. That position is what we might call the *capitalization of crime*. Many theorists also include an idea derived from the economics of John Keynes that advanced capitalist societies have an inherent tendency to oversaving, overproduction, and, thus, unemployment and underconsumption. Keynesians argue that the state can correct the problem by printing money for distribution to consumers to increase consumption, an economic policy in fact pursued by the "welfare states" we find in every major Western nation today. Marxist theorists argue that Keynesian policies do not in fact solve the problem and that unemployment will continue to grow as those policies are pursued. The state is viewed as using its powers to increasingly control lower-class people's opposition to their enforced poverty. The "repressive criminal justice system" becomes a booming industry — the "criminal justice–industrial complex" — as more and more businesses find their greatest profits are made in "fighting crime." But, of course, it is a fight they must not win, because then there would be no more profits from their "war on crime."

Richard Quinney has probably been the most consistent proponent of this viewpoint among sociologists of deviance in the United States:

> A major part of the new and growing social-industrial complex is what we can call the "criminal justice–industrial complex." Criminal justice, in all its aspects, is becoming one of the last remaining capital-investment industries. That industry finds it profitable to invest in crime is one of the final contradictions of the capitalist system (1977: 117–118).

Marxist theorists, and other sociologists as well, have argued that certain kinds of laws and patterns of law enforcement are the direct product of political action by powerful interest groups (see Douglas, 1971B; Taylor, Walton, and Young, 1973). Consider, for example, *laws of garnishment,* which make it possible for landlords or merchants to use police powers to force the employers of people who owe money to take the money out of their wages. Those laws were obviously not enacted because of political pressure from renters or those who owe bills. There are many such laws.

However, when we come to laws like those against vagrancy, the economic motive becomes far less clear. It is obvious that laws of vagrancy are enforced almost entirely against lower-class people, and that middle- and upper-class people enact them, call for their enforcement, and push to keep them on the books, but it is not clear that they do so today for economic reasons. What is gained economically by paying huge amounts of taxes to police and prison officials to keep large numbers of alcoholics in prison for short periods? Nearly one-third of arrests by police are for drunkenness, so that the cost is huge. If the economic motive were the only one at work, those who pay taxes would presumably vote to let people stay drunk (or sober) in the streets. But they don't. Why? Part of the reason may be mere inertia or lack of interest. Another part may be that some people are concerned with "standards of public decency." The reason, however, does not seem entirely clear and the economic dimension is certainly not readily apparent.

A number of criticisms can be made of social conflict theory. Although sociologists agree that social conflict can be an important factor in explaining deviance, social conflict theorists are criticized for the way in which they make use of this concept, as well as their neglect of other factors. The criticisms we now offer are directed particularly to those theories based on the premise that conflict is an inevitable process in complex societies.

Whereas structural and functional theories have been criticized for their neglect of social conflict, social conflict theories have been criticized for their failure to recognize and explain social order. Enduring, stable social situations cannot be accounted for by social conflict theories. Though each of these theoretical positions may claim to take the other into account and not to deny its importance, in actual usage each does seem to neglect either social order or social conflict.

A second criticism of social conflict theories is similar to that directed to structural and functional theories: it concerns their focus on social problems. While structural and functional theories have been criticized for accepting common-sense definitions of social problems, social conflict theories are criticized for the more general evaluative stream running through them. Social conflict theories take sides; they identify such factors as oppressor and oppressed, powerful and powerless, bourgeoisie and proletariat, supporting the position of the second in each pair. (For an excellent example of this conflict among theorists, see Howard Becker, "Whose Side Are We On?" and Gouldner's response, "The Myth of a Value-Free Sociology" in Douglas, 1970A.) Marx himself saw a necessary link between analysis and reform, and current social conflict theorists have for the most part preserved his emphasis.

A final criticism directed to social conflict theories is that they can account for only part of the data they find. In particular, to the extent that they focus on economics as the root of social arrangements, they cannot fully explain such occurrences as the vagrancy example, cited above. Critics, beginning as early as 1905 with Max Weber's criticism of Marx in *The Protestant Ethic and the Spirit of Capitalism,* argue that although economics is one explanatory variable, it is not the only one. Rather than seeing the social world as a result of economic variables, critics see the social world as itself a crucial explanatory variable.

In this chapter we have looked at some examples of the most general explanations offered to explain deviant behavior. Those at Level I explain deviance in terms that lie outside the social sphere, while those at Level II seek explanation at the societal level. All the theories we have examined deal with factors that may well contribute to an understanding of deviance, yet we see these theories as *partial* at best and not as the total explanations they claim to be. They contribute to our understanding of factors to be considered and to be investigated empirically, but our current recognition of the complexity of deviance leads us to view with suspicion any explanation that focuses on a single factor as *the cause* of deviance.

We move now to examples of middle-range theories, those which are neither purely general nor purely specific. These theories remain within the social realm in their quest for explanation, but the social features they examine are less broad than those at the societal level. As we examine these theories, we will see how sociologists have continued their search for *the cause* of deviance by looking *within* societies and social structures. When we reach Chapter 5, we will consider the issue of *causality* in the social world. Meanwhile, readers may find it useful to consider critically the idea of causality as it emerges in the next two chapters, and to consider the ways in which they view their own social behavior as *caused* by factors in the social world.

3

Middle-Range Explanations of Deviance

Middle-range theories attempt a compromise between generality and specificity. Although continuing to look to *social* factors as sources of explanation, they consider factors narrower than *society as a whole*. In this chapter we examine theories that lie at Levels III and IV of Figure 2.1. Theories at Level III seek explanations in specific features or structures of society. The features selected for analysis are usually major aspects of the society being studied. Prominent explanatory variables include urbanization, race, social class, and social relations. Theories at Level IV, which are even less general than those at Level III, turn their attention to specific groups in society.

Some sociologists have stressed the need to develop middle-range theories. Merton, whose structural theories we examined as examples at Level II, states:

> Sociology will advance in the degree that its major concern is with developing theories of the middle range and will be frustrated if attention centers on theory in the large. I believe that our major task *today* is to develop special theories applicable to limited ranges of data . . . rather than to seek at once the "integrated" conceptual structure adequate to derive all these and other theories. The sociological theorist *exclusively* committed to the exploration of high abstractions runs the risk that, as with modern *decor*, the furniture of his mind will be sparse, bare, and uncomfortable (1957: 9).

Merton thus encourages movement away from Levels I and II and toward the development of more modest theories. The latter theories are our subject in this chapter. We will devote particular attention to social disorganization theory (Level III) and theories about subcultures (Level IV). In doing so we will present major examples of such theories. Of course, work conducted within each of these theoretical frameworks is far more extensive than what we are presenting. Social disorganization theory grew out of an enormous amount of work done in the Chicago school of sociology and led to the development of theories about subcultures. We begin with a brief description of the Chicago school.

The Chicago School

In the 1920s a small group of highly energetic and creative sociologists at the newly formed University of Chicago Department of Sociology carried out a multitude of studies and created the first distinctively American theory of deviance, though they did not actually use this term. Robert Park, who motivated and directed much of this work, had served for eleven years as a reporter on the city beats of Minneapolis, Detroit, Denver, New York, and Chicago before pursuing scholarly work. The search for news in the turbulent cities of the United States gave him a sense of the excitement and mystery of urban social life which he later imparted to his many students. When he became a sociologist, he made Chicago — one of the great centers of United States immigration and industrialization — his "laboratory for discovering human nature" (Helen Hughes, 1968) and for unraveling the mysteries of social organization; he wanted to understand how any organization could come out of the extreme heterogeneity and conflict in this huge city of immigrants.

Like European sociologists examining social disintegration and deviance, Chicago sociologists conducted their studies and analyses of deviance under the background assumption that there existed in the past a more serene and organized life centered on the village or small town. Park himself had grown up in such small towns as Harveyville, Pennsylvania, and Red Wing, Minnesota. His own experience, like that of Durkheim and others, was the basis for making a fundamental distinction between what they saw as the relatively simple, highly organized, primary group life of the village and the extremely heterogeneous, disorganized, impersonal life of the city. His focus was narrower than society as a whole; it was directed toward the urban/rural distinction, even though he continued to invoke the concept of society.

For Park and most of his co-workers at Chicago, the city was a source both of excitement and mystery and of many social evils (deviance). Like United States intellectuals before them, they were ambivalent toward the city, both condemning and praising, both optimistic and pessimistic. But, although a poet such as Walt Whitman might sing the praises of Chicago's diversity and energy, the sociologists pursued their basic commitment to study urban *problems,* and for the Chicago school the main problem was deviance, rather than inequality, poverty, or the other problems social conflict theorists emphasize.

As they studied lower-class life, slums, and deviance, Chicago sociologists added a new dimension to the idea that such things were both mysterious and evil. As Matza (1969) has argued forcefully, one of their most important points was that lower-class life and the deviant patterns that existed within it were entirely *natural* — just as natural to the people involved as was any middle-class nondeviant pattern of life to the middle-class nondeviant. Indeed, they argued that most of lower-class life was essentially the same as middle-class life, merely carried out at a lower income level. One Chicago sociologist, Thrasher, noted in his description of boys' gangs:

> It must be remembered in reading the following description that the writer is presenting only one phase of the life of these communities. There are churches, schools, clubs, banks, and the usual list of wholesome institutions in these areas as well as the gangs. The gangs and the type of life described here may not even be apparent to the average citizen of the district, who is chiefly occupied in his own pursuits (1927: 5).

As Howard Becker (1963) was to conclude many years later, most of the daily life of people socially defined as deviant is spent doing very non-deviant — even humdrum — things. Gang boys might get into violent fights that resulted in deaths — a not infrequent occurrence in Chicago when Thrasher did his research — but most of the time they were "well-behaved" boys. At the same time there was mystery and excitement in their lives that intrigued and excited middle-class readers and the researchers themselves:

> It is in such regions as the gang inhabits that we find much of the romance and mystery of a great city. Here are the comedy and tragedy. Here is melodrama which excels the recurrent "thrillers" at the downtown theaters. Here are unvarnished emotions. Here also is a primitive democracy that cuts through all the conventional social and racial discriminations. The gang, in short, is *life,* often rough and untamed, yet rich in elemental social processes significant to the student of society and human nature (Thrasher, 1927).

Chicago sociology was thus characterized by its view of deviance as (1) exciting and mysterious, (2) evil, and (3) normal. These three themes recur repeatedly in the writings of the school.

The sense of awe and mystery before the vast complexity of the city's social life was not an idiosyncratic or unimportant aspect of the work of Chicago sociologists. On the contrary, this sense more than anything else motivated them to seek out all the complex forms of social life created by people in the *interstices* or crevices of the city. Even more important, it led them to become partially involved in the life they were studying, thus creating new sociological field-research methods for studying deviance. It also led them to take great pains and loving care in describing the details of the everyday life of their subjects. Whether studying gangs, hobos, or taxi-dance hall dancers* and their customers, the Chicago sociologists' excitement in penetrating and describing *life* in its natural settings often allowed them to capture that life as it was really lived rather than as distorted by the preconceptions of outsiders. The richness of the field-research descriptions in the many Chicago studies of deviance makes them a source of data even today; these books are still widely read both for their insights and their interest. It is against this background that social disorganization theory was developed. (See Faris, 1967, for a detailed historical account of this school.)

Level III. Specific Social Structural Variables as Sources of Explanation

Social disorganization theory is one of the richest sources of specific structural variables available to sociologists. These variables remain important in current sociological theory even though social disorganization theory itself has been abandoned. It may appear odd that although social disorganization theorists seem to have recognized that their theory did not fit their data, they did not abandon it. We will see the struggles that sociologists go through when their data appear to contradict "an established truth," as social disorganization theory was taken to be. It was only with the development of field-research findings about subcultures that social disorganization theory came to be abandoned. As we look at social disorganization theory, notice (1) the wide variety of social structural variables identified as explanations of deviance and (2) the struggles of sociologists to support social disorganization theory in the face of findings that contradicted it.

THE DEVELOPMENT OF SOCIAL DISORGANIZATION THEORY

Like any major body of research, the work of the Chicago school involved significant variation in the uses and interpretations of concepts. Social disorganization as a concept was used in a variety of ways and was associated with many different variables in the formulation of theory. Like other major theories, too, social disorganization theory changed over time, becoming more developed and systematic. Never-

---

* Taxi-dance hall dancers work in clubs whose patrons pay to dance with them. A popular song written in 1930, "Ten Cents a Dance" (words by Lorenz Hart, music by Richard Rodgers), portrays such an arrangement. The clubs were called taxi-dance halls because customers were generally referred and brought there by taxi drivers.

theless, there was always a core of fundamental ideas around which theories varied. These core ideas, later formulated into the systematic theory of social disorganization and deviance by Park and Burgess (1921), Wirth (1928, 1938), and others, are what concern us in this section.

One of Park's basic ideas was that human beings and their environment are interdependent. The external situation has fundamental effects on individuals and the ways in which social life is organized. One important part of this external situation is the physical environment. It tends to be most important in simpler societies, which the Chicago sociologists — unlike modern anthropologists — believed to be relatively undisturbed by social problems or deviance. (This point is very clear in Chapter 1 of Robert Faris's widely used textbook on *Social Disorganization*, 1955; for a more recent anthropological view, see Edgerton, *Deviance: A Cross-Cultural Perspective*, 1976.) But as society grows and becomes more complex and technological, the physical environment becomes less important in determining social life, while the external social situation, especially the interdependence of social groups, becomes more important. Like social conflict theorists, Chicago sociologists believed that increasing societal complexity was significant in explaining human behavior. Unlike conflict theorists, however, they saw societal complexity as resulting in the greater influence of *social* factors on human behavior.

This emphasis on the importance of social factors occurs in one of the earliest and most famous works of the Chicago school, *Polish Peasants in Europe and America*, by W. I. Thomas and Florian Znaniecki (1923). They formulated the theory of social disorganization and deviance in its broadest terms, and many of the studies done by Chicago sociologists between 1930 and 1950 drew on this tradition.

Chicago sociologists were concerned with the same general phenomena that concerned European sociologists — namely the industrial revolution and its effects on society, including massive urbanization and industrialization. They used the term *social organization* in roughly the same way as Durkheim used *social integration*. Like Durkheim, they were convinced that the degree to which individuals were involved in and committed to social relations was fundamental in determining whether they lived in accord with the values of society or violated them. Durkheim, however, believed that formal social relationships were more important than informal personal ones in explaining human behavior, whereas Chicago sociologists considered that the personal, face-to-face social relations that grow "naturally" from the interdependencies of human beings — in kinship groupings, love relations, friendships, and so on — were far more important than formal ones in socially organizing or integrating a society, a city, or a neighborhood.

The more informal, "natural," face-to-face, personal relations were called *primary relations* and the resulting groups *primary groups*. (These terms were developed by Charles Horton Cooley, 1902, 1909.) The more formal, direct, impersonal relations were called *secondary relations*. Chicago sociologists believed there was a continuum of primary and secondary relations, stretching from the total commitments of individual love to the indirect and abstract relations of membership in an international club. In general, the more primary the relations within a group, the more socially organized it was thought to be; conversely, the less primary the relations (the more secondary), the less socially organized the group was. Primary relations were thought to have a greater organizational effect on the city and on the places where such relations took place; secondary relations had far less organizational effect and indeed could coexist with disorganization.

The crucial idea of Chicago sociologists was that *social disorganization causes deviance*. The common-sense idea on which they drew was simply that the less personally and intimately involved individuals are with a social group, the more likely they are to violate its values, and indeed there is extensive common-sense support for such a view. Chicago sociologists also firmly believed that the less involvement people have with others, and especially the less they are observed in their actions, the less others can control their behavior or prevent their deviant activities. Everyone knows that children are particularly inclined to play with matches when adults cannot see them doing it. Similarly, in the midwest in the early part of this century "vice" of all sorts — hard drinking, gambling, prostitution, and so on — flourished almost entirely in big cities such as Chicago and in small "sin cities" spread conveniently throughout the region. Farmers and store clerks might not engage in such "wicked" activities in their small home towns where everyone knew them, but they could when a business trip took them to a city where none of their acquaintances could observe them. Unobserved "wickedness" had few immediate negative consequences (except perhaps on an eventual day of reckoning), so that when they went to the city they often "went wild."

According to Chicago sociologists, the more anonymous or unknown individuals are in a group, the more apt they are to violate society's rules. Shaw and McKay wrote, "Because of the anonymity in urban life the individual is freed from much of the scrutiny and control which characterize life in primary group situations in small towns and rural communities" (1942: 438). And, as we have seen, the less involved they are with society in general, the more apt they are to violate its rules. Chicago sociologists concluded that *the less involved and the more anonymous individuals are, the greater the degree of social disorganization; and the greater the degree of social disorganization, the more deviance*. This statement provides the abstract meaning of the many more graphic, and often more moralistic, generalizations Chicago sociologists made about their studies of deviance, such as the grimly moralistic picture Paul Cressey painted of the taxi-dance halls:

> Among the recreational institutions of the American city none perhaps reveals with as much clarity as many of the perplexing problems which make difficult the wholesome expression of human nature in the urban setting as does the public dance hall. In it can be found in bold relief the impersonality of the city, the absence of restraints, the loneliness and the individual maladjustment and distraction characteristic of the life of many in the urban environment (1932: xvii).

SOCIAL CONFLICT AS AN ELEMENT
IN SOCIAL DISORGANIZATION THEORY

In his 1925 article entitled "Social Problems," Lawrence Frank concluded that *all* social disorganization involved value conflicts. Conflicts — including moral ones — between the individual and a homogeneous society were basic to the idea of social disorganization and resulting deviance. A very early example is provided in W. I. Thomas's important work, *The Unadjusted Girl*:

> Preliminary to any self-determined act of behavior there is always a stage of examination and deliberation which we may call *the definition of the situation.* And actually not only concrete acts are dependent on the definition of the situation, but gradually a whole life-policy and the personality of the individual himself follow from a series of such definitions.
>
> But the child is always born into a group of people among whom all the general types of situations which may arise have already been defined and corresponding rules of conduct developed, and where he has not the slightest chance of making his definitions and following his wishes without interference. . . . Certainly the wishes in general are such that they can be satisfied only in a society. But we have only to refer to the criminal code to appreciate the variety of ways in which the wishes of the individual may conflict with the wishes of society. And the criminal code takes no account of the many unsanctioned expressions of the wishes which society attempts to regulate by persuasion and gossip.
>
> There is therefore always a rivalry between the spontaneous definitions of the situation made by the member of an organized society and the definitions which his society has provided for him. The individual tends to a hedonistic selection of activity, pleasure first; and society to a utilitarian selection, safety first. . . .
>
> It is in this connection that a moral code arises, which is a set of rules or behavior norms, regulating the expression of the wishes, and which is built up by successive definitions of the situation. In practice the abuse arises first and the rule is made to prevent its recurrence. Morality is thus the generally accepted definition of the situation, whether expressed in public opinion and

the unwritten law, in a formal legal code, or in religious commandments and prohibitions (1923: 42–43).*

Marshall Clinard and others later expanded this argument to assert that urbanization in the United States had actually produced a large increase in relativism and in conflicts over social values:

> The relativistic nature of social values in modern society, with its emphasis on individual choice, has put great strains, even in wartime, on social organization and democracy, both conditions resting essentially on general agreement about fundamental social objectives. Under these conditions the significance of laws becomes relative, some to be selectively obeyed according to whether one believes in them; others to be disobeyed if one does not. This absence of consensus on fundamental values in our society is illustrated in these pulls between group objectives and individual self-interest and disregard for personal integrity, and between national welfare and individual materialism. On the one side has been respect for law and on the other side disrespect for law if it stood in the way of individual material success, as in the case of the black market.
>   Processes of urbanization are largely responsible for this underlying lack of consensus in modern society . . . (Clinard, 1952: 330–331).

Later formulations of social disorganization theory focused increasingly on social conflict as an element in both social disorganization and deviance. Economic changes that affected everyday life, especially those which were sudden, were claimed to produce social conflict, social disorganization, and thus deviance. Paul Cressey, for example, tried to show how the rapid development of the coal industry in Harlan County, Kentucky, which greatly expanded the population and transformed jobs and other parts of life, led to widespread "vices" and helped to turn this once rural country into "Bloody Harlan" (1955). Robert Faris and other sociologists extended this argument to include many other forms of internal and external social conflict. They were very interested in how conflict between generations — what Faris termed the "loss of continuity between generations" — affects deviance (Faris, 1955: 47–50). Faris went so far as to develop a more general theory of social disorganization that was concerned with the ways in which certain forms of internal conflict generated not only deviance but dangers to the general public interest. He argued, for example, that labor union strikes can create a general social disorganization that injures the public (pp. 51–53). He even tried to show that the fall of France in 1940 was a direct result of growing social disorganization caused by conflicts among generations, between immigrants and French, between classes, and among other social units (pp. 55–60). In a

---

* Reprinted from *The Unadjusted Girl*, by W. I. Thomas by permission of Little, Brown and Company. Copyright © 1923.

way, Faris was arguing that internal conflicts in France led to deviance from the basic value of patriotic defense of the nation, an argument that was later developed independently and far more extensively by historians.

Although Chicago theorists were concerned with social conflict, they never developed a full-fledged theory of conflict comparable to that of the social conflict theorists. The relation they perceived between social conflict on one hand and social disorganization and deviance on the other was never clearly spelled out; at times social conflict appeared a cause, at others an effect. They were much more interested in policy questions — those directed to solving the social problems of crime — than in developing a thoroughgoing social conflict theory of deviance. They accepted the legitimacy of established laws and ignored the ways in which those laws themselves created conflict. The latter point was clearly recognized by social conflict theorists (see above, pp. 51–58). Chicago sociologists recognized social conflict without developing a social conflict theory.

Once they had established the existence and effects of social disorganization, the next step for Chicago theorists was to explain two occurrences: (1) why some groups have more social disorganization and deviance than others and (2) why even in disorganized groups some individuals do not commit deviant acts. We will deal with both these issues in turn and will present some of the major specific structural variables identified by Chicago theorists.

SPECIFIC SOCIAL STRUCTURAL VARIABLES TO EXPLAIN GROUP DISORGANIZATION AND DEVIANCE

Chicago sociologists believed that the more urban an area was, the more anonymous and the less involved — that is, the more disorganized — its inhabitants would be. Urban areas were described as consisting of vast hordes of strangers and of many different groups with which individuals had little direct involvement; the city was naturally more disorganized than small towns and rural areas. Therefore, it could be expected to produce more deviance.

Although aspects of the physical environment, such as slum conditions, were considered to have some independent effects on human beings and thus on deviant behavior, the social environment was believed to be more important. Because they considered both physical and social factors, theories of the Chicago school were called *social ecology** *theories of deviance.*

---

* *Ecology* is a branch of science studying the interrelationship of organisms and their environments; the term generally refers to biological or physical relationships. *Social ecology* means the interrelationships among the members of a society or social group.

Figure 3.1
Zone Maps showing male delinquency rates in Chicago for three time periods

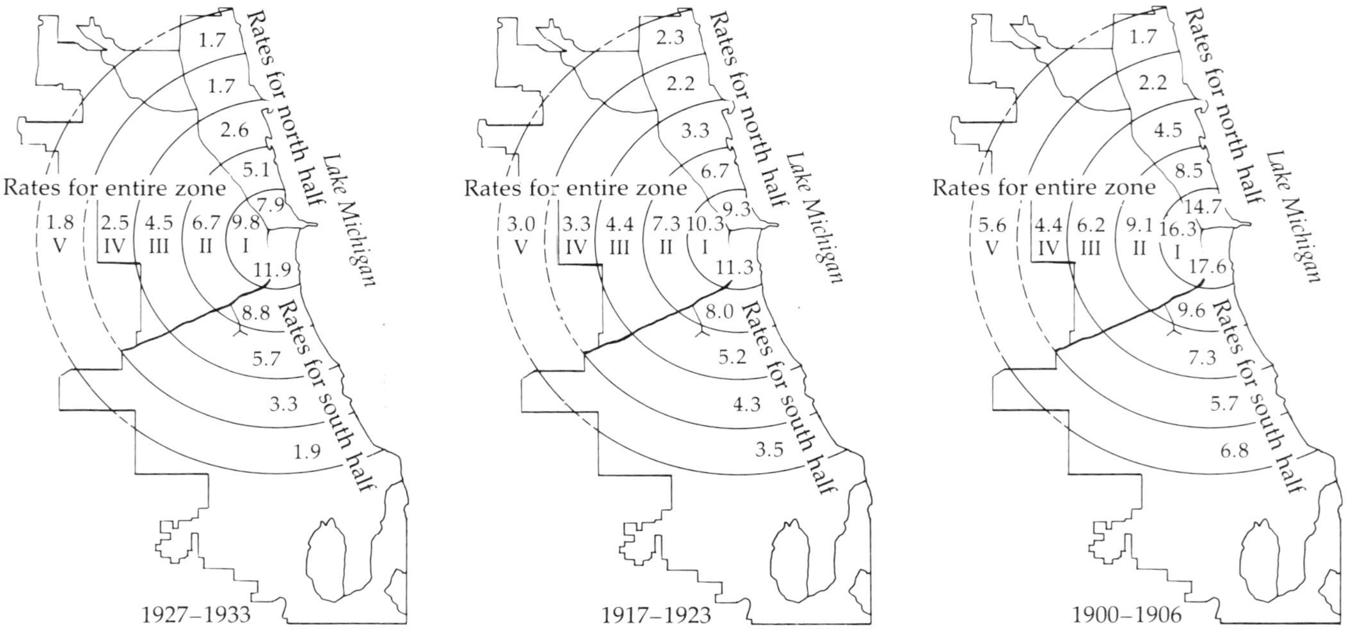

Source: Reprinted from *Juvenile Delinquency and Urban Areas* by Clifford R. Shaw and Henry D. McKay, by permission of The University of Chicago Press. Copyright © 1942.

Figure 3.2
The place of Chicago's gangland in the urban ecology.

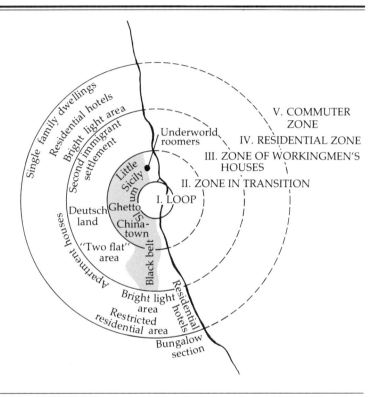

Source: Reprinted from *The Gang* by Frederick Thrasher by permission of The University of Chicago Press. Copyright © 1927.

One of the primary tools of Chicago theorists was the maps used extensively by Ernest W. Burgess and others to plot the incidence of varied kinds of individual deviance. These maps were first used to conceptualize the distribution of deviance in the city of Chicago as a whole and in particular areas of that city. Figure 3.1 is a well-known map used by Shaw and McKay (1942) in their study of juvenile delinquency. It shows one overwhelming pattern: the farther one goes from the center of the city, the lower the delinquency rate. This type of map served as the basis for *the concentric zone theory* of the distribution of crime, delinquency, and other indicators of social disorganization. Figure 3.2 is a well-known set of ecological maps used by Frederick Thrasher in developing his theory of gangs and their delinquent behavior. He constructed it by superimposing the location of the central empire of gangland on Burgess's map of the urban areas of Chicago. Thrasher's map shows that gangs and delinquency tend to occur in *interstitial* areas of the city. Interstitial areas were those which fell between what Park called *natural communities*. Natural communities, which were predominantly ethnic ones, were those which had a high degree of social organization; interstitial areas — areas that fell between highly organized areas of the city — were described as disorganized, at least relative to the natural communities.

Ecological (concentric zone) maps demonstrated that the farther one went from the center of the city, the less the deviance. More detailed maps revealed that within the city the relatively disorganized interstitial areas were most deviant. The most important interstitial areas were the so-called "transitional areas" between the highly commercial and industrial areas near the center of town and the workers' homes farther out from the center.

The final step in the development of social disorganization theory was to specify which general properties of the city caused social disorganization (Wirth, 1928, 1938). Chicago sociologists identified three major factors:

1. *The absolute size of the city.* After a town grows beyond a few hundred people, it becomes impossible to know everyone very well even a lifetime. By the time a city has thousands of citizens it is impossible for most people to have much direct involvement with all the others; and when it has millions almost everyone is a stranger to almost everyone else.

2. *The relative density of the population.* The more people who live on a given area of land, the less direct contact each can have with the others because of their sheer numbers.

3. *Heterogeneity, especially ethnic heterogeneity.* This factor was in many ways the most important to Chicago theorists. The more a city is broken up into small, tightly organized homogeneous natural communities, the less overall contact individuals have with other people in the city. Although each small community is homogeneous, the city as a whole is heterogeneous.

The interstitial areas between the natural communities are particularly high in heterogeneity and low in contact and involvement, and thus high in social disorganization. In general, then, it was argued that the greater a city's size, density, and heterogeneity — that is, the greater its urbanization — the greater its social disorganization and the higher its frequency of deviance.

We have concentrated on urbanization as the cause of social disorganization and of deviance because that is the factor Chicago sociologists emphasized. It was not, however, the only variable they studied. Some of these variables were so specific that they reached Level IX. We turn now to some of these more specific variables.

SPECIFIC SOCIAL STRUCTURAL VARIABLES TO EXPLAIN INDIVIDUAL DEVIANCE

Some Chicago theorists were quite interested in explaining why only *some* members of a group subject to social disorganization actually became deviant. In their search they identified a number of important variables and developed more and more specific theories.

Ruth S. Cavan emphasized in her book *Suicide* (1965, originally published in 1928; see also Schmidt, 1928) that individuals ultimately determine their own actions. She believed that inevitably some people in any society find that their own wishes or desires do not fit the cultural or social patterns within which they live. These people face a personal crisis regardless of the state of social organization or disorganization of the society or social group.

For many other individuals, however, social disorganization may itself be a source of personal crisis. In the face of such crises, some people are able to create their own legitimate solutions; others try but cannot do so. For the latter individuals the crisis leads to *personal disorganization,* which involves an internal lack of fit between their desires and the rules of society they have learned. This personal disorganization can lead to all kinds of deviant activities, ranging from attacks on other people to total "demoralization" or even psychotic withdrawal from the world. As Cavan argued, deviant acts such as suicide must be explained by a "social psychology of deviance" that looks at the act as the outcome of a complex process of social *and* personal disorganization:

> Suicide has appeared [here] as a function of certain social attitudes and as one resultant of a loose social organization. But suicide is more than a social phenomenon. It is also a personal experience. What groups of people are most subject to difficulties and hence tend to commit suicide most frequently? What happens to the person's emotions, ambitions, his outlook on life, before he determines to kill himself? This more personal side of suicide, the social psychology of suicide, is the [next] subject. The approach is made through a study of adjustments which people attempt to make when obstacles appear in the ongoing process of living, adjustments already shown to be more frequently demanded in an individualistic, changing social order than in a highly socialized, static social order. When adjustments fail there may occur a complete breakdown of morale, inability to satisfy fundamental interests, and consequent personal disorganization or demoralization (Cavan, 1928: 111).

Cavan thus explained why only *some* people become deviant by recognizing the independence of individual social behavior. There are a variety of routes to personal disorganization — some involve a response to social disorganization and others derive from personal circumstances.

Later study focused on the link between social and personal disorganization and minimized the individual idiosyncratic dimension. The theory that social disorganization is a major cause of personal disorganization led to a great number of studies of mental illness. Theorists argued that although social disorganization was not responsible for all cases of mental illness, it was the most important cause. In study after study it was concluded that the socially disorganized life of the city led to mental illness of all kinds. In the best known of these studies, *Mental Disorders in Urban Areas,* Faris and Dunham (1939) found that rates of mental illness were ten times greater in the central areas of Chicago than in outlying residential areas (499 versus 48 per 100,000 population per year). Later studies found the same pattern in Providence, Milwaukee, St. Louis, Cleveland, Syracuse, and many other cities. This work led directly to the very extensive studies of community life and mental illness in New Haven by Hollingshead and Redlich (*Social Class and Mental Illness,* 1958; see also 1953, 1954), and in New York City by Srole (*Mental Health in the Metropolis,* 1962), who found that mental illness, especially schizophrenia, was far more frequent in lower-class than in upper-class groups. Faris (1955) tried to show that this difference was a result of the association of class with social and, hence, personal disorganization (pp. 323–382). These studies also did a great deal to stimulate the cross-cultural study of mental illness by sociologists and anthropologists. Much of this work led to the conclusion that simpler, more homogeneous societies — that is, the ones with less social disorganization — had less mental illness, although they might sometimes have more of a particular mental illness, such as depression or manic depression.

In the latter part of Chapter 4 we will discuss theories that are attempts to explain the behavior of *any* individual and the difficulties that arise in constructing them. We will also examine some of the psychological explanations that have been offered to explain deviance.

Chicago sociologists proposed a number of variables to account for social disorganization: urbanization, industrialization, urban structure, societal complexity, primary relations, and specific city features (size, density, and heterogeneity). Although social disorganization is no longer an important sociological concept, these variables remain significant in explanations of deviance.

A variety of criticisms have been directed at social disorganization theory. At first they were based on the erroneous assumption that the theory considered only social disorganization on the societal level. As our discussion has shown, however, although the Chicago sociologists claimed to be providing explanations at the societal level, their theories were actually far more specific. Another frequent early criticism was that the theories could not explain why in a group subject to social disorganization only some individuals became deviant; as we saw in the last section, however, they tried to explain just that. These early criticisms thus seem to have involved a basic misunderstanding of social disorganization theory — a misunderstanding to which the theorists themselves contributed.

General social disorganization theory is no longer widely used in sociology for several reasons. First, the theory is linked with a way of thinking that tended to equate social disorganization with socially disapproved behavior. It did not take into account the perspective of members of so-called disorganized groups, although the Chicago researchers did gather a wealth of material from these people. Second, social disorganization itself explained far less about deviance than did the many important variables proposed by these theorists to account for social disorganization. These variables remain vital in current theories about deviance. Finally, social disorganization theory was criticized for its ambiguous treatment of social conflict. The theory is unclear about whether social conflict is a cause, an effect, or a manifestation of social disorganization. Furthermore, in issues of social conflict, Chicago theorists tended to side with the broader society and view the individual as the "problem."

It is fair to say that the data of the Chicago theorists were far superior to their general social disorganization theory. The many insights gathered in their detailed research studies serve as elements in current theorizing about deviance. Major problems arose, however, when their theories, whose explanatory power lay at Levels III, IV, and V, were applied at more general levels (I and II).

Level IV. Subcultures as Source of Explanation

It is clear that Chicago sociologists theorizing about social disorganization were repeatedly drawn by their data away from general societal explanations of deviance and toward the analysis of more specific variables. Probably the first major break from social disorganization theory and the beginning of subculture theories was a study of deviance in Honolulu by A. W. Lind (1938).

Like most great cities in the United States, Honolulu was and still is a city of ethnic groups that live largely apart. This separateness was perhaps particularly apparent in Honolulu because its inhabitants — Japanese, Chinese, Polynesians, and various Western ethnic groups — are different in appearance. Lind was unsuccessful in his attempts to apply social disorganization theory to this community of varied ethnic groups. Social disorganization theory had led him to expect that the more organized a group was, the less illegal behavior there would be.

He found, however, that certain highly organized ethnic groups displayed surprisingly high rates of specific types of illegal behavior. The more highly organized Japanese groups, for example, exhibited high rates of suicide — indeed, it seemed that the more highly organized they were, the higher the rate of suicide. Although the example of Mr. Zenzaburo and our reading of Durkheim should lead us to expect such a finding, Lind did not expect it. Similarly, the Polynesians in Hawaii had a particularly high illegitimacy rate; the more organized the Polynesian group, the higher the illegitimacy rate. Traditional Polynesian values supported sexual activity among the unmarried and did not emphasize a link between sex and marriage. Thus by following the rules of their subgroups people committed acts that were defined as illegal. But *who* had determined what was legal and what was illegal?

Lind argued that Honolulu presented a classic case: a politically powerful minority group (the Westerners) could pass laws conflicting with the values and rules of other groups that together formed the majority. Only when these other groups were disorganized could one expect a low crime rate. Lind thus concluded that social disorganization theory was flawed.

This recognition of the existence of subgroups within a society helped to undermine the idea of a homogeneous society and led to some new explanations of deviance. The idea that a subgroup might have values and activities that bring it into conflict with the laws of the larger society led to the conclusion that conformity to subgroup values may produce deviance from the values or laws of the larger society. Consequently, understanding these subgroups (subcultures) might be a fruitful source for explaining deviance. Since the dominant mode of sociological thought at the time was still that of moral absolutism, this idea seemed startling, even paradoxical. Indeed the deviants studied by the Chicago field researchers — hobos, taxi-dance hall dancers and their customers, gangs, jack-rollers,* and so on — proclaimed again and again that they saw themselves *not as breaking social rules but as following different rules and espousing different values.* They illustrated Thoreau's statement: "If a man does not keep pace with his companions, perhaps it is because he hears a different drummer." Nonetheless, the old theoretical model of moral absolutism was too powerful to allow most sociologists to entertain this new idea.

Although sociologists committed to the old model did present relatively clear statements of value conflicts by the subjects of their studies, they persisted in asserting social disorganization theory, which assumed that such value conflicts did not exist. Even after Lind had

---

* A jack-roller is someone who steals from — that is, "rolls" — someone who is asleep, generally a skid-row alcoholic who has passed out.

clearly stated the new idea of conflict between subcultures and the values and laws of the larger society, many strongly resisted it. As C. Wright Mills argued in his classic paper, "The Professional Ideology of Social Pathologists" (1942), this whole school of theorists continued to declare the *inherent pathology* of such deviant actions. Although such commitment in the face of contradictory evidence may seem unscientific, remember that both moral absolutism and social disorganization theory at the time were backed by belief and common-sense experience. (Consider the epigraph that begins Part I.) As we pointed out in Chapter 1, eliminating common-sense and taken-for-granted assumptions from scientific theories is a difficult and never-ending task. Errors that are obvious in retrospect are not nearly so apparent in the midst of the struggle. And in time most Chicago sociologists began to change their ideas. Most began by extending the meaning of social disorganization to include subculture conflicts with the larger society (see Faris, 1955), preserving the old terminology but allowing the new idea to enter their works, often with some resulting confusion. Louis Wirth, one of the foremost theorists of social disorganization, argued that subculture conflict could be considered a cause of crime only if it was actually *experienced* as conflict within the individual. Presumably the experience of conflict could produce personal disorganization and thus fit the earlier disorganization theory of deviance. Other sociologists, however, began to develop a whole new line of deviance theory into what is now known as a *subcultural theory of deviance.* Thus the classical assumptions of moral absolutism and societal homogeneity were broken.

THE CONCEPT OF SUBCULTURE: ORIGINS AND DEVELOPMENT

One of the most influential sociologists in the development of a subcultural theory of deviance and crime was Edwin Sutherland. (For a history of this development and for important articles from 1924 to 1970, see David O. Arnold, *The Sociology of Subcultures,* 1970.) In the early edition of his classic text on criminology (1924), Sutherland argued that most earlier criminology had tried to explain *all* crime in terms of some basic features of physiology, personality, or society. He saw such an approach as ultimately fruitless because *the vast number of different acts that are socially defined as crimes have little or nothing in common.* Instead, he found, through careful research, that there were natural types of crime, each of which could be defined by common properties, ideas, motives, and actions. He called these natural types *behavior systems of crime.*

The major behavior system of crime that Sutherland studied and analyzed was that of the professional thief (1937). He focused in particular on confidence artists, shoplifters, and pickpockets. Sutherland knew from the huge amount of literature on the subject that professional theft has existed in Western societies for centuries. (For a popular account of criminal varieties in nineteenth-century England, see Michael Crichton, *The Great Train Robbery,* 1975.) It was this *tradition* of crime that particularly captured Sutherland's attention.

His work has made at least two major contributions to the theoretical understanding of deviance. First, his idea of behavior systems of crime was the basis for the development of the concept of *criminal subculture.* Without using the term subculture, Sutherland found that professionalized behavior systems (subcultures) of deviance exist, are passed on from one generation to another, and operate in roughly the same fashion as nondeviant subcultures.

Second, Sutherland developed the theory of *differential association,* which detailed the way in which subcultures could affect behavior. Like many theories of deviance, this one had its origins in a very simple common-sense idea: if you associate with criminals, you are more likely to become one yourself. Sutherland argued that opportunities to associate with different groups of people, both criminal and noncriminal, vary from person to person. The more opportunity one has to associate with criminals, the greater the likelihood that one will engage in criminal activities. In a relatively homogeneous community or society there is little opportunity for differential association; in a heterogeneous community or society the opportunities increase. Differential association with criminals has two outcomes. First, it increases the possibility of one's becoming a criminal; second, it creates the foundation for criminal subcultures because criminals come to associate more with one another than with "outsiders" and their high degree of interaction leads to the development of shared meanings. Because of this differential association, according to Sutherland and others, they even develop a common language or argot that is relatively unknown to persons not in the subculture. All the shared meanings transmitted to new members constitute the criminal subculture.

Sutherland later extended the idea of differential association to many kinds of crime. He cautioned, however, that the concept could not be appropriately applied without first carrying out extensive research into the many behavior systems of crime.

Sutherland's theory of differential association has been controversial. Although it is true that a person who lives near racketeers is more likely to come into contact with them, it is not true that all those who live near or even interact with racketeers take up this profession themselves. Many people in the neighborhood choose to stay away from them as much as possible; only a few wind up doing the kinds of things racketeers do. Clearly deviance involves something more than differential association, and thus the theory is incomplete. (Donald Cressey, who helped to develop Sutherland's theory, has reviewed a mass of criticism and research bearing on the subject, 1952, 1955, 1962.)

Although there remains an obvious element of truth to the theory of differential association (see Matza, 1969, for a detailed examination of its strengths), it has not proven of great value in explaining deviance, and sociologists have generally abandoned it. It is of interest, however, because it contains a kernel of truth and because it contributed to the more theoretically useful concept of subculture.

Sutherland's basic idea of behavior systems of crime, which led more directly to the development of subcultural theory, has proven to be of far more lasting value. He himself expanded his idea to cover numerous types of crime, and the literature on criminal behavior systems is now very large. (See especially Clinard and Quinney, 1973, and, for a short bibliography, Guenther, 1976: 188–90.) Sutherland's work has greatly advanced our understanding of the specific properties of many forms of theft and their organization into enduring systems of behavior.

One of the next major works in the development of the concept of subculture and its use in explaining deviance was Thorsten Sellin's *Culture Conflict and Crime* (1938). Sellin drew heavily on historical and anthropological sources to show that in many societies the laws defining what is a crime and what is not are enacted and enforced by more powerful minority groups over the wishes and values of less powerful combinations of groups that make up a majority. This finding supports that of Lind in Honolulu described earlier in this chapter.

The laws of United States society, and the publicly enforced values of "respectability" in general, were not recognized by early sociologists as in conflict with the values held by the multitude of groups that make up our society. There were probably many reasons for this "oversight." Most important, as we have argued before, are the idea of moral absolutism and the belief that criminal laws in some way directly expressed the will of God. In addition it was believed that democracy constituted the will of the majority and — a very important idea in the United States — that all the different ethnic and class groups, with their different values, were willingly "melted" into the great American culture. A great mass of research by all the social sciences now shows that legal legislation, law enforcement, and judicial decisions in our society are affected in many fundamental ways not by "the greatest good for the greatest numbers" but by pressure-group politics, lobbying, behind-the-scenes deals, elite decisions (such as by judges on constitutional grounds, regardless of what the majority of people say or do), and by the specific political processes involved in any particular case. If assimilation (the formal term for the melting pot process) takes place, some groups are more affected by it than others. Today pressure-group politics is almost an institution, but in the 1930s it was not understood by sociologists or by most other social scientists, so they tended to follow the prevalent ideology of the "Great American Melting Pot."

Although theoretical works such as Sellin's played an important part in changing the thinking of sociologists, certain empirical studies were probably more effective. One of the most influential of all sociological works was William Foote Whyte's famous book *Street Corner Society* (1955, originally published in 1943). This book was the first of many by sociologists and others showing empirically that, contrary to what Chicago sociologists in the past had believed, the slums of United States cities were not "disorganized." One of Whyte's major points about Cornerville, as he called the Italian-American slum community in Boston that he studied, was that one could fully understand it only by seeing it as a distinct organized unit in the context of its relations with the rest of the city. Although there might be conflict between the slum and the larger city, giving the *appearance* of disorganization, the slum itself had its own organization that minimized *internal* conflict.

Since Whyte's classic study of Cornerville, sociologists and other researchers have revealed the vast complexity of immigrant subcultural life in the slums of United States cities. (See, for example, Jane Jacobs, 1963; Herbert Gans, *The Urban Villagers,* 1962.) Almost all researchers have found that these immigrant groups retain important parts of their original national cultures and build new subcultural lives in response to environmental conditions, making them in some ways deviant from values and laws of the larger society within which they must live. Such findings emphasize looking at the subcultural dimension as an explanatory variable in understanding deviance.

THE CONCEPT OF SUBCULTURE: CURRENT IDEAS

Because the various definitions of and ideas about subcultures have been the source of considerable confusion, even among experts, we need to explain what we are talking about when we invoke the concept. This section will be devoted to a clarification of the concept of subculture.

The most general meaning of subculture is *a smaller part of a larger culture.* If culture is defined as a set of shared meanings and patterns of actions that are transmitted from one generation to another, a subculture would simply be any identifiable part of such a culture. (For issues that arise in defining culture, see Kluckhohn, 1962; 1971.) Although such a definition provides a general orientation, it is too vague to give us the direction we need. Social scientists seldom use subculture in this sense. Instead they speak of a subculture as existing only if *this part of the larger culture has some shared and transmitted meanings and patterns of actions that are different or distinctive from those of the larger culture.* This idea of difference from the national culture was implicit but very important in Milton Gordon's early presentation (1961) of the basic idea and its rationale:

It is the thesis of this paper that a great deal could be gained by a more extensive use of the concept of the *sub-culture* — a concept used here to refer to a sub-division of a national culture, composed of a combination of factorable social situations such as class status, ethnic background, regional and rural or urban residence, and religious affiliation, but *forming in their combination a functioning unity which has an integrated impact on the participating individual.*

We would not refer to any group as a deviant subculture unless it shared elements of meanings and actions that violated some important larger cultural value. There is, however, a great deal of variability in the degree to which a subculture overlaps the larger culture, and we have no trustworthy rule of thumb to tell us how different a group must be to qualify as a subculture.

Another characteristic of a subculture is *subculture consciousness* — members *think* of themselves as a community of, say, addicts, deviants, or prostitutes. As Becker, Geer, Hughes, and Strauss (1961) have argued, this kind of group self-consciousness is generally reflected in the existence of specific names or labels for the group that are used, both implicitly and explicitly, to communicate the distinctive meanings of group membership. These names are generally crucial in the natural history of deviant subcultures, for they are likely to produce a big jump in the social significance of the group life.

Deviant subcultures commonly have distinctive and well-recognized *conduct norms* for their members, rules about what behavior is right and wrong for members of their subculture. John Irwin and Donald Cressey have defined a subculture as

> a set of conduct norms which cluster together in such a way that they can be differentiated from the broader culture of which they are a part. Thus, if some of the rules for behavior in the working class are different from some of the rules for behavior in the middle class, it is proper to speak of a "working-class subculture" and a "middle-class subculture," despite the fact that in these two social classes there are so many identical rules of conduct that it is reasonable to consider the two classes as belonging to the same culture (in Arnold, 1970, pp. 64–80).

Conduct norms are often very different from what outsiders expect. Professional armed robbers have strong conduct norms against using anything more than minimal violence, as we see in Letkemann's study (1973). His respondents, imprisoned armed robbers, expressed utter contempt for amateurs who used unnecessary violence.

Since the 1930s a variety of sociologists have contributed to the concept of subculture. We have seen some of the most important factors they identified. Drawing on that background, we will use the concept of subculture to apply to social groups with the following characteristics.

1. They are *identifiable* parts of the larger society, different in some but not all aspects from the larger society.
2. As a part of that society, they are subject to at least some of its rules and laws.
3. As groups with identifiable differences from the larger society, they have their own conduct norms for members.
4. They are functioning unities — that is, for at least some purposes they are capable of acting as a whole.
5. They are conscious of themselves as units in some way separate from the broader society.

Accepting these characteristics as the major components of subcultures should allow us to identify a broad range of social groups as subcultures and to examine their similarities and differences.

SUBCULTURAL EXPLANATIONS OF GANG BEHAVIOR: FREDERICK THRASHER

From the 1930s to the 1960s the study of juvenile delinquency among males was particularly popular among sociologists. Because many early theories of deviant subcultures were on this subject, we will look at these theories in some detail. It will be important, however, to look beyond the specific data and consider ways in which these theories might be applied to forms of deviance other than juvenile delinquency and juvenile gangs.

Sociologists consistently found that most illegal activities committed by juveniles that came to police attention were part of group or gang activity. Frederick Thrasher's study of 1,313 gangs in Chicago (1927), important in the development of subcultural theory, was a major leap into serious sociological research on gangs and in many ways remains a definitive work on that subject. The vast amount of research done on gangs since then has mainly added details to his basic findings, and later theoretical analyses largely deal with issues he raised.

Although Thrasher himself did not systematically consider whether gang deviance grew out of lower-class subculture, the life situation of lower-class people, or some combination of the two (an issue that later sociologists have seen as crucial), he did gather a mass of data bearing on this question. Most important, he presented a great deal of evidence showing that the gang boys he studied shared values, feelings, and patterns of action very different from those of the larger society. These different values were, however, common among many adults in their social world.

Thrasher, and others after him, found that boys generally joined gangs at an early age and often continued their participation into their late twenties or even beyond. Often, too, they then transferred their allegiance to adult clubs, especially those devoted to sports or politics, and continued as advisers to the new members of their old gangs or to new gangs in the same neighborhood. The tacit and open support by adults of much of gang life is obvious in Thrasher's lengthy considera- tion of the relations between gangs and politics in Chicago:

> The political boss knows exactly how to appeal to the gang because he himself has usually received valuable training for politics in a street gang from which he has ultimately been graduated and with which he may still retain connec- tions in an advisory capacity. The gangs and clubs of younger boys are con- sidered feeders for the older groups, and as a matter of fact, the juniors and the midgets often fall heir to the charters, the equipment, and, most impor- tant of all, the tradition of the seniors, whom they imitate.
>
> Under such conditions it is inevitable that boys in gangland regions shall have an intimate knowledge of political chicanery and corruption, not pos- sessed by boys in other districts. They often acquire attitudes of disrespect for law and tend to come to regard the whole governmental structure as largely providing opportunities for the personal emolument of successful politicians. . . .
>
> The political boss probably achieves most ready control of the gang by encouraging it to become a club, often giving it his own name for advertising purposes, such as "McFlaherty's Boosters," "O'Mulligan's Colts," etc. If he can get his name attached to a successful athletic club, he is able to attract considerable support from the "whole athletic fraternity." It is surprising how many men have been "made" politically as patrons of the sports. . . .
>
> The tendency of the gangs to become athletic clubs has been greatly stim- ulated by the politicians of the city. It has become a tradition among gangs throughout Chicago that the first source of possible financial aid is the local alderman or other politician (Thrasher, 1927).

This same pattern was later shown in even greater detail by Whyte (1943) in his study of Cornerville. Instead of disorganization, a clear pattern of organization emerges, though it is constructed on values that diverge from those of the larger society.

Thrasher also unearthed much evidence that the middle-class out- siders who came into the slum areas inhabited by the gangs came from a significantly different culture. One of the pervasive arguments in his book is that outsiders, especially social workers from social service agencies, did not share the world of meanings of the gang boys and others in the slums. In fact, one of the major goals of his book was to provide outsiders with an understanding of life *inside* the gang boys' world, in contrast to how outsiders imagined it; he continually empha- sized the fallacy of their assumptions.

Thrasher, then, had a great deal of evidence that adults and youth shared a slum subculture that contributed in some ways to the more specific gang subculture that in turn led to delinquent acts. Thrasher did not realize the full theoretical implications of his data. On one hand, had anyone asked him whether people in gang areas shared some values and ideas that were systematically different from those of the outside middle-class world, he would probably have said: "Certainly they do! Just look at all the evidence I've given showing the systematic conflict between some of their rules and ideas and those of social workers from the outside, such as Jane Addams."* On the other hand, he did not seem to realize how this finding contradicted his theory of social disorganization, which he insisted explained why gangs sprang up and were concentrated in the interstitial areas of the city. It seems obvious to us now that although immigrants to the city may have first experienced their new world as personally and socially disorganized, they proceeded to reorganize it by developing rules and ideas to fit their new situation — rules that at times conflicted with those of the larger society. Although Thrasher did not recognize this process, his data make such an insight available to us.

Thrasher's beautifully detailed picture of the gang is the basis for all the major theories of gangs and gang delinquency that followed it. Nonetheless, analysts have often criticized one or another of his explanations or, far more commonly, have failed to realize that their "new" findings were actually discovered long ago by Thrasher. Most later analysts have placed far more emphasis than he on the general subculture of poverty or of the slums. His basic picture, the natural history of gangs, was a major discovery. Some social scientists have not yet recognized its importance because they have not generally realized that the process that creates gangs is common in human societies, possibly forming the foundation for the earliest developments of social groups larger than reproductive and friendship groups.

SUBCULTURAL EXPLANATIONS OF GANG BEHAVIOR: RECENT DEVELOPMENTS

The first solid additions to Thrasher's findings were made by Shaw and McKay in *Juvenile Delinquency and Urban Areas* (1942). As early as 1928 their research had shown them that 81.8 percent of the boys brought before the Juvenile Court of Cook County, Chicago, committed their offense as members of groups. Crimes that most victimized other members of the city (in contrast to individual acts such as truancy) were even more likely to be committed as group activities. Theft, for example, was associated with group activity in 89 percent of the cases. This finding led them to focus their work on gangs. Though they continued the

* Jane Addams was a renowned social worker and social reformer in Chicago at the turn of this century.

Chicago school's concern with social disorganization, they concentrated their attention on the conflicting values within high-crime-rate areas and on the different opportunities available to the better-off and the poorer populations. In this way they contributed to our understanding of the workings of subcultures.

They found that in low-delinquency areas boys were exposed to more or less homogeneous values that opposed crime, whereas in high-crime areas in the inner city, boys had contact with law-abiding citizens, with those who favored crime, and even with highly successful criminals — in other words they had a range of choices available to them. Boys in low-delinquency areas had less opportunity for differential association.

Shaw and McKay did not find that the boys were exposed merely to vague, general values favorable to crime. On the contrary, they discovered rather specific *traditions* of criminal task-specialties transmitted from one generation to the next. There were, in short, specialized criminal subcultures, such as that of professional thievery, which inducted boys in the neighborhood and taught them their secrets of success:

> The way in which boys are inducted into unconventional behavior has been revealed by large numbers of case studies of youths living in areas where the rates of delinquents are high. Through the boy's own life-story the wide range of contacts with other boys has been revealed. These stories indicate how at early ages the boys took part with older boys in delinquent activities, and how, as they themselves acquired experience, they initiated others into the same pursuits. These cases reveal also the steps through which members are incorporated into the delinquent group organization. Often at early ages boys engage in malicious mischief and simple acts of stealing. As their careers develop, they become involved in more serious offenses, and finally become skilled workmen or specialists in some particular field of criminal activity. In each of these phases the boy is supported by the sanction and the approbation of the delinquent group to which he belongs (Shaw and McKay, 1942: 232).

Most of the conclusions that Shaw and McKay reached merely added details to Thrasher's findings. Their explanation, however, of how the subcultures developed and what motivated the boys to continue joining — despite the legal risks and the moral disapproval of many people in their lives, especially their parents — was quite different from Thrasher's explanation in terms of social disorganization. They thought that the fundamental reason for the existence of these subcultures was the relative lack of legitimate opportunity to achieve the "American dream" — financial success, luxuries, and so on — combined with the greater opportunity for illegitimate (criminal) success. They argued that social disorganization, especially the anonymity of highly pluralistic ethnic communities, simply made it all the easier for the boys to join a deviant subculture.

Though they used somewhat different terms and seem to have arrived at their ideas independently, it is obvious that Shaw and McKay were in agreement with Merton's anomie theory on the motivation for delinquency. They added the idea, however, that once the activities were established as part of a subculture they would be transmitted to others in the form of values favorable to crime and of specialized knowledge about how to commit the crimes. Once the anomie motivation became imbedded in a subculture, innovation, in Merton's terms, was accessible to a broader range of boys.

Albert Cohen (1955) drew on the concept of subculture to construct his _ambivalence theory_ of gang delinquency. He was particularly interested in the role of values in the construction of delinquent subcultures. Cohen argued that gang boys had been successfully socialized, especially by middle-class teachers, to want to achieve middle-class success. Some boys, however, found (or feared) that such success was beyond their grasp. In response they rejected middle-class values and adopted values and forms of behavior that were exactly the opposite, venting their angry frustration and repressing all thought of what they had been taught to want. Cohen tried to demonstrate that gang values and behavior are an exaggerated rejection of middle-class symbols of respectability and legitimacy. The ferociousness of the rejection suggested to Cohen the ambivalence of the boys' response, the continued secret desire for what they cannot have. Cohen's work spurred a number of critical responses, notably by Cloward and Ohlin and by Miller (whose work will be discussed below) and led to important refinements in the ways subcultural theory can be applied to an understanding of gang behavior.

Solomin Kobrin (1951) later adopted this ambivalence theory and combined it with the theory of _conflict subcultures_. He believed that once people found a way to adapt to ambivalent desires, they transmitted their strategy to others who faced a similar situation. A conflict subculture was thus available to those who saw a need for it. The ambivalence, however, remains as indicated by the fact that people continue to be sensitive to the responses of members of the larger society. Kobrin presents an important qualification, however:

> Such overtones of rebellion, on the other hand, do not characterize members of sub-culture groups who are totally excluded from participation in the dominant culture of the wider society. For example, those groups which live by systematic depredations upon property, like the criminal castes of India or the professional thieves of our own society, are relatively impervious to the negative judgments of conventional persons, and do not ordinarily resort to the kind of behavior described. Their devaluation and rejection by conventional society is not transmuted into self-rejection, since their criteria of worthiness diverge sharply from those encountered in conventional society. In

contrast, the young male who occupies the role of delinquent in the delinquency area resorts to purposive destructiveness and exaggerates the differences between himself and conventional persons precisely because he cannot exclude from his system of values the conventional criteria of personal worth. His delinquency may hence be seen as a defensive adaptation in which he creates an opposing system of values, since by virtue of his lower-class culture background he remains relatively unequipped to move toward the goals explicit in the middle-class culture of the wider society (Kobrin, 1951).

In this way Kobrin demonstrates that ambivalence theory does not provide a satisfactory explanation of all subcultural deviance. Neither does it resolve the problem of why some individuals become deviant and others do not.

Cloward and Ohlin, in *Delinquency and Opportunity* (1960), attempted to resolve some of the problems they saw with existing theories about gangs and in particular with the issue of why some boys in a situation become deviant while others do not. Drawing on the concept of *differential association* and on Merton's ideas, they identified *deviant opportunity structures,* claiming that when boys felt the ambivalence described by Cohen they would be more likely to become deviant *if the opportunity existed in their environment.*

They identified at least three major types of *deviant subcultures* in urban slum areas whose existence provided deviant opportunities to boys seeking ways out of the ambivalent situations in which they found themselves. They agreed completely with Shaw and McKay that there are *criminal subcultures* in which boys learn their criminal "trades" from older boys and men who have mastered them in the past. These are boys who, for whatever reason, find they cannot succeed by legitimate means but find that illegitimate means of success are organized in their communities. They become apprentices in crime and climb the success ladders of the many different forms of professional and semiprofessional crime.

Cloward and Ohlin also identified a second type of deviant subculture which they called a *conflict subculture.* According to them, some boys in slum neighborhoods lack both legitimate and illegitimate opportunities for success because their neighborhoods are too disorganized to have even criminal organizations. These boys seem to have the Mertonian success goals but no means to realize them. They turn to violence to express their frustration, creating a conflict subculture.

A third type of deviant subculture, according to Cloward and Ohlin, is formed by those who lack legitimate and illegitimate means to success but who do not turn to violence because they retain prohibitions against it. These boys often become "retreatists" or "withdrawalists" and form *drug subcultures.* The idea of a retreatist subculture of drug users has probably drawn more criticism than any other part of Cloward and

Ohlin's theory of deviant subcultures. Yablonsky (1962) tried to show that gangs are not built around the use of hard drugs, and particularly not around heroin use. Overall evidence indicates that most gangs use drugs only sporadically. At present it is unclear whether *any* gangs form solely around drug use. Both conflict and criminal subcultures apparently try to prevent members from becoming habitual drug users because of the presumed decrease in behavioral effectiveness that results. Most research indicates that systematic hard drug users, especially addicts, are more apt to be "loners" than members of a drug subculture. As we will see in Part II, lone drug users and lone criminals in general present a particular problem for sociological analysis.

Walter Miller's extensive research on juvenile gangs (1958, 1966, 1974) has provided further evidence of the general usefulness of subcultural analysis. Focusing on Boston, he studied the everyday activities of gangs by assigning young field workers to "run with" and "hang out with" them. These workers tried to keep highly detailed field notes on what was said and done each day. From this mass of data, Miller inferred that the boys and their families have <u>focal concerns</u> — concerns that tie together much of their daily lives — that are different from those of middle-class boys and their families. (See Figure 3.3.)

Miller found that one of the most important concerns of the boys was "toughness," which involves seeing oneself as tough (not soft or feminine) as well as displaying this characteristic to others. Miller did not, however, try to find out whether middle-class male respondents shared this concern and thus does not substantiate his claim that focal concerns are different. Although the idea of describing subcultures in terms of their focal concerns is analytically promising, Miller's work is more suggestive than definitive.

Miller has continued to study gangs and is now probably the foremost researcher in that field. His more recent work (especially that in Blumberg, 1974), has shown that many variables are required to explain the different patterns of delinquent gangs and of their activities. He has also encountered many basic problems in determining the characteristics of gangs in different cities. He has found that a vast amount of public and professional misunderstanding of gangs has been created by the mass media.

Although Miller has not proposed a general model for explaining gang behavior, he has isolated some basic variables. In his own work he has come to focus on urban structures and histories as great influences on the structure of gangs and gang activity (Level III). He has also directed attention to the processes of gang interaction (Level V).

Other recent research focuses on face-to-face interactions among gang boys and between the boys and social control agents, especially the

Figure 3.3
Focal concerns of lower class culture

Area	Perceived alternatives (state, quality, condition)	
1. *Trouble:*	law-abiding behavior	law-violating behavior
2. *Toughness:*	physical prowess, skill; "masculinity"; fearlessness, bravery, daring	weakness, ineptitude; effeminacy; timidity, cowardice, caution
3. *Smartness:*	ability to outsmart, dupe, "con";	gullibility, "con-ability";
	gaining money by "wits";	gaining money by hard work;
	shrewdness, adroitness in repartee	slowness, dull-wittedness, verbal maladroitness
4. *Excitement:*	thrill; risk, danger; change, activity	boredom; "deadness," safeness; sameness, passivity
5. *Fate:*	favored by fortune, being "lucky"	ill-omened, being "unlucky"
6. *Autonomy:*	freedom from external constraint; freedom from superordinate authority; independence	presence of external constraint; presence of strong authority; dependency, being "cared for"

Source: Reprinted with permission from *The Journal of Social Issues* from "Lower Class Culture as a Generating Milieu of Gang Delinquency" by Walter B. Miller. Vol. 14, No. 3 (1958), p. 7.

police. Gerald Suttles's important work, *The Social Order of the Slum* (1968), and Spergel's work on *Racketville, Slumtown, Haulburg* (1973) try to show the nature of urban and neighborhood structures and their effects on social interaction. Spergel has argued that different kinds of neighborhoods have very different patterns of gang activities. Neighborhoods with histories of career crime and organized crime activities tend to have gangs that steal things; more conflict-ridden slum areas tend to have gangs that engage in violence.

Subcultures and subcultural values have repeatedly been found to play a role in gang formation and behavior; they have not, however, been sufficient to explain why, even in specific neighborhoods, some boys join gangs and others do not. Having found that broad sociostructural levels of analysis do little to explain why gangs act as they do, researchers on gang behavior have focused increasingly on more specific levels of explanation.

SUBCULTURES AS AN EXPLANATION OF DEVIANCE

As we have seen, subcultural theory has been used most widely by sociologists of deviance in studies of *gang behavior*.* We will now look at some of the ways in which the idea of subcultures can be used to explain deviance in general.

Perhaps the major insight of subcultural theory is that different and at times conflicting values may exist within a society. When one part of society (generally the one that embodies the defining values of that society) is able to establish rules that apply to everyone, other parts (including subcultures) come to be labeled deviant. Subcultural theory did not explore this process in any great detail; it remained for the labeling theorists, to be described in Chapter 5, to explain how this process "creates" deviance and deviants. Subcultural theory, however, did set the stage for undermining the *assumptions* of societal homogeneity and moral absolutism.

Subcultural theory, though focusing on gang behavior, established the existence of subcultures and made a solid beginning in describing what they were like and how they influenced their members. It also recognized the conflict inherent in the existence of subcultures within a broader society.

Beginning with Sutherland, sociologists came to recognize that crime and other forms of deviance come in many different varieties and therefore may require different kinds of explanations. Subcultural theory was one such explanation, but even its proponents realized that they could not account for all deviance. Although they clearly established that subcultures exist and support deviance, and they offered valuable suggestions as to how and why such subcultures got started, they encountered difficulties in explaining why some individuals became deviant while others did not. To deal with this issue, they increasingly turned to more specific levels of analysis and in particular to social interaction as an important element in the explanation of deviance. We will explore social interaction theories in the next chapter.

Subcultural theories remain an integral part of sociology as a whole and deviance theory in particular. A number of criticisms, however, have been directed at them.

First, subcultural theorists have not yet supplied enough evidence to support the claim that subcultures share different values. Although the idea may make intuitive sense and certainly sounds plausible, sociology requires that it be backed by systematically gathered evidence. On the

* Although subcultural theory was first used in the study of crime, it was taken up in other areas of sociology, notably in studies of race and ethnic relations. Our comments here apply only to its use in the sociology of deviance.

basis of questionnaire studies of middle-class boys, for example, Short and Strodbeck (1965) assert that their respondents' values are not really very different from those of lower-class gang boys. Such abstract expressions of values, however, may have little relation to the actual behavior of individuals. Empirical research must be done on both values and behaviors of different subcultures before claims of difference or similarity can be asserted legitimately.

A second problem with subcultural theory is its inability to explain why only some of those who have access to deviant subcultures choose to join them. Subcultural theory has contributed to our understanding of the resources available to those who choose deviance, but the process of choice remains vague.

Finally, subcultural theory — particularly that derived from gang behavior — can be criticized for leaving out girls and women. Although many explanations of gang behavior rest on statements about human nature that presumably characterize both males and females, the activities of girls and women were consistently overlooked. For example, theorists asserted that children "need" to form play groups and that such play groups serve as a basis for the later development of gangs, but they neglected to document or even ask whether girls form such play groups and, if they do, whether such groups become gangs. Once again, sociologists were influenced by common-sense assumptions of their society; only recently have the activities of women and girls been the subject of research. (For a recent treatment of the subject, see Adler, *Sisters in Crime*, 1975.)

As we mentioned earlier, sociologists attempting to understand gang behavior turned toward explanations of increasing specificity. These theories, which have been developed by a variety of thinkers, will be discussed in Chapter 4.

4

Specific Explanations of Deviance

In their attempts to explain deviance sociologists have repeatedly turned to the question of *why* some individuals become deviant but others do not. No matter what variable or set of variables is identified as a possible cause of deviance, some individuals always seem to be immune to it. We have seen, for example, that not everyone who has access to criminal subcultures chooses to participate in them. Theorists operating at the highest level of generality have often set aside this problem by claiming to explain *rates* of deviance rather than particular instances of deviance; Durkheim's study of suicide is an example of such an approach. Other theorists have moved to levels of greater specificity in their search for answers.

Theories of social interaction (Level V) are the most specific *sociological* theories. *Social interaction* refers to all instances in which individuals influence one another — by means of everything from newspapers, presidential edicts, and worldwide economic decisions to fistfights and lovemaking. It includes interpersonal interaction and is a fundamental process in the development of the individual *self*. Sociologists have turned to these theories particularly when seeking sociological explanations for specific individual acts of deviance.

Some social scientists, sociologists among them, have felt it necessary to go outside of sociology to psychology for explanations of specific acts of deviance. These Level VI theories have something in common with

Level I theories, for they seek to explain sociological phenomena in nonsociological terms. Later in this chapter we will look in some detail at Level VI theories, particularly their use by sociologists. (For a penetrating examination of the distinction between psychological and sociological explanations of individual behavior see Blumer, "Psychological Import of the Human Group," in Blumer, 1969.)

Some explanations for deviance (Levels VII through IX) are so specific, so tied to unique or random events, that their claim to being scientific grows tenuous. Science is built on the perception of patterns, of regularly occurring events. A truly unique event is not subject to scientific explanation. We will, however, look briefly at some of these kinds of theories and discuss their strengths and weaknesses as explanations of deviance.

Level V. Social Interaction as Source of Explanation

According to social interaction theory, social action is *the outcome of complex interactions, both cooperative and antagonistic, among individuals and groups in society.* This theory is focused on what goes on *between* individuals. Larger social units such as social groups, subcultures, and even societies are viewed as created, sustained, and destroyed by individuals in interaction with one another.

Although social interaction theory has its roots in European sociology, notably in the work of Georg Simmel, its extensive development took place in the United States, beginning with Mead and Cooley and continuing at present in the works of Blumer, Everett C. Hughes (see, for example, 1945), and Goffman (1959). Initially overshadowed by social disorganization theory, social interaction theory nonetheless received much theoretical and empirical support from the Chicago school, whose tradition of empirical studies is carried forward today by numerous social interactionists.

Historical accounts of the development of social interaction theory usually include as part of that theory explanations based on the concepts of social disorganization and subcultures. We have chosen to deal with the theories of social disorganization and subcultures in their own right (see Chapter 3), although we recognize that social interaction theory was associated with those more general explanations. In this chapter we will examine social interaction theory as an independent theoretical explanation, discussing its most general characteristics and showing how it has been used to explain deviance. In Chapter 5 we will see how some current elaborations and revisions of social interaction theory — many of them so sweeping as to demand new names — have contributed to the new perspective.

DEVELOPMENT OF SOCIAL INTERACTION THEORY: SYMBOLIC INTERACTIONISM

Contemporary social interaction theory derives many features from *symbolic interaction theory*, developed by Charles Horton Cooley (1902, 1909) and George Herbert Mead (1934). Mead was an important theorist who belonged to and strongly influenced the Chicago school.

Symbolic interactionism emphasizes a *shared* universe of symbols, especially values, in any social group. These symbols provide the pattern or framework within which meanings and actions are interpreted by members. In his classic article, "Society as Symbolic Interaction," first published in 1962, Herbert Blumer, the originator of the term *symbolic interactionism*, explains the general orientation of the theory:

> The term "symbolic interaction" refers, of course, to the peculiar and distinctive character of interaction as it takes place between human beings. The peculiarity consists in the fact that human beings interpret or "define" each other's actions instead of merely reacting to each other's actions. Their "response" is not made directly to the actions of one another but instead is based on the meaning which they attach to such actions. Thus, human interaction is mediated by the use of symbols, by interpretation, or by ascertaining the meaning of one another's actions. This mediation is equivalent to inserting a process of interpretation between stimulus and response in the case of human behavior (Blumer, 1969: 78–79).

According to symbolic interactionism, human interaction takes place on a symbolic level, with each participant engaged in "making sense" out of what the other is doing. When participants *share* symbols, interaction may be relatively unproblematic; when they do not share symbols, however, as is likely in interactions between criminals and police or between deviants and nondeviants in general, the situation becomes problematic. Even further difficulties arise when the participants *assume* they are sharing symbols when they are not; absolutism often operates with an assumption of shared symbols.

Once subcultural theorists established the existence of different subgroups and thus of different "shared symbolic universes," they began to study these universes and their interactions with one another. Symbolic interactionism provided the theoretical framework within which such studies could proceed.

Particularly important for symbolic interactionists, and the focus of a great deal of theorizing, is the concept of the *self*. The self is seen as a social product, a result of the interactions between the individual and the surrounding social world. To clarify this process, Cooley developed the image of the *looking-glass self*. Other people serve as mirrors in which we see ourselves. What is important, however, is not how others *really* see us in some "objective" sense but rather how we *think* they see us. Thus if I think someone is angry with me, I am likely to alter both my behavior toward that person and my own self-image, *regardless of whether or not that person is actually angry.* Cooley's point here is subtle but crucial to symbolic interaction theory. If he had claimed that the self was solely a reflection of how *others* see us, he would have left no place for *individual* action. The self would have been merely a product of others, determined by their responses. We know from our own experience that this is not true; certainly we feel pressured by the responses of others, but we also have a sense of being active in the process of creating the self.

George Herbert Mead was also concerned with the development of the self and, like Cooley, did not view the individual as *determined* by external social forces. According to Mead, the self is divided into two parts: the "I" and the "me." The "me" is the repository of social ideas, beliefs, and rules as well as of past actions. The "me" provides guidance regarding socially appropriate behavior. The "I," on the other hand, is the spontaneous and acting part of the self. Because of the existence of the "me," the self can be seen as a social product. Because of the "I," the self can be seen as active, guided but not compelled by the social world. Cultural and subcultural ideas, beliefs, and values become a part of the "me" through interaction in the world; the "I" acts *against* or *in terms of* that background rather than *because of* it. One never knows how the "I" will act until after it has done so.

Symbolic interactionists study not only how the self develops but also how it operates in interaction. The sense of self is viewed as one important factor that influences human behavior. Symbolic interactionists who study deviance are particularly concerned with how deviants view themselves or *construct their self-images* as well as with the characteristics of those groups or subcultures on which they draw in constructing their self-images. Symbolic interactionists have found that through interaction with others, people may learn ways of defining their actions that have implications for their future behavior.

Alfred Lindesmith, in his study *Opiate Addiction* (1947), detailed the processes by which such learning takes place. At the time of Lindesmith's study, the general public thought of addiction as a virtually automatic process determined by the nature of the drug itself: if you take the drug, you get hooked. However, when Lindesmith compared prescription users of morphine with illegal users of the same drug, he found that addiction was not automatic. Those who had been taking morphine as a painkiller under doctors' prescriptions were able to stop using it, even when prolonged use had led to some physical dependence. Withdrawal symptoms consisted of little more than headaches, sniffles, and other discomforts not unlike those of a common cold. Why then did addiction appear to be automatic among illegal users of the drug?

Lindesmith's answer draws on symbolic interactionist theory. He discovered that unlike prescription drug users, illegal users learned from friends that withdrawal symptoms could be eliminated by continuing to take the drug regularly. They then took the drug to stop the symptoms, thereby building greater tolerance so that the next time they tried to stop they had stronger, more painful symptoms, which motivated them to take even more of the drug. In short, *the crucial difference between prescription drug users and addicts was the learned and shared symbolic meaning of the withdrawal symptoms.* Prescription drug users had not learned this method of deferring withdrawal symptoms.

Lindesmith's work illustrates the concept of *reference group,* a term first used by Herbert Hyman. A reference group is a group to which one orients or "refers" one's behavior, although not necessarily a group to which one belongs or aspires to belong. Generally the term refers to a group that one admires, the behavior of whose members one seeks to imitate; sometimes this aspect is emphasized by use of the term *positive reference group.* A *negative reference group* is a group whose behavior one strives to avoid. Criminal subcultures may serve as reference groups for those who want to join them and as negative reference groups to those law-abiding members of society who strive in every way to be unlike "those people." Being aware of an individual's reference group often helps one understand behavior that is otherwise obscure.

In his study "The Cycle of Abstinence and Relapse Among Heroin Addicts" (1961) Marsh B. Ray provides a more recent example of reference groups. Speaking of addicts and of nonaddicts, he writes:

> In the early phases of an episode of cure, the abstainer manifests considerable ambivalence about where he stands in addict and non-addict groups, and in discussions of addiction and addicts, he may indicate his ambivalence through his alternate use of the pronouns "we" and "they" and thus his alternate membership in addict and non-addict society. He may also indicate his ambivalence through other nuances of language and choice of words. Later, during a successful episode of abstinence, the ex-addict indicates his non-membership in the addict group through categorizations that place addicts clearly in the third person, and he places his own addiction and matters pertaining to it in the past tense. For example, he is likely to preface a remark with the phrase "When I was an addict. . . ." But of equal or greater importance is the fact that the ex-addict who is successful in remaining abstinent relates to new groups of people, participates in their experience, and to some extent begins to evaluate the conduct of his former associates (and perhaps his own when he was an addict) in terms of the values of the new group (in Becker, *The Other Side,* 1964: 168).

The nonaddict group can be a reference group for the addict even before he joins it — at the times, for example, when he contemplates kicking the habit. Similarly, once he comes to view himself as a nonaddict, the addict group may still exert some pull on him as a reference group.

An important development in social interaction theory was its increasing focus on all the elements involved in interaction. Whereas previous studies had been devoted to a one-sided consideration of deviants, increasing attention came to be paid to nondeviants. Studies of police interaction with gangs and with other subcultures of people that might be treated by police as criminals, and thus as deviants, led to studies of the police themselves. Researchers wanted to understand why police act as they do toward gang boys, prostitutes, and other people officially defined as deviants. More and more studies were done of the laws the police are expected to enforce, of the prosecutors and judges with whom the police interact, and finally of the politicians who use political power to create the laws within which all these control organizations work. The study of control organizations became very general, leading to studies of welfare agencies, psychiatric social workers, and many more. Those who undertook these studies were mainly interested in exploring the social interaction processes between different groups from the perspectives of all involved.

CURRENT TRENDS IN SOCIAL INTERACTION THEORY

In the sociology of deviance as well as in sociology in general, social interaction theory and in particular symbolic interactionism continue to make significant theoretical and empirical contributions. They have led to some new approaches in studying deviance. In this chapter we will concentrate on studies that remain within the interactionist perspective; in the next we will examine some of the new developments.

According to Howard Becker, an important theorist in the sociological study of deviance, the early 1960s were a turning point for symbolic interactionist studies of deviance. Becker describes why reform was needed:

> Unfortunately, the study of deviance lost its connection with the mainstream of sociological theory and research. It became a practical pursuit, devoted to helping society deal with those it found troublesome. Students of deviance devoted themselves to answering the questions posed by laymen and their elected and appointed officials. . . .
>
> In the past several years, however, all this has changed. The connections between the study of deviance and the growth of sociological theory and knowledge have been re-established . . . (*The Other Side*, 1964: 1).

Social interaction theories have helped make the study of deviance in many ways the most theoretically innovative field in sociology. Theorists no longer limit themselves to the study of illegal behavior and have greatly expanded the range of topics that they study as instances of deviance. Researchers continue to study criminal behavior — for example, check forging (Lemert, 1958), shoplifting (Cameron, 1964) and gambling (Zola, in Becker, 1964) — and criminal subcultures both inside and outside prisons (Irwin and Cressey, 1970). The increasing scope of the field, however, is suggested by studies on such topics as physical handicaps (Davis, 1962), mental illness (Goffman, 1961), nudism (Weinberg, 1970); stupidity (Dexter, 1964), and sex in public places (Humphreys, 1970; Dalph, 1978). (For representative examples of such studies, see Becker, 1964.)

A number of interactionist studies have been done on the topic of vagrancy, beginning with Nels Anderson's *The Hobo* (1961, first published in 1923). Samuel Wallace has presented the most general form of interactionist theory as it applies to "skid rowers." The following statement from his book *Skid Row as a Way of Life* (1965) suggests the issues that emerge from an interactionist perspective:

> The process of becoming a skid rower is not easy, rapid, or uniform. There are many pitfalls along the way, and the novice must be on the alert ere the Forces of Respectable Society swoop down and snatch up another hapless victim. It is a complex process whose description depends upon one's point of view. To the non-skid rower, the process appears to involve ever-increasing isolation from the larger society accompanied by ever-increasing deviance from its norms. From the point of view of the skid rower, on the other hand, the process is one of increasing participation in the life of the skid row community, and is accompanied by increasing conformity to its norms. . . . To understand the final product of this process — the completely acculturated skid rower — the investigator must recognize these dual forces of rejection and attraction within the life history of the individual.
>
> The routes to homelessness must first be examined with respect to the person's initial exposure to skid row. Since no one is born into the skid row way of life, it is critical to ask who was the skid rower before he came to skid row? Where did he come from? Where and how did he first meet up with skid row? In short, where are skid row's recruiting offices and who are those attracted to step inside?
>
> Since many are exposed to skid row but nevertheless return to respectable society, a second critical phase in the process occurs at the point of regular participation in the skid row way of life. After having been exposed to skid row, why does a novice continue to take the next step of participation in this deviant community? . . .
>
> The third and final stage in the process involves conformity to skid row values and the corresponding rejection of the values of the larger society. Just as exposure is not necessarily followed by participation, neither do all who take part in the skid row way of life become full-fledged members of its community. And to understand the entire process, the investigator must be

able to account for those who drop out at one point or another between exposure and acculturation (1965: 163–164).*

We can see that Wallace is concerned with many aspects of the situation — the perspectives of the non-skid rower and of the skid rower; the influence of the social world on the individual and the individual's response to that social world; the role of interaction in one's introduction to a deviant way of life; the significance of participation in deviant activities; and the emphasis on values and value conflict. All of these features are basic to social interaction theory.

Although present-day social interaction theorists conduct many studies within the framework of the sociology of deviance, one such theorist, Erving Goffman, has questioned the legitimacy of *deviance* as a topic of study. In "Deviations and Deviance," the final chapter in his book *Stigma* (1963B), he writes of how his study relates to the field of deviance. According to Goffman, *stigmas* — that is, attributes of individuals that are seen by members of society as discrediting to those who possess them — include physical handicaps, mental handicaps, mental illness, as well as less-visible attributes such as homosexuality, transvestitism (cross-dressing or wearing clothes of the opposite sex), illegitimacy, or Ku Klux Klan membership. In questioning the idea of deviance he states:

> Once the dynamics of shameful differentness are seen as a general feature of social life, one can go on to look at the relation of their study to the study of neighboring matters associated with the term "deviance" — a currently fashionable word that has been somewhat avoided here until now, in spite of the convenience of the label.

He continues in a footnote:

> It is remarkable that those who live around the social sciences have so quickly become comfortable in using the term "deviant," as if those to whom the term is applied have enough in common so that significant things can be said about them as a whole. Just as there are iatrogenic disorders caused by the work that physicians do (which then give them more work to do), so there are categories of persons who are created by students of society, and then studied by them (p. 140).

Goffman believes that sociologists may have given a symbolic importance to the idea of deviance that does not exist in the real world. His objection demonstrates an important aspect of social interaction theory

---

* From *Skid Row as a Way of Life*, pp. 163–164, by Samuel E. Wallace. Reprinted with permission from the author.

— its commitment to the real world of social interaction and its demand that sociological theory remain true to that world.

Goffman argues that the term deviance is being applied to phenomena that do not have enough common features to be studied as a category. Labeling theory, developed by Howard Becker, a symbolic interactionist, provides a response to Goffman's objections. Becker isolated features common to all acts of deviance, thereby justifying for him and for many later theorists the use of that concept. (We will present Becker's ideas in Chapter 5.)

GENERAL ORIENTATION OF SYMBOLIC INTERACTION THEORY

The basic idea of symbolic interactionist theory is simple enough: *the social world is constructed or created by its members in and through their social interactions.* The pattern or order within the social world is seen as resulting from the symbols, including the moral values, which members of society share through learning and living together. These shared symbolic meanings, however, must always be interpreted or *constructed* in the course of actual interactions. Social order is thus the result both of a shared symbolic universe and of concrete interactions among individuals in face-to-face situations.

The contrast between symbolic interactionism and structural theories (described in Chapter 2) is sharp. Structural theorists identify *transmitted values of society* as the basic direct cause of social order and therefore see no need to look at individual actors as independent variables determining the patterns of social life. Structuralists argue that shared meanings, and especially shared values, are sufficient to explain individual action. They argue that because social structure *causes* individual intentions or motives, these intentions cannot be independent causes of individual behavior. Symbolic interactionists, on the other hand, argue that while shared meanings are indeed important variables, they do not by any means entirely determine how individuals respond to specific situations. Moreover, individuals certainly *choose* at times to act independently of the values they share and express. The crucial difference here is that structuralists see individuals as *driven* or *compelled* to deviance while symbolic interactionists see individuals as *choosing* deviance.

In support of their argument, symbolic interactionists point out that even shared values in the United States — such values as success, equality, democracy, and fairness — are the subject of bitter controversy and conflict. The dispute is not over the validity of these values, for they are held by virtually everyone, but over what they mean in concrete situations. For example, educators who believe in "equal opportunity" disagree over the meaning of this phrase and over which actions carry it out. Teachers and administrators within a single state, city, or even school may have very different interpretations. If it were true that the shared value of equal opportunity, for example, determined how people act in concrete situations, why would there be such vast conflict over integration, busing, grades, state and federal financing of education, affirmative education programs, and so on? How could any structure of *shared* values ever produce such a complex, pluralistic set of social conflicts?

Symbolic interactionists have commonly agreed with structuralists that members of society in general share a set of building blocks consisting of values and other symbols. Interactionists insist, however, that we must observe and analyze how bricklayers and carpenters actually use those building blocks if we are to understand how some blocks wind up as part of an outhouse and others wind up as part of an International Trade Center building in New York City. The blocks may be the same, and so may all the other building materials, but the builders (the social interactors) can use them to construct extremely different buildings that have very different effects on people.

The general principle underlying the symbolic interactionist orientation is that *social meanings and actions must always be constructed to fit the actual situations in which individuals interact.* Interactionists, anticipating that meanings will be problematic, address themselves to the problem of finding out what these different meanings are. This orientation leads interactionists to concentrate on empirical studies that require close contact with those being studied. Problems may arise when the topic is deviance because researchers must become associated with, if not necessarily involved in, the deviant activities under investigation. We will discuss some of these problems of such study, as well as the kind of insights that can be gained, in Part II.

Symbolic interactionism has been criticized both by structuralists and by others on a number of grounds. A major objection has been that by focusing on interaction, the theory fails to take into account the larger features of the social world that influence social behavior, such as class, economic structure, and societal organization. Symbolic interactionists agree that it does so but disagree about the reasons for such "neglect." Some argue that symbolic interactionism can deal with the larger features of the social world, but only after the interactional dimension is fully understood. (See, for example, Berger and Luckmann, *The Social Construction of Reality,* 1966.) Others argue that the larger features of the social world cannot be studied meaningfully and that those who claim otherwise are trying to study an illusion. To those who take this position, the larger social structure exists *only as it is mediated by individuals in interaction.* (See, for example, Rock, 1979.) In any case, it is certainly accurate to say that symbolic interactionists focus on far more specific phenomena than do structuralists.

Second, one may see an implied criticism in the fact that symbolic interactionism is called social psychology rather than sociology. Certainly the term social psychology is not in itself an insult; in fact an important work in symbolic interactionism is Tamotsu Shibutani's *Society and Personality: An Interactionist Approach to Social Psychology* (1961). But when the intention of the classification is to divorce symbolic interactionist theory from sociology, it would seem that the theory is being judged inappropriate for sociological theory. The issue here is whether or not symbolic interactionism is a form of sociological theory; some who call it social psychology seem to mean that the theory is not a part of sociological theory as a whole, but rather has a much narrower application. Symbolic interactionists, as well as proponents of the new perspective, argue that social interactionist theory is as much a sociological theory as is structuralism.

Finally, symbolic interactionism has been criticized on the ground that many of its insights are not universal as claimed but rather are peculiarly American. Critics argue that it elevates the individual to a position of importance that is uncharacteristic of many societies. Even something that seems as basic to us as the sense of self may have a far broader range of manifestations than symbolic interactionism recognizes. It is certainly true that cross-cultural studies might result in important changes in symbolic interaction theory, and that such studies are rare, but interactionists themselves are cautious in the claims they make regarding the universality of their findings. By and large they think that generalizations are possible only after extensive detailed studies have established an adequate set of data.

Level VI. Individual Psychology as Source of Explanation

Psychological explanations of deviance have been vital as resources for sociologists and as a part of common-sense explanations. Keep in mind the distinction between sociology (the systematic study of the development, structure, interaction, and collective behavior of organized groups of human beings) and psychology (the systematic study of mind and behavior). Psychology is concerned with the internal workings of the mind; sociology with social behavior. If we see the two fields as distinct, directing themselves to different issues, then it is clear that although psychological explanations may be useful to sociologists, they are not *in themselves* sociological explanations.

Although it is certainly no surprise that psychologists have sought to explain deviance in terms of individual psychology and "normal" psychological processes, they often overlook the *origin* of their explanations in the study of deviants. The link between deviance and psychological theories can be seen in three facts. First, a great deal of psychological theory about the "normal" personality and its development has been derived from studies of those who are considered "abnormal" or deviant. Since Freud, psychologists have devoted much study to "abnormality" and made inferences from those data about the nature of "normality." To then make inferences from "normality" to "abnormality" may involve circular reasoning. Second, psychiatry, a service profession based on psychological theories, has been actively involved in "curing deviance." Psychological theories have been used as a basis for viewing deviance as "abnormal," "an illness," and "curable" through professional help. The distinction between "normal" and "abnormal," however, has commonly been *assumed* rather than made on the basis of established and empirical criteria. Third, psychological theory has become a part of the court process. Those accused of crimes may now be sent to mental hospitals instead of prisons; it is even possible to claim that one is not responsible for a crime because of "insanity." In this process psychological theory becomes subject to political as well as scientific considerations. These three facts demonstrate that psychological explanations are both derived from studies of deviance and also taken as *the* explanations for deviant behavior. They suggest that both circularity and absolutism are possibilities when theories are developed in such a fashion.

Sociologists have often drawn on psychological explanations both for theories and for empirical evidence. In doing so, they have encountered some problems. Sociologists in general see sociology as a distinct field of study and social behavior as guided by social rules. When they adopt psychological theories, however, they move toward *psychological reductionism*, the view that all social behavior can be explained by or "reduced to" psychological factors. In the following pages we will look at the contributions made by the psychological study of deviance, keeping in mind the social world in which such psychological factors operate.

Psychological theory, and Freudian theory in particular, has become a part of common-sense knowledge. Freudian theory has probably had greater influence on the thinking of people, especially in the United States, than any other social science theory. Even popular common-sense theories of deviance that appear on the surface to be sociological are commonly derived from Freudian theory. An excellent example of common-sense psychological explanations of deviance is provided by Robert Lindner's famous book *Rebel Without a Cause* (1944), which was made into a movie in the 1950s, continues to be popular, and has had a lasting impact on popular thinking about delinquency. The explanation of the hero's delinquency ignored social causation and focused on psychological factors — in particular, the hero's repressed rage against his parents, which he took out on society and himself. We are not denying the possibility of such an explanation; we suggest that the *assumption* of the truth of psychological explanations and the popular belief that such explanations are sufficient can block consideration of significant social factors that influence deviance. It is important for us to recognize which psychological theories of deviance we are simply taking for granted so that we can bring them to light and examine them.

EARLY PSYCHOLOGICAL EXPLANATIONS OF DEVIANCE

Psychologists have always been concerned with what we are calling deviance, though they have almost always used other terms such as insanity, nonconformity, abnormality, immorality, guilt, and crime. Although some psychologists have attempted to explain the more general phenomenon of deviance and to deal with the overall importance of deviance in human life, most have focused on *insanity* and *madness.* Indeed, much of clinical psychology and personality theory grew out of nineteenth-century studies of behavior thus labeled.

The history of psychological theory includes a wide variety of explanations of what we now call mental illness. In the seventeenth and eighteenth centuries, explanations of madness were developed by theologians and philosophers as well as by people who had to confront and come to terms with "the mad." Insanity then was popularly thought to originate within the individual. It was viewed as either a manifestation of possession by devils or witches or as a form of immorality. In the former case, treatment was in the hands of religion. In the latter, cure was seen to lie also in the hands of the ill themselves. Foucault (1965) describes a typical view of insanity and its treatment:

> At this extreme point, madness was less than ever linked to medicine; nor could it be linked to the domain of correction. Unchained animality could be mastered only by *discipline* and *brutalizing.* The theme of the animal-madman was effectively realized in the eighteenth century, in occasional attempts to impose a certain pedagogy on the insane. Pinel cites the case of a "very famous monastic establishment, in one of the southern regions of France," where a violent madman would be given "a precise order to change"; if he refused to go to bed or to eat, he "was warned that obstinacy in his deviations would be punished on the next day with ten strokes of the bullwhip." If, on the contrary, he was submissive and docile, he was allowed "to take his meals in the refectory, next to the disciplinarian," but at the least transgression, he was instantly admonished by a "heavy blow of a rod across his fingers" (p. 75).

Particularly in the seventeenth century, distinctions were not made between the insane and the criminal and vagrant; all were confined together in single institutions. What Foucault calls "the great confinement" swept across eighteenth-century Europe, confining masses of all kinds of "deviants" in hospitals and madhouses, and leading to the creation of a profession of caretakers (see also Szasz, 1970). Toward the close of the eighteenth century, treatment of madness began again to be linked with medicine, and caretakers increasingly came from the ranks of medical doctors.

With the growth of science in the nineteenth century, psychological explanations of madness were developed. Two major and competing views emerged: the *humanistic* and the *organic*. Humanistic theorists were those who explained mental illness in terms of an individual's life history, social situations, and what today we would call personality factors. Perhaps the most important scientific work of this type was the book by Esquirol (1838) on mental illness. It inspired many detailed studies of individual cases of such "immoral" behavior as suicide. Brière de Boismont (1856), for example, carefully analyzed cases of suicide from suicide notes in order to identify "types" of persons who commit suicide. Modern methodologists might disagree with many aspects of his research, but his findings were similar in important ways to those of psychologists who independently rediscovered his methods a hundred years later (see, for example, Farberow and Shneidman, 1961). Because their works were ignored by psychologists for many years, humanistic theorists influenced later psychological theories of deviance primarily through their influence on Freud and his co-workers.

Although humanistic theories were influential for a brief time, they were progressively displaced during the second half of the nineteenth century by organic theories (see the earlier discussion, Chapter 2, of Level I theories of the physical organism). Organic theories were viewed as "tough-minded," "hard-data" theories in the spirit of the natural science theories of the time. Theorists viewed all mental illness as caused by organic problems whose source lay in the physical organism. Organic theories came to dominate explanations of insanity and were not significantly challenged among professionals until the work of Freud.

It was also not until Freud that one could properly speak of *psychological theories* — those which explained mental activities in terms of the mind or *psyche* of the individual. In time these theories gained strength, and even organic theorists modified their theories along Freudian lines. We will turn now to an examination of Freudian theory, focusing on those elements that bear directly on the issue of deviance.

FREUD AND FREUDIAN EXPLANATIONS OF DEVIANCE

In considering Freudian theories of deviance we must distinguish between Freud and Freudians, as well as between what Freud said and how he actually used his ideas in his own theorizing. As we trace Freud's thought and its elaboration by later thinkers, we will emphasize these distinctions where appropriate.

Freud's theories of *superego control* and of *sublimation* have been of particular importance in psychological theories of deviance. In order to understand these theories, however, one needs some knowledge of Freud's theory of personality development and personality organization; to this end we will present a brief overview of his ideas, focusing on those which have been particularly important in explanations of deviance.

Perhaps the most widely known of Freud's ideas is the central role he gives to *sexuality* in the development and organization of the personality. One should recognize, however, the very broad definition of sexuality he was employing. According to Freud, human beings are born with a very general sexual instinct capable of being satisfied in many ways, not all commonly recognized as sexual. He states:

> As characteristics of the infantile sexuality, we have hitherto emphasized the fact that it is essentially autoerotic (he finds his object in his own body), and that the individual partial impulses, which on the whole are unconnected and independent of one another, are striving for the acquisition of pleasure. The goal of this development forms the so-called normal sexual life of the adult in whom the acquisition of pleasure has been put into the service of the function of propagation (1962: 57, first published in 1905).

On the basis of this diffuse infant sexuality, the "normal" individual will follow predictable steps to adulthood. It is understandable, however, that Freud's definition of "normality" fitted the social and moral requirements of his society. Both Freud and later theorists have minimized the importance of the initial diffusely sexual period, which might have served as the basis for theoretical acceptance of a far wider range of sexual activities as "normal." Rather they have focused on the increasing constraints that are "normally" placed on sexual behavior so that its direct expression is in male/female reproduction and its indirect expression is in a wide range of social and cultural contributions.

According to Freud, the turning point in the "harnessing" of sexuality is the resolution of the Oedipus conflict:

> It is the fate of all of us, perhaps, to direct our first sexual impulse towards our mother, and our first hatred and our first murderous wish against our father. Our dreams convince us that that is so. King Oedipus, who slew his father Laius and married his mother Jocasta, merely shows us the fulfilment of our own childhood wishes. But, more fortunate than he, we have meanwhile succeeded, in so far as we have not become psychoneurotics, in detaching our sexual impulses from our mothers and in forgetting our jealousy of fathers (1965: 296, first published in 1900).

For Freud, the Oedipus conflict is crucial in understanding human behavior. Its resolution contributes to the redirection of sexual energy to religion, ethics, society, and art; furthermore, "the nucleus of all neuroses as far as our present knowledge of them goes is the Oedipus complex" (from *Totem and Taboo*, 1913, in Brill, p. 927). The successful resolution of the Oedipus conflict involves a *repression* of desire for one's mother and of aggression toward one's father; the failur.. ..de so re- sults in a wide variety of neuroses. Successful resolution involves *iden- tification* with the rival (the father) as well as the incorporation of his view of one's self. This view serves as the basis of the *superego*, that element of the personality which punishes one for acts or even thoughts of wrongdoing through the creation of *guilt*. Because of the punitive nature of the superego, the diffuse sexual energy must be *repressed* and can manifest itself only in nonsexual forms if guilt is to be avoided. These indirect expressions of repressed sexual desires, which Freud called *sublimations*, make up the major part of our social and cultural behavior.

As the Oedipus conflict is customarily presented, it is applicable only to males. In fact, Freud states that females undergo a very different process, one that led Freud and later theorists to see a great difference between male and female personality. The process is described by Freud:

> The girl is driven out of her attachment to her mother through the influence of her envy for the penis and she enters the Oedipus situation as though into a haven of refuge. In the absence of fear of castration the chief motive is lacking which leads boys to surmount the Oedipus complex. Girls remain in it for an indeterminate length of time; they demolish it late and, even so, incompletely. In these circumstances the formation of the super-ego must suffer; it cannot attain the strength and independence which give it its cul- tural significance, and feminists are not pleased when we point out to them the effects of this factor upon the average feminine character (from *The Com- plete Introductory Lectures on Psychoanalysis*, in Brill, p. 593).

Although later Freudians have modified it somewhat, the theory of the Oedipal conflict, a pivotal one for Freud's entire conception of neurosis, remains grounded in a view of the very distinct psychological natures of males and females.

Freud himself devoted considerable attention to what we are calling deviance; in fact his theories of normal development draw almost exclu- sively on his studies of what he saw as abnormality. Freud and his followers did not see abnormality (deviance) as problematic. Like soci- ologists of that period, psychologists adopted an absolutist perspective and *assumed* that what was deviant was obvious to people in general and to theorists in particular.

Freud did much research on sexuality and presented a number of his important insights on sexual deviance in an article entitled "The Sexual

Aberrations" (in Brill). He identified what he referred to as "many deviations in reference to both sexual object and sexual aim . . ." (p. 553). His analysis demonstrated that these deviations were potentials in all human beings; his question was therefore not how such deviations come to exist but how they come to be manifested in some individuals and repressed in others. He claimed that a "tendency to perversion" is manifested when opportunities for "normal" fulfillment are blocked, either by outside circumstances or by repression under the direction of the superego.

According to Freud and later Freudians, *deviant acts are caused by processes within the individual.* Against this background two sets of Freudian theories have been developed to explain deviance: *control theories* and *defense theories.** Control theories emphasize Freud's ideas about superego control, and defense theories focus more on his ideas of repression and sublimation.

Control theories claim that deviant behavior occurs when superego controls fail, freeing individuals to act upon socially unacceptable impulses. Since Freud saw both the personality and society as constructed on the basis of impulse control, the situations in which impulses can be acted upon in socially acceptable ways are extremely limited. Although impulses may vary in strength from person to person, everyone has impulses that can manifest themselves as deviance. The point emphasized by control theories, however, is that impulses and controls are by nature in a state of tension. Situational factors may reinforce either controls or impulses, but the ultimate decision rests with the individual. When impulses are stronger than controls, deviance is likely to occur.

Defense theories also see the personality as operating through the dynamic tension of impulse and control; they differ from control theories, however, in that they believe an individual's behavior may be deviant *even when socially unacceptable impulses are repressed.* Freud believed that although impulses can be controlled, they can never be eliminated. According to defense theories, even *controlled* socially unacceptable impulses give rise to anxiety and guilt. Individuals may deal with such impulses and their attendant guilt either by concealing them behind behavior that is the opposite of that motivated by the impulses or by diverting them into other deviant channels. Thus, a male might come to terms with homosexual impulses by concealing them from himself and others behind a "macho" façade — including the display of violence toward homosexuals — or by attempting to satisfy such impulses through pornography. Control theorists, on the other hand, suggest that homosexuality, violence, or pornography occur when the

---

* We thank Robert Scott for pointing out this distinction.

controls over them fail. Control theorists hold that impulses emerge directly as deviance and defense theorists think they may also be diverted into other forms of deviance.

Control theories have been used to explain a variety of types of deviance. Some make use of the idea of the *psychopathic personality,* one which develops without a superego or conscience and thus without controls. According to Freudian theory, such individuals have not satisfactorily resolved Oedipal conflicts. The psychopath is described by Rabin (1961):

> There are two major related aspects to this notion of defective conscience. . . . The first aspect is represented in the inability . . . to apply the moral standards of society to his behavior; he cheats, lies, steals, does not keep promises, and so on. He has not absorbed the "thou shalts" and the "thou shalt nots" of his society and cultural milieu. The second aspect is that of absence of guilt. Guilt is an important part of any well-developed conscience. When a normal person violates the moral code he feels guilty; he feels unhappy and blames himself for the transgression. . . . Guilt is an unknown experience for the personality with no superego. There is none of this automatic self-punishment that goes along with the commission of immoral and unethical acts. The psychopath [sociopath] continues to behave irresponsibly, untruthfully, insincerely, and antisocially without a shred of shame, remorse, or guilt. He may sometimes express regret and remorse for the actions and crimes which he may have perpetrated; however, these are usually mere words, spoken for the effect, but not really and sincerely felt (p. 278).

Control theories have been used by many theorists to explain violence and juvenile gang behavior (see, for example, Yablonsky, 1962).

Defense theories have been equally popular in explaining deviance. One such theory that makes particularly clear the contrast with control theories is provided by Alexander and Staub in *The Criminal, the Judge, and the Public* (1962):

> This type [one neurotic criminal] was first described by Freud: a man who violates the law not because he lacks a conscience, but — paradoxical as this may sound — because he has a severe and rigid conscience, which produces in him an unconscious sense of guilt. He feels guilty because of unconscious tendencies, never carried out in reality, which go back into his early experiences in the family and which mostly emanate from his Oedipus complex, his early relationship to his mother and father. He commits crimes not so much for rational motives of material gain or from resentment against the social order, but in order to relieve his unconscious guilt feelings. With a concrete, relatively harmless transgression of the law for which he is punished, he ties his unconscious guilt for patricidal or matricidal tendencies to a much smaller offense. He is punished for this lesser crime, and the punishment relieves his guilt. He atones for a greater unconscious crime by a relatively slight punishment for some banal transgression. Such a person is clearly neurotic; his delinquency is a direct outcome of his emotional disturbance (p. 11).

In addition to control and defense theories, Freud's ideas have given rise to other explanations of deviance. Some theorists, for example, have argued that juvenile delinquency may be due not only to neurotic processes in the delinquent but to encouragement by parents acting out their unconscious, repressed impulses. A different explanation is provided by Theodore Reik, who has argued that individuals unconsciously do things to get themselves caught. Since one cannot be punished for thoughts alone, one *acts* in ways that will bring punishment. In the *Compulsion to Confess* (1959) he claims that only confession will relieve the often profound, unconscious feelings of guilt.

As one might expect, Freudian theories have been applied frequently to various forms of sexual deviance, such as prostitution (see especially Greenwald, *The Call Girl*, 1958) and homosexuality. In a careful study of 1,200 books and articles on homosexuality, Weinberg and Bell (1972) found that most were written by psychiatrists and psychologists and that most relied predominantly on the core ideas of Freudian theory. Such studies began with the basic assumption that homosexual acts are necessarily abnormal and must be explained as an outcome of neurosis. Bieber (1962) states this position very clearly: "We consider homosexuality to be a pathologic, bio-social, psychosexual adaptation consequent to pervasive fears surrounding the expression of heterosexual impulses." Such studies generally go on to show how various forms of repression of sexual drives in early childhood lead eventually to such "pathologic" or disease-caused patterns of action. Such analyses follow closely the ideas of Freud we have just examined.

Recent critics of Freudian explanations of deviance have argued that the methods of such studies have been flawed. (See especially Hall and Lindzey, 1957; and Weinberg and Williams, 1975.) Three major research problems have been recognized:

1. Many researchers have gathered their data from psychiatric patients and then inappropriately extended their conclusions to include those who have not sought psychiatric help. For example, the call girls studied by Greenwald had gone to him for psychiatric help because they felt they were abnormal or neurotic. There is no reason to assume, however, that their experiences were shared by call girls who did not seek such assistance. One could as reasonably assume that the latter were quite different. In the research process, however, neither assumption is appropriate; empirical evidence is required. We may say, then, that many studies have *generalized beyond their data*.

2. Theories based on studies of psychiatric patients often involve a *tautology* or circular argument. For example, psychological theories of violence often state that people who are violent have a weak superego that cannot control violent impulses. However, the evidence for a weak

superego is that the individual is violent *and* the evidence of violent impulses is, again, that the individual is violent. The argument goes round and round. This kind of theory cannot be proved (its truth can only be *assumed*) or disproved (it is not *falsifiable*). Control theories, in particular, have been criticized on this basis.

3. Because Freudian theory is often used so "flexibly," it is always possible to find something "abnormal" in a person's childhood that might plausibly be related to that person's adult problems. In a study of alcoholism, for example (McCord and McCord, 1956), the researchers predicted that adult alcoholics would be found to have been dependent as children. Looking at the data, however, they discovered that adult alcoholics demonstrated patterns of confident independence in childhood. The researchers did not see this finding as disproving their prediction but rather argued that the confident childhood behavior was merely a façade concealing underlying dependency.* Although this explanation may appear reasonable, science requires evidence, not mere plausibility. This criticism has been particularly directed at defense theories, those which focus on indirect routes to deviance.

Freudian theory has come under increasing attack by sociologists and other social scientists, with psychologists themselves providing some of the more telling objections. One important criticism, which at the same time supports sociological theory about subcultures, was advanced by Franz Alexander, working with Healy on a study of delinquents in Boston. In this work, *The Roots of Crime* (1935), Alexander and Healy reported that they had found many delinquents who fit the earlier Freudian model, but also a significant number who were "normal, non-neurotic criminals — professional delinquents whose Superegos have criminal tendencies" (pp. 11–12). They discovered the existence of whole subcultures with criminal values in which the superegos of members seem to support crime rather than oppose it. In such a context, crime seems not neurotic but normal.

Since the time of this study almost all sociological research has provided support for such a conclusion. David Maurer's rejection of psychological explanation and support of subcultural explanation draws heavily on his own empirical research. He writes:

> I suggest that perhaps we should go a little beyond the armchair rationalizations of modern psychology and look to the behavior pattern for some cues. Several points arise in this connection. First, the members of the criminal subcultures do not, as we would like to believe, suffer acute feelings of guilt as a result of robbing members of the dominant culture. That is their way of life; they are parasitic on the dominant culture, and have been for

* Robert Scott brought this example to our attention.

many centuries. They have no more feeling of guilt than does a fox who takes hens from a farmer. During the course of many years I have interviewed many professional criminals; I have yet to find a professional who develops severe guilt feelings in connection with any specific routine act of theft from a so-called *sucker*, or member of the dominant culture, though many learn in prison how to simulate such feelings in order to influence the parole board.

Second, because the thief is a member of a parasitic subculture, it is about as reasonable to attempt to bring him into the dominant culture via psychiatry based on conflicts thought to exist on a widespread basis in the dominant culture as it would be to transfer an old-time Sioux Indian from his culture to ours by the same method. I venture to suggest that any psychiatrist who tried to give the participants in the Custer massacre insight into their "guilt" feelings in connection with this event would have had rough going indeed. Those Sioux who exterminated Custer's force were behaving as they were expected to in their culture; they enjoyed every bit of it, and derived status from it which they carried to their dying days (1964: 16–17).*

Maurer continues his criticism, but this quotation gives a sufficient sense of its nature.

Even in the face of these criticisms, Freudian analysis remains widely used in psychiatry, psychology, sociology, other social sciences, literary analysis, and common-sense knowledge. Its position of dominance, however, has weakened and in part as a response to such criticisms, a number of recent developments in psychological theory have arisen. We turn to those developments now.

RECENT DEVELOPMENTS IN PSYCHOLOGICAL EXPLANATIONS OF DEVIANCE

Freudian theory dominated psychology for many years. Alternative psychological theories, however, have also existed, and some are now gaining in importance, though even these draw on some of Freud's insights and concerns. Of particular relevance to the study of deviance are theories of *moral development*. Our discussion of absolutism in Chapter 1 made clear the strong links between morality and deviance.

The study of moral development goes back to the classic work of McDougall, whose subject in *An Introduction to Social Psychology* (1916, 11th ed.) was "the moralisation of the individual by the society in which he is born as a creature in which the non-moral and purely egoistic tendencies are so much stronger than any altruistic tendencies" (p. 18). He later elaborates on this point: "Moral conduct is essentially social conduct, and there could be no serious objection to the use of the two expressions as synonymous; but it is more in conformity with common usage to restrict the term 'moral' to the higher forms of social conduct

* From *The Big Con*, by David W. Maurer. Reprinted with permission from the author.

of which man alone is capable" (p. 174). Works in this tradition were based on the assumption that infants were born *amoral* (without morality) and focused on the ways in which they became moral. Such works usually accepted the common-sense idea that individuals develop a set of absolute moral principles that they carry around with them as a part of their personalities or characters and that they use to determine how to act in concrete situations.

With the passage of time the idea of the absolute nature of individual morality was challenged. One of the best examinations of this issue was *Studies in Deceit* (1938) by Hartshorne and May. Their basic conclusion was that people's situations are important determinants of whether or not they will violate group rules. Individual morality seemed to them to be *situational* rather than *absolute*.

The most extensive work on moral development was done by the psychologist Jean Piaget (1932) and those who followed. Piaget's careful studies of children over many years indicated that they begin life with an amoral orientation, simply trying to satisfy their desires, a finding that fits with Freud's ideas about infancy. Met with parental punishments for certain kinds of behavior, children move to a stage of *moral absolutism*, in which they see rules as external to themselves, a necessary part of reality, or even as sacred commands. As development proceeds, children come to adjust these rules to the demands of specific situations and to view them as flexible, situational, and practical. By the age of eight or ten, children have generally replaced moral absolutism with a sense of *justice*, which involves a complex use of internal rules to achieve reciprocal or give-and-take social relationships. Modifications in morality or in one's attitude toward rules continue to develop throughout adulthood.

Piaget's general conclusion was that, as individuals interact more and more with the complex social world, moral absolutism weakens and the meanings of moral rules are increasingly determined by social context. This conclusion has been supported by many other lines of research and theory in psychology.

Personality theory, which has been a large part of modern psychology and social psychology, has increasingly emphasized the individual's *openness* to the social world and social situations and has elaborated on the idea that people actively construct their lives and selves. Gordon Allport's well-known work *Becoming* (1955) exemplifies this change in emphasis. On the basis of personality theory, Harry Stack Sullivan (1953) and others have argued that mental illness is predominantly a complex set of socially defined phenomena that grow out of social interaction. In explaining individual behavior, greater significance has been attached to factors that lie *outside* the individual.

Many studies of small-group interactions in laboratory settings have found that group pressures profoundly influence the moral decisions or

value judgments that individuals make. A further line of research concluded that people's cognitive (thought) and perceptual (visual) judgments can be guided by group pressures even in a direction contrary to
their moral commitments or common sense. Sherif's famous work
(1936) was designed to show that people in an ambiguous situation will
move their cognitive judgments into line with those of the group. In a
famous series of experiments Asch (1952) demonstrated that individuals
will adjust their perceptions of the length of a line shown to them to
agree better with the perceptions of the group they belong to, even
when other group members (in league with the experimenters) deliberately misstate the length they perceive.

The works of Sherif, Asch, and others led to a series of studies on
conformity effects, in which researchers tried to demonstrate the conditions under which individuals will conform to group standards and
decisions (Walker and Heyns, 1962; Thibaut and Kelley, 1959: 239–255;
Tagiurri and Petrullo, 1958). Faced with evidence from these and other
studies, many social scientists in the 1950s and early 1960s became
convinced that individual action was determined not by internal factors,
nor by internal moral rules, but by external factors. Freud's view of
individual determinism, which held that individual behavior is governed
by internal factors, was replaced by *social determinism,* which held that
individual behavior is governed by external social forces.

Adherents of social determinism claimed not so much that individual
determinism as a theory was unfounded, but rather that it was out-
dated. David Riesman argued in his renowned book *The Lonely Crowd*
(1950) that Americans were no longer *inner-directed* but had become
other-directed. At its extreme this view argued for the existence of adults
whose amorality (non-directedness) could cause deviance. Such arguments were particularly applied, both by psychologists and sociologists,
to sexual deviance and to violence. They spoke of *psychopaths* or *sociopaths* (terms that, strangely enough, seem to mean the same thing),
people who have clear perceptions of reality except when moral and
social obligations are involved and who often pursue immediate gratification in criminal acts, drug addiction, and sexual perversion. Such
theories are an extreme form of control theories.

The psychopath was seen as exactly the opposite of the neurotic
deviant; the former (as described in the passage by Rabin quoted on p.
110) was a deviant *without* a superego or conscience and was generally
believed to be a product of inadequate social training in morality. The
theory of the "psychopathic personality" is actually a modern variation
on the very old theory of the "egocentric" or "egoistic" personality,
which has been used for centuries to explain widespread and varied
patterns of deviance. More recent sociologists have used this theory of
the psychopathic or sociopathic personality as a source of explanation
for deviance (for example McCord and McCord, 1956; and Yablonsky,

1962). Yablonsky, in his work *The Violent Gang* (1962), saw sociopathy as the crucial determinant of gang violence and sexual deviance.

These extreme theories of the totally amoral individual pursuing momentary impulses have been generally discarded by psychologists and sociologists for a variety of reasons. First, the theories themselves are quite contradictory and confused. Often the terms psychopath and sociopath are not presented as part of an explicit theory at all, but are simply applied as labels. Second, it often seems that other explanations would much more plausibly account for the behavior under consideration. Yablonsky's explanation of gang behavior as sociopathic seems less satisfactory than those which recognize the existence of group norms among gang boys that differ from norms of psychiatrists, psychologists, or sociologists. Perhaps the most basic criticism of these theories is that they suggest that deviants and nondeviants are *entirely* different beings with totally distinct personalities. Such a finding is contradicted by a wealth of sociological data, much of which we have already examined in other contexts. Voluminous data indicate the many ways in which deviants are just like everybody else. The normality of much of their activities is reflected in the surprise people feel upon learning that a friend or acquaintance is engaged in a deviant activity. Their absence of suspicion indicates the many ways in which deviants behave normally.

As we have stated, psychologists have generally moved away from the idea of the amoral individual and a number have returned to a consideration of moral development, drawing and expanding upon Piaget. The most prominent theorist of moral development today is Kohlberg (1966, 1972; for an overview of these theories see Loevinger, *Ego Development: Conceptions and Theories,* 1976). Kohlberg has developed a *theory of moral development* that draws on Dewey's recognition of the importance of interaction between individual and environment and is based on Piaget's earlier theory of cognitive development. Kohlberg and others have expanded Piaget's concern with the development of thought (cognitive development) to include the development of the ego, emotions, and morality. Moral development, with which we are dealing here, is part of this broader theory of *developmental psychology* that addresses itself to the development of the entire personality.

Kohlberg's theory is based on the idea that *individuals progress through invariant ordered sequential states of morality.* According to Kohlberg:

> The acquisition of morality is an active change in patterns of response to problematic social situations rather than the learning of culturally accepted rules. . . . Morality is neither the internalization of established cultural values nor the unfolding of spontaneous impulses and emotions; it is justice, the reciprocity between the individual and others in his social environment (1972: 455).

Much of Kohlberg's work has been addressed to identifying these "sequential states" or stages of morality (see Figure 4.1). He claims that the stages occur in fixed order and that each is essential to the next. Although an individual may stop at any one stage or return to an earlier one, progress requires movement through each stage in sequence. No stage can be omitted. Each includes those which go before it, and thus movement through the stages is cumulative. Progress comes as one solves dilemmas with insights characteristic of the next stage. Individuals do not seek to move to new levels; they seek solutions to problems, and with new insights find themselves at a new stage. Each represents a more valuable or adequate psychological state than the one before.

Figure 4.1
Kohlberg's definition of moral stages

Preconventional level

Stage 1:   Obedience to rules and avoidance of punishment orientation; egocentric deference to persons of superior power or prestige; avoidance of acts labeled "bad"; decisions made on physical considerations.

Stage 2: Naive instrumental hedonism stage; right action is that satisfying the needs of self, and sometimes of others in exchange for favors; orientation is to equal reciprocity.

Conventional level

Stage 3:   Interpersonal concordance of good boy/girl orientation with a view toward the approval of others; oriented to pleasing and helping others; conformity to values of family and friends.

Stage 4:   Orientation to the legal and social order; maintenance of the present order for its own sake; concern with both secular and religious law.

Postconventional level

Stage 5:   Contractual orientation recognizing verbal as well as written agreements; individual rights orientation, with emphasis on avoidance of violating others' rights; decisions based on issues, rather than on group values.

Stage 6:   Universal ethical principled orientation; logical consistency in moral decision making; respect for human rights on a universal basis.

It is important to note here that stages are not based on the content of a subject's responses to a moral problem but on the logic involved in arriving at a solution. It is not the response but the rationale used that determines the moral stage. Either positive or negative responses may be given for the same basic reasons. For example, a person using stage 2 might choose or not choose to come to the aid of someone in need of help, depending upon which alternative was seen as ultimately the most beneficial to the self.

Source: Prepared by Joan Thrower Timm, adapted from Kohlberg. From her article "Group Care of Children and the Development of Moral Judgment," *Child Welfare,* Volume LIX, Number 6, June 1980, pp. 324–325. Reprinted by special permission of The Child Welfare League of America. See also Lawrence Kohlberg, "Moral Education in the Schools: A Developmental View," *The School Review,* Vol. 74, No. 1, Spring 1966, p. 7.

Moral development theory has been used to explain deviance by attempting to identify the stage at which the deviant is operating. The
following example of "Stage 2 thinking" suggests such an explanation:

> "What's in it for me?" asks the person who is reasoning on moral stage 2.
> Obviously this person is still thinking about things that affect him. He has
> his own thoughts and feelings, but now he also realizes that other people do
> too, and that their thoughts, feelings and wishes may be the same as his or
> they may be different. . . .
>
> Laws or rules are viewed as restrictions on one's actions. Stage 2 thinkers
> do not understand that laws function in a society to protect people's rights.
> A person thinking on stage 2 will obey the law to protect his own best
> interests, for example avoiding arrest. If a person can "beat the rap," how-
> ever, he is considered clever by his stage 2 thinking friends. . . .
>
> Most people reach stage 2 by the time they are nine or ten years old, and
> do not fully leave this stage until they are in their mid teens. *Juvenile delin-
> quents continue to function primarily on this stage. . . .**

This explanation suggests that a particular type of deviant, the juvenile
delinquent, is operating at a specific stage of moral development and
that movement out of this stage will eliminate that delinquency. Other
kinds of deviants can be found at other stages of moral development.
Stage 2 seems particularly applicable to juvenile delinquents. Stage 3
can be used to explain what we described earlier as subcultural and
gang deviance, since at this stage conformity is highly valued and the
approval of others is sought. Stage 4 can be used to explain terrorist
and revolutionary activities that are geared toward the establishment of
a new social order with its own authority and fixed rules. Stage 4 can
also be used to understand the behavior of those who create and enforce
laws. Although presumably deviants might be found at all the stages,
most explanations seem to place them in the earlier stages.

As an explanation of deviance, the theory of moral development can
be criticized on several grounds. First, although it focuses on the importance of the individual in interaction with the social world, that social
world seems to have a fixed and absolute character. Some viewpoints
in that social world are claimed to be better or more adequate than
others. Kohlberg's theory admits to being absolutist, explicitly rejecting
what he terms "value-relativism." Although Kohlberg's argument for
absolutism is certainly far more sophisticated than that of earlier thinkers (who *assumed* rather than *adopted* such a position), our earlier criticisms of absolutism as a framework for analyzing deviance apply here
as well (see Chapter 1, pp. 18–22). Second, this theory can be accused
of circular reasoning, which we encountered in our examination of recent Freudian theories. Kohlberg's theory itself seems to be an example

* Reprinted with permission from the author, Joan Thrower Timm, from "Moral Development in Literature, Drama and Poetry" (unpublished manuscript). Italics added.

of Stage 6 reasoning, the highest stage of moral development; those who reject his theory can be said to be at a lower stage of moral development, unable to recognize the insights available to a Stage 6 thinker. One is then taking a risk by criticizing the theory. According to the rules of scientific evidence, the proof of a theory must lie outside of the theory and not rest on a closed system of internal claims.

Like sociology, psychology is responding to criticisms of existing theories by developing new ideas, theories, and perspectives. Such issues as absolutism, value neutrality, and causality, as well as the increasing recognition that people are social beings in social contexts, have led to ideas similar to those of the new perspective that is emerging in sociology. One psychologist who in recent years has influenced both psychology and sociology is R. D. Laing. His analysis of schizophrenia (see especially *The Divided Self*, 1965) is done within the framework of existentialism, a perspective that will be described in Chapter 5. The goal of his research and clinical work has been to understand schizophrenia *from the point of view of the patient*. He recognizes both the strengths of "madness" (see also, in this regard, Perry's *The Far Side of Madness*, 1974) and the weaknesses of "sanity." About the latter he states:

> Thus I would wish to emphasize that our "normal" "adjusted" state is too often the abdication of ecstasy, the betrayal of our true potentialities, that many of us are only too successful in acquiring a false self to adapt to false realities (Laing, 1965: 12).

A similar kind of explanation of schizophrenia is presented from a phenomenological perspective by Meynell (1971). Increasingly potent in psychology is the idea that *normality and abnormality are problematic concepts*.

Similarities in recent sociological and psychological developments suggest the potential for new understanding between the fields. In the next section we will see some of the problems that have emerged when sociologists have drawn on psychological explanations. Recent trends in both fields hold promise for resolving some of these problems.

THE ROLE OF PSYCHOLOGY IN SOCIOLOGICAL EXPLANATIONS OF DEVIANCE

As sociologists moved to levels of increasing specificity in their attempts to explain deviance, they sometimes sought explanations in the field of psychology. Yet psychological theories of deviance have been repeatedly criticized for their failure to include the social world as a major factor in deviance. From Freud to Kohlberg runs a stream of absolutism, an assumption that the psychologist can distinguish between normal and abnormal, moral and immoral; psychological theory has largely neglected the role of society or the social world in creating and sustaining ideas of normal and abnormal, right and wrong, and so on. Although many psychologists claim the individual should be seen in a social context, in actual psychological theorizing that context is treated as a minor factor in no way fundamental to the *creation* of deviance.

The new perspective has returned to sociology for explanations of deviant behavior. Neither rejecting nor accepting psychological explanations, it has recognized that the goals of psychology are different from those of sociology. An understanding of deviance is sought in the structure and nature of the social world, and individuals are seen in terms of their activities in that world. The only psychological theorizing that is thought to be of direct use to sociologists is that which gives full recognition to the social world as a factor in human behavior. New perspectives in psychology may well provide such theories.

Explanations at Levels VII, VIII, and IX

In order for a science to be developed, the subject matter — whether it is history, biology, sociology, or some other — must be in some ways patterned and regular. The subject matter may be widely varied, but it must show some consistency, some regular appearance of at least some features. Science cannot study random behavior or totally arbitrary occurrences. Some thinkers have argued that history, for example, cannot be a social science because each historical event is unique. The United States has known only one "World War I" and there can never be another "World War I." Some historians have made history a science, however, by focusing on the patterns that recur through history. For example, although World War I is in some respects unique, in other respects it is quite like other wars. The recurrent aspects allow us to look at history scientifically.

Kluckhohn and Murray (1948: 35) have argued that all three elements of the following statement are true:

All human beings are:
   1. Like all other humans.
   2. Like some other humans.
   3. Like no other human.

For example, all human beings share the same physiological functions, all Catholics share certain beliefs, and no one is *exactly* like any other person. Only the first two statements lend themselves to scientific study.

The three levels of analysis to be described in this section are sometimes used to explain deviance and thus are worth considering. However, as we shall see, their focus is so specific that they cease to qualify as scientific.

LEVEL VII. CONCRETE INTERACTION PROCESSES

Explanations at this level focus on particular occurrences in interaction as causes or determinants of deviance. These explanations are exemplified by such common-sense statements as:

I never would have hit him if he hadn't said that to me.

All the guys were going to rob the candy store and I had to go along with them since they asked me to.

I didn't want to kill her but she wouldn't stop looking at me with that stupid smile on her face.

Lines similar to these are frequently found in television shows, newspaper accounts, and other media presentations. Often offered by deviants themselves, they suggest that something *specific to that particular situation* caused the behavior. If "he hadn't said that to me," if the guys hadn't "asked me to," and if she had stopped "looking at me with that stupid smile on her face," the deviant activities would not have occurred. In all these situations, the specific actions of others toward oneself are viewed as crucial.

The truth of such theories cannot be established by scientific evidence. We can never know whether or not the deviant acts would have taken place in the absence of the "instigating act" of the other person. The new perspective uses these kinds of common-sense explanations as *data*, as something to be studied, but not as valid or true explanations.

LEVEL VIII. UNIQUE PROPERTIES OF GIVEN SITUATIONS AND ACTIONS

Explanations at this level deal with factors more specific than those of Level VII, focusing on an individual responding to the external physical environment. Like Level I explanations, those on Level VIII emphasize the nonhuman factors that influence human behavior. Explanations at this level are exemplified by such common-sense statements as:

Then I saw the gun lying on the table and I picked it up and shot him.

Trouble always happens in that bar.

I didn't mean to hurt him, just scare him, but he fell and hit his head.

Many of those who propose banning the sale of handguns base their arguments on Level VIII theories, for they claim that the unavailability of guns will decrease the amount of murder, violence, and robbery. In one sense this argument is true, for limiting the availability of guns will of necessity limit their use. On the other hand, it ignores the possibility that substitutes (blunt instruments, poison, physical assaults, and knives) will be found. If you don't have a gun, you won't use it, but you may use something else. We are certainly not arguing for or against this kind of gun control; we merely say that Level VIII theories can make no predictions about its effectiveness.

In general, then, Level VIII theories state that changing the properties of a unique situation or action will change the way people respond to it. They cannot, however, predict whether these new responses will be deviant or nondeviant.

LEVEL IX. CONCRETE ACTIONS AND EVENTS

Explanations at this level are the most specific available. They are exemplified by such statements as:

> I couldn't have done otherwise.

> It was the only thing I could do.

> If you had been there, you would have done the same thing.

Ultimately this level argues that each deviant act is the result of inevitable forces and thus could not have been prevented. Such claims are more statements of fact than explanations. They also emphasize the finality of past actions, the fact that nothing can be done to change what has already happened. You can't unkill, unrob, or unrape someone. Although knowing this may have broad philosophical and moral implications, it does not add to our understanding of what happened or why. At worst, it sees human beings as powerless in the face of their world, driven by the actions and events around them.

Insights at Levels VII, VIII, and IX

Although we can question the scientific usefulness of explanations at these three levels, they do sensitize us to elements that can influence deviant behavior. One such element is the significance of whether or not resources are available to be deviant with. This idea is partly incorporated into the theory of differential association, which argues that the accessibility of criminal gangs and subcultures is a factor in whether or not one becomes a criminal. The availability of guns is a factor in whether or not one becomes an armed robber, and the environment plays a role in determining whether a person will engage in homosexual activities — the likelihood may be greater for those who live in communities where homosexuality is viewed as positive, sensible, pleasurable, and worthwhile and where partners are readily available.

Another factor which is often neglected in the explanation of deviance and which is brought to light by these levels of explanation is that deviance can be productive or fun. Thrasher argued that gang boys very commonly commit illegal acts such as vandalism because they find it exciting to do dangerous things. Sometimes deviant acts are exciting in themselves; sometimes the very fact that they are forbidden makes them appealing. For example, some people smoke marijuana because they enjoy it; they may ignore the fact that it is illegal or perhaps argue that it should be legalized. Others, however, smoke marijuana *because it is illegal or prohibited,* they might well lose interest if it became legal. This distinction, which has not generally been incorporated into explanations of deviance, is a significant one, which we will see in more detail in Part II.

We have now reached the end of our discussion of levels of explanation of deviance. We have seen the strengths and insights of earlier theories. We have also pointed out their flaws so that they will not distort our knowledge and so that we will be able to avoid these kinds of errors in future theorizing. Despite their inadequacies, these theories have drawn attention to a wide variety of factors that are clearly important to an understanding of deviance. Current theorizing, and in particular the new perspective discussed in Chapter 5, is firmly grounded in this earlier work. We will encounter more examples of all these theories in Part II, where we will see how they are used to explain specific types of deviance.

We turn now to examine the new perspective, with which we seek to preserve the strengths of earlier theories and at the same time overcome their weaknesses and errors. The new perspective is an attempt to construct a more inclusive and satisfactory explanation of deviance than the theories that preceded it.

5

The New Perspective in
the Sociology of Deviance

Since the early sixties in sociology and in the sociological study of deviance, theorists drawing on varied traditions have developed new ideas about the nature of the social world and the ways in which to study it. Different names have been given to these emerging theories: new or neo-symbolic interactionism, labeling theory, dramaturgical theory, phenomenology (phenomenological sociology), ethnomethodology, and existential sociology. Although each theory has yielded its own insights, they have also worked toward common understandings. So many ideas have been exchanged, in fact, that today the distinctions among theories are not always clear.

In this chapter we examine the theories that together make up the new perspective. As we do so, we will see some similar ideas emerging from different theories. We will then look more closely at the shared characteristics comprising the new perspective. (A detailed survey of the new perspective in sociology as a whole is given by Morris, 1977, whose book was specifically designed as an introduction.)

Although the new perspective differs in basic ways from earlier perspectives, it also draws on many strengths of the theories from which it emerged. Matza (1969), in his study of the process of becoming deviant, gives an excellent example of movement from earlier theories to the new perspective. His sensitivity to the insights of others and his ability to preserve those insights in his new formulations provide a model for cumulative theory. (We will return to Matza's ideas in Chapter 7 when we discuss the process of becoming a drug user.)

Before examining the theories that make up the new perspective, we will briefly review their common features as presented in Chapter 1 (see pp. 21–25). The new perspective posits meanings within our heterogeneous society as routinely ambiguous and subject to controversy. It focuses on what *diverse* members of society consider to be right and wrong, deviant and nondeviant, and what they think and feel about their activities. The new perspective is based on three assumptions:

1. Deviance is a construction of social actors.
2. Constructions of meanings can be problematic for members of society.
3. Sociologists' constructions of meanings are even more problematic than members' constructions.

We can now add that the new perspective is *interactionist,* based on the principle that *social meanings and actions are always, at least to some extent, constructed to fit the concrete situations facing individuals in relation to one another.* In this *situational construction of meanings,* social meanings and actions arise through individuals' interaction with other individuals and with the situations they face together. Although theories in the new perspective make different use of this principle, all accept its basic truth in some way.

Of the new theories described in this chapter, *new* or *neosymbolic interactionism* involves the least radical break with earlier traditions. It draws heavily on earlier symbolic interactionist works and the Chicago tradition. Its "newness" lies in its rejection of the evaluative dimension of earlier work, its attempts to come to terms with problems arising out of its earlier ties to social disorganization theory, and its commitment to the principle of the situational construction of meanings stated above. Since in other basic ways the "new" symbolic interactionism is much like the old in its commitment to field research, detailed consideration of people's activities from the point of view of the people themselves, and social interaction, we will not further elaborate on the theory.

It is possible to consider both labeling theory and dramaturgical theory as types of new symbolic interactionism, and in fact both remain closely tied to interactionist theories. We have chosen to examine these two theories in their own right in order to emphasize their contributions to the new perspective. In fact both labeling theory and dramaturgical theory are attempts to extend symbolic interactionism by directing attention to the multiple perspectives available in social interaction and the consequences of such multiplicity.

Phenomenology, ethnomethodology, and existential sociology grow out of very different forms of research and thought. They involve a more radical break both with other forms of sociological theory in general and with symbolic interactionism in particular. Some followers of these three theories argue that they will ultimately replace symbolic interactionism; others think peaceful coexistence is possible.

In introducing all these new theories we will focus on the ways in which they differ from one another and indicate the ways in which they overlap. Later in this chapter we will return to the issue of their similarities.

Labeling Theory

Of the theories examined in this chapter, labeling theory is the most widely known and used by current sociologists. The fundamental idea of the labeling theory of deviance is that *labeling of individuals as deviant is crucial in their becoming and continuing to be deviant.* This idea established the importance of labeling theory and contributed to the revision of older symbolic interactionism. In its original formulation the theory emphasized the labeling carried out by official agencies of social control such as police, lawyers, and judges. Later elaborations of the theory extended it to labeling by peers, group members themselves, and a wide variety of others who were involved.

Although labeling theory has become important in sociology only in the past twenty years, its origins are in much earlier work. In the late 1930s Tannenbaum drew upon legal sources and studies of delinquency by Thrasher and other Chicago sociologists to develop the first general statement of a labeling theory of deviance. Tannenbaum began by contrasting the traditional common-sense view of crime as absolute evil or absolute good with the fact of *legal relativism:* what is defined as illegal in one society is defined as legal in another. Tannenbaum then tried to show, using data from Thrasher and others, that boys who eventually become socially defined or labeled as juvenile delinquents do not start out as evil. On the contrary, they start out like anyone else, but they soon encounter social situations of intense conflict in the ethnically heterogeneous society in which they live. He recognized the way in which such situations could lead to the development of delinquent subcultures, but he went further in his analysis than the subcultural theorists did, investigating the processes by which the larger society, especially dominant political groups, controlled the legislation and administration of criminal laws. He was interested especially with the ways in which dominant political groups select certain forms of behavior as evil or deviant and thus illegal and then proceed to identify the deviants.

Tannenbaum also investigated how individuals come to define themselves as deviant and act in deviant ways, prompting officials to further define them in that way, imprison them, and so on. Tannenbaum argued (in a way that set forth the basic idea of labeling theory) that the crucial step in this whole process of definition is the official "tagging" or labeling of the individual as a delinquent and the stigmatizing effect of imprisonment. He concluded: "The making of the criminal, therefore, is a process of tagging, defining, identifying, segregating, describing, emphasizing, making conscious and self-conscious; it becomes a way of stimulating, suggesting, emphasizing, and evoking the very traits that are complained of" (1938: 19–20).

Tannenbaum's work had little effect on the development of sociological theories of deviance during his own time. Perhaps it diverged too far from the views and common-sense ideas of his day, which were characterized by a degree of absolutism and a "melting-pot" conception of a homogeneous society. In any case, it was the work of Howard Becker that introduced labeling theory into the sociology of deviance as a major idea. (For the major statement of Becker's theory, see his *Outsiders*, 1963, which includes articles published elsewhere as early as 1951.)

Becker acknowledges Tannenbaum's work, as well as that of Lemert (1951) and Kitsuse (1962) (in Becker, 1963: 9). He also draws on Lindesmith's symbolic interactionist theory of heroin use. Becker developed his ideas about labeling theory in the course of a study on marijuana use. It will help us in understanding the theory to look at his study and findings.

AN EXAMPLE OF LABELING THEORY: BECKER'S STUDY OF MARIJUANA USE

Becker found that the *social definition* of marijuana followed a path very similar to that of the opiates. In each case the social definition of the drug — the way people perceived it in terms of what it was, how it worked and how it was to be dealt with — changed dramatically over time. We can see the power of social definitions when we recognize that presumably the actual physical characteristics of the drugs have remained constant.

Marijuana use was legal in the United States until the passage of the federal Marijuana Stamp Tax Act of 1937, when it became subject to the same form of federal regulation as the opiates. Similarly, opiates were legal until the passage of the Harrison Stamp Tax Act in 1914. In both cases, people who had previously been quite legitimate citizens were socially redefined as criminal if they continued doing what they had been doing for years. Both cases, then, were obvious instances of *the social creation of deviance through the creation of new rules*. This social creation of deviance was an outcome of conflicts between groups in United States society, with some supporting the drugs and their users and others opposing them.

The fact that marijuana is far weaker in its physiological effects than the opiates makes the question of why it was outlawed all the more interesting. Street heroin users sometimes died from overdoses, and these deaths were used by officials and the media as examples of the terrible dangers of heroin, but marijuana could not kill people in this way and there was no popular conception, as there was with heroin, that using it once would create lifetime addiction. How then did marijuana become the object of political stigmatization and popular fear? Why did politicians create a new law defining marijuana use as a crime and its users as criminals? These were the basic questions Becker tried to answer.

He began by arguing that the creation of any new social rule was a creative act by certain members of society. To get some form of behavior stigmatized as deviant or as criminal requires an *entrepreneur*, someone who actively undertakes, organizes, manages, and carries out a project. Although we generally speak of business entrepreneurs, Becker spoke of *moral entrepreneurs*, those who create new social categories, complete with rules and procedures, and those who enforce those rules. The question that interested Becker was: who were the moral entrepreneurs who got marijuana criminalized?

He found that before the new federal felony law was passed, a widespread mass-media campaign had depicted marijuana as a grave danger to society, inspiring people to commit violent acts almost indiscriminately. The film *Reefer Madness* (1937) is a product of this period. The same news stories appeared almost simultaneously all over the country, all drawing on the same few cases of supposed marijuana-crazed attacks:

> One clear indication of Bureau [of Narcotics] influence in the preparation of journalistic articles can be found in the recurrence of certain atrocity stories first reported by the Bureau. For instance, in an article published in the *American Magazine*, the Commissioner of Narcotics himself related the following incident:
>> An entire family was murdered by a youthful [marihuana] addict in Florida. When officers arrived at the home they found the youth staggering about in a human slaughterhouse. With an ax he had killed his father, mother, two brothers, and a sister. He seemed to be in a daze. . . . He had no recollection of having committed the multiple crime. The officers knew him ordinarily as a sane, rather quiet young man; now he was pitifully crazed. They sought the reason. The boy said he had been in the habit of smoking something which youthful friends called "muggles," a childish name for marihuana.
> Five of the seventeen articles printed during the period repeated this story, and thus showed the influence of the Bureau (Becker, 1963: 141–142).

Becker traced the stories back to the Federal Bureau of Narcotics and argued that the Bureau had launched this campaign in order to get new laws that would increase its own social power. He saw the bureaucrats of the F.B.N. as moral entrepreneurs operating behind the scenes to create new rules that would be to their own advantage. Once this bureaucracy had been created, it looked for areas in which it could become involved, and marijuana appeared a likely candidate. This recognition of the factors involved in *the creation of rules* and *the choice of those to whom the rules are applied* distinguishes labeling theory from the earlier interactionist perspective.

Against this background Becker proposed a very general theory of the social labeling of deviance. Earlier theorists had never argued that deviance exists *only* when it is concretely and publicly labeled as deviant, but Becker argued just that. He says of deviance:

> . . . it is created by society. I do not mean this in the way it is ordinarily understood, in which the causes of deviance are located in the social situation of the deviant or in "social factors" which prompt his action. I mean, rather, that *social groups create deviance by making the rules whose infraction constitutes deviance* and by applying those rules to particular people and labeling them as outsiders. From this point of view, deviance is *not* a quality of the act the person commits, but rather a consequence of the application by others of rules and sanctions to an "offender." The deviant is one to whom that label has successfully been applied; deviant behavior is behavior that people so label . . . (1963: 8–9).
>
> Whether an act is deviant, then, depends on how other people react to it. You can commit clan incest and suffer from no more than gossip as long as no one makes a public accusation; but you will be driven to your death if the accusation is made. The point is that the response of other people has to be regarded as problematic. Just because one has committed an infraction of a rule does not mean that others will respond as though this had happened. (Conversely, just because one has not violated a rule does not mean that he may not be treated, in some circumstances, as though he had) . . . (Becker, 1963: 11–12).
>
> If we take as the object of our attention behavior which comes to be labeled as deviant, we must recognize that we cannot know whether a given act will be categorized as deviant until the response of others has occurred. *Deviance is not a quality that lies in behavior itself, but in the interaction between the person who commits an act and those who respond to it* (1963: 14).*

What deviants share, then, according to Becker, is the experience of being labeled and responded to as deviant. In Chapter 4, pp. 100–101, we spoke of Goffman's objection to the concept of deviance. Becker's views as presented here can be read as a rejoinder to Goffman.

Donald Dickson (1968) went back to look more carefully at the situation of the Federal Bureau of Narcotics at the time of the "moral crusade" that led to the passage of the Marijuana Stamp Tax Act that the Bureau was to enforce. He argued that major budgetary problems were an important motivation underlying the new legislation.

Other theorists have used Becker's labeling theory to study and explain many forms and aspects of deviance. They have, for example, tried to show that official symbolic categorizations of individuals as deviants involve two crucial processes. First, officials of the state, especially legislators, executives, and judges, create and interpret the legal categories of deviance, thus *making the rules.* Second, official agents of control, especially the police, prosecutors, and others with police powers, give their own discretionary interpretations to the rules, using those rules to separate out some and not other individuals and groups as deviant. Thus they *apply the rules.* Both of these processes of labeling have important implications for those involved (see Cicourel, 1968).

Elliott Currie (1968) used labeling theory to explain the social definition of witchcraft. Whereas Becker emphasized moral entrepreneurial work in itself without considering in detail the *motives* of the entrepreneurs and organizations doing the labeling, Currie and others have argued that such motives are very significant and that in fact to a considerable degree "moral talk" serves as a front for other motives. Currie, for example, suggests that officials who prosecuted witches gained financially from their activities; when financial gain could not be realized, prosecutions decreased.

Kai Erikson (1966) also made use of labeling theory, though within a functionalist perspective, to explain three "waves of deviance" that occurred in seventeenth-century Massachusetts: a religious heresy that challenged accepted Puritan beliefs, the Quaker movement, and witchcraft. (See the brief discussion of Erikson's ideas in Chapter 2, p. 50.) Erikson's particular concern was with *the social functions of labeling.* Although Becker and other labeling theorists focused on *how* labeling takes place, Erikson considered *what labeling did* for the social groups in which it took place. Drawing on the theories of Durkheim, Erikson concluded that labeling of deviants serves the function of redefining the boundaries of a society. Labeling and then responding negatively to deviants unites the nondeviant community and makes community values clear by contrasting them with deviance. Although Erikson made use of labeling theory, its theorists have not adopted his ideas about the social functions of labeling, since in many ways there is a basic incompatibility between labeling theory and functionalism.

Other research in labeling theory has focused on a vast array of topics. Extensive research led to its refinement and reformulation, a topic to which we now turn.

CRITICISMS AND REFORMULATIONS OF LABELING THEORY

The initial formulations of labeling theory by Tannenbaum, Becker, and others proved to be both oversimplified and overgeneralized. As the theory's limits became clear over the years, Becker (1973) revised it accordingly.

The chief criticism of labeling theory has been directed to its claim that deviance exists *only* when society, especially through its officials, labels individuals or their actions as deviant. Critics have contended that there are many forms of *secret deviance* — acts that we want to call deviant even though the individuals themselves are not publicly labeled as such. There seems to be something not quite right in saying that an uncaught murderer is nondeviant. Part of this criticism rests on a misunderstanding of Becker. He claimed, not that what he calls *secret deviants* do not exist, but instead that (1) *labeled deviants* have something in common, and (2) *secret deviants* are difficult to study and little is known about them. Later researchers have studied secret deviants and have thereby expanded both labeling theory and our general understanding of deviance.

Studies of secret or unlabeled deviants have included such topics as homosexuality, suicide, and certain forms of drug addiction when individuals participating in those activities successfully conceal their behavior and thus avoid public labeling. Carol Warren (1974), Edward Dalph (1979), and others have argued, for example, that many homosexuals are highly secretive about their sexual preferences in all their relations with the straight world. To conceal this information about themselves, they develop various strategies, including the construction of "misinformation," such as having heterosexual dates to make "straights" think they are "straight."

Suicides provide an extreme example of secret deviance. Some who take their own lives in "accidental" ways may conceal the suicide even from themselves. Many of those who kill themselves do leave notes defining their actions as suicide. "Doris, I didn't want to commit suicide, and I know how horrible people will think it is, but you leave me no choice" is a common theme in what are called "revenge suicides." Those being blamed often refuse to believe that the act is a suicide and thus avoid labeling it as such. Rather commonly, they try to hide the note and other evidence of the suicidal intent, so that officials will apply other, nondeviant labels, such as "death by accidental ingestion of a lethal overdose of barbiturates."

The criticism that labeling theory denies the existence of secret deviants, although unwarranted, has spurred studies of the application of the theory to secret deviants. Such studies have revealed the power of public labels *even when those labels are not publicly applied*. Secret deviants engage in a great deal of work to avoid labeling, and thus their behavior can be seen to be strongly influenced by the possibility of labeling.

Many recent studies have attempted to show that the involvement of officials in the creation of social rules or labels and in the uses of those labels is far more complex than earlier theorists thought. Robert Emerson (1969) and others have argued, for example, that in many states in recent years legislators and officials have "conspired," often against majority political opinion, to systematically *delabel* individuals known to be law violators. Delabeling is often done precisely because of the effect labeling would have on the future of the law violators. It is done on a massive scale in cases of juvenile delinquency in a number of states, including California, through what are known as "early diversion" procedures. The juvenile offender is "diverted" or routed around the judicial labeling process into a program that is intended to prevent further delinquency. A similar process is followed in the treatment of the mentally ill when they are routed into mental health out-patient programs rather than into prison or mental institutions. These procedures themselves may be viewed as forms of labeling, but they are intended to apply labels of lesser negative consequence for those labeled.

Recognition by officials of the significance of labeling and of the ways in which it can be manipulated is exemplified in the treatment of the "sex offenders" studied by William Henry (personal communication). The population he studied was all the male "sex offenders" in the institutions of one state, those committed for some violent sexual activity such as rape or molestation. One of Henry's first goals was to determine how differently labeled sex offenders moved through the complex set of penal institutions, and so he started following their official categorizations from the point of judicial sentencing. Much to his dismay, he discovered that approximately half of those sentenced to prison as "sex offenders" quickly disappeared from the official books when they entered the institutions. His search for these lost "sex offenders" led him to discover that they had not been actually lost, nor had they escaped. They had simply been "relabeled downward." After studying the whole system, Henry found that the explanation was simple enough. The official staff of the institutions, many of whom were psychologists and sociologists, believed that the labeling of these men as "sex offenders" would have a negative effect on the men and their self-images, especially because "sex offenders" are treated very badly, often violently, by other prisoners. The officials relabeled the men to avoid trouble and to facilitate treatment.

Research into labeling theory has repeatedly demonstrated the complexity of the processes involved. One distinction that helps to clarify them somewhat is between *primary* and *secondary characteristics* of deviance (see Ray, 1961). Primary characteristics include all those which depend on the nature of the act itself. If we take drug use as our example, primary characteristics include the need to obtain drugs by illegal means, specific effects of the drug upon the body, and the acquiring of the tools or apparatus necessary to take the drug. Secondary characteristics include all that depend on the social context in which the deviance takes place and may vary from setting to setting. Stealing money to obtain drugs is thus a secondary characteristic; presumably an independently wealthy drug user would not need to steal. The high-strung nervousness often attributed to the drug itself, and thus seen as a primary characteristic, may in fact be a secondary characteristic, related to the difficulty and dangers of obtaining drugs. Physicians with a drug habit but with ready access to drugs seldom display this characteristic (see, for example, Charles Winick, "Physician Narcotic Addicts" in Becker, 1964).

Similarly, sociologists sometimes distinguish between *primary deviance*, the deviant act desired by the deviant, and *secondary deviance*, those deviant acts such as stealing money which result from the social context of the primary deviance. One implication is that making primary deviance more acceptable and less deviant — for example, selling heroin legally at a "reasonable" price — might well reduce secondary deviance.

Labeling theory continues to be refined. It is now considered to be extremely complex and *inadequate in itself* to explain deviance. Its complexity has already been demonstrated here. Its inadequacy as a complete theory was first pointed out by critics who denied that labeling is the *only* process involved in deviance. Current labeling theorists draw heavily on other theories, particularly symbolic interactionism, to complete their explanations of deviance. Becker's more recent views are presented in the second edition of *Outsiders* (1973), where he claims that *social interaction* is the basic process underlying deviance and that one, but not the only, type of social interaction is *labeling*. When labeling takes place, whether done by friends, relatives, officials, or the public, clearly it is important to an understanding of deviance. Labeling theory, furthermore, is crucial to an understanding of illegal behavior and of the central role of officials in determining whether certain acts are deviant and who will be identified as having committed those acts. Nonetheless, there is more to deviance than labeling.

In its reformulated version labeling theory becomes a special theory or special part of either symbolic interactionism or of other theories within the new perspective. Although labeling theory cannot explain all deviance, it does provide us with a framework for understanding some fundamental processes involved in some deviance. Work on the theory continues, and we may expect continued refinements.

Dramaturgical Theory

The word *dramaturgy* refers to the art or technique of composing and presenting stage performances. Dramaturgical theory in sociology views social behavior as a theatrical performance and uses theatrical terms and ideas to explain it. As early as 1936 Ralph Linton used the term *role* to refer to expected behavior associated with a particular social position but a full-fledged dramaturgical theory begins with Erving Goffman's book *The Presentation of Self in Everyday Life* (1959). The theory takes literally Shakespeare's statement in *As You Like It:*

All the world's a stage,
And all the men and women merely players:
They have their exits and their entrances:
And one man in his time plays many parts. . . .

The theory analyzes social behavior as if it were a stage performance, complete with roles, props, scenes, frontstage, backstage, and so on. Although few theorists besides Goffman and, later, Lyman and Scott (1975) have employed it as a whole, elements of dramaturgical theory and its general perspective have had much influence on sociology, the study of deviance, and the new perspective. Labeling theory and dramaturgical theory are particularly compatible.

Dramaturgical theory has not been applied to the sociology of deviance in any extensive way, though elements of it appear in labeling theory and in existential sociology. Goffman has applied the theory to mental patients (*Asylums,* 1961); his concern, however, was not with deviance itself but with the nature of institutions. His work on stigmas, as we mentioned in Chapter 4, has direct bearing on the study of deviance though he rejects the idea itself. We will draw on some of Goffman's materials to show how dramaturgical theory might be applied to the sociology of deviance. Peter Manning (1977) has developed an entire dramaturgical theory of police work from his extensive studies of United States and British police. Since few others in the sociology of deviance have employed this theory as a whole, we will suggest here some ways in which it might be used and will show how it contributes to a new perspective on deviance.

An important element in Goffman's dramaturgical approach is the idea of the *presentation of self.* Drawing on Mead and Cooley, Goffman argues that individuals present themselves to others in ways designed to affect the impression that others receive of them; he calls this process *impression management.* (See "The Arts of Impression Management" in *The Presentation of Self in Everyday Life,* 1959.) People dramatize internal states by means of gestures, words, and actions, and in general they construct strategic presentations of appearances in social settings. We are all aware of the ways in which people try to manage the information others can gain about them. For example, if you expect visitors to your home, what you hide and what you leave exposed indicate the impression you are eager or willing to convey to visitors.

Dramaturgical theory argues that people manage information about themselves and the impressions they make for two reasons. First, since one draws one's sense of self in important ways from the ways others see that self, influencing others' views acts back on one's own sense of self. If you, for example, want to view yourself as intelligent, it is useful to be able to present yourself in such a way that others will view you as intelligent, thus confirming your own initial idea. It is far more difficult to view yourself as intelligent in the face of others who think you a fool. Second, if one wants others to act in specific ways, managing the impressions one gives may encourage that behavior in others. Thus, if you want help from others, giving the impression of your own helplessness may contribute to the provision of that aid.

The idea of impression management is a large contribution to sociological understanding because it provides an alternative to *sociological determinism*, the idea that all human behavior is caused or determined by social forces that lie outside the individual. Impression management is a concept that allows sociologists to recognize the ways individuals can manipulate the social environment by using social rules and expectations. If you know all the rules of etiquette, then you are able to give the impression of being either very polite or very impolite, depending on how you use those rules.

Two aspects of impression management, as the idea was developed by Goffman, are important to recognize. First, others may view you as *giving an impression* even when you don't intend to. Thus, men in Italy may walk arm in arm without notice, but if Italian men continue this practice in the United States, they may give the impression of being homosexual. Behavior will be interpreted and impressions gathered by others *regardless of the intent of the actors themselves.*

A second aspect of impression management, and one that has caused a great deal of confusion, is the idea of *manipulation* that seems to characterize dramaturgical theory. Critics such as Messinger et al.(1962) have claimed that, while people do sometimes intentionally manipulate their own behavior in order to manipulate others, much more commonly they act out of other motives. The criticism is that Goffman presents people as far more calculating and, in a sense, evil than they really are. In fact such criticisms are based on a misunderstanding of Goffman, who enphasizes that social behavior can be studied *as if* it were manipulative but nowhere claims that it really is like that. Quite to the contrary, he states that:

> At one extreme, one finds that the performer can be fully taken in by his own act; he can be sincerely convinced that the impression of reality which he stages is the real reality. . . .
>
> At the other extreme, we find that the performer may not be taken in at all by his own routine (1959: 17).

To obtain the insights provided by the dramaturgical approach, we must keep in mind the "as if" quality of the analysis and the fact that it does not claim that individuals need to be consciously aware of what they are doing. In this way we can see that both con artists setting up an elaborate confidence game and those who strive to be open and honest ("up front with everyone," "letting it all hang out") are involved in impression management. (Lyman and Scott, 1975, do, however, view life as drama in a far more literal sense.)

Dramaturgical presentations appear to be at least one fundamental goal in certain forms of deviance. Presenting oneself as deviant to others may be of direct value to the deviant. Consider the well-known behavior of *flaunting* one's wickedness. (See Hunter Thompson's descriptive accounts of *Hell's Angels,* 1966.) Certainly there are people who build important parts of their lives around flaunting their deviance for the pleasure of producing shock or outrage in others. For example, a study of the nude beach (Douglas and Rasmussen, with Flanagan, 1977) disclosed a young woman who took delight and seemed to derive feelings of pride from shocking others with her sexual casualness. When she later became a masseuse, she derived pleasure by telling strangers about her work and then watching their looks of shock and temporary befuddlement. This shock value was a fringe benefit of her job and a primary goal in certain everyday interactions in which she took part.

There are a variety of reasons for wanting to give the impression that one is deviant in some way. It may be a display of independence and a claim that one is not dominated by social rules. In "adolescent rebellion," for example, although the deviant activities — such as drug use, violations of curfews, and drinking — may be valued in themselves, part of their appeal may lie in their being deviant. Juvenile male gangs, as we might expect, often use forms of deviance to present themselves to each other and to outside audiences as "MEN." Drug-using gangs may rank members in prestige according to the legal danger of the drug behavior they engage in. The harder the drug, and thus the greater the danger of police action, the higher the user's social status. It is precisely because of the police and their attempts to enforce drug rules that this pattern of deviance can exist.

In dramaturgical terms, deviance may also be seen as a way of protecting the self from external assaults. Goffman, in *Asylums* (1961), was struck by the ways in which the staff of the mental hospital he studied systematically stripped patients of their "symbolic armor," the meaningful forms of clothes and behavior that maintained their self-images and self-respect before they were committed. The patients responded to this symbolic assault by developing a shared underlife, a deviant subculture of shared meanings and behavior that deviated from and subverted the official (staff) culture. They presented themselves to the staff as submissive and nondeviant but communicated to each other in secretive ways that in fact deviated from the official world's rules.

Dramaturgy seems particularly useful in understanding attempts to control deviance, especially in our media-oriented society. The self-presentation of the one charged with enforcing rules is clearly a main element in the control of deviance. Adults know common-sensically the importance of a stern manner in dealing with recalcitrant children. For centuries law enforcers have used specialized symbolic devices to inspire fear, awe, veneration, and so on in potential law-breakers. There was quite a dispute about precisely this practice in the early history of the United States. The British tradition of judicial practices that the United States inherited involved extensive use of symbols of sternness and aloofness, which commonly communicated the "majesty of the law" and the "superiority of the judges" to the accused. Such symbols as black robes, wigs, and gavels certainly inspired awe, fear, and submission in many a defendant. The more traditional American party, the Federalists, generally supported the continued use of these symbols in court proceedings. John Adams argued quite explicitly that they would inspire awe, submission, and a sense of dignity. The more democratic, antiauthority forces led by Jefferson generally opposed these symbols and insisted that judges should dress like ordinary people and that the court rooms should simply be like other rooms, thus egalitarian. For the most part, the Adams forces won that argument, and the ancient symbols are still widely used in legal proceedings.

The idea of public punishment as a dramatization supplements Durkheim's idea (Chapter 2, pp. 44–45) that such punishment is a way for law-abiding group members to reaffirm their commitment to group values. Dramaturgical theory allows us to see the processes involved in this reaffirmation, both for law-abiders and for law-breakers. The growing importance of the mass media has greatly expanded the use of dramatization by would-be enforcers.

An excellent example of this kind of dramatization is provided by a popular police practice, the "police sweep" or the "clean-up-campaign." This activity pits "moral crusaders" (Becker's term) against some "force of evil," such as prostitution, drug dealing, or auto theft rings. A variety of motives may underlie the behavior of these "moral crusaders." A politically ambitious police chief may want to gain publicity and present himself as a crusader against "evil"; the concern of ordinary citizens may generate a grass-roots crusade; or a newspaper might decide that a "cause" would increase circulation. Whatever the motivation, the next step in the process is extensive media coverage. Day after day local newspapers, television, and radio present stories about the "urban blight of streetwalkers" or the "crazed drug dealers seducing our children" or the "nationwide ring of car thieves." The police saturate the streets with plainclothes officers, sometimes using decoys who try to gain access to the illegal goods or services. The conclusion usually consists of mass arrests, often in a variety of places on the same night. Police normally contact the media days in advance so that they can be ready with cameras and presses. When the police make their sweeps, the cameras are rolling and get beautiful shots of the forces of evil "being hauled off to prison." Sometimes hundreds of people are charged with law violations, though often most of the charges are later reduced or dropped.

Dramatizations of this sort have many interesting effects. Seldom do these sweeps and media campaigns have lasting effects on deviant activity. In the short run the result may be increased caution on the part of deviants or a temporary change in the area of operation. In time, however, deviants seem to return to their former activities and base of operation. Such dramatizations do, however, present the police as active, vigilant, and thoroughgoing in their pursuit of crime.

It is easy to say that such dramatizations are simply ways for police to cover up the bad job they are doing, but the situation is more complex than that. First, the dramatizations do have the immediate effect of curtailing criminal activities. Second, they allow the police to respond to the pressure of moral crusaders in a way that does not generate overwhelming pressure from those who want the illegal goods and services, since they will in time return to the marketplace. Third, the dramatization assists police in dealing with public expectations that they cannot meet. Peter Manning (1975) and others have clearly documented that in fact the police cannot do much to solve most forms of crime. If they do not apprehend criminals at the time of the crime, the probability that they will ever do so is extremely small. At the same time, the police are subject to intense public pressure. What are they to do? Dramatizations seem to reduce public pressure and allow police to proceed with their routine of a mixture of arrests and unsolved crimes. (We will return to the topic of police work in Chapter 11.)

We do not know in detail the effect of such dramatizations on deviance. We may speculate that it decreases deviance to some extent, but empirical research is necessary before we can make any assertion. We do know that in England around the end of the eighteenth and beginning of the nineteenth century, when pickpockets were publicly hanged, pickpockets worked the crowds attending the hanging. But did more pickpockets work the crowd when a murderer was being hanged? We do not know. Dramatizations do not eliminate deviance; beyond that we can say no more. Such dramatizations, however, do have their effects on public opinion, police work, and many other elements related to deviance.

Dramaturgical theory may help us understand deviance and its control as personal "productions" with implications for both self and others. In itself an insufficient explanation, it holds promise of contributing to a full explanation. It makes us aware of some ways in which individuals "act" in and on the social world, thereby serving as a corrective to earlier theories of individuals as merely "acted upon."

Phenomenology and Ethnomethodology

Philosophy can be defined as a discipline that analyzes the grounds for fundamental beliefs and the concepts that express them. Sociology, in its early attempts to establish itself as a distinct science, divorced itself from philosophy, but recent sociologists have recognized the importance of a philosophical grounding for sociology. The new perspective is concerned with articulating the philosophical bases of its sociological theories. In their search for an appropriate philosophical system to provide a foundation for sociology, some sociologists have turned to phenomenology and others to existentialism — both of which have contributed to the development of the new perspective — as well as to other forms of philosophy that will not concern us here, such as ordinary language philosophy and Marxist philosophy.

Phenomenology is a school of philosophy developed by Edmund Husserl.* Out of phenomenology grew existentialism, which we shall look at later in this chapter.

Sociology grounded in phenomenology is termed *phenomenological sociology*. It draws heavily on the work of Husserl and one of his students, Alfred Schutz (see especially 1967B). Schutz was particularly concerned with applying phenomenology to the study of the social world, and his work is widely used by sociologists.

Phenomenological sociology is reputed to be difficult to understand, in part because of the convoluted language used, and is often misunderstood, yet the basic ideas are quite straightforward. Earlier sociologists, as well as scientists in general, assumed that the social world has meaning *independent of the meanings given to it by those acting in that social world*. Thus, for example, early sociologists "knew" what was deviant even when those they called deviant disagreed with them. Phenome-

---

* *Ideas,* 1913, is one of Husserl's major works; a gentler introduction to the complex works of this thinker is *The Idea of Phenomenology,* 1907. See also Kohak, *Idea and Experience,* 1978, for a clear and careful exposition of Husserl's thought.

nological sociology, on the other hand, says that we can understand the social world only through the meanings it has for the actors in it. *The social world does not have intrinsic meaning; it makes sense only in terms of individuals' experience of it.* We can understand individuals' behavior only when we understand the ways in which they see the world. Furthermore, we are in no position to claim that one way of looking at the world is in any absolute sense better than another way. *Phenomenological sociology is an attempt to understand the social world and social actions as they are experienced by social actors in concrete situations.*

An important part of the work of phenomenological sociology is the detailed *description* of the social world from the perspective of those being studied. Theorizing is based on such descriptions and searches for their general characteristics. In this process researchers adopt a perspective very different from the common-sense perspective that we use in everyday life and that Schutz calls the *natural attitude*. In the *phenomenological attitude* our concern is with learning the actors' views of their world *without ourselves making a judgment about that world*. Letkemann, for example, provides the following description by a bank robber who with his associates has just entered the bank and instructed the bank personnel to lie down on the floor:

> So they are froze there — their reaction is one of very extreme fear and they drop on the floor and sometime we select the strongest person — the manager especially or another teller which is very big — a six footer, or something like that, you know. And we won't say a word, we just walk up to him and smash him right across the face, you know, and we get him down. And once he's down the people, the girls especially, they look at him and they say, "My God — big Mike, he's been smashed down like that — I'd better lay down too, and stay quiet" (1973: 110).

Phenomenological sociologists seek this kind of understanding from the participants' point of view and do not make judgments about it. Whether or not it is "right" to "smash him right across the face" is an issue that arises, if at all, only in the participants' terms. Though they may find the behavior objectionable from their personal standpoint, as phenomenological sociologists, they have nothing to say on the matter. In this way they scrupulously adopt the principle of value neutrality (see Chapter 1, pp. 15–18).

Research in this tradition focuses on two questions:

1. How do individuals make sense out of their world?
2. What is the relation between the meanings they construct and the situations they face?

Description always precedes analysis and theory, since description is problematic and requires a great deal of careful research.

Research in phenomenological sociology is still relatively new and developing. Its scope is illustrated by the works of Schutz and, in terms of its current status, in Psathas's *Phenomenological Sociology* (1973). Its use in the sociology of deviance is limited but growing. Since there are few studies upon which we can draw to provide examples, we will describe in general terms the way in which phenomenological sociologists might approach the study of deviance.

That which is characteristic of any sociological theory is the kind of questions it asks. Different theories ask different kinds of questions. A phenomenological sociological study of suicide would ask: What does suicide mean to the persons doing it? What do they think about their world? Why does suicide seem a reasonable action in terms of that world? What do they think the outcomes of their suicide will be? Do they in fact see what they are doing as suicide? These questions could be asked of both suicides discussed in Chapter 1 — Dick Kenyon's and Taki Zenzaburo's. A wide variety of information would be collected to answer these questions — documents, records of interviews with friends, relatives, and acquaintances, and any other materials that appeared relevant. Having developed a body of descriptive materials about a number of suicides, the researcher would analyze them in terms of common features and unique features, working toward some general statements about the nature of suicide. Unlike psychology, which would be concerned with individuals and their choices of suicide, phenomenological sociology is concerned with *suicide as a social phenomenon.* Researchers would not be concerned with whether or not it was "right" to commit suicide but would concentrate on *what it was like.*

Some studies of the sociology of deviance have grown out of phenomenological sociology, most notably the work of Aaron Cicourel (1968). He examined offical statistics and the way in which they are used to construct a world, with important implications for those who become a part of that world. Warren and Johnson (1972) and Warren and Ponse (1977) have used a phenomenological perspective to describe "the gay world," asking such questions as: "What does 'gay' mean to those in the gay world? How do they arrive at and use those meanings?"

ETHNOMETHODOLOGY

Many of the studies of deviance that draw on phenomenological sociology are ethnomethodological studies. *Ethnomethodology* is derived from the basic ideas of phenomenology. Most ethnomethodologists also see themselves as phenomenologists. Ethnomethodology is a part of phenomenology in much the same way labeling theory is a part of symbolic interactionism. The term was developed by Harold Garfinkel (1967; see also Hill and Crittenden, 1968) and refers literally to folk (ethno-) methods as distinct from scientific methods. Garfinkel claims that in our everyday, common-sense life we have methods for carrying out our daily social affairs and that these methods are subject to study. There is some confusion in the literature, since ethnomethodology refers sometimes to everyday methods themselves and at other times to the study of those methods. We will use the term in the second sense and define *ethnomethodology* as *the sociological study of people's everyday methods for acting in the social world.*

Of particular interests to ethnomethodologists are people's *accounts*, the ways in which they make sense of or account for their behavior. (See Scott and Lyman, "Accounts," 1968.) An example of the study of accounts is provided by Wieder (in Turner, 1974, see also Wieder, 1974) in his study of a halfway house for narcotics-addict felons on parole. He identified a code of behavior among the residents, which they referred to as "the code" and used to account for their behavior. For example, one element of the code was "Above all else, do not snitch" (p. 145) — that is, do not squeal on another individual. Wieder found that

> When talking with residents, staff and I often had a relatively friendly line of conversation terminated by a resident's saying, "You know I won't snitch" (p. 153).

This statement served to inform Wieder and the staff that the resident would not further discuss the topic and that this decision could be *accounted for by the code.* As is typical of ethnomethodologists Wieder, however, was not satisfied with simply seeing the statement "You know I won't snitch" as the use of the code as an account. In his analysis (p. 153) he shows the statement's multiple meanings and lists the following elements that it includes:*

1. It describes what has just happened: You asked me to snitch.
2. It says that the resident will not answer the question or pursue the conversation.
3. It gives the reason for the resident's action.
4. It brings to attention the relationships that made up the conversation — staff and residents — by implying "For *you* to ask *me* that would be asking me to snitch."
5. It reminds staff that they and residents are different.

All these meanings are included in the simple statement, "You know I won't snitch." Such a statement thus can serve as a rather full account of behavior once its multiple meanings are known.

Now that we have seen what an account is and how it operates, we

---

* Since ethnomethodological language is often difficult for those who are not familiar with it, we have paraphrased these five elements.

can redefine ethnomethodology, in terms an ethnomethodologist might use, as *the study of the ways in which people present themselves to each other as rationally accountable.*

Ethnomethodologists are particularly concerned with rules and their use in everyday life. Donald Zimmerman (1969A, 1969B), for example, studied the uses of organizational rules in a welfare agency in California. What he found of that organization seems to be true of organizations in general: activities occur that an outsider would regard as violations of organizational rules or as deviance but that, within the organization, are not viewed or treated as violations. Insiders seem to assess rules in terms of the practical activities they are designed to guide; when rules interfere with those practical activities, then the rules are "reinterpreted" rather than "broken."

An example will help to clarify the point. Universities often have ironclad rules about grade changes: grades can be changed *only* if there has been a clerical error. New faculty members often follow that rule literally and find themselves in trouble with both students and administrators. Experienced students and faculty understand that professors can change any grade for just about any academic reason and simply call it an error due to clerical mistake. Administrators in fact expect faculty to do just that, though they would never say so. It is unclear how the official rule was established, how it is justified, or why it continues, but it is certainly important for faculty to learn *both the rule and how it is used:* knowing just the rule is certainly not sufficient for practical activities. In ethnomethodological language we would say that faculty interpret the rule's meaning in the context of the practical situations they face in order to accomplish the accepted legitimate goal of giving correct and just grades.

A number of ethnomethodological studies of deviance have been done, and work in this area continues. A sampling of titles of these works will suggest the range and complexity of topics and the detailed ways in which they are approached:

Egon Bittner, "The Police on Skid Row: A Study of Peace Keeping" (1967).

Kenneth Stoddart, "Pinched: Notes on the Ethnographer's Location of Argot" (in Turner, 1974).

Harold Garfinkel, "Passing and the Managed Achievement of Sex Status in an Intersexed Person" (in Garfinkel, 1967).

Peter McHugh, "A Common-Sense Perception of Deviance" (in Douglas, 1970A and Dreitzel, 1970).

Arlene Kaplan Daniels, "The Social Construction of Military Psychiatric Diagnoses" (in Dreitzel, 1970).

Clearly, ethnomethodology is concerned with *everyday action in the social world* — the multiplicity of little things that go into the construction of social behavior. *Social behavior and the social world are viewed as accomplishments achieved by the participants.*

A great deal of criticism has been directed to phenomenological sociology and ethnomethodology, some of it quite hostile. (See, for example, Coser, 1975.) Some criticism seems based on the idea that both approaches require a new understanding of the nature of science, conceiving it as far more tentative and problematic than it is customarily seen to be. Indeed, phenomenological sociology and ethnomethodology do call for a new view of science, and they claim that such a view is both necessary and fruitful. Implicit in both, furthermore, are criticisms of earlier theoretical approaches, criticisms which we have indicated throughout Chapters 2, 3, and 4. Certainly there is disagreement among sociologists about the nature of science, but the call for a new view does not seem legitimate grounds for criticism.

The language of phenomenological sociology and ethnomethodology has often been attacked. Coser (1975) and others have argued that "esoteric language" covers up "trivial ideas," and that "obscure jargon" is used to create a group of "insiders" who are the only ones who "really understand." There is no question that the writings in these two approaches are difficult to read; the issue is whether or not there is a *sociological* or general intellectual reason for the style adopted. Adherents claim that since what they are talking about is generally taken for granted, and thus not talked about, a vocabulary is not readily available. Furthermore, to distinguish between common-sense and sociological talk about common sense requires linguistic distinctions that are not always easy to construct. A sense of the linguistic problems that arise may be gained if, for example, one tries to describe in clear prose the *taste* of coffee.*

Since phenomenological sociology and ethnomethodology are relatively new, it is difficult to assess the legitimacy of criticisms directed toward them. The ultimate test of their theories lies in the insights produced. We see phenomenological sociology and ethnomethodology as making important contributions to the new perspective.

Giddens has summed up the contributions of phenomenological sociology and in particular of ethnomethodology as follows (1976, in *Phenomenological Sociology Newsletter*, pp. 5–6):

1. They "place the notion of agency once more in the forefront of sociological theory. By the idea of agency, I mean the thesis that

---

* A problem brought to Waksler's attention by Richard Mendelsohn, Lehman College.

human society as produced by human individuals is a creative and skilled production, that the sustaining of even the most trivial kind of encounter between individuals, whether of verbal dialogue, or interaction is a creative phenomenon of the same order as the speaking of a language is a creative phenomenon."

2. They recognize "the significance of language as a medium of practical activity . . . . language is a mode of doing things." (See our earlier description of Wieder's work on "the code.")

3. They recognize the importance of seeing action in terms of time and place or of "the temporal and contextual locating of actions."

4. They place "in the forefront the significance of common sense, not merely as an obstacle, not merely as a series of beliefs which have to be undermined, have to be transformed, which social science can merely dispense with, but as a medium whereby social life is constituted as meaningful at all."

Existential Sociology

Existentialism is a school of philosophy developed by Jean-Paul Sartre as a response to what he saw as the limits of phenomenology. Existentialism differs from phenomenology in the central role it gives to *emotions, perceptions, conflict,* and *absurdity,* ideas we will develop in this section. Phenomenology, on the other hand, focuses on experience and on reflection on that experience, thus giving a central role to symbolic or cognitive thought. Existentialism and phenomenology share a concern with seeing *individuals in the world,* rather than detached from it, and thus give a primary place to *interaction.* While there are important differences between the two philosophical approaches, and thus between phenomenological sociology and existential sociology, their similarities and unique contributions have become a part of the new perspective. Existential sociology, a more recent development with a small number of followers, promises to make important contributions to our understanding of the social world and of deviance. (See Tiryakian, 1962, and Douglas and Johnson, 1977A.)

Sartre's basic insight existentialism, on which he constructed, was: "Existence before essence." He meant that we are alive, feeling, perceiving, and acting *before* we have symbolic experiences (essences). A newborn feels hunger and reaches for the breast; perceiving the breast between its lips, it sucks and swallows. The *feeling* and *perception* seem to explain the behavior; it seems unnecessary to suggest that the infant analyzes (symbolizes) its condition and formulates a plan that will lead to its satisfaction. While reaching for the breast may be viewed as instinctive behavior, existentialists argue that patterns of perception and feeling lead to adult action as well. According to existentialism, *feelings — specifically, situated drives and emotions — are the ultimate determinants of human action. Values and beliefs become effective determinants of action only when (1) they have been fused with feelings through experience and (2) they give direction to the expression of those feelings.*

Sartre's analysis of antisemitism provides an example of this process. According to Sartre, it can arise in two ways. First, it can be taught by others who are antisemitic, so that one comes to share their ideas even though one may never have had any experiences, negative or positive, with Jews. Second, it can emerge through having negative experiences with Jews and perceiving them as a threat. Sartre argues that the first way arouses relatively little negative feeling so that it can be readily eliminated by direct positive experiences with Jews. The second way, on the other hand, engages one's feelings directly. Deep emotions result that provide the grounds for one's behavior in such a way that even positive experiences with Jews seem to have no effect on one's antisemitism. Feelings come to guide behavior in a way that mere abstract learning cannot. This analysis shows how existentialists give a central role to *feelings* as an explanation of human action.

Existentialists also argue that *conflict is a necessary part of all individual human lives and of all social interactions.* In this way they share many of the concerns of social conflict theorists (see Chapter 2). Since, however, existentialists see conflict as only one of a number of elements basic to the explanation of social behavior, they cannot properly be called social conflict theorists. Existentialists are concerned with both intrapersonal (within the person) and interpersonal (between people) conflict.

As an example of intrapersonal conflict, consider the simple activity of going to the beach. Common-sensically we might think this event nonconflictful, assuming that one likes to go to the beach, but existentialists would claim that it must involve some conflict. Going to the beach requires giving up many things that might be done in its place. Even if these activities are less pleasurable, they nonetheless have some value and must be renounced. There is always the conflict that "you can't have your cake and eat it too." Moreover, there may be some "after-beach costs," such as sunburn, fatigue, salty skin, or wet hair. If alternatives to going to the beach are tempting, the conflict will be greater, but even without them there will be some conflict.

Quite understandably, existential sociologists are more concerned with interpersonal than with intrapersonal conflict. They have focused especially on the conflictful nature of public behavior, drawing to some extent on dramaturgical theory (from sources such as Goffman's *Behavior in Public Places*, 1963A) but adding a conflict dimension that is largely missing in that theory. One dramaturgical concept they have found particularly useful is that of *front*, the public presentation one makes that conceals one's private self. For example, much of *The Nude Beach* (Douglas and Rasmussen, 1977) is devoted to unraveling and exposing the convoluted layers of frontwork nude beachers use to hide their sexual motives from a public that would be outraged by such behavior. Existential sociologists argue that *it is the pervasive conflicts of civilized life that lead to the development of pervasive frontwork to hide private activities from public view.* The public realm is where interaction between people of different backgrounds is most frequent. Public realms are the ones presenting the most potential for conflict and thus the most incentives for hiding one's discrepant ideas in order to minimize that conflict. The more a society is made up of heterogeneous groups or subcultures, the greater the potential for conflicts. To avoid conflicts, frontwork becomes extensive (Douglas, 1971B).

In the United States and in Western societies generally the separation between private and public life is clearly defined and even legally supported. The "right to privacy" in a sense legitimates a difference between private and public behavior. Absolutist or totalitarian societies attempt to destroy the boundaries between public and private life in order to prevent private differences that might subvert absolutist power. In absolutist as well as in homogeneous societies fronts and private selves tend to merge, while in heterogeneous societies they are more clearly distinguished.

Existential analysts argue that *the necessary conflicts of life, even at the individual level, make cognitive contradictions and even absurdities inevitable.* This idea is developed at some length by Lyman and Scott in their book, *A Sociology of the Absurd* (1970). They feel that the term "sociology of the absurd" ought to be applied to what we are calling the new perspective. The following statement suggests the central place of their views in the new perspective:

> The term "absurd" captures the fundamental assumption of this new wave [of sociological thought]: *The world is essentially without meaning.* In contrast to that sociology which seeks to discover the *real* meaning of action — a sociological reality, such as the *functional* meaning of social behavior — this new sociology asserts that all systems of belief, including that of the conventional sociologists, are arbitrary. The problems previously supposed to be those of the sociologist are in fact the everyday problems of the ordinary man. It is he who must carve out meanings in a world that is meaningless. Alienation and insecurity are fundamental conditions of life — though they are experienced differently by individuals and groups — and the regular rehumanization of man is everyman's task (1970: 1).

Here the differences between existentialism on one hand and phenomenology and ethnomethodology on the other become clear. All agree that human beings provide *rational accounts* of their behavior. Existentialists, however, look behind such accounts to the feelings that are thought to motivate them. The problem that arises is philosophical, not empirical. Feelings and thoughts are not directly available to us; we know only what others disclose and what we infer. What, if anything, lies behind rational accounts is an issue that we must leave unresolved for now. But we must remember that phenomenologists and ethno-methodologists *assume* the self-sufficiency of these accounts, whereas existentialists *assume* that accounts derive from feelings.

Existential sociology has been used most extensively in the sociology of deviance. Some existential analysts have argued that people may get involved in deviant activities through a series of slow steps by which they change their feelings toward what they are doing. Initially they may deceive both themselves and others until they develop new feelings that allow them to overcome and finally escape feelings of guilt and shame when committing deviant activities.

Many prostitutes, for example, enter the profession only after a step-by-step process in which they increase their "casual sex lives," test the responses of others to their activities, and hide their sex-for-money activities from those who would shame them for their behavior (Rasmussen and Kuhn, 1976). Shame is a powerful drive which all humans seem capable of and which is used in all societies as one particularly effective means of deterring deviance. To become deviant in the face of feelings of shame involves avoiding that shame until new feelings can be created that will negate it. Overcoming it is difficult, but it can be done.

Lyman and Scott exemplify the existential study of deviance in their article "Paranoia, Homosexuality, and Game Theory" (in Lyman and Scott, 1970). Their concern is with what deviants themselves think about their activities. They suggest that deviants may provide a rich source of data to sociologists on the nature of the social world, since deviants for their very survival must develop a heightened awareness to their environment.

Perhaps the most important contribution of existentialism to the new perspective is a recognition of perceptions and feelings, realms of experience long neglected by sociologists. Hochschild (1975) in an article entitled "The Sociology of Feeling and Emotion: Selected Possibilities" attributes this neglect to the following conditions:

> Perhaps the main reason sociologists have neglected feeling is that, as sociologists, we are members of the same society as the actors we study, and we share their feelings and values. Our society defines being cognitive, intellectual, or rational . . . as superior to being emotional or sentimental. . . .
>
> Another reason for sociologists' neglect of emotions may be the discipline's attempt to be recognized as a "real science" and the consequent need to focus on the most objective and measurable features of social life (p. 281).

This statement reminds us how much has been taken for granted and unexamined by earlier sociologists. Each section in this chapter has brought to light elements that have heretofore been concealed to us because we *assumed* them rather than *investigating* them. The new perspective recognizes the pervasiveness of taken-for-granted ideas and the seemingly unending task of bringing them forward for examination.

General Features of the New Perspective

The various theories examined in this chapter emphasize different aspects of the social world and in some ways conflict and disagree with one another, yet we think they share sufficient similarities to comprise a "new perspective." They share the three assumptions listed on the first page of this chapter and described in Chapter 1. In addition, the following statements would be generally agreed to by the theorists included in this chapter:

1. Social behavior is based on social interaction — that is, on interaction between and among individuals.
2. Social meanings and actions are constructed to fit concrete situations.
3. The general process of labeling or social definition is an important element in social behavior.
   a. Deviance is a social creation.
   b. Significant factors in explaining some kinds of deviance include the labeling of deviants as deviants, the creation of new social rules, and the activities of moral entrepreneurs.
4. Human beings both act in the social world and are acted upon by it.
5. The social world is a social creation. Social behavior and the social world are *accomplishments* achieved by the participants.
6. Impression management is an important feature of social interaction.
7. People's accounts of their behavior are themselves social productions.
8. The social world does not have intrinsic meaning; meaning is *granted* by social actors.
9. Sociology has in the past neglected areas of study that are worthy of consideration; of particular significance are the social rules of everyday life and emotions (feelings).
10. Value neutrality is a main goal in sociological research. It is, however, exceedingly difficult to achieve and may sometimes have to be renounced in the search for truth.
11. Philosophy is important for the grounding of sociological theory.

We have phrased these statements in the general terms in which they characterize the new perspective. Each of the special theories we have examined in this chapter would emphasize some of these statements, minimize others, and present yet others with considerably more specificity.

Much of the disagreement among these theories derives from their having been developed to deal with different types of deviance. The first formulation of labeling theory by Becker, for example, was based largely on the study of drug violations. This topic lends itself to an emphasis on laws and the bureaucracies that pass and enforce them, since in the United States the link between drugs and the law is strong. Existential theory, on the other hand, has based its theories on the violation of sexual rules, which are made and enforced both through laws and in many other ways. Such studies are more apt to see laws only partially representative and to focus on deep feelings of threat and dread, lust and excitement, as important factors in the understanding of sexual deviance.

The development of varied theories is fruitful for sociological understanding. Given the wide range of behavior that in some place at some time is seen as deviant, we will need a broad and flexible set of explanations if we are to make sense out of the many and varied forms that deviance takes.

THE NEW PERSPECTIVE AND LEVELS OF EXPLANATION

Returning for a moment to Figure 2.1 (pp. 32–33), we can see that the new perspective does not seem to fall at any one level of explanation. Rather, it *seeks that level most appropriate to the type of deviance to be explained*. As a sociological perspective it restricts its analysis to Levels II through V but draws on other levels and the expertise of other sciences for data and for possible explanatory materials. Nonetheless, the new perspective is grounded in the study of the *social* world and the *social* factors operating in that world.

One criticism we have repeatedly directed to earlier theories of deviance is that they remained committed to a single level of analysis even when their data indicated the need for movement to another level. The new perspective attempts to remain flexible in its search for sources of explanation, moving from the most universal features of the social world to specific characteristics of concrete situations and interactions.

In Part II, when we examine different types of deviance and the varied explanations offered of them, we will have the opportunity to compare earlier theories with the new perspective. The strengths of the new perspective's multilevel approach should then become evident.

MORALITY AND RULES IN THE NEW PERSPECTIVE

Although the new perspective aims toward value neutrality in the collection and presentation of its data, the moral values (morality) and rules of those being studied are especially important elements of the data gathered. Since they present particular problems in research and analysis, we will take a look at them before concluding our presentation of the new perspective.

We will begin with these everyday definitions:

Morality — conformity to ideals or principles of right human conduct.
Rules — prescribed guides for conduct or action.*

We might say that morality tells us what to do and rules tell us how to do it. An absolutist perspective, and perhaps a common-sense perspective as well, might suggest that morality is derived from some necessarily true system, such as religion or natural law, and that rules for behavior follow from morality in a straightforward fashion. In this view, morality precedes rules and rules precede action. This view characterized much of early sociology and led to the view that deviance was simply any action that violated morality.

In the new perspective, deviance is seen as enormously more complex. Studies within this perspective have disclosed both the problematic nature of morality and the routine departure from the progression from morality to rules to action. The absolutist perspective simply does not accurately represent the processes in routine everyday behavior.

Moral conflicts in recent years have become increasingly evident in the United States. Important moral issues have been raised by black power advocates, hippies, women's liberation, the Watergate scandal, and the gay pride movement, to name but a few. And increasingly it is difficult to obtain public consensus on what is right and what is wrong. The old assertion, "It's as clear as the difference between black and white," sticks in one's throat nowadays. These events and the reactions to them became a great stimulus to the development of new ideas both at the common-sense level and in the social sciences. They contributed in particular to the ideas that make up the new perspective in the sociology of deviance, for they established very clearly that *morality is situational*. As the new perspective sees it, moral issues that arise in any given situation are problematic both for participants and for researchers. Sociologists must study morality; they cannot simply assume a moral position. Furthermore, understanding the moral concerns of participants is a useful resource for sociologists seeking to explain behavior.

The new perspective also recognizes that there is a crucial and neglected link between morality and deviance: defining something as deviant may be in itself a moral judgment, and generally a negative one, suggesting that to be deviant is to be wrong, bad, evil, and the like. While sociologists in the new perspective attempt to use the term deviance in a value-neutral way, not making judgments about the "goodness" or "badness" of deviance, they have come to see the importance of recognizing that people in general often do use the term in a negative or pejorative way.

* By permission. From *Webster's New Collegiate Dictionary* © 1980 by G. & C. Merriam Co., publishers of the Merriam-Webster Dictionaries.

For example, the moral entrepreneurs Becker speaks of seem to believe, at least to some extent, that the behavior they are seeking to eliminate is wrong; this is why they are called *moral* entrepreneurs. Is deviance, however, always viewed as wrong? If you call something deviant, are you also calling it wrong? While people in everyday life may answer these questions "Yes," there is evidence to suggest that sociologists must answer "No." This evidence consists of instances of activities that in all other ways seem to fit our definition of deviance as a violation of values and rules and yet are publicly defined either as good or as nondeviant.

Everett Hughes has argued that attention to "bad" deviants has obscured the existence of "good" deviants, those who violate the rules in positive ways or whose very rule-following is so consistent as to violate our expectations for people in general. The example Hughes raises is saints, whose very "goodness" violates the rules of behavior for "everyday people." Following this reasoning, we might consider as deviant the person who receives an "A" on an exam that everyone else fails. If everyone failed, the exam might be considered at fault, but the presence of one "A" undermines such an explanation. "Curve-breakers" are often viewed as deviant even though their behavior in itself may not be defined as "wrong."

Dorothy J. Douglas's unpublished study of nuns as sexual deviants (1969) provides another piece of evidence here. Some readers might want to argue that "it isn't right" to call nuns sexual deviants on the basis of their celibacy, and yet if we do not attach a negative meaning to the term we can gain insights into the workings of the social world by investigating this kind of deviance as well. Deviance may be linked with a negative value in common-sense usage, but the new perspective suggests that sociologists keep deviance and morality distinct, recognizing the existence of both positive and negative deviance and the possibilities of studying both forms.

A major element in the new perspective is the broad definition given to the idea of "rules." Earlier sociologists were particularly concerned with formally stated rules such as laws, but the new perspective extends to include both informally stated rules, such as those told to Wieder as part of "the code" (see above, p. 143), and taken-for-granted rules, those which are not stated even though they are followed as if they were. Taken-for-granted rules have been examined particularly in the dramaturgical and ethnomethodological approaches.

The following two statements about rules, taken from a study of rules and rule use by Douglas (1971A), suggest this expanded conception of rules:

> Social rules are the criteria that normal members of the society are expected to make (sincere) use of in deciding what to do in any situation for which they are seen as relevant (p. 141).

The members of our society make use of rules to adequately achieve their purposes at hand (p. 221).

Both these statements indicate that rules are to be *used* rather than *followed*. This distinction can be illustrated by the way in which students construct excuses to explain absence from class.

Given a situation in which they are expected to attend classes, students who miss a class may be called upon to justify their absence. The earlier absolutist perspective might suggest that there are a limited number of adequate reasons for missing classes; all other reasons are inadequate or inappropriate. An examination of actual student excuses suggests a different process: students are aware of the distinction between adequate and inadequate reasons for missing class and construct their excuses in terms of adequate reasons, *regardless of the "real" reasons for their absence*. Examples of student excuses often used include: "I overslept," "My car broke down," "I was sick," "I was in the infirmary." Readers might well suspect, however, that such a list does not exhaust all the possible reasons for missing class. The excuses listed all embody a value placed on attending classes and a recognition of the rule that one attends class as long as one is physically able to do so. It seems likely that people in fact miss classes because other values assume greater importance — "I wanted to see a friend," "I was in the midst of a heavy affair," "I was reading a good book" — or because one didn't feel like it, or for no reason at all — yet these kinds of reasons are seldom offered by students as excuses.

This example demonstrates that rules can be used in a variety of ways, not only to guide behavior but also to explain behavior in a socially acceptable though not necessarily true way *after* it has occurred. We are not here saying that people lie, but that people *use* rules as required by situations. Student excuses can be seen at least in part to be required of the situations in which they take place, a way for students to meet the requirements of other situations while not jeopardizing or threatening the student-teacher relationship.

In the new perspective rules are viewed not as static but as dynamic and changing, used by participants to meet situational requirements. Rule use itself is social behavior, and the rules themselves may be modified in the process of being used. While the *accounts* we give of our behavior might suggest that our actions are always guided by rules and the morality from which they are derived, detailed study of that behavior discloses quite different processes. While there certainly are occasions in which our behavior seems to be an outcome of rules we are following, there also seem to be occasions on which rules do not become an issue until after we have acted. When we ask: Why did I do that? we can generally come up with reasons, but are those the reasons that in fact motivated the behavior? The answer is not clear, and the new perspective attempts to recognize the existence of such ambiguity.

Our considerations in this section lead us to an obvious but often unrecognized characteristic of social rules that distinguishes them from physical rules: *Social rules can be broken.* Though physical rules cannot be violated and in this sense are absolute — one cannot defy gravity — social rules by their very nature can be and are violated. In fact, social rules arise only in situations where they could be violated: "No swimming" signs appear next to lakes, not in deserts. And they appear because of the expectation that if such actions were not prohibited, they would occur — people would swim in the lake. Furthermore, the existence of signs or of rules in general does not prevent behavior but merely forbids it. Anyone can break social rules. Breaking rules does leave one open to punishment and even to identification as a deviant, though such a result is merely possible, not inevitable. One may break a social rule and not get caught; presumably readers can supply their own examples here. It is this possibility of breaking social rules and even perhaps getting away with it that makes deviance an inevitable feature of social life.

The question of the origin of morality and rules has only recently become a topic of intensive sociological research. The earlier absolutist perspective did not permit even the raising of such questions but simply assumed that both derived from religion, natural law, or some other sphere of absolute truth. Becker's study of the origin of marijuana laws is an important contribution to the topic of origins. Further work is needed, however, particularly in the area of nonlegal rules and associated values. While the process of the development of rules and morality is not yet fully understood by sociologists, their source seems to lie in the workings of the social world and in the processes of social interaction in concrete situations.

Concluding Note to Part I

Each of the wide variety of theories we have examined in Part I contributes by explaining some kinds of phenomena and is weak or irrelevant in explaining others. Any all-inclusive theory of deviance will have to preserve the insights of earlier theories, and perhaps of some as yet uncreated, in order to explain the full gamut of phenomena that can be called deviant. We see the new perspective as a promising movement in the development of a general theory of deviance. Our major commitment, however, is to *the understanding of deviance as a social phenomenon*, not to any specific theory. Our best chance of advancing our theoretical understanding of deviance lies in being continually open to the world of experience, however that experience displays itself.

PART II

VARIETIES
OF DEVIANCE

There was a time when I merely listened attentively to what people said and took for granted that they would carry out their words. Now I am obliged not only to give ear to what they say but also to keep an eye on what they do. — Confucius

Having considered in Part I the many *explanations* offered for deviance, in Part II we will concentrate on *activities* that have been or can be seen as deviant. Our presentation will be guided by the new perspective, which entails some problems we must recognize at once.

First, from the point of view of the new perspective in general and of labeling theory in particular, any activity is deviant *if it is so defined by others.* Clearly, we cannot consider *all* deviance and thus we have had to make choices. We have been guided in our selection by our desires to present a wide variety of types so that readers can apply our analysis to other instances in which they are interested; to consider topics "traditionally" dealt with in the sociology of deviance; to include topics of current popular concern so that common-sense and sociological approaches can be compared; to consider topics on which there is extensive literature as well as those on which data are sparse; and to present topics that the authors themselves find interesting — an option that value neutrality allows us.

A second problem is that many of the topics we have included have not been studied, or not studied intensively, by sociologists who adopt the new perspective. In such instances we have drawn on whatever sources we have available — studies done in other perspectives, popular accounts, novels, media presentations, and so on — and have made clear the tentative nature of our formulations.

While viewing data from the new perspective, we have also included discussions of sociological work conducted from a variety of other perspectives. The strengths and weaknesses of different theoretical explanations of deviance will emerge as we consider their applications to particular instances. We will mention some of these as we proceed, but readers should themselves recognize such issues even when they are not emphasized.

In Part II we will consider a wide range of activities, some of which will seem to readers more *self-evidently* deviant than others. The new perspective, however, demands that we justify *all* our choices and demonstrate *why* and *in what ways* the activities under consideration can be considered deviant. In this process, a moral issue will arise. Earlier views of deviance, as we have indicated, took for granted that deviance is wrong. The new perspective, on the other hand, advocates what Matza (1969) has called an *appreciation* of deviance, an understanding of the deviant activity *in its own terms.* Such an approach is often *misunderstood* as support for deviant activities. We want to emphasize that the new perspective is committed to *value neutrality* (as described in Chapter 1) and *neither* advocates nor condemns any deviant activity. It is certainly likely that readers will see some forms of deviance as "reasonable," "good," "okay," and "not really deviant" and others as "bad," "sick," "kinky," and the like. Readers should recognize that such moral evaluation flows from their own moral and ethical principles and, though personally important, is not a part of sociological explanation. Readers may find it instructive to become aware of their own moral stances on different kinds of deviance and the consequent effects on their understanding. Our goal, as sociologists, has been to remain faithful to the data and to allow readers of all moral persuasions to come to their own moral conclusions. Our task here is a sociological, not an ethical, one.

As we did in Part I, we will continue to direct your attention to the ways in which sociologists work to achieve understanding and the processes by which theories are developed. We will also compare commonsense and sociological perspectives. Our focus will be on sociological explanation as a process that emerges from study rather than as a currently existing body of established facts.

6

Sexual Deviance

In Chapter 1 we developed an ostensive definition of deviance as *any thought, feeling, or action that members of a social group judge to be a violation of their values or rules* (p. 10). In all societies we know of, sexual behavior is regulated in some way. No society allows totally free sexual activity. Because all societies have rules governing sexual behavior, all societies will have rule-breakers and thus sexual deviants. Our subject in this chapter is such sexual deviants, however they are defined by the societies in which they act. We will explore the varied rules that have existed, the ways in which they have changed, and the many ways in which they have been broken.

Our focus in this chapter will be on sexual activity that has a physiological component. We will not consider the broader issues of sex role behavior, sexual stereotyping, or other cultural elaborations based on perceived differences between the sexes, since such consideration would further complicate an already complicated subject. We will restrict ourselves to activities that relate to such sexual behavior as prostitution, pornography, sexual pleasures, and sexual responses in general.

We begin by looking at some of the ways in which sexual behavior in general and sexual deviance in particular have been studied by the social sciences. Next we consider the moral climate in which decisions are made about sexual deviance in the United States today. Then we turn to sociological studies of sexual deviance: first, two topics that have been studied extensively by social scientists and are popular with the media — prostitution and pornography; second, two topics that emerge from the new perspective — deviant and nondeviant sexual pleasures and social rules restricting sexual activities.

Sex as a Topic of Scientific Study

In Western societies of earlier centuries, the intense privacy of the topic of sex and the strong restrictions against public discussions, displays, and acts involving it resulted in its virtual exclusion from "respectable" science as a subject of investigation. Early social scientists found it necessary to provide extensive justification for any scientific concern with sex and to emphasize the *scientific* nature of their work. Krafft-Ebing published his renowned work, *Psychopathia sexualis*, in 1886 in Latin to keep it from falling into the hands of those who might use it for erotic rather than scholarly purposes. Parent-Duchatelet published some remarkably advanced studies of prostitution as early as 1848, but he did so within the framework of "medical hygiene." Freud encountered both opposition to his work and questioning of his "real" motives.

Social pressures directed against those studying sex have continued during the present century. Bronislaw Malinowski implored his fellow anthropologists to remember that "Man is an animal, and, as such, at times unclean, and the honest anthropologist has to face this fact" (1927: 6). Reflecting on his experience in psychology in the 1930s, Wardell Pomeroy (in Farberow, 1963) described how strong were professional taboos against studying sex even within psychology:

> As an undergraduate thirty years ago, I was warned by my psychology professors that there were two areas of study that were fraught with danger. One was the study of hypnosis, and the second was the study of human sexual behavior. Further inquiry as to why these areas of research were dangerous was met with frosty stares, much harrumphing, and evasion. Dismissal of researchers in at least two psychology departments in the early 1930's because of studies on human sexual behavior could not help but increase the anxiety of psychologists contemplating work in this field. Despite Freud and his followers, Havelock Ellis, German sexologists, and others, only five psychologists had published anything approaching good statistical data on human sexual behavior prior to 1940 (p. 22).

When Alfred Kinsey started publishing his studies of "normal" sexual behavior (1948), considerable controversy arose over his work in spite of the antiseptic medical attitude he adopted, perhaps because he did not also adopt the moral tone of earlier researchers. Even today researchers studying sex have been publicly criticized. (See, for example, responses to Douglas and Rasmussen, *The Nude Beach*, 1977; Laud Humphreys, *Tearoom Trade*, 1970; and Gay Talese, *Thy Neighbor's Wife*, 1980.)

Public repression and the norm against talk about intimacy with non-intimates has made it particularly difficult to study sex, and especially to observe sex directly, even now. Almost all studies of sex have relied on indirect data, obtained mainly through interviews with "patients," as Freud did, or through a wider selection of interviews, as Kinsey or, more recently, Hite (1976) has done. Sex researchers have undoubtedly made great progress in recent years in understanding sex, but there are still severe constraints on observing the most important aspects of sex — the most intimate and also the most characteristic features of sexual behavior. Only rare works, such as those by Masters and Johnson (1966), have begun to contribute to our understanding of sexual behavior through direct observation, and even here the framework remains a medical one in which social dimensions are largely unexamined.

In spite of these restrictions, sexual deviance nonetheless is one of the few forms of deviance that has been studied in some way or other by almost all sciences. Few disciplines dealing with human beings have not generated at least some extensive studies of sex. Historically the first major studies of sex were medical. Our most extensive current knowledge is of the physiology and biology of sex. Anthropology began extensive comparative studies of sex norms, sex roles, and sex behavior in the last century (Westermarck, 1912) and has continued to devote some attention to the topic. (See, for example, Ford and Beach, 1951, and the selection of articles in Marshall and Suggs, *Human Sexual Behavior*, 1971.) Though sociology was comparatively late in beginning to study sex, sociologists are now engaged in a variety of studies of the subject. Historical studies of sex include such major works as Otto Kiefer's *Sexual Life in Ancient Rome* (1934), Lawrence Stone's *The Family, Sex and Marriage in England 1500–1800* (1977), and Vern Bullough's *Sexual Variations in Society and History* (1976). Today, and for some time past, psychological studies of sex have been extensive, rivaling medical studies for dominance. The psychological influence has been so pervasive that it has been adopted by other social sciences as well.

Early researchers in sexuality seemed to have little difficulty in distinguishing between "normal" and "deviant" sexual activities. Researchers began with firm ideas of what sexual deviance was and expected to find simple explanations for a wide spectrum of sexual deviance. These confident, simplistic expectations have been undermined by later research. As an example, we will consider the history of the study of homosexuality, reviewing the many ways in which homosexuality has been "explained" by social scientists.

EXAMPLE: A HISTORICAL OVERVIEW OF THE STUDY OF HOMOSEXUALITY

Homosexuality, like other forms of sexual deviance, was first studied by doctors. Their goal was simple: to find representative homosexuals, study them medically, and thereby determine the biological cause of this "obvious pathology." The search was for a Level I explanation based on the nature of the physical organism and its presumed malfunctioning. Researchers began by defining homosexuals as those who practice sexual acts with members of the same sex, and they implicitly assumed that people were *either* exclusively homosexual or exclusively heterosexual. They saw homosexuality as a *state of being* rather than as an *act subject to choice*. Furthermore, they implicitly assumed that the identification of people as homosexual was nonproblematic and thus that researchers, members of society, and homosexuals themselves would agree on who was homosexual. Conversely, heterosexuality was viewed as nonproblematic and a self-evident characteristic of those who possessed it. Later research has proved all these assumptions false.

For example, Kinsey's studies (1948, 1953) disclosed that 37 percent of the males and 13 percent of the females studied had at least one sex act with a member of the same sex leading to orgasm between adolescence and old age. Ten percent of the males and 6 percent of the females were predominantly homosexual in their sex acts for at least three years between the ages of 16 and 55; 4 to 6 percent of the males and 2 to 3 percent of the females were exclusively homosexual in their sex acts from adolescence onward. Although a number of critics have questioned Kinsey's work, it does seem to establish that homosexuality is not necessarily either an exclusive orientation or a lifetime commitment. Its situational nature seems to suggest a social rather than a biological source of explanation.

Other studies have arrived at findings similar to Kinsey's (see, for example, Weinberg and Williams, 1975). It is particularly striking that in the United States, where homosexual acts were strongly stigmatized at the time of the studies, both men and women admitted to homosexual acts. A further important finding is that most of these persons were defined by themselves and by others as heterosexuals, not as homosexuals. The issue of self-identification of homosexuals has been studied by Warren (1974), Ponse (1974), and others and found to be complex. Both those who engage in homosexual acts and those who do not do so but are aroused by the idea may consider themselves "gay," while others who engage in homosexual acts may view themselves as heterosexual. Reiss (1961) found that boys who engaged in homosexual sex for pay were adamant in avowing their heterosexuality. Humphreys, in his study of impersonal sex in public restrooms (1970), describes those he studied as follows:

> Many men — married and unmarried, those with heterosexual identities and those whose self-image is a homosexual one — seek such impersonal sex, shunning involvement, desiring kicks without commitment (pp. 1–2).

It now appears certain that distinctions are to be made among those who see themselves as homosexual, those who are seen by others as homosexual, and those who engage in homosexual activities. The confounding of these three elements in earlier studies was simplistic and distorted the data.

The search for a biological cause for homosexuality has been extensive but largely unsuccessful. Sex has such obvious biological aspects and is so obviously related to powerful emotions and drives that it has seemed reasonable to search for the biological bases of sexual behavior, both deviant and nondeviant. Some homosexuals have themselves argued for the biological nature of their preferences, saying that homosexuality for them is "natural." Some studies have found a somewhat greater tendency for male twins from one egg (identical twins) to both be either homosexual or heterosexual, thus suggesting some genetic basis for sexual choice, but such studies are neither definitive nor undisputed. Hormonal studies have found factors associated with various aspects of homosexuality, but again the findings are ambiguous.

Some of the most extensive work done on the biological bases of homosexuality has been conducted by John Money, a professor of medical psychology and pediatrics. Having reviewed the literature on hormones, he concludes:

> The most likely explanation of the origins of homosexuality, bisexuality, and heterosexuality of gender identity is that certain sexually dimorphic traits or dispositions are laid down in the brain before birth which may facilitate the establishment of either of the three conditions but are too strongly bivalent to be exclusive and invariant determinants of either homo- or heterosexuality, or of their shared bisexual state. The primary origins of the three conditions lie in the developmental period of a child's life after birth, particularly during the years of late infancy and early childhood. . . . Once the pattern is established in the early development years, however, it is remarkably tenacious. The hormones of puberty bring it into full expression (Money and Ehrhardt, 1972, p. 244).

Whatever its role in sexual activity, biology does not seem sufficient to allow us to explain the existence of either homosexuality or heterosexuality.

Again drawing on the biological model, some researchers have argued that since heterosexuality has such obvious importance in reproduction, homosexuality must be either biologically unlikely or socially prohibited. Such an argument sounds plausible, but is not supported by the facts. Anthropologists have found homosexuality in most societies, in varied forms and with varied frequencies, with responses ranging from strong prohibition to encouragement, and even with legitimate social positions for adult homosexuals (Davenport, 1965). What reproduction seems to require is simply that *some* people at *some* times engage in heterosexual activities. Once this condition is met, homosexuality seems to provide no particular "reproductive threat." In this regard, Money and Ehrhardt state:

> Any mammal is capable of homosexual behavior, in the sense of performing part or all of the act of mounting on a member of the same sex. . . . This kind of behavior is widespread in the animal kingdom. . . .
> Farm animals or wild animals observed in homosexual behavior are, almost without exception, also able to breed. In other words, they are bisexual. . . . They exhibit homosexual behavior more often in childhood than in adulthood, and more often when sex-segregated than not (1972, p. 236).

Current evidence seems to suggest that while the biological existence of sexual impulses is certain, the object of those impulses is not biologically specified in any fixed and determined way. The choice of sexual object — of the opposite sex, same sex, or even of nonhuman objects — seems to be influenced in important ways by individual experiences and social contexts. Current research in sex and in sexual deviance has moved from Level I explanations to more specific and more social sources of explanation. (For studies that focus on the social aspect of homosexual behavior see Hooker, 1965; and Leznoff and Westley, 1956; both reprinted in Gagnon and Simon, 1967.)

CURRENT KNOWLEDGE ABOUT SEXUALITY AND SEXUAL DEVIANCE

Different forms of sexual activity seem to involve quite distinctive combinations of biological, physiological, psychological, and social factors. In this section we will present and describe these general factors.

There is no question that there is a basic biological component to sexual activity. Gender (male or female) and sexual impulses are genetically inherited among all mammals, though both are subject to modification through psychological and social influences. Sexual impulses are not as basic, as powerful, as unidirectional, or as aim-specific as those drives directly associated with self-preservation — that is, the drives for air, food, water, elimination, and sleep. Sexual impulses are far more affected by social situations than are more pressing or basic drives, though all drives are to some extent modifiable by personality and culture. It is possible for individuals to go through life without engaging in any form of direct sexual behavior, though such abstinence is rare. Nonetheless, the sexual impulse may be a particularly powerful motive for action, especially when it is not at least minimally gratified in some way. Millions of individuals and massive social organizations, such as the Catholic Church in medieval Europe, have attempted to minimize the possibilities of gratifying sexual impulses in particular individuals or groups without ever achieving more than temporary success. While select groups, such as nuns, priests, and ascetics, have managed to enforce rules of celibacy for their members, (1) there has always been some deviance even among certain of these group members; (2) sexual impulses have been given other modes of expression, as in the erotic fervor of the writings of St. Theresa of Avila; and (3) such rules have been applied only to a restricted population. St. Paul advised realistically that although celibacy was the most virtuous path, those who could not sustain it ought to marry, for "It is better to marry than to burn." We have every reason to believe that Freud's findings are correct: social situations may repress the expression of sexual impulses, but the impulses themselves continue to exist and to seek expression, if not directly then indirectly (but see Foucault, 1980). Social situations do more in fixing the timing and specific form of sexual behavior than in determining whether or not sexual impulses will be expressed. The social world *shapes* the sex drive; it neither creates nor destroys it.

Any type of socially defined sexual behavior consists of a constellation of biological, psychological, and social components, any one of which may predominate. Returning to our example of homosexuality, we may identify a number of subtypes depending on which component seems most important. Some relatively infrequent forms of homosexuality seem strongly influenced by biology, such as *hermaphroditism* (possession of reproductive organs of both sexes) or other birth anomalies (less accurately called birth "defects") in sexual organs that seem to be associated with hormonal-neural anomalies. Most subtypes of homosexuality, however, seem far more affected by social experience than by biology. Important social experiences that may affect homosexuality include early child-rearing practices (see Gagnon in Gagnon and Simon, 1967), early introduction to homosexual behavior, or severe and lasting constraints on the availability of heterosexual partners, as for prisoners, members of the military, and boarding school students. Yet again homosexuality may be chosen as an alternative to unsatisfactory heterosexual experiences or as a political statement valuing intersex solidarity. Even in a specific situation such as prison there may be a variety of reasons for engaging in homosexual activities: preference for such activities, despair of access to partners of the opposite sex, fear of aggression by others who will rape them if they do not submit (see Kassenbaum and Ward, 1971; Giallambardo, 1966). Even in similar situations, a variety of motives may come into play.

Current knowledge about sexuality emphasizes these aspects:

1. Sexuality, both deviant and nondeviant, involves biological, psychological, and social factors.
2. Different types of sexual activity involve different constellations of biological, psychological, and social factors.
3. While the existence of sexual impulses is a biological fact, the satisfaction of those impulses can occur in a wide variety of ways that are governed by psychological and social rather than biological factors.

4. Sexual impulses can be satisfied in a wide variety of ways, but it appears that the drive to satisfy them *in some way* is strong. Diversion of sexual impulses and their *indirect* satisfaction is not uncommon; suppression of sexual impulses seems to require great and constant effort.
5. The social world shapes the sex drive; it neither creates nor destroys it.
6. A large number of biological, psychological, and especially social factors affect sexual behavior — when, how, and why it occurs.

The earlier absolutist distinction between "normal sexuality" and "sexual deviance" has been refuted by numerous studies, which indicate instead the wide range of sexual behavior of which human beings are capable and the importance of psychological and social factors in the construction of ideas of sexual "normality" and "abnormality." In the next section we will see the ways in which both ideas about sexuality and sexual activities themselves have undergone changes in the public realm.

The Sexual Revolution

It is commonly argued that the United States is in the midst of a "sexual revolution." In considering this claim, we will gain some knowledge of the moral climate within which current public and private decisions about sexual deviance are made.

What is meant by "revolution"? The term suggests a sudden, radical, or complete change, a change that is in some sense fundamental. There can be little argument that at least some changes in sexual values and behavior have taken place in the United States and continue to take place. But has change been sudden, radical, and complete, or has it instead been gradual and emerging?

A further question arises in discussing a "sexual revolution": are we talking about *changes in behavior* or about *changing attitudes toward behavior?* Changes in either can be revolutionary; we must, however, specify what we mean. When, for example, we speak of a "revolutionary" change in homosexuality, do we mean that there is more homosexual activity now than in the past, or that the public is more aware of homosexuality, or that public attitudes toward it have changed?

Clearly the biological bases of human sexuality have remained virtually the same throughout human history. Nonetheless, there have been developments that directly affect the biological dimension of sexuality. Those who speak of a "sexual revolution" often cite the development and widespread availability of contraceptives as a source of radical change in sexual relations. While methods of preventing pregnancy have been known for centuries, current knowledge and the increasingly widespread availability of devices and methods now make it routinely and easily possible for one to *choose* whether or not one wants to conceive a child and, *as a separate decision,* whether or not one wants to engage in sexual relations. In a sense there has always been an element of choice, for one could always refrain from sexual relations or educate oneself about existing methods of contraception, but today such a choice is more readily available to a large proportion of the population.

It does seem clear that knowledge about sexuality, and especially public knowledge, has been increasing — in Western societies at least — since the time of Freud. It is not clear, however, whether this growth of knowledge represents a "revolution," partly because of its slow and emerging character and partly because we don't know its effects on actual behavior. That we now know about a wide variety of sexual activities does not mean that the activities themselves have recently begun.

Freud's studies on sexuality began a new era in the public consideration of sexuality as a human activity, and they met much public disapproval. The Kinsey revelations had similar effects, possibly more so because Kinsey studied what was going on among the "normal" population while Freud had focused on those who might be dismissed as "mad." Kinsey's findings that somewhere around 50 percent of the men and 30 percent of the women studied admitted to having had at least one adulterous affair came as a shock to many. Did Kinsey's material, however, document the beginning of a sexual revolution or a practice that had been going on for centuries? We do not have the data to answer this question, but it seems likely that Kinsey simply publicized already existing practices. Subsequent studies have come up with similar findings, suggesting that these proportions of adultery may have a certain stability through time rather than indicating any great change in sexual activity.

If nearly half the married people know that they themselves have been involved in such violations of public rules, why do they seem shocked to find that so many other people are doing the same thing? There seem to be two reasons: misinterpretation of the findings, and belief that one's own acts are exceptions and idiosyncratic. Many people interpret the findings to mean that 50 percent of men and 30 percent of women are having affairs *at any one time,* whereas the studies indicate that *over many years of marriage* those percentages of people had engaged in adultery. At any one time the proportions are considerably smaller. Rasmussen (1979) has found that casual sex affairs in general tend to be bunched up in one period of a person's life, generally toward the termination of a marriage. Adultery is often both effect and cause of a deteriorating marital relationship that is often resolved by separation or divorce.

The second reason that research findings may shock people is that deviant activities are usually carefully hidden from public view by *fronts of respectability,* so that even those involved in the activity do not know how extensive it is. Secret deviants often assume that they are either the only deviants or members of a small category; to find they are just a few among many changes the meaning of what they are doing. It is also important to remember that some who engage in deviant activities disapprove of those very activities.

Shock is often displayed at findings about the frequency of masturbation, and this activity may serve as a useful example of the social effects of research findings. Children who know of the negative social evaluation of masturbation, and engage in it nonetheless, characteristically see themselves as "the only ones" to engage in such "sinful" acts, assuming that others either do not have such urges or overcome them. As one of the respondents in the Hite report states (1976):

> I definitely "discovered" masturbation by myself, although I believe that my parents' selectively negative reactions helped me to focus my interest on this forbidden part of my body. At first, I just enjoyed exploring. Gradually, as I became older, the feeling that I was doing something shameful and bizarre became part of the pleasure. . . . When I was about ten, a girl my age had a bout of serious illness. My father told me that her illness, of which she had almost died according to him, had been caused by her doing "that." So I began to realize that perhaps other children masturbated too, but still couldn't quite believe it — it was such a crazy thing to do (p. 71).

This experience of being "the only one" — "the only creep in the whole world!" — or one who "has something wrong" seems common among both boys and girls. When, however, in adulthood, one learns of the frequency of masturbation engaged in by others, along with shock may come a feeling of relief that one is not so "bad" after all. Another respondent in the Hite report states:

> Yes I enjoy masturbation physically, but only recently psychologically. Before other women began to talk about it I was sure there was something wrong with me for needing it. . . . I resent not learning how to masturbate until I was an adult. I was too much of a prude to experiment and invent it until I had already been married for several years. I could have had a lot better time in adolescence if I had (p. 66).

The dissemination of knowledge about what others do may change one's individual quirk to an experience held in common with others. One may still choose to reject the experience, to view it as deviant and to be avoided, but the recognition that others also engage in it seems to enhance the possibility that one will view it as an option that one may choose. The absence of knowledge coupled with fronts of respectability works to limit such choice.

In discussions of "the sexual revolution," a great deal of attention is given to premarital virginity. In 1939 a famed psychologist proclaimed the end of premarital virginity on the basis of a study he conducted:

> In contrast with the slow tempo of many cultural changes, the trend toward premarital sex experiences is proceeding with extraordinary rapidity. . . . In the case of husbands the incidence of virginity at marriage is 50.6 per cent in the oldest group and only 13.6 per cent in the youngest. The corresponding drop for wives is from 86.5 per cent to 31.7 per cent. If the drop should continue at the average rate shown for those born since 1890, virginity at marriage will be close to the vanishing point for males born after 1930 and for females born after 1940 (Terman, 1939: 321–322).

Studies from Kinsey on (see, for example, Hunt, 1973) have revealed that only 30 percent of women over 55 report that they had sexual intercourse before marriage while 80 percent of women under 25 report such activity. Such figures do seem to suggest a change of revolutionary proportions, but further investigation reveals instead a slowly emerging change, for all of the major studies have found that almost exactly 50 percent of women at all ages report that their only premarital intercourse was with the man who became their husband. While it does seem clear that premarital virginity is changing as a value, the husband as a woman's one and only sexual partner continues to be a valued and supported arrangement among 50 percent of women studied. Further findings that 34 percent of women had intercourse with a total of two to five partners and only 13 percent with six or more suggests a slow increase in premarital sex with non-future-husband partners rather than a revolutionary change.

There does seem to be a clear pattern in the United States of increased variety in marital sex practices and in the amount of postmarital sex (that which occurs after divorce or the death of a spouse), though here too the changes are slow and have emerged over a somewhat extended period. Reports by married couples and divorced men, as well as, to a lesser degree, by divorced women, suggest both increased variety and frequency of sexual activity. Much of this apparent increase, however, may lie simply in people's increased willingness to talk about such activities, because such talk seems to be losing some of its deviant character.

An idea that has gained much popular attention in recent years is that the "sexual revolution" has brought about an enormous increase in the numbers of people who engage in "swinging" or "mate-swapping." Study suggests, however, that what has increased is the number of people who now know about the existence of "swinging." The practice has long existed and indeed may not even have expanded much in recent years. Though books, articles, television programs, and films about swinging did sell and may well have attracted some recruits, evidence suggests that much of the excitement was *voyeuristic*, derived from seeing and hearing about swinging rather than engaging in it. Public recognition may have provided support for those already participating, but there is little evidence that "swinging" itself increased significantly. The rhetoric of swinging may be used for seduction (Douglas and Rasmussen, 1977) or swinging may be used as a last-ditch marital effort prior to separation or divorce (as happened in the Major case described in Talese, 1980), but the incidence of swinging as a valued activity engaged in by married couples for pleasure seems to be relatively low, certainly not of revolutionary proportions. (On the topic of swinging, see, for example, Varni, 1972.)

Homosexuality comes closer to exemplifying a revolutionary change — again, perhaps primarily in public recognition of activities that have probably existed since human life began. Of the significance of this movement Humphries (1972) says:

> Whether the movement is viewed as having originated in 1950 or in 1969, its rate of growth is astounding when examined in the light of the tenacious resistance of American norms surrounding homosexual behavior (p. 8). . . .
>
> Whatever the relative success of the movement, however, it will have changed American society. Thousands, perhaps millions, of Americans will have moved out of the closets, into the streets. These persons, the closets, and the streets can never be the same again (p. 12).

While homosexuals' public avowal of their preferences ("coming out of the closets") may be viewed as a significant social change, there is little evidence that the *amount* of homosexuality has increased along with its *visibility*. Studies show pretty consistently that the predominance of homosexual experience occurs during the experimental stage of adolescent sex; that only about 10 percent of boys and 5 percent of girls have such experiences during adolescence; that a significant proportion of homosexual activities take place among those who are predominantly heterosexual and who are in single-sex institutions such as boarding schools, prisons, or military establishments; and that the overall figures for those who are homosexual by choice during a significant part of their adult life shows no appreciable change.

A modest case can be made that changing views in the United States toward homosexuality constitute a revolutionary change; the case is stronger when limited specifically to female homosexuality or lesbianism. We can assume that female homosexuality is no newer than male homosexuality. Perhaps its increased visibility is largely a matter of increasing public recognition. The association of female homosexuality with the issue of women's rights, however, may increase the revolutionary character, the appeal, and the extent of such activity, for it can be seen as both emotionally satisfying *and* politically correct. Thus the number of female homosexuals may increase because of increased positive support for such activities. One woman cited by Hite argues,

> I am currently thinking of lesbianism as an alternative to abstinence, and to men in general, because they are not very liberated sexually or emotionally or any other way, and I can't stand it any more (1976, p. 415).

Although data here are particularly sparse, the change that is taking place may go beyond mere greater visibility.

Our conclusion, from a historical and sociological perspective, is that changes in sexual practices and attitudes in the United States have generally been slow and emergent rather than revolutionary. The major change we see is in *public attitudes toward sexuality.* There seems to be a decrease in absolutist stances and an increase in public awareness of sexuality. The trend toward more open and explicit discussion has led many people to believe that there has been an enormous increase in both the quantity and variety of sexual behavior, yet research evidence indicates a surprising consistency in sexual activities over time.

We should not, however, minimize the importance of this trend in public discussion. Activity that was formerly private or locally restricted has now entered public awareness and become part of the knowledge of a multitude of people. This knowledge provides people with alternatives that they had not seen before. One can see an alternative without choosing it, but the availability of alternatives does make choice possible. Also, however, it may make choice necessary where formerly it was not. Virgins, for example, may now need to *justify* their stance, whereas in the past mere *assertion* of that stance was viewed as sufficient. Change may both increase and decrease choice.*

While we do not see a sexual revolution, we do see continuing change in both sexual behavior and sexual attitudes.

Two "Typical" Examples of Sexual Deviance: Prostitution and Pornography

Prostitution and pornography can be called "typical" examples of sexual deviance in that both are publicly labeled as deviant in the United States and in many other societies as well, both are illegal in the United

---

* We thank Nora Lerdau for bringing this point to our attention.

States, and both have been widely studied by social scientists as sexual deviance. In the two case studies below we will consider the many explanations that have been offered for these phenomena and the criticisms of such explanations from the new perspective. We will see the ways in which earlier scientific explanations depended on the Western sexual values we have just been considering. Both activities, it has now become clear, are far more complex and problematic than was previously assumed.

A CASE STUDY OF PROSTITUTION

At first it might seem that prostitution is easy to identify. The term's most common meaning in everyday life is *any sexual act where the recompense is neither sexual nor affectional.* Such a definition *assumes* that "normal" sex is engaged in for sexual or affectional rewards or pleasures somehow intrinsic to the act itself. Any other motives, therefore, entail sexual deviance or prostitution.

This view embodies a very limited idea of "normal" sex and a very broad idea of prostitution, whereby all of the following could be called prostitutes:

Men or women who engage in a single act of sex for a specified amount of money.

Men or women who engage in a single act of sex for nonmonetary rewards, either gifts or other considerations.

Men or women who engage in a single act of sex as payment for goods or services such as a night out on the town.

Spouses who engage in sex acts as a part of their obligations as spouses.

Spouses who engage in sex acts in return for economic support.

In common usage, however, the term prostitute is applied in a much narrower sense to women who sell sexual favors to men and receive monetary rewards for the acts themselves. Far less frequently, the term is applied to males who sell sexual favors to homosexual males (see Reiss, 1961). Seldom is the term applied to males engaged in heterosexual activities or to males or females engaging in marital sex.

Since people who "use" sex to get material advantages other than direct money payment customarily hide that fact from others and even at times from themselves, it becomes difficult to assess motives and thus to decide who the prostitutes "really" are. Working in the new perspective, Rasmussen (1979) has argued that a broad spectrum of patterned activities could be considered as *sex for nonsex reasons.* Since being a "prostitute" is seen as shameful by many people in the United

States and in many other societies as well, a great deal of creativity may go into concealing both from others and from oneself the nonsex motives for engaging in sexual activities.

Even what seems more clearly and obviously prostitution — the direct selling of sexual acts for money — involves a complex and wide range of roles and activities, from "sidewalk hostesses" who walk the streets to "stables" of girls under the control of a pimp to employees of "whore houses" to upper-class call girls, from bar girls and waitresses who supplement their salaries with the cooperation of their employers to prostitutes who sit behind picture-windows in small storefront houses and look appealingly at passersby, from host and hostess services to "whore ranches" along the highways of Nevada, to gay prostitution in nude baths, and so on. While monetary rewards may be of primary importance in these activities, sexual and affectional rewards may also be sought and found. Masseuses have reported being at times sexually aroused, even at times to orgasm, by customers, though some masseuses also reported that they tried to avoid *appearing* aroused (Rasmussen and Kuhn, 1976).

It is sociologically difficult to identify prostitution, yet such identifications are routinely made in everyday life by those who are concerned with prostitution — either as an evil or as a desirable service. In some form or other prostitution has been recognized throughout history and all over the world. The somewhat scanty historical data even suggest that prostitution in big cities has not varied greatly in frequency over time. There have been alternating phases of repression and toleration of prostitution, but the major effect has been not on frequency but on visibility.

Official Christian morality has always opposed prostitution, but in practice big-city prostitution was rather open and tolerated in Christian societies until the sixteenth century, when venereal disease became a major public problem. At that time public authorities began denouncing prostitution and took stern measures to eliminate it. Success was limited except in England and a few other societies, where it was largely eliminated from public view though it continued to thrive under cover. By the nineteenth century official enforcement of rules against prostitution had become lax even in England and the United States, and nations such as France had rather wide-open houses of prostitution in major cities.

Later in the nineteenth century, Victorian England and the United States launched campaigns to suppress prostitution and other moral "evils." Industrialization, mass education, and the growing size of the middle class seem to have been associated with increased repression of deviance in general and of sexual deviance in particular. The very Protestant ethic that supported industrialization also supported a Puritanical morality (Weber, 1905); these views, typical of the middle class, came to have more and more social effect as the size of the middle class increased. We offer this Level III explanation for the suppression of prostitution, based on the social structural variables of class and ideology, as a hypothesis only, not as an accepted theory. Whatever the explanation, prostitution in urban areas did shift from a public to a secret activity thereby moving away from official control and becoming associated with other underground activities.

Waves of repression and toleration of prostitution continued during the twentieth century. In urban areas today the trend seems to be toward toleration, and prostitution is becoming increasingly visible. There are even some strong movements to legalize prostitution. Nonetheless, sex for direct money payment remains illegal in the United States, and every now and then local enforcement officials try to ride a moral wave into political office by launching a "clean-up campaign" against prostitution.

Traditional studies of prostitution have focused on men's approaches to female prostitutes for sexual favors in exchange for money. Since researchers began collecting survey data on prostitution there has been no major change in the proportion of men reporting the use of prostitutes' services. Kinsey (1948) found that approximately 69 percent of men interviewed reported going to prostitutes at some time in life; the figure varies little today. Today, however, we have more data about types of customers and their reasons for going to prostitutes. Traditional social science explanations saw men going to prostitutes because they could find no alternative release for their sex drives. This *pressure-release theory,* a Level VI explanation drawing on individual psychology, is a modified form of classical Freudian theory. It conceives of sexual energy as a fixed feature of human biology that demands some form of release. It further assumes that women seldom encounter this problem, presumably because they possess less sexual energy. This theory led researchers to expect that prostitutes' clients would be mainly young men, the unmarried, those who were married but separated from their wives by military or other activities, and others who for some reason such as deformity were excluded from marriage. Current research indicates that most customers are middle-aged and married. There seem to be no major class distinctions — workers in overalls, middle-class bankers in pinstriped suits, and international entrepreneurs seem to have equal recourse to the many forms of sex for money. The pressure-release theory does not seem to account for the facts, since men who presumably do have alternative means of release (wives) or who experience lessened pressure (owing to age) nonetheless seek the services of prostitutes.

A second explanation for the existence of prostitution has been developed by Kingsley Davis (1939) and falls at Level II, focusing on social structure and function. Davis argues that the family is the basic unit of society, serving the multiple functions of socializing and controlling children, providing cooperative economic activity, and providing sexual gratification. Not all families, he argues, in fact fulfill the functions assigned to them; not all marriages are, for example, sexually satisfying. When a marriage fails to fulfill this latter function, Davis sees two alternatives: (1) the marriage can be dissolved and another established or (2) sexual gratification can be sought outside marriage. The first alternative requires the breakup of a family; the second does not. Davis concludes that prostitution serves the social function of providing an alternative form of sexual gratification, thereby allowing marriages to continue and the social structure to remain stable.

By looking at some criticisms of Davis's theory, we can see both its weaknesses and the factors that need to be taken into account in any explanation of prostitution. Four major criticisms are:

1. *Divorce rates.* Divorce rates have been slowly rising in the United States for about a century, while there is no evidence that rates of use of prostitutes' services have declined. Higher divorce rates and lower rates of use of prostitutes' services would support Davis's theory. Although many factors are involved in divorce, and thus evidence does not refute Davis's theory, the relation between prostitution and divorce remains unestablished.

2. *Causes of divorce.* Extramarital sex is one of the most common direct causes of divorce. While not all extramarital sex involves prostitutes, visits to prostitutes by married men are certainly a form of extramarital sex. Rather than resolving marital tensions, extramarital sex seems to indicate a deteriorating marriage. Rasmussen (1979) sees extramarital relations as a crucial "end-game" *cause* of divorce rather than as a salvation of the marriage.

3. *Women's sexual gratification.* Davis's theory, and many early explanations of prostitution, do not consider the issue of women's sexual gratification. Women are customarily seen either as having more moderate sexual impulses than men or as being more easily satisfied. Nonetheless, the evidence indicates that women often find marriages sexually unsatisfying. In most studies since Kinsey, in fact, almost half of women respondents report that intercourse does not normally give them orgasmic release. Yet women almost never have recourse to male prostitutes, and they report far fewer homosexual or masturbatory acts and a lower incidence of extramarital relations. Women seem to have learned to live without sexual gratification in ways that men presum-

ably have not. Davis fails to explain why males seek sexual gratification outside marriage far more often than females. He maximizes the importance of sexual gratification for males while minimizing it for females, drawing on common-sense ideas that embody a double standard, one standard for men and another for women. Sociologists certainly must take such common-sense views into account, but they need to move beyond them if they are to develop theories that will account for *all* the data.

4. *Prostitutes' services.* Rasmussen and Kuhn (1976) and Rasmussen (1979) have concluded from their studies that the majority of prostitutional sex is not intercourse. Though popular accounts of prostitution such as Xaviera Hollander's *The Happy Hooker* (1972) overplay the amount of "kinky" sex demanded by customers, evidence suggests that the majority of prostitutional acts consist of oral sex, and other forms of nonintercourse sex are frequent. A frequent reason given by clients to prostitutes for their preferences is that their wives won't do such things and they desire them and thus purchase them. The desire here is not for general release of sexual pressure but for specific kinds of alternative sex practices. Rasmussen has concluded that customers are motivated by a general desire and search for *greater* sexual pleasure, not for simple release from pressure. Some of this greater pleasure comes from sex with a new partner and some comes from the very fact that sex with prostitutes is socially forbidden. Davis saw sexually frustrated men seeking prostitutes to give them release; Rasmussen sees men who may even be regularly and routinely satisfied increasing their sexual desire by contemplating the forbidden act of sex with prostitutes and then proceeding to satisfy that sexual desire.

Although we cannot accept Davis's theory, examination of it has sensitized us to the many and varied elements that need to be considered in explaining prostitution. Much research is flawed by a narrow conception of prostitution, uncritically adopted from common-sense thought, which restricts it to sex for money and focuses on women's providing sexual services to men. If we view prostitution more broadly as engaging in sexual activities for nonsex reasons, we are able to study a far broader range of activities, to make comparisons, and to see both similarities and differences. Whether or not we choose to call this broader range of activities prostitution, we are able to recognize the varied motives and activities involved in sexual behavior. Such an approach is characteristic of the new perspective.

Even studies of prostitution in its more narrowly defined sense can give more attention to prostitutes' experiences and perspectives. Jackman, O'Toole, and Geis's article, "The Self-Image of the Prostitute" (1963, in Gagnon and Simon, 1967), considers the value systems of prostitutes in themselves and in relation to the value system of the broader society. The authors of this modest study offer a tentative conclusion:

> Personality factors, early socialization, childhood sexual experiences, and adult marital relations are insufficient explanations of recruitment to prostitution. The selection of prostitution as an occupation from available alternatives must be sought in the individual prostitute's interaction with others over a considerable time span (p. 146).

Bryan's study of "Apprenticeships in Prostitution" (1965, reprinted in Gagnon and Simon, 1967), illustrates the application of the new perspective to the study of prostitution. Although Bryan uses the narrower definition of prostitution, he explicitly renounces the Freudian theory that pervades study of this topic in favor of an interactionist perspective that emphasizes *becoming* deviant. Bryan views prostitution as an occupation and considers the processes involved in selecting and joining the profession. He sees apprenticeship as important for developing a clientele rather than for "learning the trade," and he suggests that apprenticeship is called for by the secrecy rather than the complexity of the work. Nowhere in his article does Bryan speak of prostitution as right or wrong, good or bad, evil or blessing, but rather he sustains value neutrality in his consideration of the *work* of prostitutes.

As the new perspective continues to guide research studies, we can anticipate more detailed studies of the activities involved in prostitution, consideration of a broader range of relevant activities, and studies of those who make and enforce rules and laws that restrict such activities. Such studies promise to increase our understanding both of prostitution and of deviance in general as well as of the workings of the social world.

A CASE STUDY OF PORNOGRAPHY

The most basic common-sense definition of pornography is *any sexually arousing written, pictorial, or otherwise representational material.* Studies of pornography thus far have focused almost entirely on pornography itself and those who use it, giving little attention to those who produce, finance, pose for, or in other ways contribute to its creation. Future studies may find it fruitful to consider the latter as sexual deviants.

Defining pornography has been difficult both for researchers and for public officials. Legal conflicts over the nature of pornography have been extensive and highly emotional, yielding a whole literature on that subject alone. (See, for example, the discussion of the law and pornography by the Commission on Obscenity and Pornography, 1970A.) Over many years United States courts have given clear and distinct definitions of pornography, only to find that they lead to unintended consequences, such as the legal suppression of various art forms, or that they are readily subverted by those who want to produce pornography. The Commission on Obscenity and Pornography despaired of defining pornography in any clear, unproblematic way and opted to consider all erotic materials (erotica):

> In the absence of well-defined and generally acceptable definitions of both obscenity and pornography, the Commission conceptualized the relevant stimuli as erotic materials, sexual materials, or sexually explicit stimuli over a range of media (photographs, snapshots, cassettes, files, and written materials in books, magazines and typewritten stories) which are capable of being described in terms of the sexual themes portrayed: e.g., "a man and woman having sexual intercourse," or "mouth-sex organ contact between man and woman" (1970A: 181).

An important issue arises from various attempts to define pornography: those who see pornography as sexual deviance and as evil seem to be arguing that people ought not to be sexually aroused by "material" but only by people, and in particular by one's spouse. Further, they argue that the public availability of pornography sexually arouses those who do not want to be aroused but cannot help themselves. To a lesser extent they are also concerned with those who want to be aroused; the latter are generally judged to be "abnormal" or "sick."

Others, however, identify a number of types of sexually arousing material. Pornography, as one type, is designed specifically for arousal and eliminates all material not directly related to such a goal. Other, nonpornographic, types include works that have artistic value or "redeeming social value"; in such works sexual arousal is viewed as a byproduct rather than a primary goal of the material. Such observers may regard pornography as sexual deviance while seeing other types of material as both nonpornographic and nondeviant.

Still others identify as pornography materials that are sexually arousing *and* "degrading" to the participants. Of particular concern here has been the use of women in pornography. For the most part women are the "raw material," not the audience, of pornography. Whether the sexual activity portrayed is between males and females, males and males, or females and females, the audience addressed is almost exclusively male. Female subjects of pornographic materials serve primarily as objects for male sexual arousal.

Ultimately the term pornography is used in a negative way. Rather than arguing that pornography is good, people are more likely to argue that specific material is not pornographic. This evaluative dimension contributes to the problem of establishing a useful definition. We might here tentatively define pornography as *sexually arousing material that is*

judged wrong, recognizing that the same material may be judged pornographic by some and not pornographic by others.

The use of sexually arousing materials has not been widely studied.
Its use, however, appears to be situational, either to enhance sexual
enjoyment or as a substitute when alternatives are unavailable. An important element in its use is the *satiation effect,* the lessened arousal that
results from continued exposure to the same stimuli. Behind the satiation effect is what psychologists call the *adaptation level effect:* the human
nervous system adapts to a given level of perceptual stimulation so that
in time that level of stimulation causes less and less arousal. To get back
to the earlier, higher level of stimulation, the stimulus itself must be
greatly increased.

The satiation effect is well known by the successful producers of
pornography. They know that to keep their audience as well as to
increase it, they have to move to ever more extreme degrees of exposure, explicitness, and so on. People who work in the pornography
industry show the ultimate in the satiation effect because they are oriented toward sexual acts day in and day out for many hours a day.
Before long the sex acts themselves do not arouse them sexually and
they may come to focus more heavily on the romantic aspects of sex.
Rene Bond and Winston Hill found a good example of the satiation
effect in their interview with a young woman "stag movie" star:

> *Is there any stimulation provided by being in front of the camera, or from having all
> these people around — I mean an exhibitionist thing?*
>
> Oh, for some people there is. But that kind of thing gets old very quick. I
> mean big deal, it makes no difference.
>
> *How many different guys have you worked with? A lot?*
>
> I would say so. Not an awful lot. There really aren't that many different
> guys. A guy will only last in the business three or four months.
>
> *Why is that?*
>
> Well, see, when a guy first gets into the business, the idea of making love
> to a number of different girls is exciting to him, he really digs it. But after he's
> been in the business a while, making love to just any girl — well, pretty soon
> she's got to start being a really nice person. She's got to be good looking —
> he's got to like her. I mean there's got to be something else besides just that
> she's a new chick. Because they don't get turned on. They just can't do it.
> (Bond and Hill, 1974, p. 69.)

The problematic and changing contents and social meanings of pornography have produced tremendous difficulties for the law and for
law enforcement in the United States. Courts tried until the 1970s to
solve the problem by defining "pornography" as any material that is
sexually arousing in a harmful way or, even more commonly, sexually
arousing but "without redeeming social value." Had the pornography

industry remained static, it might have been legislated out of existence. The industry, however, responded to court decisions by reworking pornography so that it met the letter if not the spirit of the new laws. Thus sexually arousing material would be put into the context of "socially redeeming" material. Many of the most obviously pornographic films use as settings clinics or doctors' offices, present lectures or "medical information," and in other ways portray what could legally be called "socially redeeming material," though viewers know that they are seeing "dirty movies."

In general the United States has moved toward greater explicitness in the portraying of sex and sexuality. During World War II, pin-ups such as Betty Grable were viewed as erotic if not pornographic; the sexual excitement was derived from exposure of the legs and from certain suggestive posings of a halter-and-shorts clad model. Pre-*Playboy* nudes were hardly nude at all. Until the late 1960s, nudes in "men's magazines" were *airbrush nudes*, nudes whose pubic hair had been airbrushed from the photographs. Now such magazines are both more explicit and more readily available.

The explicitness with which sex and sexuality are portrayed has changed to various degrees throughout the nation. The South has changed very slowly, except in isolated places such as New Orleans. California, though not Orange County, changed very rapidly and became the "porn capital of the United States," a title angrily disputed by habitués of Times Square in New York City. State courts have adopted a policy of allowing pornography to be defined by local areas in terms of their own standards. The problem of definition is not thereby solved but is simply shifted to local officials, since local areas have many of the same conflicts and changing standards as states. Some local courts have resorted to questionnaire survey studies of local moral standards. They hope to learn whether community members favor leniency or whether they feel that pornography should be removed from the community and those involved forced out of business, sent to prison, or otherwise punished. This method has its limits. As one gay New Yorker told Douglas:

> One morning this cop knocked at my door — complete with uniform and gun. He was doing a survey of local moral standards. He started asking me questions about whether I was offended by the gay bar just down the street. Well, needless to say, I felt I'd damned well better be offended or this guy might get suspicious of me.

Identifying local standards is difficult, and in many cases uniform standards may not exist. If there is variability on the local level, on the federal level it is virtually impossible to establish criteria for moral standards and for pornography in particular.

While prostitution and pornography are both deviant phenomena in terms of Western sexual morality, they are of quite different types. Prostitution involves sexual activities that are condemned by some, approved of by others, and engaged in by those who may either condemn or support the activities they engage in. Pornography involves sexual activities that are far more ambiguous in terms of both what "ought to be" and what "is." In subsequent chapters we will see deviance of both types. Deviance of the first type can perhaps be explained in terms of higher-level theories, because it is a part of the established social structure and can be considered in terms of social structural variables, but deviance of the second type seems to require more specific levels of explanation. Official attempts to define pornography on the local level demonstrate the specific nature of this second type of deviance.

In the next section we look more closely at sexual deviance in terms of the new perspective. Researchers who adopt this perspective ask different kinds of questions and may choose much broader topics in order to encompass all the data.

Sexual Deviance in the New Perspective

In this section we use the new perspective to consider phenomena closely related to sexual deviance; initially their relevance may not be apparent. Our first example is of eroticism and sexual pleasures in both their nondeviant and deviant forms. We draw particularly on existentialism and its concern with the *feelings* that underlie human behavior. Our second example explores the ways in which deviance is "created" by those who identify and respond to it. Here we draw heavily on labeling theory. These two examples will illustrate how the new perspective might "make sense out of" sexual deviance.

EROTICISM, SEXUAL PLEASURES, AND SEXUAL DEVIANCE

The new perspective recognizes the reality of continuity between nondeviance and deviance, so that any consideration of the one must include the other. In this section and the next we will consider eroticism and sexual pleasures in both their nondeviant and deviant forms and then consider how particular activities come to be put in one category or the other.

Those who study sexual behavior have been struck by the extremely matter-of-fact approach that nonhuman animals take to sexuality. Even our closest primate relatives, the chimpanzees, who seem to enjoy many of the same kinds of sexual pleasures that humans do and demonstrate excited anticipation of sexual activity, engage in sexual behavior with notable casualness. (See Goodall, 1967 and 1971, esp. pp. 91–92, for illuminating accounts of chimpanzee sexuality.)

In no known human society are sexual relations conducted with the casualness that other animals display. Except in isolated instances human sexual behavior is preceded by thought and engaged in privately. Nonetheless, societies vary considerably in the seriousness with which they engage in sexual activity, the degree of pleasure they experience, and the specific sources of sexual pleasure they recognize. If we are to maintain value neutrality and not be *ethnocentric* (applying our own societal standards to the rest of the world), then we must recognize that human beings are capable of a wide range of sexual pleasures, many of which seem to be foregone because of societal restrictions rather than personal inclination. *Social* rather than *biological* or *natural* rules seem to be a major source of the distinction between deviant and nondeviant sexuality.

We consider here the broad range of sexual pleasures found among humans, and in particular *eroticism* (sexual arousal). We will examine the sources of such arousal and the social rules that define what is and is not sexually pleasurable. We will become aware of the dilemma faced by those who are sexually aroused by what their society or social group says should not be arousing.

Societies vary greatly both in what they identify as erotic and in their evaluation of erotic feelings as good or bad. All societies attempt to limit both erotic stimulation and the acts it leads to. Violations constitute sexual deviance from the viewpoint of those who hold to those limitations.

In the United States the nude body, especially the genitalia and mammary glands, has long been viewed as erotic, and the many rules governing public nudity are directed toward its perceived erotic possibilities. In societies where nudity, partial or total, is common, the nude body is not viewed as particularly erotic. A respondent from tribal Africa told Waksler:

> I can't understand U.S. males' preoccupation with breasts as sexually exciting. Females in my society never cover their breasts and males are not sexually aroused by the sight of breasts. We find the sex act sexually arousing.

The eroticism of the nude body seems to depend on the body's being generally hidden in all but sexual situations.

What is viewed as erotic is not what is customarily and readily available, for, as we saw earlier, the satiation effect comes into play, weakening eroticism. Since what is forbidden is not likely to be readily available, it may keep its erotic potential. What is forbidden *because it is sexually arousing* is particularly likely to be viewed and responded to as erotic. Acts and objects that some societies see as both harmless and nonerotic may be viewed as both dangerous and highly erotic in societies that so define them and forbid them. John Messenger's study, "Sex and Repression in an Irish Folk Community" (in Marshall and Suggs, 1971), provides a number of examples:

> Nudity and physiological evacuation are considered sexual in Inis Beag. Nudity is abhorred by the islanders. . . . Only infants have their entire bodies sponged once a week, on Saturday night; children, adolescents, and adults, on the same night, wash only their faces, necks, lower arms, hands, lower legs, and feet. . . .
>
> Despite the fact that Inis Beag men spend much of their time at sea in their canoes, as far as we could determine none of them can swim. . . . They have never dared to bare their bodies in order to learn the skill. Some women claim to have "bathed" at the back of the island during the heat of summer, but this means wading in small pools with skirts held knee-high, in complete privacy. Even the nudity of household pets can arouse anxiety. . . . In some homes, dogs are whipped for licking their genitals. . . .

In Inis Beag the very act of undressing is viewed as highly sexual. If this attitude strikes one as extreme, it may be helpful to remember that the sensuality of stripteasers involves the simple act of undressing. Such public undressing is sexually arousing because it is uncommon and forbidden. Stripteasers are not in great demand at nudist camps or nude beaches.

Outsiders expect that "everyone" at a nudist camp or beach will be wildly excited by nude bodies; that in fact is true primarily of newcomers. Male newcomers sometimes "give themselves away" by getting erections in front of thousands of people. Most people, however, soon "cool down." In an effort to minimize eroticism, conventional nudists generally prohibit adornments of the nude body or partial concealments that would "excite" interest (see Weinberg in Douglas, 1970A).

Examples can be readily offered of the erotic effect of both concealment and unavailability. In past centuries women in Western societies wore long skirts that concealed their legs and even ankles; female legs and ankles were considered extremely erotic objects. A woman could throw a man into a state of frenzied arousal by revealing a delicate ankle or a dimpled knee. Flirtation — whether carried out by "making eyes," "teasing," "being suggestive," or some other method — involves promising something beyond what is said or done. The process may entail eye motions, facial expressions, body movement, or other body language and may be enhanced by clothing style. Both the promise and the likelihood of fulfillment may be ambiguous. The promise may even be denied, leaving the other without either satisfaction or release. Flirtation, by nature, involves the promise of what is concealed and apparently unavailable.

We have been discussing objects and acts that are socially acceptable or understandable as sources of pleasure and that indeed are forbidden *because of* their perceived erotic possibilities. One learns simultaneously that such an object or act is *both* forbidden *and* desirable. We shall now consider acts and objects which are viewed as nonerotic or nonsexual and which may be forbidden or may not even be recognized as sources of pleasure. Those who respond sexually to such acts and objects make up a somewhat different category of sexual deviants, those who take pleasure from what is viewed as an inappropriate or unimaginable source.

DEVIANT EROTICISM AND DEVIANT SEXUAL PLEASURES

Although in Western society the nude body is considered erotic, its appeal is regarded as largely restricted to someone of the opposite sex and within a certain age range. These restrictions apply even in pornography, where scenes of women making love are designed to be sexually arousing to men but not to women. The love of older men for young boys, extolled by Plato, is currently viewed in Western society as a perversion of what is "natural." Even in the heterosexual sphere, it is expected that a certain age range sets limits to sexual desire. The male who remarked to Waksler about a girl's desirability, "She's too old; she's got breasts already," was expressing a preference clearly deviant by United States standards.

Those whose eroticism and sexual pleasures are derived from pain are also deviants by United States standards today. *Sadism,* deriving sexual pleasure from the pain of others, and *masochism,* deriving sexual pleasure from pain to oneself, are eloquently depicted in the works of de Sade, from whom the term sadism derives, and more recently in Pauline Reage's *Story of O.* One of the common "kinky" customers of prostitutes is the man who wants to whip or be whipped. Sadism and masochism may not be popular forms of sexual orientation in the United States, but S&M bars do exist; whips, chains, and other paraphernalia can be purchased in stores or through mail-order catalogues; and explicit ads for partners appear in newspapers and magazines, as illustrated in Figure 6.1.

The activities we have considered so far involve the bodies of other persons. *Fetishism,* by contrast, refers to sexual pleasures derived from objects. Some such objects seem obviously associated with sex, such as underwear; others, such as shoes, seem less directly related. That fetishism is "abnormal" or "sick" is implied by psychological references to it as *displacement* or as the use of *symbolic equivalents.* The assumption is that neither underwear nor shoes could provide any *inherent* sexual pleasure, so that they must be used as a substitute for something else. Fetishism may indeed occur when other alternatives for sexual expression are not available. Adolescent males are known to use lingerie as an

Figure 6.1
Advertisements for sadistic and masochistic partners. W means white; M, male; F, female; Cpls, couples; B, bndg, bndge, bondage; D, Dom, dominant, dominance; Mstrses, mistresses; B, black; G, gay; Lovrs, lovers; Slm, slim; Exper, experienced; end, endowed; bi, bisexual. The newspaper in which the ads appeared is widely read by college students.

Source: Reprinted with permission from *The Boston Phoenix.*

exciting symbol of women's sexuality, but once they have access to women they commonly choose to engage in sexual relations. There do appear to be some people, however, for whom the fetish is the sex object of choice. A shoe fetishism that served both as a substitute and as a sexual pleasure was described in a news note in *Parade* magazine (September 9, 1979):

> For the past 3½ years, Japanese police in Yokohama have received reports of a shoe thief. Recently a 19-year-old coed saw a man making off with her new $50 boots.
> Later that evening, she noticed him lurking near her apartment house and notified the police. They arrested the man, a 42-year-old unemployed worker from Kanagawa, searched his room and found 127 pairs of women's shoes, including the latest models.
> Explained the thief, "I have neither the courage nor the money to marry. Looking at women's shoes and engaging in fantasy, that's all I have in life."*

According to Norman Cameron (1963), women's shoes are the most common male fetish.

Many other sources of eroticism and sexual pleasure violate rules for what "ought" to provide such arousal and pleasure. These deviant pleasures may be derived from simple observation of the sexual acts of others *(voyeurism)*, anal intercourse *(sodomy)*, sexual relations between a

---

* Reprinted with permission of the author, Lloyd Shearer, *Parade Magazine,* September 9, 1979.

man and a boy *(pederasty)*, sexual relations with animals *(bestiality)*, sexual relations with the dead *(necrophilia)*, exposing one's genitals in public *(exhibitionism)*, and presumably from other activities for which names are not readily available. Of particular sociological significance in the existence of such deviant sexual pleasures is not only their violation of social rules for behavior but their *violation of rules about feelings, namely about what one finds pleasurable.* There seems to be public agreement that such activities *cannot be pleasurable* and that those who claim to find such pleasure are deluding themselves and are mistaken. The new perspective makes no such assertions, taking seriously the statements of participants themselves that they indeed take pleasure in such acts. Although self-deception can occur, it must be documented carefully, for the claim that *I* understand and *you* are deceiving yourself undermines value neutrality. In the absence of concrete evidence of self-deception, theorists in the new perspective take seriously participants' definitions of situations.

In this section we have looked at data in the area of eroticism and sexual pleasures and have suggested the kinds of issues that arise when such phenomena are considered from the new perspective. In the next section our concerns will be more theoretical, demonstrating the relation between deviant sexual behavior and the process of officially "creating" such behavior. We will look at varied ways in which sexual deviance has been "explained" by earlier theories and then at the insights that emerge from the new perspective.

SOCIAL RULES, STIGMATIZATION, AND SEXUAL REPRESSION

A wide range of explanations have been offered for sexual deviance. Theories based on the nature of the physical organism, the process of psychological development, and the needs of society have been particularly popular. Theorists have asked: *Why* do people engage in deviant sexual acts? The new perspective leads to a different set of questions, redirecting our search for explanation. The question of *why* people engage in deviant sexual acts *assumes* that such acts are wrong and in need of explanation. The new perspective makes no such assumption; instead, it poses such questions as the following:

Why are certain kinds of sexual behavior defined as deviant?

Why are certain kinds of sexual behavior socially controlled?

Why is it viewed as important to control the sexual activities *engaged in by other people?*

Why do some people feel that they should use police or other powers to repress other people's sexual activities?

The question of *why* people engage in deviant sexual acts directs us to the individual; the questions listed above direct us to the social world, and in particular to the activities of those who create and enforce rules relating to sexual behavior.

In considering the issue of sexual repression, the new perspective is particularly concerned with the ways in which official rules come about, the reasons given for the creation and enforcement of such rules, the ways in which rules are applied, and the stigmatization process that takes place when individuals are labeled "sexually deviant." Since the new perspective has not been applied extensively to the study of sexual deviance, we will not be able to provide definitive answers to the questions above. We will, however, suggest the lines along which future research might proceed in providing empirical answers.

We begin by looking at traditional explanations of sexual deviance. It is clear that for the most part they do not address the kinds of questions that emerge from the new perspective.

TRADITIONAL EXPLANATIONS OF SEXUAL DEVIANCE

Judeo-Christian absolutism. The traditional, absolutist, Judeo-Christian explanation of sexual deviance, embodied in early social science explanations, was based on the belief that the sole function of sexuality was reproduction and its sole place was within marriage. Any other use of it was both unnatural (dirty, perverted, abnormal) and immoral (naughty, wrong, bad, evil). The unnaturalness and immorality of nonreproductive nonmarital sexuality was simply *assumed*. This type of explanation, invoking as it does the nature of the physical organism, falls at Level I.

This traditional explanation overlooks the problems of definition we have been considering in this chapter. It also assumes the existence of shared and common values and ignores the possibility that those who engage in "forbidden" acts may have different values. This tradition is still embodied in psychological explanations that focus on "curing" sexual deviance and in sociological explanations that consider sexual deviance "harmful" to society. Its main feature is that questions such as those above and derived from the new perspective are nonproblematic; all four can be answered in the same way: because those sexual activities are wrong and unnatural.

Freudian guilt theory. A second type of explanation, the *guilt theory* based on Freud's ideas, provides a more detailed explanation for *why* certain people seek to control the activities of others. A Level VI psychological theory, it maintains that those who have learned to feel guilt over their own deviant impulses will seek to repress the expression of those impulses by others. If, for instance, people learn that pornography is wrong and, even though tempted, they repress their desires to enjoy it, then they will be at least as harsh toward others' interest in and use of pornography as they have been toward themselves. This analysis has made its way into common-sense explanations, and it is often argued, for example, that those who are most antihomosexual are those who have most strongly repressed their own homosexual desires. As we will see, there are various reasons for seeking to control the acts of others, and while guilt may be one reason, it is certainly not the only one. A more serious problem is that guilt theory in no way explains why some acts come to be viewed as deviant in the first place; guilt theory retains its ties to an absolutist theory of perversion (unnaturalness).

Freudian sublimation theory.   A fuller type of explanation of sexual deviance, this one at Level II, is based on the ideas Freud developed in one of his last works, *Civilization and Its Discontents* (1930). This *civilized sublimation theory* maintains that sexual energy exists in all individuals in limited amounts; the more it is dispersed in direct sexual activities, the less is available to do the work that societies require. Freud saw creative work, science, art, and a variety of other social and cultural activities as "fueled" by repressed sexuality. Freud theorized that societies that do not repress sex in all forms other than those directly related to reproduction become corrupt and uncreative, doomed to decline and eventually disappear, to be replaced by more creative and sexually repressed societies.

This theory has contemporary adherents. Bruno Bettleheim, for example, has stated:

> If a society does not taboo sex, children will grow up in relative sex freedom. But so far history has shown that such a society cannot create culture or civilization; it remains primitive (Commission, 1970, p. 625).

This theory, intuitively sensible as it may seem and compatible with common sense, is not supported by empirical evidence. Given its pervasiveness, we will here offer some observations that refute it:

1. Athens in the fifth century B.C., one of the most creative societies in the history of the world, was not subject to severe sexual repression, and the least repressed of Athenians, the aristocrats and well-to-do freemen, were the very people who produced that flowering of economic, scientific, humanistic, and artistic creativity for which Athens became known.

2. Imperial Rome (31 B.C. to 476 A.D.) is quite often presented as a highly unrepressed *and* uncreative society, at least in Greek terms, lending seeming support to Freud's theory. But the Romans had never been very creative in science, the humanities, or the arts; they were certainly more creative in those ways in the Imperial Age than they had been at earlier times; and Roman creativity was always focused on the practical

arts of war and law. Although this example does not refute Freud's theory, it certainly does not support it.

3. Women, highly repressed in many societies, have not been recognized in those societies as the most highly creative. Rather, the less repressed men have been acclaimed as the creators of much that is important in the arts and sciences of civilizations. While increasing numbers of women are being "rediscovered" in history as artists, scientists, and contributors to creativity, Freud's theory would lead us to look for them in the forefront, where we definitely do not find them.

4. Creators often are deviants. Many of the most creative Western artists and writers through history have been far more sexually deviant, in word or deed or both, than other members of their societies. The bawdiness of Chaucer and Shakespeare, or of Joyce and Miller, did not prevent their being far greater writers than John Wesley, the famous Methodist.

The evidence, then, does not support the idea that sexual repression leads to greater creativity. Short of the obvious fact that those who spend all their time debauching are not apt to get anything else done, there seems to be little positive connection between repression and creativity.

Social victimage theory. As the shortcomings of absolutist and of psychological theories have been recognized, an explanation of sexual deviance based on the idea of social harm or *social victimage* has been developed. This Level II explanation is based on the assumption that certain forms of sexual deviance harm society by encouraging behavior that threatens its members. This explanation deals specifically with types of sexual activities termed *victimless crimes,* such as pornography (a solitary activity) or prostitution or adult homosexuality (activities that involve consenting adults). Who, the critic inquires, is being harmed by such activities? Social victimage theory replies that these activities harm society indirectly by leading those involved to other acts that directly harm others. Thus it is argued that reading pornography may lead aroused readers to rape or that homosexual activities may lead to the seduction of heterosexuals and even children.

While the social science position on the application of the social victimage theory to pornography is to reject it, the theory remains popular enough in common-sense terms to influence official laws and practices. The popularity of the theory in the face of such strong evidence against it suggests that those who hold it do so for reasons other than truth; it may be used to justify repressive practices that are engaged in for other motives.

The social victimage theory may also be extended to argue that people repress those activities by which they themselves or others close to them may be victimized. Women do not want to be raped, children do not want to be molested, heterosexuals do not want to be seduced by homosexuals, celibates do not want to be sexually aroused. While there is certainly some truth to this idea, it is interesting that in many instances those who make and enforce the laws are *not* those who are potential victims. Only recently have women become involved in preventing rape; children do not march against molesters; and celibates often withdraw from the political arena. Furthermore, many of those involved in rule-making and rule-enforcing seek being victimized by going to pornographic films or bookstores, by being available to homosexual advances and irately rejecting them, and by seeking out in other ways that which "ought to be" unavailable. This sort of activity cannot be explained by the idea of victimization; further explanation of another sort seems called for.

EXPLANATIONS OF SEXUAL DEVIANCE
FROM THE NEW PERSPECTIVE

A full explanation of sexual deviance has not yet emerged from the new perspective. Here we will indicate some lines along which research might proceed. Although we recommend this approach, we also recognize that its value cannot be firmly established until more extensive empirical evidence has been collected.

The new perspective recognizes, without adopting any of them, a wide variety of common-sense explanations for the repression of sexual deviance. Its aim is to understand why such sexual repression takes place at particular times and places, how the processes work, and what the consequences are. Common-sense ideas are used as data, not as explanation. Thus the new perspective is concerned not only with sexual deviants but with those who create and enforce rules that limit the sexual activities of others. Earlier explanations focused on the sexual deviants themselves.

As we have said, one vital way in which the new perspective differs from other approaches is in the *kinds* of questions it asks and the *kinds* of activities about which it is concerned. Gagnon and Simon, in their book *Sexual Deviance* (1967), provide some useful examples of the application of the new perspective to such deviance. Rather than focusing on the *differences* between deviants and nondeviants, they state: "We feel that the most extreme deviant still shares more in common with the rest of humanity than he holds as unique attributes" (p. vii). Further, "Given the right circumstances, we are all potential deviants" (p. vii). Drawing heavily on labeling theory, they recognize that such an approach requires attention to many issues that have been overlooked in the past: "It requires going beyond merely describing and categorizing behavior to the task of tracing out the complex processes of societal definition, the emergence of the deviant self-conception by a so-labeled actor, and the contingency-laden career that follows the labeling experience" (pp. 2–3).

Simon and Gagnon themselves have done a modest study, "The Lesbians: A Preliminary Overview" (in Gagnon and Simon, 1967), in which they draw on labeling theory and suggest the kinds of analysis made possible by such an approach. They discuss the simplifying process that goes on when labeling takes place, and they caution sociologists against engaging in such simplification themselves, as when one talks about "*the* homosexual" or "*the* lesbian" rather than recognizing the variety of forms such activities may take. They also devote considerable attention to the nonsexual activities of those labeled "lesbian," such as family interactions, earning a living, making friends, and constructing a sense of self. As is characteristic of the new perspective, their study recognizes the complexity of social behavior in both its deviant and nondeviant forms.

Howard Becker's study of the creation of laws against marijuana (1963), although not concerned with the issue of *sexual* deviance, can be used as a useful model for the study of rules directed toward sexual activities, and it is likely to be used in just such a way as studies are conducted within the framework of the new perspective. Becker directed his attention to those who create rules (whom he identifies as *moral crusaders*), the reasons that they give and that can be inferred from their activities, those who enforce the rules (whom he terms *moral enforcers*), and the multiple reasons that underlie their actions. These factors can be applied to a wide variety of kinds of deviance, and they hold particular promise for our understanding of sexual deviance and of social responses to it.

For example, Becker's approach allows us to see that moral crusaders and moral enforcers may act on the basis of *belief* in any of the traditional explanations presented above, using such explanations as ideological support for their activities, while at the same time we as sociologists can recognize the practical and situational factors involved. The social response to prostitution in the United States displays a pattern of repression followed by tolerance followed by repression and so on, explicable less in terms of ideological changes than of situational exigencies. Reckless (1961) has described this pattern as a *lid-on, lid-off theory of social responses to prostitution* (see also Rasmussen, 1979). This cyclical activity cannot be explained by any of the traditional theories proposed earlier. Rasmussen, however, has found that the repression phase of the cycle generally comes just before and during political campaigns; after the elections, tolerance of such activities increases. While politicians as a category may indeed favor sexual repression, it does seem that this commitment fades after election day.

Tolerance or repression of sexual activities appears to be *a social act,* directed toward activities that are not *by nature* but by *definition* immoral or unnatural. Descriptive studies of those called sexual deviants have indicated that what some call immoral others see as moral and that what some view as unnatural others engage in quite "naturally." Changes occur over time as well: homosexuality in the United States is less "immoral" and more "natural" today than it was 50 years ago, and premarital sex may be engaged in casually and with little sense of evil by more people than in the past.

Given the heterogeneity of United States society, it is not surprising to find diversity in beliefs about sexual activities. What is surprising is the force with which some people seek others' support for their views. In addition to the political reasons for such activity, we will suggest here an idea that emerges from symbolic interactionism and labeling theory: the breaking of any social rule is a threat to that rule, for it demonstrates to everyone that breaking it is at least *possible*. Even the severest punishment cannot prevent people from realizing that such rule-breaking is possible. We discussed this idea earlier when we noted that learning that others masturbate, even if one views it as wrong, moves the act from the idiosyncratic to the shared realm and thus to the realm of the possible. Moral enforcers seek to eliminate the rule-breaking of others because it challenges the very rule itself.

Although the new perspective has not yet produced a great deal of specific analysis of sexual deviance as a social phenomenon, descriptive studies and the perspective itself lead to the following ideas:

1. Human beings are capable of a vast array of sexual activities.
2. Out of the range of possible sexual activities, all societies encourage some and discourage others. The kinds of rules established range from those of celibate groups such as monks and nuns, which forbid even sexual reproduction, to those of permissive and libertine groups. Even the latter groups set some restrictions.
3. There are various reasons why sexual activities of certain types are restricted. The reasons that group members offer may conceal other purposes. There may be important nonsexual reasons for such restrictions, such as political or social reasons.
4. An understanding of sexual deviance requires knowledge of both rule-breakers and rule-makers.

The new perspective has been limited in its study of sexual deviance by the problems in the scientific study of sex mentioned at the beginning of this chapter. The present climate in the United States makes such studies somewhat more feasible, and we expect more research in this area. We expect continued study of "sexual deviants" themselves, particularly as they see themselves, and an extension of serious attention to the labelers, the rule-makers and enforcers, and to the social implications of existing rules. Without minimizing the moral commitments of those who make and enforce rules, we anticipate that other reasons will be found for their actions, reasons that suggest benefits they personally derive by making and enforcing rules *for others*. We expect the power dimension to be particularly important, for rule-making and rule-enforcing are acts of those who have power. Ultimately, however, we do not know what we will find until we conduct the studies; what we present here, though based on current knowledge, remains speculative.

7

Drugs

As a way of life, a social problem, an individual choice, and a source of personal destruction, drug use has long been a topic of discussion and debate in the United States. Although public concern has ebbed somewhat, perhaps owing to overexposure and the resulting satiation effect, the issues surrounding drug use and abstinence remain important in the sociology of deviance. The subject has been studied in some detail from a variety of perspectives, and data and analyses are abundant.

In this chapter we will refer to earlier studies but our primary focus will be on the insights offered by the new perspective and, in particular, by labeling theory and phenomenological sociology, which have made major contributions to our understanding of this topic. The issues we will consider — the problematic meanings associated with drugs and drug use, the labeling of drugs and drug users, the experience of drug use, and the process of becoming deviant — are all characteristic of the concerns and approaches of the new perspective.

Problematic Meanings and Social Conflicts over Drugs

Although it has existed since ancient times, there is little doubt that drug use, both legal and illegal, has been growing rapidly in much of the world, both East and West. As a consequence, many new problems have arisen in the creation and enforcement of social rules concerning this practice. The subject is the source of much controversy and neither professionals nor the general public seem to be able to agree on which kinds of drug use are deviant and which are not. What is feared and despised by part of the population may be trusted and commended by another part. What is defined today as criminal drug use may have been accepted in the past and may be encouraged in the future. In fact, as Erich Goode writes, the very word "drug" is so emotionally freighted in the United States today that any discussion of drugs is likely to involve implicit moral judgments calling for major political commitments (Goode, in Blumberg, 1974: 166).

Conflicts over the moral meanings, effects, characteristics, and uses of drugs crosscut most social groups and social categories* in the United States. Within any subculture we may find some who approve of the use of heroin or other opiates, some who share the broader societal disapproval, and some who disapprove most strongly. For example, while heroin use is high in some lower-class black communities, many residents strongly disapprove of it, perhaps in direct response to the threat posed by heroin's greater availability. Even among drug users, some drugs are frowned upon. Troy Duster's (1970) study of heroin users (in Douglas, 1970A) showed that those who preferred heroin for its euphoric effects and, when it was unavailable, used barbiturates or "barbs" to stave off withdrawal symptoms nonetheless stigmatized the latter drugs, calling them "goofballs." In the following discussion of drugs keep in mind that opinions and views on drug use vary widely.

DEFINING DRUGS

Although the dictionary lists a number of definitions for "drug," we will initially define it here as *a substance other than food intended to affect the structure or function of the (mind) or body*. We have selected this definition as a starting point because, unlike such definitions as "a substance intended for use in the diagnosis, cure, mitigation, treatment, or prevention of disease" or "a substance that causes addiction or habituation," it is nonevaluative.† It is not, however, always easy to determine whether a substance is "other than food" — that is, to distinguish food from drugs. Are vitamin pills food or drug? What about alcohol? Although we will continue with the definition offered above, we recognize its limitations. A further distinction will, however, prove useful in our consideration of deviant drug use: that between *psychoactive* and

---

* A *social group* is a social unit involving interaction among members and with the potential for being identified as a group by members and nonmembers. A *social category* is an abstract unit based on the possession of one or more common characteristics. A party and a church are both social groups; all twenty-one-year-olds or all left-handed people are social categories.

† Definitions by permission from *Webster's New Collegiate Dictionary* © 1980 by G. & C. Merriam Co., publishers of the Merriam-Webster Dictionaries.

nonpsychoactive drugs. *Psychoactive drugs* are drugs that directly alter the states of the central nervous system, especially those which alter conscious experiences of cognition and perception (hallucinogens) or emotion (mood-altering drugs). Figures 7.1 and 7.2 describe some major psychoactive drugs. Most drugs are nonpsychoactive or have minimal effects on the central nervous system. Societal rules and laws primarily control the use of *psychoactive* drugs; the use of *nonpsychoactive* drugs is less likely to be considered deviant.

Psychoactive drugs have aroused much social and moral controversy and are the focus of most social science research on drugs. We have little systematic knowledge about social rules for nonpsychoactive drugs because very few studies have been made of them. We should recognize, however, that the vast majority of drugs being used medically and sold over the counter (without prescription) in the United States today are nonpsychoactive by medical definition. Some of these drugs may actually have some psychoactivity for some people but without evidence we can only speculate.

Members of the medical profession disagree over how to determine and enforce social rules for nonpsychoactive drugs. For example, some medical experts argue that antibiotics are overused — that is, used to the point where they become harmful to the body. They claim that bacteria develop strains resistant to the antibiotics and that antibiotics kill off large numbers of bacteria that the body needs to work well and be healthy. If they are widely used for minor ailments, they become less useful against major problems. These experts argue that social rules ought to control the use of these drugs.

Social scientists, medical researchers, and the general public agree on the need for more knowledge of nonpsychoactive drugs. As rules governing their use are created, rule-breaking and thus deviance will become possible. Current concerns about deviance, however, focus mainly on psychoactive drugs, with which we will be concerned in the remainder of this chapter.

EFFECTS OF PSYCHOACTIVE DRUGS AND DRUG USE

If the definition of drugs is problematic, the nature of the effects of psychoactive drugs is even more so, for biological, psychological, and social factors are entwined in ways that are difficult to identify and separate. The problematic nature of psychoactive drugs contributes to the social controversies over drugs that rage in our societies today. Drugs such as strychnine or potassium cyanide that have obviously fatal effects are not generally subject to social controversies. Drugs in general, however, and the psychoactive drugs in particular, are characteristically somewhat problematic in their effects.

Drugs have different effects on different individuals. Some people

Figure 7.1
Major psychoactive drugs: their uses

Drug type current users[a]	Most common trade name	Legal status[b]	Prescriptions per year[c]	Medical use	Street names
Narcotics (522,000 users)	Codeine	II	744,000	Analgesic, cough suppressant	Schoolboy
	Demerol	II			Demies
	Dilaudid	II			Little D
	Heroin	I		Analgesic	Smack, junk, downtown
	Methadone	II			Meth, dollies
	Morphine	II			M. Miss Emma, morph
	Opium	II	1,601,000	Paregoric	Blue velvet, black stuff
	Percodan	II		Analgesic	Perkies
Related analgesics	Darvon	IV	34,000,000	Reputed painkiller	None
	Talwin	IV			Ts
Barbiturates and related sedatives (1,060,000 users)	Amytal	II	375,000		Blues, downers
	Nembutal	II	1,702,000		Yellow jackets, yellows
	Phenobarbital	IV	7,910,000		Phennies, purple hearts
	Seconal	II	1,507,000		Reds, F-40s
	Tuinal	II	1,173,000		Rainbows
	Doriden	III	2,195,000	Sedation, relief from tension, anesthetic	D
	Noludar	III	1,324,000		Downers
	Placidyl	IV	1,878,000		Dyls
	Quaalude, Sopor, Parest, Optimil, Somnafac	II	1,352,000		Ludes, 714s, Qs, sopors
Minor tranquilizers (1,360,000 users)	Dalmane	II	12,795,000	Relief of anxiety, muscle tension and the symptoms of alcohol withdrawal	Tranks, downs
	Equanil/Miltown	IV	9,751,000		
	Librium	IV	15,340,000		
	Serax	IV	3,525,000		
	Valium	IV	57,084,000		
Alcohol (92,300,000 users)	Beer, wine, spirits	None		Nighttime sedation, to improve appetite and digestion; pain-killer, to relieve anxiety	Various trade names

Category (users)	Generic/chemical name	Class[b]	Figures	Medical use	Slang names
Major tranquilizers	Mellaril	None	7,187,000	Control psychotic episodes reduce hallucinations	None
	Thorazine	None	4,749,000		
Inhalants (375,000 users)	Amyl nitrite	None		Smooth muscle relaxant, controls heart spasms by lowering blood pressure	Poppers Locker Room, Rush
	Butyl nitrite	None			
Amphetamines and related stimulants (1,780,000 users)	Nitrous oxide	None		Anesthetic	Laughing gas
	Benzedrine	II			Bennies black beauties
	Biphetamine	II	5,5000,000	Weight control (no longer recommended), to combat fatigue, depression, narcolepsy and hyperactivity in children	Copilots
	Desoxyn	II			Dex, speed
	Dexedrine	II			Meth, crank
	Methedrine	II			
	Preludin	II			Uppers
	Ritalin	II			
Cocaine (1,640,000 users)	Cocaine hydrochloride	II		Local anesthetic for eye surgery. Used with narcotics to treat intractible pain	Coke, snow, uptown, toot
Caffeine (unknown)	Caffeine	None	(16 pounds per person per year)	Headache pain (in combination with analgesics)	Coffee, tea, cola, chocolate, No-Doz
Nicotine (64,570,000 users)	Nicotine	None		No medical use	Various trade names
Cannabis (16,210,000 users)	Hashish	I		Under study for treatment of glaucoma, asthma, side effects of cancer medication	Kif, herb, Honey
	Hash oil	I			Grass, ganja
	Marijuana	I			
Hallucinogens (1,140,000 users)	LSD	I		No current use	Acid
	MDA	I			The love drug
	Mescaline	I			Cactus
	Peyote	I			Buttons
	Psilocybin	I			Magic mushrooms
Related (6,000,000 users)	Ketamine hydrochloride	None		Anesthetic	Green
	PCP phencylidine	II		None for humans	Angel dust, krystal; DOA (dead on arrival)

[a] Source: National Institute of Drug Abuse. Figures represent current users in 30-day period, except for PCP, which is total, past and present.

[b] Federal penalties for trafficking: Classes I, II (15 years/$25,000), III (5 years/$15,000) and IV (3 years/$10,000).

[c] Source: National Prescription Audit via NIDA. In most cases, figures represent total number of prescriptions and refills from May 1976 to April 1977.

Source: Reprinted by permission from Playboy (September 1978).

Figure 7.2
Major psychoactive drugs: their effects

Short-term effects of average dose

Codeine, Demerol, Dilaudid, Heroin, Methadone, Morphine, Opium, Percodan:
Masks pain by creating mental clouding, drowsiness, and, in some patients,
mild to extreme euphoria. In contrast, some users experience nausea,
vomiting, an itching sensation. Methadone similar to other opiates but lasts
24–36 hours (compared with 2–4).

Darvon, Talwin: Talwin produces anxiety and hallucinations.

Amytal, Nembutal, Phenobarbital, Seconal, Tuinal: Relaxation, sleep; used
recreationally, the drugs are "like alcohol without the calories," producing
mild intoxication, loss of inhibition (sexiness or aggressiveness), decreased
alertness, and muscle coordination.

Quaalude, Sopor, Parest, optimil, Somnafac: Similar to barbiturates, except users
claim to feel euphoria without drowsiness. Reputed aphrodisiac.

Dalmane, Equanil/Miltown, Librium, Serax, Valium: Mild sedative effect produces
sense of well-being, ability to cope. May cause headaches and in rare cases an
increase in anxiety and hostile behavior.

Beer, wine, spirits: Relaxation, euphoria, loss of inhibition, increase in
confidence, talkativeness, mood swings, decreased alertness, and motor
coordination.

Mellaril, Thorazine: Heavy sedation, relief from anxiety, disorientation, an
unpleasant trancelike stupor.

Amyl nitrite, Butyl nitrite: Relaxation, euphoria, rapid heartbeat, dizziness,
headache. Users claim that it heightens orgasm.

Nitrous oxide: Giddiness, intoxication, drowsiness.

Benzedrine, Biphetamine, Desoxyn, Dexedrine, Methedrine, Preludin, Ritalin:
Decrease in appetite, Dramatic increase in alertness and confidence, mood
elevation. Improved physical performance and concentration, lessened sense
of fatigue. Feeling of anxiousness, or "being wired."

Cocaine: Similar to amphetamines but subjective reports claim the drug is
smoother, more intensely felt. This may be due to route of administration,
more rapid onset of drug, and shorter duration of effects.

Caffeine: Wakefulness, enhanced mental capacity, increase in heartbeat and
reaction time, ability.

Nicotine: Relaxation, mild stimulation, increase in heartbeat.

Cannabis: Relaxation, euphoria, altered perception, fascination with visual and
auditory phenomena, laughter.

LSD, MDA, Mescaline, Peyote, Psilocybin: Users compare altered state of perception to religious, mystical experience. Rapid, drastic mood changes possible. With the exception of MDA, the hallucinogens usually produce visual and sensory distortion. MDA is reputed to be an aphrodisiac.

Ketamine hydrochloride, PCP phencyclidine: Varies from pleasant, dreamlike state to confusion, paranoia, sense of dying, losing touch with your body, psychotic states, assaultive behavior.

Short-term effects of large amount

Codeine, Demerol, Dilaudid, Heroin, Methadone, Morphine, Opium, Percodan: Effects of lower dosage are exaggerated; greater insensitivity to pain, increased sedation, nodding (a dreamlike state of relaxation, with total awareness and the appearance of sleep) or, paradoxically, a drive state of clarity and energy. Toxic overdose produces unconsciousness, slow and shallow breathing, cold and clammy skin, weak and rapid pulse. When mixed with any other depressant, may cause death.

Darvon, Talwin: Darvon has relatively low lethal dose.

Amytal, Nembutal, Phenobarbital, Seconal, Tuinal: All effects of lower dosage will be exaggerated, plus slurred speech, shallow and slow respiration, cold and clammy skin, weak and rapid heartbeat, hangover. Unconsciousness may move beyond sleep to coma and death.

Doriden, Noludar, Placidyl: Longer acting than most barbiturates; consequently, the effect of an overdose is difficult to reverse. Often fatal.

Quaalude, Sopor, Parest, Optimil, Somnafac; Similar to barbiturates, except users may exhibit restlessness and excitement — rather than sedation — prior to convulsions.

Dalmane, Equanil/Miltown, Librium, Serax, Valium: Similar to barbiturates but considered less toxic: drowsiness, blurred vision, dizziness, slurred speech, stupor.

Alcohol: Effects of lower dosage are exaggerated; nausea, double vision, vertigo, staggering and unpredictable emotional changes (some people get hostile, some friendly), stupor, unconsciousness, severe hangover, rarely terminal.

Mellaril, Thorazine: Anxiety, rigidity of muscles, confusion, convulsions, possible respiratory arrest, and heart failure.

Amyl nitrite; Butyl nitrite: Severe headaches, nausea, fainting, stupor.

Nitrous oxide: Unconsciousness from oxygen deprivation, hallucinations.

Benzedrine, Biphetamine, Desoxyn, Dexedrine, Methedrine, Preludin, Ritalin: Profound overstimulation, acute paranoia, agitation, insomnia, fear, irritability, sharp rise in blood pressure, fever, chest pain, headache, chills, stomach distress. Death from overdose is very rare.

Cocaine: Similar to amphetamine reaction; however, initial rapid pulse may become slow and weak, rapid breathing may become shallow and slow. Possible convulsions, acute stomach pain, circulatory failure, and respiratory collapse; death from overdose is rare.

Caffeine: Stomach disorders, restlessness, insomnia, irritability, heart palpitations.

Nicotine: Headache, loss of appetite, nausea. Effects vary, depending on tolerance.

Cannabis: Confusion of time sense, inability to carry out mental tasks, sense of strangeness and unreality about self and surroundings, fear of dying, anxiety, panic, unwelcome introspection, hallucinations.

LSD, MDA, Mescaline, Peyote, Psilocybin: May exaggerate effects of low doses, increasing duration and intensity of trip. Possible panic, nausea, tremors, vomiting.

Ketamine hydrochloride, PCP phencyclidine: Exaggeration of the effects of smaller doses, plus sweating, flushing, drooling, visual distortions, muscle rigidity, and rarely seizures, coma, and death in combination with other drugs.

Long-term effects of chronic use or abuse, withdrawal symptoms, if any

---

Codeine, Demerol, Dilaudid, Heroin, Methadone, Morphine, Opium, Percodan: Physical addiction (users take drug to avoid the discomfort of withdrawal sickness), lethargy, weight loss, inhibition of ejaculation and erection, loss of sexual interest. Withdrawal symptoms: restlessness, irritability, tremors, loss of appetite, panic, chills, sweating, cramps, watery eyes, runny nose, nausea, vomiting, muscle spasms.

Darvon, Talwin: Similar to narcotics, including withdrawal.

Amytal, Nembutal, Phenobarbital, Seconal, Tuinal: Excessive sleepiness, confusion, irritability, severe withdrawal sickness. Warning: While tolerance to sedative effect increases, tolerance to lethal dose does not increase. A user may increase dosage to fatal level while attempting to regain previous high. Withdrawal symptoms: anxiety, insomnia, tremors, delirium, convulsions, and infrequently death.

Doriden, Noludar, Placidyl: Similar to barbiturates.

Quaalude, Sopor, Parest, Optimil, Somnafac: Similar to barbiturates; however, while people who use barbs may substitute Ludes for the "down," Lude freaks seldom use barbs.

Dalmane, Equanil/Miltown, Librium, Serax, Valium: Impairment of sexual function. Withdrawal symptoms indistinguishable from barbiturates. May appear one to two weeks after use stops (due to slow elimination of drug from body).

Alcohol: Light to moderate drinking does not have a serious effect on longevity. Chronic heavy use may cause malnutrition, impotence, ulcers, brain and liver damage, delirium. Withdrawal symptoms similar to barbiturate withdrawal.

Mellaril, Thorazine: Slowing of movement, rigidity, and painful muscle contractions. May cause dyskinesia (permanent disabling of motor coordination).

Amyl nitrite, Butyl nitrite: No known long-term effects, no withdrawal.

Nitrous oxide: Possible damage to bone marrow after 12 hours' continuous use.

Benzedrine, Biphetamine, Desoxyn, Dexedrine, Methedrine, Preludin, Ritalin: Tolerance develops rapidly. Psychological dependence and preoccupation with drug is usual. User may suffer from paranoia, auditory, visual, and tactile hallucinations (the feeling of bugs crawling under skin). Withdrawal symptoms include fatigue, hunger, crashing (long periods of sleep), disorientation, severe depression.

Cocaine: Economic disaster. Extensive long-term snorting may damage nasal tissue (can be minimized by rinsing with water or salt water). Prolonged use has been reported to cause effects similar to amphetamine abuse — particularly paranoia and hallucination (coke bugs).

Caffeine: Stomach disorders, increased chance of heart attack. Withdrawal may produce mild anxiety, drowsiness, headache.

Nicotine: Has been linked to cancer, lung damage, heart and respiratory disease. Withdrawal: nervousness, increase in appetite, sleep disturbances, anxiety.

Cannabis: Much ado about nothing: Long-term use of very heavy doses reported to cause impairment of concentration, memory, alertness, and the ability to perform complicated tasks. Contradictory studies abound.

LSD, MDA, Mescaline, Peyote, Psilocybin: Slight withdrawal: irritability, restlessness, insomnia. There is no medical consensus that the hallucinogens have any long-term effect. Many users report lower energy level day after use.

Ketamine hydrochloride, PCP phencyclidine: Some evidence of memory loss, inability to concentrate, insomnia, chronic or recurrent psychosis. Withdrawal may produce short- to long-term depression.

Source: Reprinted by permission from Playboy (September 1978).

can with minimal effects drink amounts of alcohol that will leave others sick and without control of their actions. Laws that punish people for having specific blood alcohol levels* are thus inherently subject to social

* Blood alcohol levels are usually expressed as grams of alcohol per liter of blood. Drunkenness is commonly described quantitatively as 1 gram of alcohol per liter of blood.

conflict and may punish some who have greater control over their behavior than do others who go unpunished. Similarly, alcohol or other
drugs may make some people aggressive and others affable. These complex individual variations are found with most drugs, which is why
doctors encounter so many unexpected adverse drug reactions. Browse
through the *Physicians' Desk Reference (PDR),* an annual compilation of
information on drug products, to see the wide variety of potential drug
reactions. The variability of drug reactions poses an interesting problem
in the sociology of deviance: is it taking drugs that is viewed as deviant
or is it the effects of those drugs? If certain drugs are stigmatized because they make people lose self-control, why are they stigmatized even
for those upon whom they do not have that effect? This problem is
concealed by the common-sense assumption that any drug has the same
effect on everyone; abandoning that assumption discloses the problematic nature of the existing rules.

Our knowledge of the effects of drugs is limited by the incomplete-
ness of our biological knowledge. The body is an extremely complex
system that is in no way fully understood scientifically. Changing one
part of this system commonly changes many other parts whose intricate
interrelations are only partially understood. Introduction of any drug
produces a variety of effects, only some of which are currently known.
Common-sense knowledge about drugs is constructed on an assumption of far more knowledge in the scientific world than scientists would
admit to.

Knowledge of drug effects is also complicated by lag effects, adaptive
effects, the placebo effect, and drug interactions. The *lag effect* refers to
the time between drug use and drug effect. Especially if this interval is
long, behavior may not be recognized as an effect. *Adaptive effects* refer
to the ways in which the body adapts to a drug taken over time, thus
curtailing or otherwise modifying the drug's effects. This process is
often noted in the addictive drugs, where one's *tolerance level* is raised.
The body slowly adjusts its operations to keep them normal at a given
level of the drug. Any increase or decrease in dosage in terms of the
tolerance level will produce noticeable effects; dosage at the tolerance
level will not. The *placebo effect* refers to the body's ability to produce
effects even in the absence of the "cause." Those who smoke oregano
thinking it is marijuana often display the same effects as those who are
indeed smoking marijuana. Oregano, the *placebo* or substance chemi-
cally incapable of causing the evident effects, is, however, capable of
producing its effects *when one thinks it is marijuana.* This placebo effect
provides an important element in the symbolic interactionist theory to
be described below that views marijuana smoking as socially learned
behavior.

A final complicating factor is *drug interactions.* Doctors only recently have come to see that taking drugs together may significantly change the effects of each drug. Much drug use involves use of more than one drug at a time (polydrug use). Some common drugs such as alcohol can *potentiate* or increase the power of other common drugs such as barbiturates. Many have died from modest amounts of alcohol and barbiturates *taken together;* the interaction of the drugs multiplies the depressant effect of each. Some drug addicts find this property of potentiation very useful. A commonly used combination of psychoactive drugs is a small amount of an amphetamine (an upper or stimulant) with a small amount of heroin or methadone (depressants) to produce a multiplication of the depressant high associated with heroin. This combination, known as BAM, is much cheaper than straight heroin and produces similar effects.

If drugs produced the same effect in everyone, social conflict over drug use would revolve around whether or not that effect ought to be produced in that way. The multiplicity of effects muddies the social issue, for the stigmatizing of any one drug may be the stigmatizing of a whole variety of effects, some of which might be even judged positively by those doing the stigmatizing. Against this background it is not surprising to find the stigmatization of drug use a complicated and variable process.

The application of a significant amount of bias to the complicated question of drug effects can produce vast controversies. Stir in political movements and motivations, and vast social conflicts can result — as in fact they have in the United States concerning drugs.

Stigmatization of Drug Use

Erving Goffman, a symbolic interactionist theorist whom we discussed earlier (pp. 100–101 and 135–136), developed the concept of *stigma,* an attribute of individuals that is discrediting to those who possess it. A stigma makes an individual different from others and in some sense "less desirable." Stigmatization takes place when one is recognized as possessing a stigma. Goffman emphasizes that we all possess attributes that are potential stigmas but stigmatization emerges through the process of social interaction. Goffman's primary concern is with the stigmatized themselves — how they are distinguished and how their stigmas affect identity and interaction. (See Goffman, 1963B.) Our concern in this section is with attributes and the ways in which they come to be viewed as stigmas. How have certain kinds of drug use come to be stigmatized?

One of the remarkable facts about psychoactive drugs is that they were not highly stigmatized or even very controversial in the last century (see Lindesmith, 1965; Musto, 1973). Most people in the United

States today are so used to the idea of the opiates (opium-based narcotics) as "killer drugs" that they find it hard to believe that in the nineteenth and even early in the twentieth century opiates were widely used in common, nonprescription forms sold at the corner drugstore and advertised in family magazines. (See Figure 7.3.) Paregoric and laudanum were in frequent use for children's teething problems. Indian hemp (marijuana) seeds were a regular ingredient in birdseed, useful for making caged birds sing.

Before 1937 and the passage of the Marijuana Tax Act, drug regulation in the United States was slight, but since then both federal and state government agencies have imposed progressively sterner controls on drug use. The recent move in some states to decriminalize marijuana use by making it a misdemeanor rather than a felony has been overwhelmingly offset by increased regulation of the introduction of new drugs and increased control over many forms of tranquilizers, barbiturates, and other psychoactive drugs.

Although some other nations are very stern in government controls over specific drugs, few if any seek to control as many kinds of drugs as the United States does. In Mexico the government sometimes imposes severe penalties for certain forms of drug violation, such as cocaine dealing, largely as a response to political pressures imposed by the United States government, but such repression is most commonly directed against United States citizens. Use of drugs among Mexican citizens is less sternly limited, and fewer drugs are stigmatized.

The extensive efforts in the United States to regulate the use of psychoactive drugs, in marked opposition to the value placed on individual freedom, has intrigued many social scientists and led to a number of studies and theories. Social scientists are in general agreement that both the regulation and the use of drugs is governed by a number of major variables interacting over time. Though there is less agreement on what those variables are, most sociologists consider *definitional processes* to be of major importance: the way in which drugs are defined and characterized is a crucial factor in understanding both regulation and use.

Sociologists thus agree that in the United States there are social processes that work toward stigmatizing specific psychoactive drugs as *dangerous*. Stigmatizers seem to feel that such drugs pose a *threat*. This feeling of threat, often approaching dread, leads to stigmatizing drug users by calling them "drug fiends" or "dope fiends." In addition, some stigmatizers stand to gain by the stigmatization process. Government agencies, for example, may find that their budgets depend on the continued stigmatization of a drug. It is not always clear which comes first, perception of threat or creation of an agency that then creates its own "work." (This process has been studied by Becker, 1963.)

Although sociologists have some understanding of the process by which drugs come to be stigmatized, they have encountered far more

Figure 7.3
Legal opiates of grandmother's day

One of the largest markets for opiates in the country was the soothing syrup trade, aimed primarily at infants who were giving their parents a hard time by crying and carrying on, or who made the mistake of appearing sickly. This genre of medicines included preparations which were known as baby syrups, colic cures, infants' friends, teething concoctions and so forth. Parents were put at ease by labels which assured that the preparation "Contains nothing injurious to the youngest babe" and that "Mother need not fear giving this medicine to the youngest babe, as no bad effects come from the use of it." Laws were passed to prevent such claims appearing on preparations which did, in fact, contain addictive and toxic dosages of opiates, but then, as now, the laws were quickly circumvented by quick-thinking entrepreneurs. A representative list of products offered to distraught parents of uptight infants looks something like this:

Dr. James' Soothing Syrup Cordial — Heroin
Children's Comfort — Morphine Sulphate
Dr. Fahey's Pepsin Anodyne Compound — Morphine Sulphate
Dr. Fahrney's Teething Syrup — Morphine and Chloroform
Dr. Miller's Anodyne for Babies — Morphine Sulphate and Chloral Hydrate
Dr. Fowler's Strawberry and Peppermint Mixture — Morphine
Gadway's Elixir for Infants — Codeine
Dr. Grove's Anodyne for Infants — Morphine Sulphate
Kopp's Baby Friend — Morphine Sulphate
Dr. Moffett's Teething (Teething Compound) — Powdered Opium
Victor Infant Relief — Chloroform and Cannabis Indica
Hooper's Anodyne — The Infant's Friend — Morphine Sulphate
Mrs. Winslow's Soothing Syrup — Morphine Sulphate

Source: Bill Drake, *The Cultivator's Handbook of Marijuana*, 1st ed. (revised), pp. 26–27. Copyright © 1979. Reprinted by permission of the Wingbow Press. We would like to thank Ann Herrick for bringing this quotation to our attention.

difficulty in determining why *some* drugs and not others have been stigmatized. We turn to that problem now.

In fact, the effects of some drugs are so obviously negative that stigmatization is unnecessary. Control of the most highly destructive psychoactive drugs, those that "destroy the mind" or "drive one mad," is based simply on the general perception of them as dangerous. Although researchers have discovered great numbers of powerful drugs that have deadly effects, we seldom hear about them because no one is interested in using them.

The drugs that are more highly stigmatized are those whose effects are more ambiguous, so that they can be *defined* by some as negative and dangerous and by others as positive and pleasurable. The most stigmatized of all drugs is probably heroin; yet, if its effects were as "purely" debilitating or dangerous as its stigmatizers claim, few other than the suicidal would consider using it. Heroin is stigmatizable precisely because it has great attractions (euphoria) and merely possible, hence problematic, catastrophic consequences. The general public, those with no direct experience of heroin, perceive it negatively as having catastrophic effects. On the other hand, researchers who have studied heroin seem to support the claims of users themselves that none of the major effects of heroin are dangerous to life as long as the purity of the drug and its dosage are known and carefully controlled. Some side effects, such as constipation, drowsiness, and possible decrease in sexual desire, may be viewed as unpleasant, but studies of heroin addicts over many years show that the drug has no detectable organic effects that are dangerous. (Extensive evidence is reviewed in the National Commission on Marihuana and Drug Abuse, 1972.) Those who do research on heroin sometimes forget how negatively it is viewed by the general public and even by doctors themselves. One major heroin researcher told Douglas about a talk he gave to a medical group. He was as shocked at their response as they were at his proposal that heroin be legalized.

Many of the characteristics attributed to heroin users seem to result not from heroin use but from its illegality. Readers should recall the distinction we made in Chapter 5 (pp. 133–134) between primary and secondary characteristics of deviant activities. The secondary characteristics of heroin use derive from the impure quality of illegal street drugs, the difficulties of obtaining it, the money-saving devices used by both addicts and sellers, and other factors related to the drug's illegality. These factors may certainly have great consequences for users; such consequences are not related to the nature of the drug itself.

The view of the general public, in spite of research findings, remains negative. Fears remain that heroin is irresistible, that one use will lead to addiction, and that at least a life of misery and at worst death from an overdose will result. Those who hold such a view are those who passionately stigmatize the drug, its users, and especially its sellers. They both believe and perpetuate the "myth" of the drug pusher who hooks children, leading them into a life of misery and degradation. Medical research shows that drugs such as "street" barbiturates, those produced and sold illegally, are far more powerful than "street" heroin, far more addictive, and far more likely to be dangerous when used by those who are not knowledgeable about their characteristics. It is not commonly known, for example, that sudden withdrawal from high levels of barbiturates can produce *grand mal seizures,* violent spasms of the whole body, and almost instantaneous death. Withdrawal from street heroin is never fatal. Nonetheless, the medically more dangerous drugs, street barbiturates, are less stigmatized by the general public than heroin because *heroin is perceived, in common-sense knowledge, as more dangerous.* It is the perception of danger that has significance for stigmatization.

A recently stigmatized drug, formerly viewed as normal but now increasingly seen as a threat, is tobacco, particularly in the form of cigarettes. As the scientific finding that cigarettes are a major cause of heart disease and cancer has slowly spread to the general public, the move to stigmatize cigarette smoking and cigarette smokers has grown. More and more people are turning those looks of scorn, once restricted to "the evil" and "the perverts," upon formerly "innocent" smokers. The impact of this new stigma is particularly strong on those who are not yet smokers and thus do not have vested interests in the practice. College students in particular are not starting to smoke. Doctors and medical personnel are also increasingly becoming nonsmokers. Interestingly, it is doctors who most commonly know that opiates are safe when administered medically and they have a high rate of opiate use and addiction. Some estimates put doctor addiction rates in the United States at 1 percent or more; by contrast, the official number of addicts in the general population is about 250,000, which is only 0.1 percent of the population, one-tenth as many as for doctors.

Another reason that some and not other drugs come to be stigmatized is related to the characteristics of the users themselves. Lindesmith (1968), Duster (1970), and others have argued that the use of heroin, cocaine, and marijuana by deviant groups such as prostitutes, gamblers, mobsters, and jazz musicians was important in leading the general public to perceive such drugs as dangerous and evil because of their association with dangerous and evil groups. Stories about the drugs and stories about the stigmatized groups showed remarkable similarity.

Political processes are also major factors in the stigmatization and destigmatization of drugs in the United States. On the one hand, politicians may follow what they see as public opinion and legislate accordingly. On the other hand, there may be other political advantages to stigmatizing or not stigmatizing drugs, such as supporting or undercutting existing government or business agencies or policies. Coalitions of political or business interest groups may, for purposes quite unrelated to drugs, create or enforce drug laws. Gusfield (1967) and Timberlake (1963) have shown, however, that stigmatization is not effective when high percentages of the public have direct experience of a substance as nondangerous and as pleasurable. Criminalization of alcohol by the Prohibition Amendment to the Constitution, for example, did not succeed in publicly stigmatizing alcohol; rather it created a huge number of deviants — bathtub gin producers and speakeasy clientele. Politicians soon found it vote-worthy to destigmatize alcohol, and the Prohibition Amendment was reversed.

Governmental labeling of behavior may be a significant variable in the social stigmatization of drug use, but at other times it may have little effect, as in the case of alcohol. Lawmaking remains an important, though not the sole, factor in making once nondeviant behavior into deviant behavior and vice versa. In extreme social stigmatization such as that directed toward heroin use and some other forms of drug behavior in the twentieth century, official labeling certainly requires strong public support. Media and government labeling seem of particular importance when the general public has little direct experience with the drug being stigmatized.

Nature of United States Drug Laws

Protestantism in general and Puritanism in particular have indirectly nurtured United States drug laws. Religious groups frequently oppose, though with varying severity, the use of any drugs, including alcohol and tobacco. Drug use has been called un-Godly, the corruption of the flesh, and the work of the Devil. Although such direct prohibitions have certainly supported the United States stance on drugs, more significant for our understanding is the "Protestant ethic" so eloquently described by Max Weber (1905), which emphasizes hard work, seriousness, deferring of gratification, and planning for the future. Drugs are seen as a particular threat to the Protestant ethic in two ways. First, drug use may lead one away from the "virtues" and into playfulness, lethargy, a casual attitude toward work, the seeking of immediate gratification, and concern with the present rather than the future. Second, drug use is viewed as an inappropriate means, the assumption being that the individual ought to be able to achieve any such results by an effort of will, on one's own, and not with "artificial aids." Thus even if amphetamines ("speed") might make one work hard, they would still be devalued because hard work "ought" to come from personal effort. This set of beliefs has become an important part of United States culture; even with the waning of religious commitment such beliefs have retained their strength as "the American way."

Joseph Gusfield (1967) and others have sought the explanation for drug repression in religion, though focusing less on religious ideas and more on religious groups. They argue that for centuries middle-class Puritan society had repressed alcohol use. When Catholic immigrants, and particularly hard-drinking lower-class Irish, grew numerous in United States cities late in the nineteenth century, descendants of the Puritan tradition feared for the preservation of their own values. The Prohibition Movement grew out of the desire of Protestants to "clean up" the slums and repress the alcohol use taking place there (see Timberlake, 1963). These Irish–Catholic urban groups posed not only a value threat but also a political threat to Protestants, for their numbers and their political sophistication made it likely that they would gain political control over city politics. Protestant groups were successful in having the Prohibition Amendment accepted and also seem to have played a role in the passage of laws prohibiting nonmedical use of the opiates.

Although religious beliefs and conflicts clearly encouraged the repression of drug use in the United States, the most severe repressive measures have come more recently, during the period when Puritanism has waned. If religion has helped in establishing drug repression, what has caused its continuation?

First, the Protestant ethic, which opposes drug use, remains a feature of United States culture. Second, repressing certain groups and their activities has proved to be an effective way of gaining political control. Consider, for example, that those drugs used by the lower classes and by blacks are subject to greater repression and greater law enforcement than those drugs used by the middle and upper classes and by whites. Third, once drugs become illegal, sources for acquiring them become limited and direct experience with them is minimized. Public officials can thus disseminate their own views of the drugs when it suits their political purposes to control their use.

Why has it been politically advantageous to control drug use? The argument that officials have acted out of simple bureaucratic motives of self-aggrandizement has not generally held up under close examination. Officials seem to have been responding to larger, more powerful, and more pervasive social forces beyond their own personal motives. Let us consider some of these forces.

Political control of drugs is partly the result of concern over the effects of drugs on the work force — business and government officials view drug use as detrimental to the efficient operation of bureaucratic industrial society. There is, for example, a great deal of literature on occupational alcoholism, almost all of it financed by government and supported by business. Business executives generally believe that the use (on or off the job) of drugs such as heroin, other opiates, and cocaine would obstruct efficient business activity. It is not clear, however, whether they developed this belief through direct experience with workers on drugs or whether they simply drew on common knowledge. The strength of the assumption, however, is evident from the fact that little government-sponsored research has been done on ways of using drugs to heighten work efficiency.

Richard Brown (1978) has proposed another reason for the repression of drugs. He has tried to show that political figures and others with access to power have repressed *unregulated* forms of drug use so that regulated drug use can be taxed. Furthermore, if certain drugs are defined as illegal, legal alternatives can corner the market. One might, for example, expect self-interest to lead those involved in the legal business ot making and selling alcohol to support the continued illegality of marijuana. Clearly those involved in the repression of drugs are profiting by it psychologically or materially. We need further studies in order to discover the political and business advantages of such actions.

Drug laws in the United States were not all written at one time or with a single rationale. Rather, they have developed over the years in response to public opinion, political activities, business interests, and, to a far lesser extent, scientific knowledge. Some were originally adopted for reasons far different from those which keep them on the books today. In the study of drug use as social deviance, the biggest gap in sociological knowledge concerns why particular drugs came to be defined as they did. Because scientific statements on the harmlessness of drugs do not seem to fundamentally affect public views, we know that drug repression involves a wide variety of factors that seem to bear little relation to the nature of the drug itself.

Drug Use and Secret Deviance

We have been dealing with drug use that is publicly defined and recognized as deviant and have focused on psychoactive drugs that are illegal. In this section we will look at drug use in general and discuss some drugs that have not been singled out for labeling as deviant and some users who have not been labeled as deviants.

In our discussion of sexual deviance we saw that many of its forms are not new but have always existed; what is new, at least in the United States, is public recognition of such acts and controversy over whether or not they "ought" to be labeled deviant. For drugs and drug use, the picture is quite different. Increased medical use of drugs, increased production of new drugs, and increased street availability of psychoactive drugs all indicate that drugs and drug use are far more widespread and varied than ever before. Most of the increase has been of nonpsychoactive drugs; psychoactive drugs have not, however, been far behind, and these are the ones that involve the most intense social conflict over rules and thus the most potential for deviance.

The variety of available drugs has been greatly affected by the scientific-technological revolution. "Natural" drugs have always existed. Alcohol, tobacco, marijuana, the opiates, and cocaine are natural products of plants. Opiates are also produced by the human body itself as a counteractive to pain. The contribution of science and technology and of biochemistry in particular has been the production of synthetic drugs such as barbiturates and tranquilizers and their resultant availability in pill or capsule form. The consequence of the availability of synthetic drugs that is particularly significant for the sociology of deviance is the "normalizing" of the taking of psychoactive drugs. Normalization takes place in two ways. First, since taking pills is an accepted custom in the

United States, taking drugs for a "high" rather than for a therapeutic effect can be easily hidden both from self and others. The apparatus involved in taking heroin or cocaine "looks" deviant in a way that pill taking does not. Second, pills can be obtained through legal channels in a way that illegal drugs cannot. One can get high on pills left over from "legitimate" medical treatment; one is less likely to have leftover heroin or cocaine.

Many of those who take pills for their mood-altering effects do not think of what they are doing as drug use and addiction. Few other practices reveal so clearly the capacity of human beings to indulge with a clear conscience in self-delusion and "blindness to the obvious" (see Gustav Ichheiser, 1970). Indeed the contradictions in drug beliefs, rules, and actions are so pervasive and so extreme that one might argue for the existence of an *intentional social blindness*, a desire of members of society *not to see* certain activities. Anyone who studies drugs in the United States today is presented with an almost endless spectacle of mind-boggling contradictions. The most fervent moral opponents of "drug fiends," the most dedicated law-and-order types who want all "drug addicts" imprisoned for life and view them as "human vermin," are among the most frequent addicts of barbiturates, tranquilizers, or dozens of other soporific (sleep-inducing) drugs that produce "highs."

When Douglas and a team of field researchers began a study of drug crisis intervention for the National Commission on Marihuana and Drug Abuse (1972), they were in their own way "socially blind," unaware of the pervasiveness of drug use. They knew, of course, that alcohol use was widespread, but, like most people, they did not recognize the similarities between the immense and growing use of legally prescribed psychoactive drugs and the use of illegal street drugs. In fact, they had not thought initially of barbiturates, tranquilizers, and so on in terms of their mood-altering properties. Yet when one compares street addicts and users to prescription-drug addicts and users, remarkable similarities emerge. The main difference between the two lies in the possibility of prescription-drug users' *seeing themselves and others' seeing them* as nondeviant. Feelings and bodily states are very similar between the two categories; social definition, on the other hand, distinguishes sharply between the two.

Psychoactive drug use by prescription has been increasing over the past quarter century by approximately 7 to 8 percent per year. Recent research has shown that there are hundreds of thousands of *prescription addicts;* in all likelihood they outnumber illegal addicts. By the late 1970s some 300 million prescriptions for psychoactive drugs were being filled each year, though what proportion of this usage was primarily for medical reasons and what for mood alteration is not known. Almost two-thirds of these prescriptions go to women, an indication that women prefer this "respectable" medical form of "high" to alcohol, two-thirds of whose users are men. Prescription by doctors of psychoactive drugs for women also indicates that doctors view women as "in need" of such drugs, a view strongly contested by those who argue that a restructuring of sex roles is what is needed. In general young people use more stimulants such as the amphetamines; "bennies" (benzedrine) are popular among students studying for exams. Older people use more depressants.

There are a variety of ways for obtaining prescription drugs for use as mood alterers. The easiest is to receive them for a "legitimate" medical complaint and then continue their use once the complaint has passed. This is a common introduction to the mood-altering properties of drugs. Once the desire for such drugs is established, a number of methods are available for obtaining them. One can go from doctor to doctor, claiming the set of symptoms for which the drug is customarily prescribed. Thus diet pills are in much greater demand than the number of people dieting would lead one to expect. Some doctors are recognized by prescription-drug users as particularly open to such approaches, and such "pill doctors" are important sources of drugs. Drug nonusers who have obtained supplies for past ailments may be willing to part with their leftovers. There is also a black market for prescription drugs. No one knows what quantity of prescription psychoactive drugs is sold on the streets, but street sales of barbiturates are known to be huge. Most illegally sold prescription drugs are manufactured in the United States, shipped either legally or illegally to Mexico and other countries, sometimes in huge quantities, and then illegally transported back to the United States for street sale.

The greatest expansion has taken place in the use of legal, prescription, and over-the-counter drugs, but illegal drug use, both of illegally obtained prescription drugs (especially barbiturates, tranquilizers, and morphine) and of illegal drugs (marijuana, cocaine, and so on), has also increased greatly and rapidly. The use of illegal drugs seems to have been significantly less up until the early 1960s, being mainly restricted to certain ethnic groups (such as marijuana use by Mexican-Americans in the Southwest and heroin use by lower-class urban blacks) or to small subcultures (marijuana use among jazz musicians). In the 1960s there was a large increase in the use of illegal drugs by young people, especially by college students and affiliated street people. Marijuana was the best known and most widely used of the illegal drugs, though its use varied throughout the United States. In some areas of California and the Northeast it is claimed that over 50 percent of the young have used it while that figure drops to 10 percent or less in some areas of the South and Midwest. Frequency of use also varies, with a large proportion of users being experimental (even one-time users) or infrequent, weekender types. Use of the more powerful illegal drugs, notably LSD, peaked in the late 1960s and began to recede rather rapidly, more or less in direct proportion to the waning of campus protest movements. Marijuana use peaked a bit later and followed a slower decline. By the late 1970s cocaine was replacing marijuana among college students as the preferred euphoric, second only to alcohol, while other legal drugs, either legally or illegally obtained, such as amphetamines, remained more stable, presumably because they were used for the practical purpose of staying awake when exam catastrophes loomed. Marijuana and alcohol use seem to be inversely related among college students, increased use of the one being accompanied by lessened use of the other.

To some extent our perception of drug use as having markedly increased in the recent past may result from increased knowledge about drugs. Evidence strongly suggests, however, that drug use has in fact increased. Another factor involved is our recent recognition of the use of legal prescription drugs for purposes other than alleviating or correcting medical symptoms. This activity we call *secret deviance*, for it can pass as nondeviant activity even among the deviants themselves. Recognition of such usage as deviance has, however, increased our perception of deviant drug use. Certain segments of the United States population, especially the elderly, are in large proportion highly sedated — hooked on medical prescriptions. Furthermore, a large proportion of the population now has direct experience with psychoactive drugs and thus the opportunity to define such drugs positively for their mood-altering effects. Critics of such drug use often blame doctors for prescribing the drugs without sufficient care rather than blaming drug users themselves. While there seems to be some public consensus that use of prescriptive drugs for "highs" is a deviant activity, there seems to be a reluctance to define users themselves as deviant.

Widespread use of prescription drugs for "highs" similar to those produced by illegal drugs blurs the lines between illegal-drug users and prescription-drug users. Why is the former category deviant and the latter not? What does it mean when a barbiturate-taking official legislates against heroin? Once again we see the importance of social definitions in the determination of what is deviant. Public pronouncements about drug deviance and social problems commonly overlook the crucial fact that taking drugs to alter one's consciousness is a pervasive practice in the United States. An alcohol high and a Quaalude* high

---

* Methaqualone (Quaalude, Sopor) is a psychoactive drug with a sedative-hypnotic effect. It is used medically to produce sedation or sleep. Recreationally it is claimed to have aphrodisiac properties, to produce euphoria, and to promote unreserved interpersonal relations. Mild overdoses usually cause depression, but restlessness and excitement may result. See Figure 7.1.

may be indistinguishable physically and indeed the two substances may even be taken together (a potentially fatal combination) to intensify effects, but socially they are worlds apart because of the way in which social definitions conceptualize each of them.

Experience of Drug Use

Deviant drug use, particularly drug use in violation of laws, is nowadays commonly called "drug abuse." While the term "drug abuse" is customarily presented as if it were a scientific one, it is actually a moral or value construction. The moral dimension gives a special twist to a basic question asked in many studies: How does a person become a drug abuser? Suspending moral judgment and asking instead: How does a person become a drug user? directs one to a much more common-sensical and everyday realm. One can become a drug user in a variety of ordinary ways: a friend told you the usefulness or pleasantness of an over-the-counter drug; someone advertised it and you thought: Why not try it?; someone was taking it when you were present, offered you some, and you saw no reason why not; or a doctor prescribed it, it worked, and you continued using it for the same problem or when you sought its effects. The question of why a person *abuses* a drug is exceedingly difficult to answer, for it seems that few if any people intentionally set out to *abuse* a drug.

Actually, all the extensive research on illegal use of drugs reveals that most people use illegal drugs or use drugs illegally for roughly the same reasons people use legal drugs legally. There are, as one would suppose common-sensically, multiple paths to drug use and convoluted motives and patterns of use, nonuse, and polydrug use, many of which are very ordinary. Because many researchers have failed to realize that illegal use is apt to be like legal use in many basic ways, a great deal of effort has been wasted on the search for the "secret cause" of this "evil action" and there has been much fruitless controversy over "*the* real cause" of "drug abuse," "*the* real motive," "*the* basic pattern of use," and the like. But there is no "*the*"; there are multiple causes, motives, and patterns. Moreover, few of these causes, motives, and patterns are very mysterious to anyone who has observed everyday patterns of legal drug use.

Although we have often argued in this book that common-sense explanations must be investigated by social scientists and cannot be simply assumed to be true, at times some social scientists get caught up in their own theorizing and overlook the very useful explanations available in the common-sense world. Such explanations need empirical verification, but they are worthy of consideration, because they emerge out of the very experience that is being studied. A great deal of drug research has assumed a dichotomy between "us" and "them," non-users and users, and has failed to explore the common features that underlie deviant and nondeviant drug use.

Becker (1963) some time ago pointed out the obvious but often over-looked fact that *availability* of a drug is a crucial part of the process of becoming a deviant drug user. For example, high school students in the 1950s had an extremely low chance of getting hold of any marijuana, no matter how hard they tried. By contrast, high school students in the 1970s had an extremely high chance of coming into direct contact with marijuana and being offered a sample, though of course this opportunity varied considerably from one part of the country to another. Thus we might argue that some people do not use certain illegal drugs simply because they have never been asked. Readers might examine their own experience for the opportunities they have had to try illegal drugs and the chances they have had to either accept or refuse. One reason for the widespread use of marijuana today is simply its availability.

How does a drug come to be available? How did marijuana during the period from the 1950s to the 1970s go from being almost unavailable to readily available? A number of explanations have been offered. Maybe the Russians were trying to produce a generation of American drug addicts. Maybe greedy pushers "hooked" a whole generation. Some people indeed believe such theories. Evidence indicates, instead, increasing direct experience with the drug. There were always some areas of the country, especially along the Mexican border, where marijuana was available. Californians surfing in Mexico began using Mexican marijuana. There were also some college students associated with jazz and rock musicians who began using and sharing it. As such small "youth subcultures" came to be viewed as less deviant, their practices, including marijuana smoking, were taken up by others. By the 1960s marijuana smoking had become an important part of the political counterculture of the young, both as a source of "expanded consciousness" and as an illegal activity that expressed rejection of "the system." In this process, availability of the drug continued to increase, and such increase made direct experience and use more likely.

Availability of a drug, however, does not explain its use; availability is necessary but not sufficient. Marijuana had a number of characteristics that, in addition to its availability, made it the drug of choice among 1960s youth. The very weakness of its physiological effects made it appealing to those who were afraid of stronger drugs, such as LSD or cocaine. Regular users of marijuana may, however, switch to other drugs, particularly cocaine, if marijuana is temporarily unavailable, and thereby gain experience with other drugs. Everywhere we can see the element of *choice*; users *choose* to use; they are not *forced* into drug use either by the nature of the drug itself or by social circumstances.

Another explanation for the increasing choice of marijuana focuses on the pleasure that many perceive in its use and the absence of any *evident* deleterious effects. Direct experience seems to encourage use. The great explanatory power of the pleasure principle in understanding drug use necessitates our considering it in some detail.

THE PLEASURE PRINCIPLE

It is remarkable how often the pleasure aspect has been overlooked in social scientists' search for an explanation of drug use. Common sense, however, suggests that many people take drugs, whether legal or illegal, because they make them feel good or at least better than they felt before. In this section we will examine the pleasurable aspect of drug use. Uncertainty in the scientific literature over the chemical, physical, and psychological processes involved in "addiction" suggests that an understanding of the social dimension may contribute to an explanation of drug use. Our presentation will be intentionally one-sided, emphasizing that which seems amenable to explanation in terms of pleasure.

Freud no doubt was right that in order to understand some forms of behavior we must "go beyond the pleasure principle," but the mistake of most drug researchers has been in ignoring the pleasure principle altogether. In their search for the mysterious "cause" behind the "evil" behavior of "drug abuse," they have focused on neurosis, psychosis, psychopathy, and sociopathy without considering that some drugs make many people feel good. Nonetheless, psychoactive drug experience has many roots in the pleasure principle for most, if not all, users (see Becker, 1963). Failure to recognize this fact has led to multibillion-dollar mistakes in social policy. Such policy has sought to develop ways of weaning users away from euphoria-producing drugs. Again and again researchers have discovered "miracle drugs" that will "cure" "drug abuse" only to find that the substitute drug was effective only to the extent that it, too, produced a high. Cocaine was originally hailed as the "solution" to opiate addiction, only to become a "problem" in its own right. Similarly, heroin has been used as a solution to morphine addiction and, most recently, methadone as the solution to heroin addiction.

Initial research on methadone indicated that the drug did not have the potential to produce euphoria and might prove useful in weaning users away from heroin. Since medical personnel did not normally take methadone themselves, it took them some time to learn that methadone was effective as a heroin substitute because it produced euphoria and could be obtained legally and without great difficulty. Many heroin addicts using methadone and experiencing a methadone high kept this fact from medical personnel, who would be likely to discontinue supplying methadone once they saw it was a substitute drug rather than a cure.

Just as the pleasure principle has been consistently downplayed or even ignored in explaining psychoactive drug use, so the obverse side, the pain principle, has been consistently overplayed. Under the assumption that evil causes evil, researchers looked for social evils (poverty, broken homes), psychological evils (neurosis, masochism), and physiological evils (withdrawal pains) to explain drug addiction. Contradictory evidence, such as the high rates of opiate addiction among doctors and entertainment stars, hardly the socially deprived, has been long in surfacing.

Even the pain of withdrawal symptoms has been greatly overestimated. The writhing, sweating agony customarily pictured in the media, though possible, is certainly not common. Although this picture may be publicly useful in scaring people away from drug use, its uncritical acceptance in scientific research as a model of the withdrawal process seems inappropriate. Ray, in "The Cycle of Abstinence and Relapse Among Heroin Addicts" (1961), found that doses of drugs used by street addicts are generally too low to produce severe withdrawal symptoms. In fact, heroin addicts commonly detox themselves — that is, they take their doses down in stages to avoid withdrawal symptoms as a way of reducing their tolerance and making it possible to achieve a high state with less heroin, hence less money. Ray also shows that the return to heroin, though perhaps motivated by some physiological components, is heavily dependent on the social relations of those involved. Media emphasis on the return to drugs as an avoidance of the pain of withdrawal seems to us one-sided; important also is the seeking of pleasures that had been found with drug use.

The importance of the pleasure principle in explaining drug use is indicated in the common comparison made by drug users of a drug rush or high and sexual orgasm. Given the perceived similarities of the two experiences, it is not hard to see why drug users "crave" the drug and return to it regardless of their sincere good intentions to "kick the habit."

Social scientists doing drug research tend to *assume* that the drugs' physical nature *causes* their use or physically compels users to continue, but we argue that the pleasurable outcomes of drug use *sought* by users are a major component of their actions. Our evidence for this claim is that under certain circumstances drug users *choose* not to take drugs, a choice that would not be possible if physical compulsion were the main motivation behind drug use. Even if one takes drugs to avoid withdrawal pains, one does so as a matter of choice — one could do otherwise.

We have spoken already of the way in which heroin users withdraw themselves from the drug in order to lower their threshold of tolerance. The infrequent use of cocaine injection in spite of the strong euphoria thus produced further demonstrates the dimension of choice. Cocaine users give three reasons for their choice to inhale ("snort") rather than inject ("shoot"), reasons suggesting that there are considerations beyond the pleasure principle. First, the rush euphoria is not without later cost; it is followed by a down period. If one keeps injecting to get the rush, the down period can become a depressing "crash." Second, the pleasure of cocaine use requires foregoing other pleasures; if one is high on cocaine, one limits the experiences that cocaine inhibits. Third, there is actually a kind of fear of becoming too involved with the drug precisely because it is so euphoric; there is a fear of getting *too* high. Although indeed there may be cocaine users who fit the picture of the drug fiend — driven to take the drug in greater and greater quantities and helpless in the face of the "need" — such people are seldom encountered in the flesh. Far more commonly they appear in tales told by others. Cocaine users studied by researchers seem to make more reasoned choices. They seem to fear not the physical addiction to the drug but the addiction to the pleasure produced by the drug. The experiencing of *too much pleasure* is seen as dangerous because of the strong motivation it provides for continued and increased drug use.

Clearly there are some people who are always high on some drug or another, but they comprise but a small portion of those who use drugs. The "always high" in fact seem to be a deviant category among drug users, stigmatized as undependable. A study of high-level drug dealers indicated that they were commonly unwilling to work with persons who could not control their drug use. It was seen as too dangerous and risky. (See Adler, Adler, and Douglas, forthcoming.) Further research on the "always high" is clearly needed. Tales about such users are useful as warnings to others but are not in themselves adequate scientific evidence. We speculate that such users are far rarer than stories about them suggest.

Those whose drug use would be considered "normal" by other drug users seem to be generally conventional in other respects. Many are neither rebelling against society nor withdrawing from it. Often they differ from nonusers but marginally. Many aspects of their lives, like those of most persons called deviant, are basically nondeviant. Drug use is held within bounds set by their own subcultural rules, which guard against their becoming total "druggies." In fact, Erich Goode's findings about marijuana users seem equally applicable to other drug users: "The image of the potential and present potsmokers as 'wild thrill seekers' has no basis. Most of the users interviewed were cautious and apprehensive about trying marijuana, and would not have made the leap unless they had been convinced that it would not harm them" (1970: 126).

The idea that drug users are in many ways nondeviant, following rules in drug use and limiting pleasures, has led sociologists to explore the process of becoming deviant as a "normal" one rather than as "something going wrong." Let us look now at some sociological explanations of this process.

Process of Becoming Deviant

It seems that relatively few people begin drug use on their own. It seems to be not a solitary choice and activity but a social one. Erich Goode (1970), for example, found that only about 4 percent of his respondents started using marijuana alone, and even these probably had some prior contact with other users or at least with a supplier. Contact with others using the drug seems to be crucial for most people in determining whether they "take the leap"; the words and actions of other users are important in defining or redefining drug use as a worthwhile activity.

Howard Becker, in an article entitled "Becoming a Marijuana User" (1963), was the first to emphasize the important learning or socialization dimension of drug use. Marijuana, at least in the "commercial" form available on streets of the United States, is one of the weakest drugs used to achieve "highs" and thus is highly susceptible to social definition. Becker studied the ways in which people learn how to use the drug, how to define the effects, and thus how to continue use; those who do not *learn* how to enjoy it are not likely to continue using it. According to Becker, in learning to use marijuana for pleasure:

> The first step in the sequence of events that must occur if the person is to become a user is that he must learn to use the proper smoking technique so that his use of the drug will produce effects in terms of which his conception of it can change (1963: 47).

However,

> Even after he learns the proper smoking technique, the new user may not get high and thus not form a conception of the drug as something which can be used for pleasure (1963: 48).

According to Becker, the user must not only feel effects but be able to point out such effects and recognize them as the result of drug use. New users learn how to recognize such effects as hunger, heightened susceptibility to laughter, and distorted sense of time as drug-related and pleasurable. The latter step, learning to view the effects as pleasurable, is a necessary part of learning to use marijuana. As Becker says,

> Marijuana-produced sensations are not automatically or necessarily pleasurable. The taste for such experience is a socially acquired one, not different in kind from acquired tastes for oysters or dry martinis (1963: 53).

In summary, Becker states:

> No one becomes a user without (1) learning to smoke the drug in a way which will produce real effects; (2) learning to recognize the effects and connect them with drug use (learning, in other words, to get high); and (3) learning to enjoy the sensations he perceives. In the course of this process he develops a disposition or motivation to use marihuana which was not and could not have been present when he began use, for it involves and depends on conceptions of the drug which could only grow out of the kind of actual experience detailed above. On completion of this process he is willing and able to use marihuana for pleasure.
>
> He has learned, in short, to answer "Yes" to the question: "Is it fun?" (1963: 58).*

Becker thus sees marijuana smoking as a social phenomenon to be explained in the framework of symbolic interactionism. Becker also recognizes the significance of the pleasure principle in drug use.

Goode (1970) and others have further developed the idea of *learning* drug use. Becker largely takes for granted that the new user trusts the more experienced ones and accepts what they say. Goode has focused on the importance of users' *convincing* newcomers that they have nothing to fear, a process in which the newcomer may be quite active. Some people in fact encounter a drug, have it available to them, and nonetheless do not try it. In these "negative" cases, Goode found that the newcomers did not trust or like the experienced users and did not accept their redefinition of the drug. Even those who had developed curiosity and had little fear of the drug itself would commonly not turn on until asked to do so by users whom they both trusted and liked, suggesting that other users are significant not only in initially defining drug experiences but as a part of the context in which drugs are enjoyed.

Goode identified five elements important to a person's decision to use drugs: these are the person's (1) perception of danger or lack of danger, (2) perception of the drug's benefits, (3) attitude toward users, (4) closeness to those who advocate the drug's use, and (5) closeness to those who are trying to turn them on (1970: 127). These factors can combine in different ways in any given situation. Sometimes a liking for the user, especially a sexual liking, will count more but usually it is less influential.

Participation of those who are not fully experiencing the effects indicates the importance of the social context in which marijuana is smoked. Some people try repeatedly to get high on marijuana and fail, even with

---

* Quotations reprinted with permission of Macmillan Publishing Co., Inc. from *Outsiders* by Howard S. Becker. Copyright © 1963 by The Free Press of Glencoe, a division of Macmillan Publishing Co., Inc.

expert teachers whom they like and trust, and yet may continue to smoke just as "social drinkers" drink to be sociable. Adler and Adler document this social participation by children, "tinydopers":

> Theories of child development . . . agree that prior to a certain age children are unable to comprehend subtle transformations and perceptions. As we will see, the full effects and symbolic meanings of marijuana are partially lost to them due to their inability to differentiate between altered states of consciousness and to connect this with the smoking experience. Yet this does not preclude their becoming avid pot users and joining in the smoking group as accepted members (1978: 91).

Adler and Adler offer an example of such social dope-smoking:

> "Big Ed": The Diaperdoper — Big Ed derives his name from his miniature size. Born three months prematurely, now three years old, he resembles a toy human being. Beneath his near-white wispy hair and toddling diapered bottom, he packs a punch of childish energy. Big Ed's mother and older siblings take care of him although he often sees his father who lives in a neighboring California town. Laxity and permissiveness characterize his upbringing, as he freely roams the neighborhood under his own and other children's supervision. Exposure to marijuana has prevailed since birth and in the last year he advanced from passive inhalation (smoke blown in his direction) to active puffing on joints. Still in the learning stage, most of his power is expended blowing air into the reefer instead of inhaling. He prefers to suck on a "bong" (a specially designed waterpipe), delighting in the gurgling sound the water makes. A breast fed baby, he will go to the bong for oral satisfaction, whether it is filled or not. He does not actively seek joints, but Big Ed never refuses one when offered. After a few puffs, however, he usually winds up with smoke in his eyes and tearfully retreats to a glass of water. Actual marijuana inhalation is minimal; his size renders it potent. Big Ed has not absorbed any social restrictions related to pot use or any awareness of its illegality, but is still too young to make a blooper as his speech is limited (1978: 92).*

We are suggesting, not that the drug itself has no effects, but that the social context is a fundamental factor in understanding drug use. The study of "tinydopers" suggests that marijuana smoking is more easily learned when one does not have to "unlearn" prior negative views of the drug. An important aspect of adult learning of drug use involves learning that the drug is "o.k." after all. In this process, other users, particularly those whom one likes and trusts, seem of great importance.

Use of legal psychoactive drugs, on the other hand, can more readily

---

* This quotation and the preceding one reprinted with permission of The Society for the Study of Symbolic Interaction from "Tinydopers: A Case Study of Deviant Socialization," by Patricia A. Adler and Peter Adler. *Journal of Symbolic Interaction*, Vol. 1, No. 2, Spring 1978.

be a solitary activity because one does not need to *learn* that they are okay but only that they are pleasurable and can be diverted from their prescription purpose to pleasure. Users of prescription drugs may not even be aware that they take the drugs "in order to" get high; they may use a variety of other reasons that mask their adherence to the pleasure principle. Learning to use drugs seems a more complicated process when the drug already has a "bad reputation" and must first be redefined. In such a process, others play an important role.

David Matza (1969) has used Becker's ideas and those of a wide range of other sociological theorists to construct a general theory of *Becoming Deviant,* the title of his book. His phenomenological perspective draws on Becker's symbolic interactionism and labeling theory but goes beyond to a more fundamental recognition of the role of experience in becoming deviant. We will apply his more general theory to the process of becoming a drug user.

According to Matza, becoming deviant involves the processes of *affinity, affiliation,* and *signification.* He constructs these on the basis of earlier conceptualizations to which he adds his phenomenological commitment to the individual as *an actor in the world. Affinity* refers to conditions that set the stage for drug use — interest, availability, alternatives, opportunities. Matza rejects the idea that circumstances *cause* drug use or any other deviance; affinity tells us only about probabilities, chances, and likelihoods. *Affiliation* refers to the process of conversion, of choosing drug behavior, or, as Matza puts it, "a process in which a willing subject, an affiliative other, and a signifying other ordinarily share or collaborate" (1969: 104). Affinity provides one with what Matza terms "the invitational edge," the opportunity to try a deviant act; affiliation involves accepting the invitation of another who has already crossed over. Signifying or *signification* refers to the fact that deviant behavior is *labeled* as deviant, and thus the deviant actor must orient behavior in terms of disclosure or concealment. Secrecy and revelation become possibilities. As Matza states it,

> To become deviant is to embark on a course that justifies, invites or warrants intervention and correction. By definition, then, to deviate is to run the risk of apprehension. . . . Thus, deviation is actionable activity (1969: 155).

Here we can see a basic difference between the use of legal drugs for "highs" and the use of illegal drugs; only the latter are publicly actionable. Users of prescription drugs can conceal their deviance even from themselves in a way that those who use illegal drugs cannot. Even those who feel strongly that euphoric drugs ought to be legalized must recognize that *they are not legal* and their illegality has important consequences for users.

In this limited discussion of Matza's work we cannot do justice to the beauty and complexity of his theory. We do, however, want to emphasize a major theme of this chapter and of the new perspective: that deviant activity is a process in which some people *choose to do* what others have labeled deviant. Drug use is not *caused* by the physical nature of the drug itself or by external conditions or by the pressure of others. All these factors may be significant, but drug use is a *choice* made by individuals acting in the social world.

There are a multitude of reasons that people can give for why they take drugs. We have emphasized the scientifically neglected dimension of the search for pleasure. Pleasure may be found in religious ecstasy, through alcohol, in sexual activities, by means of drugs, or in many other ways. Choice depends upon opportunity, inclination, and willingness to choose. Recognizing the pleasure dimension of drug use will allow future researchers to consider the similarities as well as differences between those who seek pleasure through drugs and those who seek such pleasures in religious, sexual, or other ecstasy.

Woven into the fabric of United States society is the view that drug taking for pleasure is evil. This view is incorporated in the "War on Drugs" being waged at home and abroad. Enormous sums continue to be spent in efforts to stop the drug flow; programs to curb drug abuse continue to expand; and laws remain relatively harsh. Simultaneously, the illegal supplying of drugs has become a multimillion-dollar business in which many people make huge profits. The interaction of complex structures that seek to control and to provide drugs supports the preservation of the status quo and the continuation of "business as usual." The illegal status of a wide range of drugs provides work for existing institutions while encouraging the development of new sources of drugs and creative substitutes for drugs; it also serves as a target of rebellion for those who want conflict with authorities. "Drug abuse," a value-laden concept that does not advance scientific understanding, is accepted by the public as a real phenomenon and as a justification for official policy. The study of drug use as deviance, considered from the new perspective, brings into focus the difference between common-sense knowledge and scientific knowledge and demonstrates the ways in which common-sense knowledge affects our day-to-day lives.

8

Violence

In discussing sexual deviance and drugs we drew heavily on the new perspective for the details of our analysis. Now we return to the idea of *levels of analysis* (see Figure 2.1, pp. 32–33). Certainly we cannot even survey the voluminous literature in the social sciences on the topic of violence. We have chosen to include material that demonstrates the many *levels* of theories that have been developed and the problems that arise in seeking to explain the many forms that violence takes. The new perspective will help us to frame the questions we ask and the criticisms we offer.

We begin with data on *collective violence,* acts of violence committed by group members acting together, as in warfare, riots, and panics. Rather extensive and reliable data are available, but missing from such accounts — a significant omission from the new perspective — are subjective details about the events, such as reasons given for such violence or how participants saw their experiences. The reasons we have are primarily those expressed publicly by officials, providing at best only a partial and biased view.

We will consider collective violence from its most extensive expression by mobs and crowds to its narrower expression by gangs. We will then examine forms of violence that may be either collective or individual, such as assault and battery, homicide, and rape, concluding with the clearly individual act of suicide. Extensive but again only partial data are available on individual violence both in sociology and psychology. Learning about individual violence, however, involves one rather serious research problem: identifying those who engage in it, for their activities frequently go unnoticed except by the victim. The more public quality of collective violence makes it easier to identify. Those who engage in individual violence are often more highly motivated to conceal their activities, and there is general agreement that *reported* instances of violence are far fewer than instances of *actual* violence. Rape, which we will consider later in this chapter, is an example of individual violence that is often concealed; an unknown but presumably large proportion of rapes go unreported to officials and even untold to others.

Violence illustrates the complex and often contradictory nature of social rules, rule violations, and social reactions to rule violations. Important distinctions are made, for example, between legal and illegal violence. In both popular and social scientific literature emphasis is usually placed on illegal violence: violence that is officially stigmatized. Far less commonly do discussions of violence consider war, official military actions, and other activities engaged in by public officials such as the police, the FBI, and the CIA. Although the scarcity of data will limit our discussion of such topics, *all* kinds of violence ultimately must be included in any complete and accurate picture of the phenomenon.

In much of the world today, permissiveness increasingly characterizes attitudes toward sex, drugs, and a variety of other forms of deviance. At the same time, tolerance for many kinds of violence seems to be decreasing, though war and other official forms of violence continue to be tolerated or even approved. Furthermore, it is not always clear in which situations violence will be viewed as deviant and in which nondeviant; in fact, the same situation may be subject to both views by different definers. The complexity of the problem is captured in these lines by Wolfgang Borchert:

> When the war was over, the soldier came home.
> But he had no bread.
> Then he saw a man who had.
> He killed him.
> You mustn't kill people, you know, said the judge.
> Why not, asked the soldier.*

There is some evidence of a slow decrease in most forms of illegal violence within the United States over recent decades, though some such as terrorism or mugging may have increased. The most striking change has been the rapid increase in social disapproval of violence, particularly in its illegal forms, and in repressive social reactions toward

* From *The Man Outside*, Copyright © 1971 by New Directions Publishing Corporation. Reprinted by permission of New Directions and used by Rogers (1977).

it. Social definitions of deviant violence have been expanding to include more and more forms of action, while definitions of nondeviant violence have been contracting; this development has led many people to believe that there has been a great upsurge in violence. Deviant violent acts and those who commit them have also been increasingly stigmatized.

The kinds of acts subject to *criminal* penalties such as imprisonment have also expanded rapidly. More and more states have been passing laws with *mandatory sentences*, sentences that judges must give to *all* breakers of the law at issue. With mandatory sentencing, judges cannot use their discretion in the sentencing procedure but must sentence uniformly. Some states now have mandatory sentencing for such acts of violence as the use of a gun in the commission of another crime. A number of states have strong "anti-gun laws," laws to control or prevent the sale of cheap hand guns, such as "Saturday night specials."* And some of these same states, interestingly, are at the same time legally destigmatizing sex among consenting adults and drug use.

It is apparent that crimes of the educated middle to upper-middle classes are becoming increasingly destigmatized (but see Chapter 11 on "White-Collar and Official Deviance") whereas the violence they particularly dread is becoming increasingly stigmatized. Since certain lower-class groups and subcultures are more likely to engage in, make use of, and even approve of the kinds of violence that are becoming increasingly stigmatized and legislated against, it is they who are most affected by the increasing social disapproval of violence and the consequent legal steps taken to control it. Because these trends are rather recent, we do not yet know what their specific effects may be, but the movement suggests that those who make rules are concerned with destigmatizing that which they wish to engage in and stigmatizing that which they fear. Keep in mind, then, the important issue of *who* makes rules and *who* is affected by those rules as we consider various kinds of violence.

Nature of Violence

The term *violence* has been used to describe behavior, either *overt* or *covert*, and either *offensive* or *defensive*, which involves the use of force toward others. Four types of violence can thus be identified: (1) *overt violence* — violence that is visible, such as fighting; (2) *covert violence* — violence that is concealed or not directly acted out, such as threat be-

---

* A Saturday night special is a cheap, small gun that can be easily purchased; it is commonly used in armed robbery and personal assault and then disposed of. Its name comes from its frequent use in Saturday night disputes.

havior; (3) *aggressive violence* — violence that is initiated not for protection but for gain, such as mugging; and (4) *defensive violence* — violence initiated for self-protection. Both aggressive and defensive violence may be either overt or covert.

Threat behavior is much more pervasive than overt violence, and defensive violence is much more pervasive than aggressive violence. Threat behavior communicates to others the supposed intention to use overt violence *if* necessary. The one issuing the threat need not *really* intend to be violent; others need only believe in the truth of the threat and the threatener's ability to carry it out.

With threats, small numbers of people can control others. Threat, considered as a form of violence, is an important element of *power*, the ability to carry out one's wishes even in the face of opposition (Weber, 1958). Threats are particularly effective when demonstrations are given of one's willingness to carry them out. Terrorists, as we shall see later in this chapter, recognize and act on this fact. When Spartacus and his slave-revolutionaries were finally defeated and captured by the Romans, they were crucified on posts along the main road so that other slaves would see the mile upon mile of mutilated bodies and would themselves be "motivated" not to revolt.

Police forces draw heavily on threat behavior (which we referred to earlier as self-dramatization; see pp. 138–140), as when heavily armed police cars are driven through areas of potential trouble before that trouble has manifested itself. When such threats alone are ineffective, overt violence, quick and extreme, is commonly used to back up the threats. We are familiar with media presentations of the bad guys holed up in a building and the good guys surrounding them and calling "Come out with your hands up or we'll shoot." Traditionally either the threat is taken seriously and chagrined wrongdoers come out with hands raised or the threat escalates into overt violence and the building is riddled with bullets by the forces of good.

Harvey Greisman (unpublished manuscript) has shown how the common-sense language we use to discuss violence is actually tied in to our basic ideas of legitimate and illegitimate dominance relations. He demonstrates that the same behavior is defined differently depending on whether it is enacted by revolutionaries or officials. Revolutionaries are involved in "terrorism," while police or intelligence forces engaging in the same kinds of behavior are not called "terrorists" by the mass media, by other officials, or by the public in general. Greisman argues that this symbolic distinction is made because the state powers are implicitly assumed to be legitimate and rational. When the state's police kill someone, their action is *assumed* to be based on some rational consideration of the goals they are trying to achieve, such as silencing a dangerous enemy of the state; when individuals commit the same acts on behalf of their unofficial causes, they are *assumed* to be acting as "terrorists" and to have no rational understanding of the means and ends associated with their acts. Regardless of any *real reasons* for actions, these assumptions are made, according to Greisman, on the basis of the legitimacy or illegitimacy of the groups involved. "Terrorist murders" are viewed as illegitimate and a threat to society in a way that "police murders" are not.

Some conflict theorists (notably Quinney, 1970 and Chambliss, 1969) have argued that official uses of force and threat are every bit as "violent," and often more so, as illegal violence such as armed robberies. These theorists claim that official force should be called violent in the same way individual criminal or deviant acts are. Some theorists have even argued that business actions involving potential danger to individuals — the sale of dangerous drugs, automobiles that are "unsafe at any speed" (Nader, 1965), or potentially lethal toys — should also be labeled as acts of violence.

Such analyses as those of Greisman, Quinney, and Chambliss are clearly helpful in revealing the basic variety of social meanings embedded in the term "violence." They demonstrate that use of the term, even by social scientists, often misses these underlying meanings. It is vitally important for sociologists to get at such social meanings, though in doing so we have to be careful not to overextend the term and not to ignore its common-sense, everyday uses and their social implications. Crucial questions for sociologists are: What terms do various groups in our society use to deal with the phenomena we are calling "violence"? What do groups mean by those terms? Why do they use the terms? How? With what effects?

We should keep in mind Walter Miller's caution:

> The term "violence" is highly charged. Like many terms which carry strong opprobrium, it is applied with little discrimination to a wide range of things which meet with general disapproval. Included in this broad net are phenomena such as toy advertising on television, boxing, rock-and-roll music and the mannerisms of its performers, fictional private detectives, and modern art. Used in this fashion the scope of the term becomes so broad as to vitiate its utility severely (Miller, 1966).

Miller chooses to resolve this problem in his own work by restricting his considerations to forms of violence defined as "criminal" by the state. Conflict theorists would, of course, argue that such a view gives tacit support to official definitions and neglects the possibly contradictory views of those not in power. Since the study of violence has not yet thoroughly focused on other definitions, in this chapter we will have to content ourselves with public and official ones, but in doing so we will attempt to provide alternative conceptions wherever possible. Certainly there is need in sociology for studies of violence as a whole, in both its illegal and legal manifestations.

Collective Violence

The rapid development of democratic forms of life and government in Europe and the United States that began in the eighteenth century convinced many social theorists that the masses had become an overwhelmingly important factor in Western societies. This belief led to the development of the Level II sociological theory of the *mass society*. (For extensive treatment of this theory and its application to deviance, see Rosenberg, Gerber and Howton, 1971.) Mass society was conceived of as one in which the values and forms of social organization that had previously bound individuals to each other had been destroyed, primarily by urbanization, industrialization, bureaucratization, and democratization. Works such as Ortega y Gasset's *The Revolt of the Masses* (1961) saw the "power of the masses" as a new force that would transform the social world in potentially beneficial ways. Most theorists saw such changes as leading instead to individualization and a general decline of social control, with individuals no longer effectively constrained by other members of society. Such theorists saw the result as social disorganization and, consequently, extensive deviance.

Unlike social disorganization theorists, however, mass-society theorists focused on forms of deviance that they believed were specific to this movement to a mass society. These specific forms they termed *collective deviance,* defined as that deviance committed by a mass of people gathered together, people who shared properties though they were not organized socially in terms of values or political goals. Of particular concern to these theorists, and illustrative of the kinds of issues they had in mind, was crowd deviance, especially panics and riots. By crowds they particularly meant violent crowds such as those that had played such an important part in the panics, riots, and revolutions in Europe from the eighteenth century on (see Rude, 1964). Theorists saw these crowds as made up of strangers who suddenly came together in a mass in city streets. Such crowds were viewed as having no formal organization and no common goals. Any common direction or coordination was viewed as an outcome of "milling around," spontaneously emerging in a concrete situation.

Gustave Le Bon, whose book *The Crowd* (1895) remains the classic statement of this theory and one of the most influential works of social theory ever written, presents his ideas boldly:

> Up to now these thoroughgoing destructions of a worn-out civilisation have constituted the most obvious task of the masses. It is not indeed to-day

merely that this can be traced. History tells us, that from the moment when the moral forces on which a civilisation rested have lost their strength, its final dissolution is brought about by those unconscious and brutal crowds known, justifiably enough, as barbarians. Civilisations as yet have only been created and directed by a small intellectual aristocracy, never by crowds. Crowds are only powerful for destruction. Their rule is always tantamount to a barbarian phase. A civilisation involves fixed rules, discipline, a passing from the instinctive to the rational state, forethought for the future, an elevated degree of culture — all of them conditions that crowds, left to themselves, have invariably shown themselves incapable of realising. In consequence of the purely destructive nature of their power, crowds act like those microbes which hasten the dissolution of enfeebled or dead bodies. When the structure of a civilisation is rotten, it is always the masses that bring about its downfall (Le Bon, 1960: 17–18).

In Le Bon's unsympathetic statement we can see evidence of a moral and political position that obscures the perspective of participants.

Le Bon and many theorists who followed him attributed crowd violence to the irrationality, emotionality, and imitation of individuals cut off from the social constraints of social organization. Individuals in crowds were thought to imitate each other, thus reinforcing and amplifying one another's emotionality and irrationality. Such analyses were done almost entirely from an outside perspective, using as data general descriptions provided by onlookers, who, though, were often sympathetic to the activities of the crowds.

Recent work on crowds done from the perspective of insiders (crowd members and participants) discloses a much different picture (see Berk, 1974 and Wright, 1979). Even the panic that takes place in a situation such as a burning theater, often cited as an instance of crowd irrationality, appears from the point of view of participants a far more sensible act. As Roger Brown writes, "The famous mad rush for the fire exit is a fairly rational reaction when others have stepped out of line and threaten to block your way" (1965: 842).

Fortunately there are now a number of fine studies of collective violence based on direct social scientific observations, though studies based on participant observations from inside crowds are not extensive. These studies show a picture of collective violence fundamentally different from that painted by Le Bon and his successors. Each instance tends to be extremely complex and to involve many more variables than Le Bon recognized. Although Le Bon's views of the importance of the crowd's emotions and their immediate situation in determining what happens have been substantiated by recent work, the remainder of his theorizing has not held up to empirical investigation. (For a general treatment of collective behavior, see Lang and Lang, 1961; Turner and Killian, 1972.)

Recent studies have demonstrated that in general collective violence grows out of concrete situations that are preceded by a more extensive time period during which shared ideas, values, goals, and problems develop and come to be recognized. Shared problems are of particular importance and may involve feelings of danger, resentment, or outrage. An immediate problem may spark a mass uprising, but even then there must be some history that sets the stage for common action. Uprisings may be the spark that starts violence, but the cultural kindling must have accumulated before the spark can have much effect. Some sociologists, most notably Charles, Louise, and Richard Tilly (1975), emphasize the importance of the "political mobilization" that makes the spark of uprisings bigger and revolutions more successful, but more sociologists are likely to agree with analysts such as Ted Robert Gurr (1970) that individuals who rise up must in some way first perceive the background situation as one that is unjust, feel moral outrage, and then respond with anger against the source of the outrage. Furthermore, they must also perceive the immediate, concrete situation they face as one in which they can express their outrage with an amount of danger they are willing to risk.

Recent theorists (Turner and Killian, 1972; Smelser, 1963) have suggested that even when crowds are initially made up of strangers who have only a general cultural background in common, such as being American or Russian, specific crowd norms tend to emerge as a result of the nature of the situation itself and of the feelings aroused. Sam Wright (1978) has found that collective violence can grow out of crowds with all degrees and types of shared cultural ideas and social organization. Some crowds are relatively unorganized in the beginning, and organization emerges slowly. Others start out with a core of would-be leaders who may or may not be effective in sustaining organization. Often different elements in the crowd are vying for control. Some so-called crowd riots are actually previously planned acts of violence brought about by highly organized groups. The National Commission on the Causes and Prevention of Violence (1969) concluded from its study that it was not, however, organized "Leftist conspirators" among the demonstrators — as was widely believed at the time — but the Chicago police themselves, who produced the violence at the Democratic National Convention of 1968. The Commission spoke of "The Chicago Police Riot."

Current research indicates that crowds are by no means *necessarily* violent but comprise settings conducive to violence *if* there are some shared and long-standing issues that can unite a crowd and *if* the concrete situation itself makes violence appear a sensible response. Sociologists, who now generally agree that crowds even when rioting display a certain degree of social organization, have come to focus increasing attention on what happens within crowds. Interaction among participants is seen as fundamental in crowd activity, and work has been done on the way in which information is passed among crowd members (see Shibutani, 1970). Such Level V theories often bear strong similarities to the theories that emerge from the new perspective.

Terrorism

While terrorism may be carried out by one person, far more customarily it is engaged in by a *group* acting in concert, and thus it is a form of *collective violence*. Most social scientists who have attempted to explain terrorism as collective violence have constructed very general quantitative theories of the Level II and III type, in much the same way as Durkheim and the structuralists who followed him tried to explain all deviance in terms of very broad structural variables. As, however, Laqueur (1977) concluded from his review of the political science literature: "[T]he results . . . far from proving anything, have been quite negative and no truly scientific (that is, predictive or explanatory) theories have emerged" (p. 142). In the absence of in-depth field research studies, Laqueur used fictionalized accounts of terrorism for his data, drawing especially on works of former terrorists or other insiders, such as Dostoevsky (see, for example, his *Notes from the Underground*). Such an approach, while incomplete, does provide a useful and important base for further research. In this section we will focus on what existing data tell us about the *nature* of terrorism and the descriptive features that have been identified. We will not detail existing theories, based as they are on scanty data.

Terrorism is a particularly difficult topic to study in the mode of value neutrality. The very term "terrorism" embodies an evaluation, for both social science research and the mass media apply the term to *any form of politically inspired violence carried out by any nonofficial source*. Politically inspired violence carried out by public officials is omitted from such a definition, even when the only difference in activities may be the official or nonofficial status of those acting.

A number of insights on terrorism emerge from historical case studies and the reports of insiders. Many types of violence are called "terrorism," but an overall definition particularly useful for scientific purposes has come from the definitional work done by Yonah Alexander. He concludes (1976: 3) that the second of two definitions offered by the *Oxford English Dictionary* fits the specific phenomenon that most concerns people when they speak of terrorism in the world today: terrorism is *"a policy intended to strike with terror those against whom it is adopted; the employment of methods of intimidation: the fact of terrorizing or condition of being terrorized.''* The actual *use* of violence is seen as a particularly effective *threat of future violence*, since it makes clear that one's threats are not idle and that one is prepared to carry them out.

We must be sure to distinguish terrorism from the apparently similar but motivationally different idea of *revenge*. While revenge, or the threat of revenge, may instill terror, the intent of revenge is retaliation for perceived past wrongs, while the intent of terrorism is to instill fear of future harm. Many of the current verbal disputes between Israelis and Arabs are over the very issue of which country is engaged in terrorism and which in revenge.

Research has demonstrated that a crucial element of terrorism, which makes it so powerful a strategy in certain situations, is its effectiveness in producing an extreme state of pervasive fear even among those who are indirectly or incidentally the object of terrorist attacks. Terrorists normally concentrate their efforts on very specific forms of action that can be experienced by very wide segments of a given public as highly threatening to members of that public *personally*. The apparent randomness of the attacks, in terms of both when and where they will occur, enhances the fear perceived by potential objects of attack. Since no one can predict to whom or where or when it will happen, it could happen to ME! That's exactly how people who are successfully besieged by a terrorist campaign come to feel, with a result that giving in to terrorist demands takes on a rather persuasive appeal. The probability of being harmed or killed by such an attack may well be small, yet the randomness and the inability to make accurate predictions of one's own chances seem to increase the terror.

The responses of the target population of terrorism can be seen clearly in this account:

> At Lod International Airport in Tel Aviv, the passengers have just landed on an Air France jet. They are milling about on the lower concourse, waiting for their luggage. The conveyor belt begins to move and after a while the bags appear, moving in slow succession as passengers step forward and take two valises off the belt. The crowd is beginning to thicken. Suddenly the three pull grenades and Czech-made machine guns from their cases and with businesslike deliberation begin lobbing the grenades and raking the crowd with bullets. People scream and cower in terror. The terrorists slip in the blood and fall. One is accidentally shot by a companion, one is killed by his own grenade, and one is arrested. By the time the guns have stopped, twenty-four travelers lie dead; seventy-six others are wounded. Hours afterward, while the world is still numb with shock, Israel's political enemies step forward to claim credit for the act. The Popular Front for the Liberation of Palestine announces that the massacre is the work of one of its units, part of the extension of the Palestine struggle into the civilian heart of Israel, where everyone, national and foreigner, soldier and noncombatant, is seen as the enemy of the displaced Palestinian (Schreiber, 1978: 15).

Though current discussions often seem to assume that terrorism is new, in fact it recurs throughout history. In the same area of the world almost 2000 years ago a group called the Zealots were active (A.D. 66 to 73). Zealots opposed the subjugation of Judea to "idolatrous" Rome. They demanded religious "purity" and vigilantly sought out those committing acts that were sacrilegious or that provoked anti-Jewish feeling. They mixed with large crowds at city marketplaces and upon seeing an "offense" would suddenly draw knives from under their clothes and stab unsuspecting offenders. Their methods drew on earlier practices of organized assassination. In time the Zealots became organized as a political party, opposing the rule of Herod. From the viewpoint of ordinary people the attacks often appeared random and inspired a general terror; the Zealots themselves regarded their acts as religiously motivated and supported by the Bible.*

Increasingly researchers have become aware that the possibilities of terrorism are significantly enhanced by the existence of the mass media, for ultimately the effectiveness of terrorism rests on a broad-based public fear. Media coverage expands the public who can see themselves as potential victims of terrorism and thus increases the range of the potential threat. As Schreiber said, the *world* was "numb with shock" over the attack in Tel Aviv; the world for the most part was unaware of the attacks by the Zealots.

It is not uncommon for the news media to provide live coverage of terrorist attacks, a policy that terrorist groups exploit, since public attention has always been vital to their aims. The more extreme the acts of violence, the more pain inflicted, the more drama and attention, and the more that fear is experienced directly, the more effective is the feeling of terror that is the goal of terrorism. The mass media, however, merely make terrorism more effective; the mass media do not *create* terrorism. Terrorism can succeed wherever the public can learn of the requisite acts and feel threatened and terrorized by them.

While terrorism has not been analyzed from a dramaturgical perspective, it seems to particularly lend itself to such an approach. Terrorism is "propaganda by deed," as nineteenth-century anarchist terrorists used to call it. It is propaganda that makes use of demonstration or dramatization. Theorists and others have long argued that throughout history the poor have used collective violence in the form of urban riots and rural rebellions as a way of demonstrating or dramatizing their discontent. With no other effective means of communicating with those

---

* Data from *The Jewish Encyclopedia*, Isidore Singer, Projector and Managing Editor, New York and London: Funk and Wagnalls, 1901.

in power, and no longer willing to endure, groups have resorted to collective violence as a *threat* and a way of bringing about change.

The involvement of mass media in publicizing these displays makes each act of violence far more effective, and thus such displays become more appealing to those considering dramatizations and terrorism. The media in this way *amplify* deviance. Such amplification works, however, only in the short run because of audience boredom and the pressure of keeping audience ratings high. This process is another instance of the satiation effect described in our discussion of sexual deviance. Mass-media coverage is most effective when terrorism is a short-term process, based on quickly aroused terror and immediate satisfaction of demands.

Terrorism is usually carried out by a small number of people. Sometimes they are trying to force the general public or public authorities to give in to some specific demands. More often they employ terrorism to force officials to use severe repression, repression that will alienate wide segments of the public from the government and thus set the stage for revolution. Terrorism can thus be a way to provoke governments to "official violence" in a dramatic way. The Black Panthers drew this kind of response, and some segments of the public seemed for a time more outraged by police violence directed toward the Panthers than it was by the Panthers' violence. If a nation already has widespread alienation, public awareness of official violence might tip a society to revolution. Such an outcome, however, is merely a possibility, and not necessarily a strong possibility.

Official terrorism — violence and threats of violence by official sources in a society — is seldom viewed by social scientists as either terrorism or violence, and yet the new perspective leads us to see it as worthy of consideration in this context. A classic example is official terrorism directed toward slaves — exemplified both in early Rome and in the United States under slavery, two of many possible examples. Execution of some slaves serves as a "reminder" to the others. Whether or not it was intentional, the televised police extermination by gunfire and flames of the Symbionese Liberation Army in Los Angeles certainly must have given pause to others considering attacks on police. The danger to officials in such encounters is that in order to successfully overcome terrorists, they must use terrorist tactics and thus display themselves as more similar to terrorists than they would like to appear.

State terrorism has been official policy in many totalitarian states, such as Nazi Germany and Stalinist Russia. While secret police attacks are presented as being directed only at enemies of the state, official conceptions of such "enemies" are sufficiently vague to discourage many with potentially deviant ideas of any kind. As Adolf Hitler put it so bluntly in *Mein Kampf*, "The one means that wins easiest over reason: terror and force." While, as Laqueur and other systematic students of terrorism have recognized, many instances of terrorism do succeed in terrorizing, and even occasionally in achieving more general political goals, most terrorists ultimately fail in their goals. Becoming desperate, terrorists may give up all pretense of trying to achieve concrete goals and may become ritualists of violence, worshipping it for its own sake. These generalizations appear to hold both for official and nonofficial terrorism.

In considering terrorism and violence, it is important to recognize that terrorism is not violence; rather, it is a political method that *uses* violence. Terrorists view violence not as an end in itself but as a way of displaying the power of one's threats. The use of violence is also an effective way of displaying the violence of "the other side," "the enemy," or opponents in general. When violence becomes an end in itself, it can no longer be called terrorism.

Data on terrorism are too scanty to allow us to explain the phenomenon in any depth. Both practical and moral considerations make direct observational study difficult at best. The information we do have makes it clear, however, that terrorism is viewed very differently by insiders and outsiders. Theorists have yet to make extensive use of participants' perspectives.

Gang Violence

Like terrorism, gang violence involves a *group* acting in concert. We have considered in earlier chapters explanations for the existence of gangs and for the activities in which they engage. Let us reconsider Chapter 3, pp. 82–89, as background to the data to be presented in this section. Some of the explanations presented there to account for gang behavior in general have also been applied to gang violence.

Level II explanations of gang violence often draw on Merton's theory of deviance and anomie (see Chapter 2, pp. 45–49) and view violence as innovative, retreatist, or rebellious behavior. Level IV explanations based on differential association (see Chapter 3, pp. 78–79) tend to explain gang violence in terms of the basis of participation in already existing violent gangs. In this section we will focus on Level VI explanations, popular in sociology in the past and still a part of common-sense explanations, and on some recent Level IV theories.

In Level VI explanations gang violence is often attributed to the evilness of the individuals or to some personality defect. Lewis Yablonsky, in his book *The Violent Gang* (1962), presents a clear example of a Level VI explanation:

> Today's violent delinquent is a displaced person — suspicious, fearful, and not willing or able to establish a concrete human relationship. The formation

of the violent gang, with its impermanence, its possibilities for hollow glory, its limited expectations of any responsibility on the part of its members, is all-inviting to youths who have difficulty fitting into a more integrated and clearly defined world. . . .

A prime function of the modern gang is to provide a channel to act out hostility and aggression to satisfy the continuing and momentary emotional needs of its members. The gang is a convenient and malleable structure quickly adaptable to the needs of emotionally disturbed youths who are unable to fulfill the demands required for participation in more normal groups. They join gangs because they lack the social ability to relate to others, not because the gang gives them a "feeling of belonging. . . ."

In a single act of unpremeditated intensity he establishes a sense of his own existence and impresses this existence on others. No special ability is required to commit violence — not even a plan — and the guilt connected with executing the act of violence is minimized by the gang code of approval — especially if the violence fulfills the gang's idealized standards of a swift, sudden, and senseless outbreak. This is the gang's classic form (p. 3–4).

Yablonsky thus explains gang violence in terms of "defective" personalities (see also McCord and McCord, 1956, for a similar explanation.) Theories that attribute violence, or any other behavior, to the "totally amoral individual" and to "defective personality" have, for the most part, been discarded by current psychologists and sociologists alike. As Hakeem (1958) has argued, such theories are contradictory and confused and for the most part have been used to explain patterns of behavior that could be accounted for more plausibly by noting the existence of group norms that simply happen to conflict with those of psychiatrists, psychologists, or sociologists.

A great deal of field research in the past twenty years on gangs in their natural settings, learning about members' perspectives, has led to a number of explanations at Level IV. Researchers have failed to find an abundance of "defective personalities," and a number of their conclusions contradict both common-sense ideas and previous theories. They have certainly found gangs that fight one another and gangs that attack members of the public, but they have found also that the amount of violence committed by even the most violent of gangs is comparatively small in terms of the popular picture and other gang activities. For less violent gangs, violence is even more infrequent.

In his extensive field research study of Boston boys' gangs, Walter Miller (1966) identified 228 violent offenses committed by 155 boys and 138 court charges for 293 boys over a twelve-year period. Only a minority of the gang boys he studied were engaged in any violence at all. Even for those who engaged in violence, it was an occasional act. Most of the violence involved no weapons. Other boys rather than the general public were the victims. While he later found (Miller, 1974) that there was somewhat more violence among gang boys in Philadelphia, the general picture remained similar. Miller has concluded that "violence appears neither as a dominant preoccupation of city gangs nor as a dominant form of criminal activity," even for the toughest of gangs.

Even though Miller claims that the popular image of gangs does not fit with empirical evidence, he certainly does not deny the existence of gang violence. Having established that it is less frequent and less important than the public imagines, he proceeds to seek an explanation for the violence that does occur. He begins with recognition that boys in gangs are more violent than nongang boys, citing in particular the existence of gang wars. He attributes the existence of violence to a lower-class *focal concern* with "toughness." (See Chapter 3, pp. 88–89 for a discussion of *focal concerns.*) Wolfgang and Ferracuti (1967) use a similar explanation when they speak of *violent subcultures.*

The ideas of *focal concerns on toughness* and *violent subcultures* seek to explain violence as an activity that groups may come to value for what it indicates or accomplishes. Males in the United States, for example, often use violence as a way of indicating masculinity. Whether or not one avoids violence is certainly influenced by whether such action is seen as that of a pacifist or of a "chicken." While in the United States many whites stereotype blacks as violent, many blacks stereotype whites as bad fighters.* We saw earlier that middle-class lawmakers are far more concerned with stigmatizing violence than with stigmatizing drug use. Such stigmatization should not, however, lead us to assume that all groups in the United States abhor violence. Some groups see it as a reasonable and even valued response *to specific situations.*

Any group that successfully socializes its members to feel a high degree of "dishonor" over insults or other acts may thereby encourage both threats of violence and actual violence. The classic instance is in the emphasis on "machismo" both among Latins and in related forms among men of many societies. Evidence of this sort led Wolfgang *et al.* (1962), Clinard and Quinney (1973), and many others to argue for the existence of subcultures of violence in the United States, particularly among the lower class. Wolfgang later summed up his findings and those of many other researchers, arguing that most violence occurs in lower-class groups who have a subculture of violence and, consequently, develop a "front-lines" readiness to meet violence with violence, which makes violence much more likely.

> On the basis of these findings thus far, it is obvious that homicides are principally crimes of passion, or violent slayings that are not premeditated or psychotic manifestations. Emerging out of the data is a theory that suggests a conflict between the prevailing middle class values of our society and the values of a subsocial or subcultural group. Previously we have referred to this

---

* From a student paper by Sandy V. Lee.

group as constituting a "subculture of violence." If there exists a subculture of violence, then we must further propose that the greater the degree of integration of the individual into his subculture the higher the likelihood that his behavior will often be violent; or, we may assert that there is a direct relationship between rates of homicide and the degree of integration of the subculture of violence to which the individual belongs . . . (Wolfgang and Ferracuti, 1967: 27).

While Wolfgang's subcultural theory is clearly an instance of a Level IV explanation, it bears interesting similarities to Durkheim's Level II explanation of suicide.

In one of the most interesting works on gang activities, Short and Strodbeck (1965) tried to understand why gang boys sometimes get involved in shootings. To an outside observer the activity may well appear irrational because of its potentially serious consequences. Short and Strodbeck found that from the standpoint of some gang boys in specific situations, potential punishment by officials is so much less likely than is loss of reputation among other gang members if one avoids violence that the shooting becomes rational or reasonable in the eyes of the one who does it.

An important idea that emerges from recent sociological studies is the discrepancy between research findings and media pictures of gang violence. Why is there such a discrepancy? What are the sources and reasons behind media presentations? Why do the media present a public image of gangs and gang violence as more serious, more frequent, and wider ranging than is found in empirical studies? Even the most violent of gangs do more than engage in violence, media evidence notwithstanding.

The new perspective recognizes that people engage in behavior *that seems reasonable to them.* If one sees violence as a method of achieving certain ends, then one can see people as *choosing* to engage in it rather than being driven to it by inner forces. If one can choose violence, then presumably one can choose nonviolence if the latter more effectively achieves one's end. How one defines the situation affects one's decision.

From the Level IV explanations we have been considering comes the important finding that one does not need to see gang violence as an irrational response of defective personalities and that, indeed, such an explanation does not fit the data. Observational studies suggest that gang violence is commonly a response to perceived threats. Further research on reasons given by those who engage in violence seems potentially fruitful. What the media present as "random violence" or violence with no reason may turn out to "make sense" to those who engage in it.

Assault and Battery and Homicide

Assault and battery is a legal category referring to illegal acts involving threats to apply and the actual application of physical force to another. It can range from verbal attacks to murder. *Homicide* is any killing of another by one's own actions. *Legal* or *justifiable homicides* are generally those committed in defense of self, others, or property. *Criminal homicides* are all homicides forbidden by law. The distinction between legal and criminal homicides is not always clear and customarily requires court proceedings. There are three major forms of criminal homicide: *Murder* is the illegal killing of a person with "malice aforethought" or with a "guilty mind," either with or without premeditation and planning. *Voluntary manslaughter* is any illegal homicide without "malice aforethought" but in which the individual did "intend" to attack the victim. *Involuntary manslaughter* involves the death of another arising from negligence but not from intended attack. In this section our remarks will pertain to all forms of criminal homicide except involuntary manslaughter, which is excluded because our focus is on violence, not death. Since most social science studies of assault and battery and homicide deal with those acts as they are legally defined, we will be restricted to such data; we want to emphasize, however, that such definitions present numerous problems, as evidenced by the extensive court procedures and court documents developed to clarify confusions.

Assault and battery and homicide are viewed officially as individual acts even when they result from collective activities. Court procedures are concerned with the responsibility of each individual involved. In our discussion we will follow this usage, recognizing that these individual acts may occur within a group context, as with the kinds of collective violence we have considered up to this point.

United States courts have formulated detailed methods for making determinations of assault and battery and of homicide. The new perspective emphasizes that legal methods are *one way* of conceptualizing violence, not *the only way*. The legal system *makes assumptions* based on evidence, but these are not the only assumptions that might be made. Thus, to determine that an individual has committed murder, the court must establish *malice aforethought*. In legal language "malice aforethought" is said to exist when it is legally established that the accused (1) intended to kill either the victim or another, or (2) intended to inflict serious bodily injury on the victim, or (3) did not intend to kill but engaged in conduct of extreme recklessness, or (4) killed in the course of committing some other felony, such as theft, or (5) killed a policeman while resisting arrest (Clinard and Quinney, 1973: 25–26). The difficulty in all these criteria is the issue of *intent*. Intent *cannot* be observed but must be *inferred* on the basis of observable behavior. "Real" intent remains obscure and can certainly be inferred on bases other than those used by the legal system.

The distinction between murder and voluntary manslaughter is not clear-cut. Murder is generally viewed as something that one intends; voluntary manslaughter is seen as an unintended *result* of one's actions, as when others are victims of sudden outbursts of anger, not of carefully premeditated actions. Clinard and Quinney have argued that the difference between assault and murder is primarily one of outcome rather than intention:

> In general, murder and aggravated assault are similar, for both involve the use of physical force to settle an argument or a dispute. In aggravated assault there is an attempt to cause a person injury or even deprive him of his life. Nearly all murders thus represent some form of aggravated assault, the chief difference being that the victim died. In fact, serious assaults are invariably considered felonies as they cover such behavior as an attempt to inflict severe injury or to kill, including assault with a deadly weapon, assault to commit murder, or assault by shooting, cutting, stabbing, maiming, and so forth. Whether the behavior results in injury, or is only an attempt to cause injury, it is still aggravated assault. In most cases it is probably the element of chance that prevents the offense from sliding over into criminal homicide by the death of one of the parties (1973: 26).

The procedures involved in determining the legal category into which individuals fit are an important focus of the new perspective. Cicourel's *The Social Organization of Juvenile Justice* (1968) documents the procedures of identification of offenders, arrest, and disposition of cases. Harold Garfinkel's article, "Some Rules of Correct Decisions that Jurors Respect" (in Garfinkel, 1967), elaborates on the use of common sense to interpret the absolute criteria provided by the courts. The common-sense view that the categories of assault and battery and homicide are clear-cut is denied by the evidence and by the difficulties involved in making determinations. If the process were so easy, courts would have little work to do.

Assault and battery and homicide are crimes that particularly captivate the public imagination. Detective stories and murder mysteries are widely read forms of literature, and television programs on assault and murder are also popular. Magazines and movies of the "True Detective" type have numerous fans. This great public interest is paralleled by the great deal of study social scientists have devoted to such crimes. Unfortunately, their findings have been skimpy, in part because of the difficulties in directly observing the activities and in part because of the unavailability for study of those who "get away with it."

Mass-media presentations of homicide focus on premeditated homicide (murder), inspiring popular images of the "evil perpetrator" and the "innocent victim" so familiar from television series of the Perry Mason type. Since few members of the public have direct experience of homicide, they tend to make use of the available entertainment "information." The stereotypes they develop of homicide perpetrators and victims serve as a basis for their attitudes and for public and private action. The result is widespread public misinformation about crime.

The relative rarity of all highly violent forms of behavior (particularly of murder), the obvious incentives for perpetrators to hide their behavior, and the moral restrictions that researchers are likely to feel have fairly well prevented social scientists from conducting studies by direct observation. They have fallen back on two major sources of data, both having severe limitations.

First, they have used official statistics. These records, quite obviously, include only activities *that are known about*. Because for many reasons those involved are often highly motivated to conceal such activities, many such acts do not appear in official statistics. How many of the people who "disappear" each year *might* be homicide victims buried in the deserts, woods, or mountains? Every year many such bodies are discovered. It seems likely that instances of assault and battery, which are easier to hide than homicide, are concealed even more often.

Second, social scientists have used case studies of those convicted of violence as a way of understanding violence in general. Problems arise in this kind of data as well. Some of those studied may brag and exaggerate their exploits while others conceal at least some of their activities. Boasters, such as Charles Starkweather, Charles Manson, and Gary Gilmore, are likely to receive extensive media coverage, which reinforces the popular image of the murderer as "totally evil." Those who conceal their activities are generally not subjects of mass-media portrayal.

The accounts that convicted offenders give to social scientists often are marred by omissions. The problems in studying those convicted of violence are made clear by the work of Lonnie Athens (1974), who conducted in-depth interviews with imprisoned violent offenders. By cross-checking with prison records, Athens was able to document that two of the twenty-five respondents were clearly lying — either to prison officials or to the interviewer. In addition, three admitted to the interviewer violent crimes they had previously denied to officials. How many others were lying? Letkemann's study of armed robbers (1973), alternatively, provides important data on violence through the case-study method, and this researcher seems to have overcome some of the problems of concealment and lying. Nonetheless, we cannot assume that no concealment was involved. An even more serious problem with case studies of violent crime, however, is that *they provide information only on those convicted*. They tell us nothing about those who have engaged in such activities but have not been convicted. *There is no reason to assume that the two categories are identical.*

In spite of the difficulties in obtaining data, and though information about those who are not convicted remains sparse, social scientists do have some knowledge about many *kinds* of violent acts committed and the circumstances surrounding them. From this knowledge some patterns emerge. We will look now at some of the descriptive findings; then we will turn to theoretical explanations.

The great majority of all known assault and batteries and homicides are committed against someone known intimately, and they occur in situations where interaction between perpetrator and victim becomes increasingly emotional in quality, building rather quickly to a violent act. Such acts are referred to as *crimes of passion*. Whether the violent act results in homicide or mere assault or battery depends heavily on such factors as availability of lethal weapons, relative strength of the opponents, and even available emergency medical care. Thus a recent decline in the homicide rate in Boston was attributed to advances in emergency medical care. There do not appear to be important situational differences between most cases of homicide on the one hand and assault and battery on the other. Even who will be perpetrator and who victim may not be clear until the conclusion of the event. (See Wolfgang and Ferracuti, 1967, for a general review of evidence on crimes of passion.)

Contrary to the popular fear of "crime in the streets" and of "mindless and meaningless" violence by "cold-blooded muggers," all available information suggests that the greatest threat of violence today, and perhaps throughout history, is from someone known very well. Relationships that are sexual tend more often than other relationships to generate highly destructive violence. Studies throughout the Western world demonstrate that recurrent disagreement and conflict over long periods between two people who are closely involved, most commonly in sex and love but sometimes in friendship or family intimacy, comprise a setting conducive to violence with a potential outcome of death to one of the participants.

The pattern we have been describing applies to *known* instances of assault and battery and homicide. There is no reason to assume that it applies to unknown instances, and in fact the latter may well be quite different. The very fact that those involved in violence are known to one another increases the possibility that they will be identified by the police if the incident comes to public attention. When one spouse dies violently, the other spouse is always at least a potential suspect. Those known to the victim are more likely to be caught by the police. Violence among strangers is more likely to go unpunished because of the problem of identifying the perpetrator. Far less is known about violence among strangers, but it may well follow patterns quite different from those of the crimes of passion we have described here.

A variety of explanations have been offered to explain assault and battery and homicide. Some theorists recognize a common thread in homicide and suicide, where both are viewed as outcomes of violent feelings (a Level VI explanation). Homicide involves turning feelings outward toward others, while suicide turns the same kinds of feelings inward against oneself (see Henry and Short, 1954). This and similar theories suggest a pattern worth further study. They may, however, be flawed by reliance on official statistics and by the absence of information about secret deviance.

Both psychological explanations (Level VI) and subcultural explanations (Level IV) have been used to explain assault and battery and homicide in much the same way they have been applied to gang violence. We will not further elaborate them here. Neither of these kinds of explanations seems sufficient to explain the existence of homicide or assault and battery for the same reasons we found them inapplicable to gang violence.

What does seem to be the case is that all human beings are capable of violence; some are more capable than others, some have more resources available than do others, and certain situations either encourage or discourage violence. People differ, too, in terms of what they see as adequate reasons for violent acts. Detailed research is needed that takes this broad variety of factors into account. Readers might find it instructive to consider situations in which they might find it reasonable to respond violently.

Regardless of what social factors may be linked to individual violence, there appears to be a very clear pattern of social interaction involved, and thus Level V explanations seem particularly important. The popular image of the "evil" perpetrator and "innocent" victim has been largely discredited by social science research. Rather, perpetrator and victim commonly appear to be involved in a social encounter where the acts of each affect those of the other. Such is clearly the case when perpetrator and victim know each other, but it may also be of significance in acts of violence involving strangers. In some cases victims have been known to exhort perpetrators to attack them. The role of the victim in the production of criminal violence has been studied by a number of social scientists, among them Stephen Schafer. In his book *The Victim and His Criminal* (1968) Schafer urges the study of the criminal-victim relationship:

> Crime is not only an individual act but also a social phenomenon. . . . it is far from true that all crimes "happen" to be committed; often the victim's negligence, precipitative action, or provocation contributes to the genesis or performance of a crime (p. 152).

We will return to this issue in the next section when we consider rape as violence. The point here is not that the victim is to *blame* for any resulting violence but that violence emerges in *interaction between* perpetrator and victim. (See Wolfgang, and all the many essays in the four volumes of Drapkin and Viano, 1974, for a discussion of victim involvement.

Today sociological studies of assault and battery and homicide, particularly within the new perspective, focus on them as violent acts that share similarities and differ primarily in their different outcomes (insult, physical injury, or death). The view of the violent as "mad" or "insane" is giving way to a view of violence as a method of coming to terms with a situation in which both perpetrator and victim are involved. Increasingly, too, sociologists are recognizing that there may be important distinctions between known acts of violence and unknown or concealed acts and that one cannot generalize to the latter on the basis of knowledge about the former. Meanwhile, social rules and laws against violence are growing more stringent, and we can expect greater numbers of people, who for their own reasons choose violence, to be labeled deviant. The role of lawmakers and law enforcers in this process are coming under increasing sociological scrutiny. The existence of media violence suggests that not only specific subcultures but United States culture as a whole has an interest in violence that undermines the very stigmatization process that is taking place. We expect that continued research on violence will provide us with evidence related to all these considerations.

Rape

Rape is a particularly value-laden topic both for the general public and for social scientists. It is also complex and ambiguous, involving as it does elements of both sex and violence. Emotions and ambiguity, together with a general lack of valid and detailed evidence, make rape a difficult topic for sociological study. In this section we will suggest ways of considering the topic so as to maintain value neutrality while respecting the phenomenon's complexities. We will draw particularly on the new perspective, contrasting it to the Level VI explanations that are commonly offered. Common-sense explanations will also be considered.

Our subject here is legally referred to as *forcible rape*, any act of sexual intercourse in which one partner uses some kind of force to make the other submit. We will not consider *statutory rape*, sexual intercourse in which the raped partner is below the legally prescribed age of consent — generally sixteen, eighteen, or twenty-one — and in which violence is not involved. (Continental European law avoids this linguistic problem by distinguishing between *rape* and *fornication with a minor*.)

Legal definitions of rape in the United States generally assume that the rapist is male and the victim female, though we will not make such an assumption. Homosexual rapes are not uncommon in male prisons, and the issue of women raping men has come in for some current discussion. Legal definitions of rape also often exclude other forms of forced sexual behavior, classifying them not as rape but as "assault," "crimes against nature," or some other category. Our discussion will be somewhat restricted by the fact that most of the available data refer to men raping women.

A subject of much public controversy has been the issue of "acceptable" evidence for rape. With other forms of violence, such as assault, the victim's word is generally relied on, but the rape victim is customarily viewed as a far less reliable source of information. Some states require that medical tests be taken to confirm the presence of semen before the charge of rape can be made. In some societies, Israel for example, the charge of rape cannot be made by police unless the victim's testimony is supported by other testimony. In the United States, if there is not sufficient evidence for a charge of rape, a charge of assault may be made:

> In one case believed to be rape, the medical examination failed to reveal the presence of semen in the victim. Later, after any such evidence would have been washed away, it was found that the victim had a ruptured colon. The detectives, while treating the case as one of rape, could not use the penal code designation for rape (261 PC) because of the wording of the rape law. However, since the victim was badly beaten, the detectives could use the attempted homicide statute (217 PC). In this particular case they added armed robbery and everything else they could think of that could possibly meet the legal requirements. Thus, even though the detectives could not officially treat the assault as rape, they worked it as such using other laws (Sanders, 1977: 187).

Social controversy over forcible rape has often been carried on, especially in the mass media, in highly confusing and inflammatory words. Two very different images are popular, that of the "mad rapist" and that of the "normal human male." We will look at each of these in turn.

The "mad rapist" image, particularly popular in the mass media, involves the idea of violent rape by a stranger, an act whose shocking quality makes it newsworthy. Victims of such rapes may be unable to keep the event secret from the press. Mass rapists, those who rape a number of women, receive the greatest media coverage and also seem to serve as the model for the "mad rapist" image. The Boston Strangler, the Hillside Rapist, and others serve to provide data for the image. This image generates a multitude of protective responses and widespread fear, a response similar to that achieved by terrorism though without any overt goal or purpose. Women are afraid to walk the streets at night, lights are left on, locks are quadrupled, and all the everyday feelings of fear are experienced. Violent rapes by strangers are, however, extremely rare events, a small fraction of all homicides, of all assaults, and even of all rapes.

The second image of the rapist, that of the "normal human male," focuses attention on the victim as provoker or seducer and the rapist as only responding as "any normal male" would. This image was particularly popular in the past and is often accepted in common-sense thinking. Many of those males who currently hold such a view do not, however, see it as applicable when their own wives, girlfriends, or daughters are rape victims. In this image, provocative women are seen as the *cause* of their own rape, men in some way being helpless in the face of such provocation. An alternative form sees the rape not as *caused by* the woman so much as *just punishment* for her seductive behavior. Such women are thus considered to *deserve* rape because "they asked for it."

Both of these images, the "mad rapist" and the "normal human male," are not only part of common-sense ideas but have been invoked as elements in social science explanations. The following passage, drawn from a sociological examination of the topic by Clinard and Quinney (1973), makes use of psychological explanation (Level VI) and shows the reworking of the "normal human male" image to focus on the woman as "wanting it." In this passage the authors argue that many, if not all, rape victims really want some degree of force used against them as a way of avoiding guilt and as a way of coming to terms with "female ambivalence" and "female masochism":

> The victim of forcible rape often appears to have much to do with the fact that she is raped. Amir found that 19 percent of the forcible rapes in his Philadelphia study were victim-precipitated in the sense that the victims actually, or so it was interpreted by the offender, agreed to sexual relations but retracted before the actual act or did not resist strongly enough when the suggestion was made by the offender or offenders. The role of the victim was also crucial when she entered a situation in which sexual stimulation was pervasive or made what could be interpreted as an invitation to sex relations. In over half the rapes the victims displayed submissive behavior. Moreover, 19 percent of the victims had an arrest record and 56 percent of them had been charged with some sort of sexual offense (Clinard and Quinney, 1973: 42).

In a well-known social science study of rape, *Patterns of Forcible Rape* (1971), Menachem Amir stated baldly "In a way, the victim is always the *cause* of the crime . . . ," (p. 258) and, somewhat more modestly, "If the victim is not solely responsible for what becomes the unfortunate event, at least she is often a complementary factor" (p. 26). Speculations of this kind, almost always based on no *direct* evidence of rapists' and victims' perspectives, though perhaps influenced by rapists' justifications, tend to reinforce the popular view of rape as victim-provoked. There is little doubt that many people, including some social scientists, firmly believe that any woman who gets raped is the cause at least in the sense that she put herself in a situation where it was likely to happen and she should have known better. A similar line of reasoning would maintain that banks *cause* hold-ups by accumulating money that arouses the greed of bank robbers.

An interesting outcome of the image of rape as victim-provoked is that *victims* have come to be stigmatized in the popular imagination both as deviant and as the cause of the deviance of others. The victim is viewed as "dirty." The same boyfriend or husband who wants to kill the rapist might avoid his girlfriend or wife because of what she had "done." With this possibility, as well as the problems of establishing evidence of rape, many rape victims choose not to report rapes to authorities and may conceal the event from friends and acquaintances as well. The end result is that official statistics on rape are extremely biased and incomplete. Such biases have led some social scientists astray, have reinforced the image of victim provocation, and have thus reinforced the process of victim stigmatization.

Though official statistics on rape present a distorted picture, they do provide some information useful for a sociological understanding of the phenomenon and suggest that the image of the "mad rapist" and that of "the normal human male" are inaccurate. Officially reported cases of rape commonly involve perpetrators and victims who know one another to some degree, from casual acquaintances to relatives. Whether or not unreported rapes involve strangers to a greater extent, the very fact that some rapes involve those who know one another seems to undermine the idea of the "mad rapist." Most studies of official statistics find that somewhere between 50 and 65 percent of reported rapes involve some previous acquaintance (see, for example, Amir, 1971). Obvious exceptions are found in patterns of rape such as hitch-hiking rapes.

Generally police must rely predominantly on the testimony of alleged perpetrators and victims. Even medical examinations that show the presence of semen indicate only that sexual activity has occurred, not that it has been a result of force. Alleged perpetrators are often able to provide plausible accounts of provocation and even actual consent given by alleged victims. Similarly, almost all the alleged victims give plausible accounts that contradict perpetrators' accounts. It is clear that the common-sense theory held by police will have much influence on their understanding of what happened. Whether that theory favors perpetrator or victim, it will affect police response, since they are caught in the middle of a very problematic situation (see Sanders, 1977 and 1980). If they merely take the word of the alleged victim, they may be sued for false arrest by the alleged perpetrator. If they take the word of the perpetrator, they will be accused of oppressing women and letting criminals go free.

There is some evidence that until recently police have been somewhat more willing to dismiss the victim's story than that of the perpetrator, perhaps because the police themselves believed in the idea of victim provocation. Strong critics of police investigations claim that the police still dismiss a high percentage of rapes with little investigation or even stigmatize the victim in a way that leads to the dropping of charges against the perpetrator (see Susan Brownmiller, *Against Our Will*, 1975: 343–386).

While there are few studies of the ways in which police investigate rape, some have found that the police view rape as a major crime that is worth investigating. Police are also aware, however, of the many difficulties involved in constructing a "good" case, and they may focus on the more unambiguous cases that come before them. They are also aware of claims of rape that are later retracted by victims; such cases, whether or not they are frequent, are likely to lead police to doubt the victim's word when independent evidence is not available. Sanders (1977 and 1980) found that police feel that they have to interrogate alleged victims intensively to locate problems in testimony that might be significant in court. Sanders's studies were done in two different cities of California; Rasmussen (personal communication) found similar processes in a study of detectives in the eastern United States. Nonetheless, an unusually high percentage of alleged rapists — about one-half to three-fourths of those apprehended — are unprosecuted or found innocent.

Continued criticisms of police practices and court outcomes by women, and particularly by rape victims, suggest that they view the situation somewhat differently from the way the police do. Further study of victims' perspectives would provide important data about rape and the way the situation appears from the victim's point of view. One idea that has emerged from women's criticisms has been to support and encourage the idea of women fighting back. An all-day workshop in Boston in 1973, "Women Against Violence Against Women" (see Shapiro 1973), considered the ways in which women might use violence as a defense against rape. While attempts have been made to change court procedures, efforts have also been directed to preventing the actual event through defensive action by the potential victim.

Rape between strangers may be ambiguous, especially to outsiders such as the police; when participants know one another, even more complex questions arise about whether or not *rape* has occurred. Some researchers, especially Kurt and Sandra Weis (in Drapkin and Viano, 1974), have concluded that in a majority of cases in which males use some degree of force to achieve sexual intercourse, they have done so in the face of conflicting information provided by both participants. Especially in a heterogeneous society and with an assumption of important social differences between the sexes, different assumptions and expectations may lead to differing interpretations of what is going on. This situation is made even more problematic by common-sense views of women that see them as sexually available, a view that is held by many men and can be used by them to explain their behavior as not being rape. Such views include the idea that women like to be forced or "taken," that they "don't really mean it" when they object, or that by a wide variety of acts they "asked for it." A woman who accepts an invitation to go to a man's apartment may simply be accepting a dinner invitation; he may have been offering a dinner and bed invitation; and force may determine whose definition of the situation predominates. The real problem in analyzing such a situation rests with the extent to which there really are two views of the situation and the extent to which one of the participants is "intentionally" misunderstanding. In a broader sense, it is particularly difficult to ascertain the extent to which those who are accused of rape really believed that the victim didn't mind and the extent to which they merely offer such statements as justifications for their behavior. We as sociologists cannot make such a determination; we can, however, advise caution in uncritically accepting the explanations offered by perpetrators as "real reasons." On the other hand, it is important to recognize such data as the finding of William Henry (personal communication), who has spent years studying imprisoned sex offenders, that even rapists whom he got to know very closely continued to insist, as they generally do in court, that the victim "really wanted it and enjoyed it."

The outcome of the foregoing considerations is that the less women are viewed as wanting to be forced into sexual relations, the more rape there is. Rape then can be viewed as occurring not only between strangers but even between people engaged in amorous activities. Even when force is used after a significant amount of "petting" or foreplay, one can still speak of rape *if one takes seriously a partner's claim* that sexual intercourse was not wanted or intended. Reports and experiences in the United States indicate that females are far more likely than males to stop foreplay prior to sexual intercourse and that males are more likely to use their strength to threaten or constrain females to have intercourse after foreplay. At what point in this process, and from whose point of view, are we speaking of rape? The decision one makes on whether or not rape has occurred depends less on the actual situation than on the perceptions and beliefs we bring to it.

An issue that has recently received public attention in the press is that of rape by a spouse. Such cases involve claims that husbands use force to achieve sexual intercourse with wives who do not desire sexual intercourse at that time. In such a situation it is extremely difficult to determine who wants what, and when such situations are viewed retrospectively the problems multiply, yet the legal process requires just such a determination. Social science in any event requires that the same criteria be applied to all participants: one may choose to accept or reject the words of both, but to take the word of one over the other and claim that perspective as the true one violates rules of scientific reasoning.

Rape that occurs as the outcome of an amorous setting or that takes place between spouses seldom reaches the police and courts and thus rarely appears in official statistics. Whether or not the few cases that have recently been made public are the vanguard of a new attitude or merely isolated instances is not clear. What such cases do indicate, however, is a changed common-sense view that recognizes the possibility of rape *in any circumstances where one partner is forced to engage in undesired sexual relations.*

A consideration of rape discloses a particularly difficult problem for sociologists, namely the inaccessibility of the minds of others. Sociologists, like members of society in general, must rely on external behavior as an indication of what others mean. In situations of rape, it is frequently, perhaps always, the case that the participants publicly disagree about what went on. Perspectives of perpetrators and victims are significantly different, and there are no known sociological techniques to determine who is right. The resolution of this problem by the new perspective, based on the recognition that more than one point of view exists, is to focus on participants' views of the matter and not attempt to determine who is right. Attention is devoted to multiple perspectives and the ways in which they are used by societal members. The role of sociologists in studies of rape, then, is not to take sides but to recognize and document the many sides to the same story.

Suicide

In this chapter we have considered broad forms of collective violence such as crowd behavior and terrorism and have moved to more and more individual forms of violence. Suicide serves as a logical end-point to this consideration. The killing of oneself, which we call suicide or, literally, "self-murder," has been the focus of a wide range of responses from extreme stigmatization to high praise. As we consider such responses, we may find it useful to keep in mind two underlying questions: Is all suicide violent? Is the very taking of one's own life a violent act?

The view of suicide as a moral act under certain circumstances was strong in Japanese culture, especially during the Tokugawa Period (1603–1867). We began Chapter 1 with an illustration of suicide (*seppuku* in Japanese) performed as a moral act. Of such an act Nitobe says:

> Now my readers will understand that *seppuku* was not a mere suicidal process. It was an institution, legal and ceremonial. An invention of the middle ages, it was a process by which warriors could expiate their crimes, apologise for errors, escape from disgrace, redeem their friends, or prove their sincerity. When enforced as a legal punishment, it was practised with due ceremony. It was a refinement of self-destruction, and none could perform it without the utmost coolness of temper and composure of demeanor . . . (Nitobe, 1969: 116).

Rules for performing *seppuku* and for the circumstances under which it was suitable were carefully detailed. The moral code of the warriors *(samurai)* considered suicide neither as a means of escape nor as a response to despair but a way to respond morally to certain specific circumstances.

Although *seppuku* is not now commonly practiced in Japan, the ideas associated with it remain a part of the culture. In recent years, when some Japanese youths were arrested for their involvement with activities of the Palestine Liberation Front, the father of one of them said publicly that he "ought to" commit suicide because of the disgrace brought upon him by his child, but he does not seem to have actually done so. Those who do commit suicide nowadays not uncommonly leave behind indications that they did so "for the good of others," rather than out of despair or as punishment directed toward those left behind.

The widely read and respected Japanese author Yukio Mishima (1925–1970), concerned with the decay of Japanese culture after the American occupation (1945–1952), saw *seppuku* as an intrinsic part of that culture and devoted considerable effort to preparing himself for such an act. He says:

> I cherished a romantic impulse towards death, yet at the same time I required a strictly classical body as its vehicle; a peculiar sense of destiny made me believe that the reason why my romantic impulse towards death remained unfulfilled in reality was the immensely simple fact that I lacked the necessary physical qualifications. A powerful, tragic frame and sculpturesque muscles were indispensable in a romantically noble death. Any confrontation between weak, flabby flesh and death seemed to me absurdly inappropriate. Longing

at eighteen for an early demise, I felt myself unfitted for it. I lacked, in short, the muscles suitable for a dramatic death. And it deeply offended my romantic pride that it should be this unsuitability that had permitted me to survive the war (Mishima, *Sun and Steel*, 1970: 27–28).

Mishima carefully trained his body and on November 25, 1970, performed publicly the act of *seppuku* in order to dramatize his critique of the Westernization of Japanese culture. One of his followers served as *kaishaku* (see Chapter 1, p. 6). Mishima hoped through his act to arouse Japanese conservatives to action, but he seems to have been unsuccessful.

Western history discloses a variety of views toward suicide. In ancient Greece and Rome suicide was apparently regarded with considerable ambivalence: some suicides were lauded and others stigmatized. The response seemed to depend on the situation in which it took place, on the intentions of the person committing suicide, and on the consequences of the act for others. In the Roman Empire (31 B.C.–A.D. 476) the dominant religious philosophy of the middle and upper classes, Stoicism, strongly favored most forms of suicide and saw it as the last bastion of freedom and dignity for people of courage.

There was some ambiguity about suicide in the early days of Christianity in Europe. Those who condemned suicide argued that the fall from grace through the eating of the apple in the Garden of Eden resulted in suffering as a part of life; only God could put an end to either suffering or life. Those who took their own lives were apparently trying to get away with less punishment and to usurp God's power to decree death. Other Christians, however, saw certain kinds of suicide as moral and even praiseworthy. Avoidance of rape was seen as a suitable reason for suicide, a reason that was also accepted in traditional Japan. The Christian Saint Pelagia, when a girl of 15, jumped from her roof to avoid rape by soldiers, and her act contributed to rather than detracted from her sainthood. There was a period in early Christianity, in fact, when many sought death as a way to martyrhood and Heaven. Some facing legal action directed against their Christianity taunted their captors to receive a sentence of death. Some heretical Christian sects even engaged in mass murder reminiscent of the Jonesville massacre in Guyana:

> Direct and deliberate suicide, which occupies so prominent a place in the moral history of antiquity, almost absolutely disappeared within the Church; but beyond its pale the Circumcelliones, in the fourth century, constituted themselves the apostles of death, and not only carried to the highest point the custom of provoking martyrdom, by challenging and insulting the assemblies of the Pagans, but even killed themselves in great numbers, imagining it would seem, that this was a form of martyrdom, and would secure for them eternal salvation. Assembling in hundreds, St. Augustine says even in

thousands, they leaped with paroxysms of frantic joy from the brows of overhanging cliffs, till the rocks below were reddened with their blood (Lecky, 1955: Vol. II, 49).

St. Augustine apparently was deeply shaken by such mass suicides and took a strong negative view of suicide. His view came to be accepted as official Church doctrine.

It came to be common practice in some parts of Europe to drag the body of a suicide through the streets to a major intersection and then mutilate it, hang it from a tree, or drive a stake through its heart. Murder was not dealt with so severely. The body of a suicide was often handled with extreme ritual care to avoid pollution. It might, for example, have to be removed from the house where the suicide took place by being dragged through a special hole constructed in a specific part of the house. Burial commonly took place in unconsecrated ground. Laws prescribed some of these sanctions. The property of a suicide might be confiscated so that family and relatives felt the effect of the "sinful" act.

The view of suicide as morally wrong was dominant until the seventeenth century, when some Protestant intellectuals began the slow process of destigmatizing suicide that continues into the present day. At first only a few major intellectuals publicly expressed their opposition to the extreme treatment of the bodies of suicides. By the nineteenth century more and more people openly talked about suicide and supported the rights of individuals to take their own lives in certain situations. Some of the Romantics openly portrayed courageous acts of suicide in their novels, poems, and plays. Public debate over suicide was extensive throughout the nineteenth century. As Albert Bayet (1922) has shown in his extensive historical study of this period in France, the more educated, urban, and secular people came to feel that suicide in certain situations, such as to escape disgrace or great pain or for "romantic" reasons, was justifiable. The less educated, more rural, and more church-oriented continued to stigmatize all forms of suicide, though among them public response became less severe than it had been.

In the twentieth century in most Western nations there has been a rather steady social destigmatization of suicide. For example, while laws still exist prohibiting suicide, those who attempt it and fail are seldom treated as lawbreakers and the issue may not even arise. The idea that individuals who are terminally ill may choose to die, or even receive medical assistance in dying, is now an important and controversial issue. The fact that such an issue can be publicly raised suggests that suicide has become less stigmatized. Two important moral points arise here: (1) Should individuals have the right to take their own lives? (2) Under what circumstances should they have the right? There seems to be some movement toward answering "Yes" to the first question; finding answers to the second is proving more difficult.

Suicide was an early topic of social science investigation, and a great deal of theorizing was done on the basis of official statistics. Officials started collecting and reporting statistics on suicide as early as the seventeenth century (see Douglas, 1967). Statistical studies of suicide, which usually fall at Level II and III, have continued to the present (see, for example, Gibbs and Martin, 1958; Henry and Short, 1954; Gold, 1958). Many recent studies can be found in the *Journal of Suicide and Life-Threatening Behavior*). Official statistics on suicide are generally both invalid and unreliable; a number of studies within the new perspective have disclosed their particularly distorted nature.

If early sociologists, and many later ones as well, had examined the processes of gathering official statistics instead of uncritically accepting them, they would have seen that the ways in which coroners, medical examiners, and other officials go about deciding whether a given death is a suicide are complex labeling procedures with important *social* dimensions. At first it might seem easy to decide whether one has died by one's own hand, the hand of another, or by accident, but in fact such determination involves a variety of medical and social factors. First, we can see that if suicide is viewed as immoral, there is strong incentive for coroners, medical examiners, other officials, and survivors to interpret ambiguous cases as not suicide. Second, survivors who find unacceptable the suicide of someone close to them may deny or even conceal the fact, for example, by hiding pills or other suggestive evidence. Third, there may be financial incentives for denying suicide, as where insurance companies do not pay death benefits in the case of suicide. Finally, some of those who commit suicide attempt to do so in a way that does not look like suicide. There is no way of knowing, for example, how many car accidents are in fact suicides. Given all these factors, it is not surprising that official statistics are inaccurate.

In many ambiguous situations, the dilemma of the doctor determining whether or not suicide has occurred is similar to that of the police determining whether or not rape has occurred. And like the police, doctors are influenced by the common-sense theories that they hold about what is the likely meaning of a situation.

The social sciences have produced a wide range of theories seeking to explain why people commit suicide. In Chapter 2, (pp. 42–45) we looked at some detail at Durkheim's Level II explanations based on the idea of social cohesion. Now we will employ the new perspective to look at common-sense reasons given for suicide, explanations that tend to be at Level VI. How do people in the United States explain suicide? What reasons for suicide do they find sensible? How do those who commit suicide explain their act?

Depression is frequently cited as a "cause" of suicide and is accepted in common sense as an "adequate" reason. While many of those who are depressed do not kill themselves, there is evidence that those who do commit suicide are depressed. Depression, however, does not seem adequate as a full explanation. In an important work on suicide Jean Baechler (1979) has tried to show from a wide-ranging review of cases that depression is associated with a general tendency of some people to "give up" in the face of great situational problems. Karen Kenyon attributed her husband's suicide (described at the beginning of Chapter 1) to such factors when she wrote:

> It was not the act of a madman, but the act of someone scrunched in, crumpled, thwarted by his job, and by life. It was the act of a man who just didn't fight back, who just didn't, couldn't talk about what troubled him.

"Loss of job" and "loss of loved one" are often cited as important "reasons" for suicide. There are many, however, who lose job, loved one, even both and do not choose to take their own lives.

Those who commit suicide often see their actions as a way of "going to God," of leaving this world and its sufferings for a better world, a world generally believed to be one of bliss or at least peacefulness. Even in those cases where suicide is viewed as a sin, there is likely to be an expressed hope that forgiveness will occur. Revenge is another common motive cited by those committing suicide and recognized by others as well. It is not unusual for husbands or wives to leave the kind of suicide notes that will lead others to blame the surviving spouse.

The "reasons" for suicide we have been discussing are closely tied to United States culture and in particular to its emphasis on individualism. Such reasons would make no sense in traditional Japan and would have been dismissed as "wrong" by early Christianity. As explanations of *suicide in general* they are clearly in error. Systematic study of reasons given for suicide would seem a fruitful line for further research.

Let us return now to the questions: Is all suicide violent? Is the very taking of one's own life a violent act? The material we have examined here makes these questions more difficult to answer because they have become more complex. Suicide in the midst of overwhelming depression may seem violent in a way that reasoned suicide in the face of terminal illness does not. Jumping off a building may seem violent in a way that taking an overdose of barbiturates, perhaps the most common method of suicide, does not. If one views all suicide as wrong, perhaps one may see it as violent, but if one accepts suicide as morally proper in certain situations, then it seems less violent. Perhaps in future study the distinction between violent and nonviolent suicide should be considered. In any case, by considering suicide we have moved clearly to the end of our discussion of violence and perhaps a bit beyond it.

Concluding Remarks on Violence

In this chapter we have discussed a wide range of activities and explanations for them. Let us consider now some of the main issues that emerge from our discussion.

Violence may be either a group or individual activity, and we have considered both collective and individual violence. We find that participants can generally provide explanations for their acts; "mindless violence" is not typical and may even be nonexistent. Furthermore, while especially in the United States violence is being increasingly stigmatized, official violence is often condoned, unofficial violence such as vigilante action is often at least tacitly approved of, and media presentations of violence are well-received by many.

A wide variety of explanations have been offered for violence. Many of them deny the experience of the participants themselves and substitute political or moral positions in terms of which events are evaluated. The issue of multiple perspectives emerges clearly in this chapter. Whether we are talking about "evil terrorists" or "enlightened revolutionaries," "mad rapists" or "normal human males," "rape victims" or "seducers," "suicides" or "accidents," it is clear that the perspective we choose significantly influences the picture that emerges. The new perspective encourages us to recognize these differing perspectives without espousing any of them if we are to produce sociological knowledge that respects its data. We cannot legitimately criticize earlier theorists for taking sides if we simply take different sides.

The importance of the media in developing and disseminating views of violence, and of deviance in general, emerges in our discussion of the way the media facilitate terrorism, portray gang violence, and create images of rapists and victims. Mass-media images enter into understandings of the social world, particularly for those who do not have direct experiences of the activities to be explained. Clearly violence exists whether or not the media recognize it; what the media contribute are images of the activities that seem to influence public attitudes and behavior.

A key problem related to violence, as well as to deviance in general, is that of the importance and ultimate impossibility of knowing others' "real" intentions. Many distinctions that we want to make, including whether any act is deviant or nondeviant, may rest on what the individuals involved *intended*. Intent, however, is not observable but can only be inferred from observable behavior. Since individuals can alter their observable behavior and thus conceal their intent, intent is always uncertain. We must be aware of this state of affairs if we are to recognize not only the strengths but also the limits of sociological research.

If we decide to respect the data we study, we may at times feel that we are engaged in a very frustrating task. Answers do not come easily. We find that the boundary between deviance and nondeviance continues to shift; every time we think we have it established, it moves. There is a real appeal to the idea of simply settling on one answer, almost any answer, as long as it will allow us to say: now we know. Yet the understanding we are after seems to require that we dismiss absolute answers and continue to examine the often vague, ambiguous, and even contradictory social world in which we live in a way that will respect that vague, ambiguous, and contradictory character.

In this book so far, and further on, there are many criticisms of the theories and ideas of others. We have sought to preserve the strengths of what they have done, but their failings too are instructive. Sociology in this respect is in the position of Edison, who confronted an assistant marveling at the bewildering total of his failures — 50,000 experiments, for example, before he succeeded with a new storage battery: "Results? Why, man, I have gotten a lot of results. I know fifty thousand things that won't work."

9

The Many Faces of Dishonesty: Amateur Dishonesty and Amateur Crime

Social scientists have only recently begun to examine the *many* ways in which dishonesty is manifested and to recognize its presence not only in deviance but in "normal" everyday life. Because at first they thought of it only in terms of "bad guys," they began with a narrow Western middle-class perspective, studying those who break property laws. They focused on public law-breaking, such as juvenile gang thefts of hubcaps or cars, liquor store holdups, and other property violations that are widely known and open to observation. Later they became aware of less public violations, such as political corruption and business deviance, forms of dishonesty that are usually known only to insiders and are less subject to police involvement. Only recently, beginning with the neosymbolic interactionism of Erving Goffman, have sociologists come to recognize how pervasive dishonesty is in "normal" everyday life. (See, for example, Goffman's article "On Cooling the Mark Out," in which he applies a concept from confidence games to analyze everyday life.) Just as Machiavelli's recognition of the pervasiveness of dishonesty (see *The Prince*, 1905, written in 1513) led to condemnation of Machiavelli and rejection of his ideas, Goffman too is often criticized for being "too pessimistic" or for taking an unjustly negative view of people's motivations.

We will first examine everyday dishonesty and then begin to consider those whose everyday or occasional activities are both dishonest and illegal. The latter category includes both *amateur criminals,* lawbreakers whose activities are largely situational, and *professional criminals,* those whose illegal activities are organized as a way of life. We will consider professional criminals in Chapter 10. In Chapter 11 we will consider dishonesty in the business and professional spheres and among those involved in making and enforcing laws. Clearly, we will not be able to consider all the forms these activities take. We have included varied types of dishonesty that can serve as models for the analysis of types we have not considered. We have drawn on research data where available; for important topics where data are scanty we have drawn on available resources and suggested lines for further study.

The new perspective provides the rationale for the organization of these three chapters, allowing us to see similarities and differences among the many forms of dishonesty. Our view of dishonesty as a factor in everyday life is characteristic of the new perspective and its recognition of the continuity between deviant and nondeviant activities. While we draw on the work of earlier theorists, our major concern is with the variety of reasons people give both for their dishonesty and for redefinitions of their actions as not dishonest. We continue to focus on individuals as *actors* in a social world rather than as pawns *acted upon* by social forces. We begin with a brief consideration of the nature of honesty and dishonesty and then start our survey of the many faces of dishonesty with a consideration of *self-deception,* the ways in which individuals are *dishonest with themselves.* In this way we will be able to see that both honesty *and* dishonesty are basic features of social life.

Nature of Honesty and Dishonesty

> Cochise was a famous Apache Indian chief. He wished to maintain a peaceful coexistence with the white settlers who were moving into the traditional Indian lands of Arizona. A man who kept his word, Cochise remained peaceful until an incident for which he was mistakenly blamed caused an all-out war. Peace was eventually restored, in part because of the trust between two men — Cochise and a white man named Tom Jeffords. . . . The story gives ample evidence of the overwhelming importance of truth and trust. Cover statement on a children's book entitled *The Value of Truth and Trust: The Story of Cochise* (Ann Johnson, 1977).

The virtues of truth and honesty and the evils of falsity and dishonesty are important social themes — portrayed in children's literature, exemplified in the mass media, taken for granted by most people, and taught as major precepts by religions throughout the ages and the world. Given the many overt rules that support honesty and discourage dishonesty, one might expect that it would be easy for us to examine dishonesty as deviance and to see honesty as rule-abiding behavior. The issue, however, turns out to be far more complex, as we shall demonstrate in these and the next two chapters.

Honesty can be defined as *fair and straightforward conduct guided by truth and facts. Dishonesty* can be defined as *conduct intended to defraud or deceive by altering or ignoring truth and facts.* Honesty in some degree is a basic value in all social groups and seems to be necessary for their existence. Durkheim's claim that society is a *moral order* asserts that some degree of honesty is a *precondition* for the existence of society. Honesty is in fact a characteristic of *both* deviant and nondeviant groups. Honesty in dealing with one's fellow deviants is as stern a rule among deviant groups as is the rule to be dishonest with one's opponents. (An excellent fictional account of a thief's honesty is Boyle, *Boston Blackie,* 1919.) The reason for honesty among deviants is simple: it protects the deviant group in the face of dangerous assaults by outsiders. If, for example, drug dealers lie to one another and tell the truth to the "narcs," then it becomes difficult for drug dealers to do business with one another and the entire drug community becomes vulnerable to "busts." A big drug dealer studied by Adler, Adler, and Douglas (forthcoming) put out a "contract" on a dealer who was telling the truth to the "narcs" — stern enforcement indeed, but not uncommon as a response to "informers." Informing, snitching, squealing, or in other ways "telling the truth" to inappropriate others, whether the police, the teacher, parents, or others defined as "outsiders," is customarily viewed as a deviant activity by insiders, threatening their activities and group cohesion.

Rather than viewing dishonesty as deviant and honesty as rule-abiding, people seem to follow a taken-for-granted rule that supports honesty in dealing with "one's own kind," however they are defined, and dishonesty in dealing with outsiders, particularly when they pose a threat. Both honesty and dishonesty may be either deviant or nondeviant. Cooperation and conflict, altruism and selfishness, and honesty and dishonesty are basic to social life, and thus there are social rules governing the circumstances under which each is appropriate. Breaking such rules is what constitutes deviance: being dishonest when honesty is recommended *or* being honest when dishonesty is called for.

Dishonesty is a particularly important tool in situations of conflict and can be effectively used to minimize it. As early conflict theorists recognized, there are conflicts within any society, subculture, or social group. Parents and their children have serious conflicts, and sibling conflicts are common. Dishonesty can be used to minimize such conflicts by concealing those factors over which conflict can take place. Those involved in a wide variety of deviant activities frequently conceal their activities from family members. The literature on deviance is filled with instances of deviants going to great lengths to conceal their activities from their parents or children, even when the deviants are convinced of the basic "rightness" of their activities. Readers might find it instructive to consider those activities that they conceal from their own families.

Although dishonesty can be effective in minimizing conflict, it can also destroy social groups, since they all depend on a certain degree of honesty, such that people can trust others to be and do what they claim (see Henslin, 1976, for a discussion of trust from the new perspective). Discovery of dishonesty can be a shattering experience for a group and its members. The very possibility of dishonesty provides the reason for strong rules supporting honesty; at the same time conflict management seems to require a certain degree of dishonesty. We find, then, both rules that favor honesty at all times and simultaneously allowances for certain kinds of dishonesty, often justified as "not *really* dishonest." This recognition of the social uses of dishonesty and its consequent acceptability discloses dishonesty as at times rule-abiding and honesty as deviant.

For example, "white lies" are clearly dishonest in the sense that they are designed to defraud or deceive. Nonetheless, they are socially justified because they are thought to be well-intentioned. Adults enthusiastically "lie" to children about the existence of Santa Claus yet for the most part would not call their own activities "dishonest." In social usage, then, fraud and deceit are not viewed as dishonest *if they are intended to be good for others or are altruistically inspired.* It is only when fraud and deceit are viewed as harming others or as selfishly inspired that one speaks of "real dishonesty."

As soon as one moves away from an absolutist conception of honesty as always good and dishonesty as always bad, it becomes possible to recognize different conceptions of dishonesty. The example of Cochise with which we began this chapter is revealing of these different views. While white Americans long insisted that it was the "redskins" who were liars and cheats, thieves and worse, and thus basically dishonest, the Indians insisted equally that it was the whites who possessed precisely those attributes. With any groups in basic conflict with one another, each sees the other as dishonest and one's own group as honest, engaged only in that deceit and fraud which is called for or necessary. Here we might reasonably rephrase Becker's statement of the labeling theory of deviance to say that *honesty and dishonesty are not qualities of acts themselves but emerge as labels through interaction of different individuals or groups.*

Self-Deception

Nothing reveals better the problematic nature of honesty and dishonesty in human life than *self-deception* — being dishonest with one's self. Dishonesty toward others has been recognized throughout history as a means of controlling others and fulfilling one's own desires, and was even developed into an explicit political philosophy by Machiavelli

(1513). Self-deception has emerged as a significant issue only in the recent past.

The "rational man" theory, which has dominated Western thinking about the self for the past two hundred years, generally ignores or even questions the very possibility of being dishonest with one's self. This theory sees humans as "rational beings," able to recognize their desires, calculate how to fulfill them, control them when fulfillment would be disadvantageous, and in general act "reasonably." This view became an important part of the social sciences as they developed and remains an important explanatory element even in theories that also attempt to recognize the existence of "nonrational" behavior. The image of humans as rational has perhaps been most pronounced in economic theory, but to varying degrees it still pervades the social sciences. Marx, for example, accepted the idea of self-deception in his idea of *false consciousness* — exemplified in the failure of the proletariat to recognize the *real* causes of their condition — but such false consciousness was seen as an abnormal state, one fostered by the bourgeoisie, and not a normal human condition.

Freud was the first social scientist to systematically explore the role of self-deception in human action, and Collins and Makowsky call him the "Conquistador* of the Irrational" (1978). Freud, his followers, and other psychological theorists have argued that self-deception is a method used by the *unconscious* realm of the mind to conceal the threatening desires it harbors as well as to provide some fulfillment of them in ways that do not produce guilt. Dreams are a prime example of such deception for, as Freud argues, they express far different ideas than they appear to. (See in particular his *Interpretation of Dreams,* 1900.) However, psychoanalytic theory, and psychoanalytic practice in particular, focus on bringing unconscious ideas to consciousness *so that they can be considered rationally.* It is the unconscious that is seen as the source of mental illness and of neuroses and psychoses. The movement toward normality is a movement toward rationality. Here, too, the "rational being" idea is evident, though as a goal toward which to strive rather than as an inherent characteristic of all human beings.

The evidence for the existence of self-deception is strong, but how it works and what it does is far more ambiguous. Freudians see it as an important outcome of sexual repression, Adlerians see it as related to power or dominance drives, and some recent sociologists see it simply as one possible way of dealing with the social world. Self-deception can probably be found to some degree in any situation that poses a threat to the self, though clearly it is but one of a number of possible responses. Individuals clearly differ in their perceptions of threats to the

---

* Conquistador is a Spanish word meaning conqueror.

self and in their responses to such threats. Societies and social groups also differ in the degree to which they encourage, tolerate, or prohibit self-deception.

For a number of reasons sociologists have commonly failed to consider the issue of self-deception. First, the whole idea of self-deception contradicts the rationalist view of human beings on which the social sciences were founded. In order to consider self-deception, sociologists must question all the research and theory that assumes that human beings are exclusively rational. Second, since science itself is based on rationality, how can it study irrationality and itself remain rational? While to some extent Freud came to terms with this problem in his descriptive work, psychoanalysis nonetheless studies and treats irrationality as a departure from rationality rather than as a phenomenon in its own right. Critics of psychoanalysis, in particular Laing (1965) drawing on a phenomenological and existential perspective, recognize the loss of knowledge resulting from this failure to take irrationality seriously as a topic of study in its own right. (See also Foucault, *Madness and Civilization,* 1965.) A third deterrent to the study of irrationality and in particular self-deception is the problem of determining when people are engaged in self-deception. If they are successful in self-deception, then they cannot tell us about it; sociologists, meanwhile, as outsiders, cannot ever *know* that another is engaged in self-deception. Much of the current controversy about recruitment to religious cults such as the "Moonies" (see Chapter 12 for a discussion of this and other religious groups) is over whether the recruits are deceiving themselves, have discovered a new truth, or are being deceived by others.

There is probably no more problematic research activity than that of *inferring* self-deceptions. And research on this topic necessarily involves *inference,* the drawing of conclusions on the basis of what are taken to be indicators, since we can never know directly the experience of another. Sociologists investigating self-deception can *know* that they are deceiving themselves but can only *infer* such activity in others. The importance of the process of inference is emphasized in the new perspective and was largely neglected by earlier social scientists. (For a discussion of the problems of inferring self-deception, see Douglas, 1976: 93–103.) In spite of the difficulties, sociologists who adopt the new perspective recognize the existence and importance of self-deception in everyday life. Goffman has dealt indirectly with the issue of self-deception in his analysis of socially accepted, everyday methods of making inferences. He has been criticized, however (see especially Messinger et al., 1962), for his failure to distinguish between those who deceive both themselves and others and those who deceive only others. Others in the new perspective have focused on ways in which people go about deceiving themselves (see, for example, Scott and Lyman,

"Accounts," in 1968). The work of the ethnomethodologists is also concerned with people's talk about their activities and the many processes they engage in through talk, including self-deception. (Garfinkel's experiment in the counseling of students illustrates how a problematic situation can be understood through the use of self-deception: Chapter 3 in *Studies in Ethnomethodology*, 1967.)

Sociologists within the new perspective recognize that one cannot *know* when others are engaged in self-deception, but they also recognize that self-deception is a feature of everyday experience that needs to be considered in any full study of social activity. Some sociologists (especially the neosymbolic interactionists, dramaturgical theorists, and ethnomethodologists) are currently focusing on the ways in which people talk about, theorize about, and deal with self-deception in everyday life while others (especially the phenomenologists and existentialists) are focusing more on the experience of self-deception. Both sets of researchers are trying to move beyond the absolutist perspective that sees others who disagree with that absolutist perspective as deceiving themselves.

Although the findings of these new approaches to self-deception are limited, it is now apparent that self-deception may play an important role in the process of becoming deviant.

Self-Deception and the Process of Becoming Deviant

One can become deviant in a wide variety of ways, not all of which involve self-deception. One may become deviant by engaging in one's usual behavior after the rules have been changed. In Massachusetts, for example, in the past there were no rules requiring safety equipment to be worn by motorcyclists, and many rode without protective head covering. Then a law was passed making the wearing of a helmet mandatory. After its passage all motorcyclists in Massachusetts who rode without helmets were lawbreakers, even those who did not know about the law. In such circumstances, self-deception does not seem to arise as an issue. One does not think one is wearing a helmet when one isn't. When, however, one becomes deviant *through choice*, deciding to engage in conduct that one in the past agreed was deviant, self-deception may be useful to ease movement into the new activity. In fact, research indicates that *self-deception is often crucial in the early stages of becoming deviant*.

A strong control in any society or social group against deviant behavior is members' beliefs that deviant behavior is *wrong* and that engaging in it will result in guilt, shame, or both. In the United States certain forms of behavior, including public nudity, prostitution, homosexuality, and murder, are particularly stigmatized and associated with intense guilt. Those members of society who have been socialized to accept the prevailing rules will feel considerable shame and guilt over engaging in any of these activities *at first*. When, however, such people are faced with situations encouraging such behavior — when, for example, a person wants to go nude in public, work as a prostitute, engage in homosexuality, or murder someone — and here we see the importance of differential association (see Chapter 3, pp. 78–79) in providing opportunities for such encouragement — they are at the "invitational edge" (Matza 1969). They have the opportunity to accept the invitation to deviance, to step over the edge, and in choosing to do so they may make use of self-deception.

Those who want to enter into activities that they have been socialized to stigmatize may find it helpful to develop new definitions of situations that can serve as justifications and explanations both to others and to themselves. Self-deception serves as a useful bridge between old and new definitions and is often of great importance in the first phases of engaging in new behavior. In time, if the behavior comes to appear "less wrong" or its advantages particularly desirable, and it thus continues, self-deception may decrease as those involved deal with powerful feelings of guilt and shame a bit at a time. The gradual reduction in self-deception and recognition of one's own motives is expressed in the words of a country rock song:

> The devil made me do it the first time.
> The second time I done it on my own.*

Not much sociological research has focused on the processes of self-deception, but fruitful areas for future research have been identified. Hiding reasons both from others and oneself and at the same time constructing moralistic fronts to justify one's acts, drawing on conventional morality to do so, may well be revealed as a common way of stepping over the invitational edge into deviance. This process allows guilt and shame to be controlled until they can be expressed and overcome. Paul Rasmussen (1979; Rasmussen and Kuhn, 1976) has found these processes very important in the transformation of college women into "sex masseuses." The presence of this process in becoming deviant in other ways awaits future research, but in this chapter and the two that follow we will indicate evidence of its potential extent.

One thing becomes clear when we consider self-deception: people explain their behavior in different ways at different times. The reasons given for deviant behavior seem to depend upon a wide variety of factors and thus are meaningful only in the context in which they appear. "Real reasons" may always be elusive, but recent work suggests

---

* "Black Rose," Billy Joe Shaver. Copyright © 1971 ATV Music Corp. Used by permission. All rights reserved.

that those engaged in deviant activities are able in retrospect to give reasons for beginning those activities that they did not, at the time, give to others or perhaps even to themselves.

Dishonesty with Others: Evasions, Lies, and Fronts

In heterogeneous societies, in which moral disagreement is unavoidable, members of society may find it to their advantage to *appear to follow* rules with which they do not agree. Dishonesty in public may serve as a form of *protective coloration*, like the color changes of a chameleon. The importance of protective coloration is recognized by both amateur and professional criminals, but the method is used daily in many small ways by everyone. The presence of moral entrepreneurs ready to speak out against rule-breakers may provide an important incentive for *appearing to be* a rule follower even when one is not. Goffman has pointed out (1959) that avoiding the disruption of social situations may *require* dishonesty. Dishonesty may thus both protect the rule-breaker and preserve the social situation from disruption.

Evasion is a common form of dishonesty, one that people may view as "not really dishonest" because it does not involve outright lying. *Silence* can be used as a form of evasion when it involves not speaking out in circumstances where to do so would disclose oneself as a rule-breaker. When a professor asks a classroom of students, "Have you all done the reading?" the silence that often follows indicates evasion by those who have not done the reading. When the professor chooses to interpret the silence as an affirmative answer, the evasion is successful, at least temporarily.

Avoiding the situation is a form of evasion in which at least one of the parties involved chooses not to bring up subjects or enter situations in which rule-breaking can be disclosed. For example, most teenagers know that there are some major moral disagreements between themselves and their parents. Some choose to fight over every disagreement every time it comes up, and others even make sure that the disagreements do come up; still others develop a kind of moral detente or disengagement in which the parties develop an unspoken agreement: "I won't bring it up if you don't and if it comes up by accident we'll just ignore it." By avoiding certain topics both teenagers and parents allow rule-breaking to go unnoticed. Another example of this type of evasion is the choice by rule-breakers to avoid places where they will be identified as rule-breakers. Those who are under the legal drinking age may avoid drinking in bars known to be frequented by their parents' friends.

Evasions allow people to avoid giving untruths; **lying** is the intentional giving of untruths. Unlike misinformation, which involves untruth given unintentionally, lies involve intention; the distinction, however, is not always clear in practice, and those who lie may choose to *appear* merely misinformed. Different degrees of lying are accepted in the United States: white lies and fibs are distinguished from "real lying." Older adults who lie about their age are joked about but are not considered "real liars." Those who lie about their age to get government benefits, on the other hand, are seen as more culpable liars. The reason for the lie seems to affect the seriousness with which it is taken. All lies, however, whether serious or trivial, involve dishonesty. Given that absolute honesty on all occasions is virtually impossible, and that those who insist on it are themselves viewed as deviant, dishonesty can be viewed as a common social activity, one with which everyone is familiar. Moreover, although social rules attempt to limit the occasions on which lying is appropriate and to discourage lying that is not for the benefit of others or for the preservation of social situations, once people learn to lie effectively the controls lose effectiveness and the borderline between good and bad lies becomes increasingly vague.

Front is a concept elaborated by Goffman within the context of his dramaturgical approach. He defines it as

> that part of the individual's performance which regularly functions in a general and fixed fashion to define the situation for those who observe the performance. Front, then, is the expressive equipment of a standard kind intentionally or unwittingly employed by the individual during his performance (1959: 22).

A front involves setting, appearance, and manner, all of which contribute to its construction. Fronts may be true or false, but in either case they conceal *back-regions*, places where work is done that violates public stereotypes represented by the front. Since the concept of front may be somewhat difficult to grasp initially, we will provide examples to clarify it.

If we view a front as a public presentation of what one is, then we can look at a wide variety of social roles as fronts. Much of the controversy over Richard Nixon's behavior involved his violation of the *front* of the presidency. His deals, his behind-the-scenes activities, and his use in private of four-letter expletives were not unique in politics, as many of his supporters have argued, but their disclosure to the public violated public views of the presidency and the reality of the front that was being presented. The front was not false, for Nixon was still the president, but the front concealed activities backstage that disclosed the front *as a front*.

The sociology of deviance is generally more concerned with fronts that conceal activities different in kind from the one presented by the front — the massage parlor that is really a house of prostitution, the bakery that conceals a numbers game, the business executive who is really a con artist, the customer who is really a shoplifter. It is important to recognize, however, that such "false" fronts can be learned and presented in much the same way as "true" fronts.

The recognition of fronts as routine social productions has led sociologists to a number of insights: the "natural" discrepancies between private and public behavior; the role of dishonesty, deception, and deviance in everyday life; and the continuity between the world of normal nondeviant activity and the worlds of deviance. It is now clear that many of the techniques used by deviants, both criminal and noncriminal, can be learned through participation in everyday life. Increasingly sociologists using the methods of participant observation have uncovered the day-to-day activities obscured by fronts. Particularly in heterogeneous societies, with many potential conflicts over what is deviant and what is not, there can be many reasons and motives for any individual or group both to violate the rules of some other important individual or group and to conceal these violations from public view; fronts are a means for such concealment. Field research along these lines has disclosed that the moral image of absolute honesty presented in public by a wide variety of individuals and groups is not and probably cannot be accurate.

False fronts are particularly threatening to social cohesion. When fronts conceal not only discrepant activities but different activities entirely, that trust on which the social world is based is challenged. Henslin, for example ("Trust and the Cab Driver," 1976) observes that cab drivers may be upset by those who present themselves as customers and turn out to be poor tippers or bad fares but are most threatened by those whose front of customer conceals aims of assault or robbery. Similarly, it may be disturbing to learn that a surgeon jokes around in the operating room, thus violating the front or public image, but it is quite different when one learns that the person performing surgery is not really a surgeon at all. When fronts cannot be trusted — when they are in fact false — social behavior is seriously threatened. We may like to assume that we can tell the difference between true and false fronts, but in fact the distinction between the two is not at all clear, and many of our decisions are based on trust. As long as that trust is customarily warranted, the social world is relatively predictable, but if that trust is threatened, the social world becomes unpredictable and even dangerous. Readers might consider how they would respond if, for example, they learned that specific people in their daily life were not what they appeared to be.

Evasions, lies, and fronts are common in daily life in the United States. The "socially sophisticated" member of a conflictful, heterogeneous society who must daily traverse moral minefields develops a "moral radar" to detect these moral mines and avoid them. David Riesman (1950) might have called such people "morally other-directed," oriented toward the moral standards of others and adjusting their behavior accordingly. Such orientation provides protective coloration and avoids "useless conflict." Though some moral standards may be openly opposed, many are too powerful for one person to confront or else appear to be too fixed and unchangeable to be worth challenging.

It seems that people *try to choose the minimal form of dishonesty that seems available to them in the situation at hand*. In this way they decrease their risk of being severely stigmatized, reduce the amount of shame they feel, and minimize the possibility of serious punishment. In day-to-day life, however, it is seldom, perhaps never possible to avoid dishonesty, and thus one is always in a position of being labeled deviant *if others choose to apply that label*. With evasions, lies, and fronts, particularly true fronts, others often choose to overlook the dishonesty involved.

Dishonesty with Others: Tricks, Rhetorics, and Seductions

The techniques called tricks, rhetorics, and seductions involve the participation of others and in a sense their *cooperation* in a way that lies, evasions, and fronts do not. Those who are "duped" by the latter three may be viewed as innocent, while those who "fall for" tricks, rhetorics, and seductions may be seen as sharing the blame for the dishonesty involved. As we shall see in the next chapter, confidence games similarly involve some assumption of "guilt" on the part of the person conned.

Tricks are words, acts, or devices used to lead others to *infer* untruths. Whereas lies are the explicit statement of untruths, tricks involve doing things or setting things up so that people make an incorrect inference in such a way that the trickster can claim innocence. The simplest example, and a useful model for understanding subtler social tricks, is the magic trick. The magician leads observers to believe that things can appear and disappear through techniques that give an appearance of reality to that which is false. The magician need not claim that what is being done is true; that inference is drawn by the observer.

Tricks are probably as ancient as the human species. The complexity of any society, even the simplest, means that any individual can understand only part of what goes on and is ignorant about the remainder. This ignorance is the raw material of the trickster. Even tricksters can be tricked in areas outside their own area of expertise. Tricks involve specialized knowledge limited in its public availability. What appears as a trick to an outsider may be readily explained by the insider. Many conflicts between Western medical technology and tribal medicine involve each viewing the other as a trickster.

The successful trickster does not risk being taken as either a braggart or a liar but merely lets others infer from what they see that something special is taking place. Almost everyone tries to trick others at some times, though with differing degrees of skill and success. Makeup and wigs can be seen as tricks, and beauty and fashion magazines provide voluminous advice on how to conceal "undesirable" features. Whether one wants to appear older or younger, successful trickery does not involve making such a claim, and thus lying, but simply *appearing to be* the desired age and letting others draw "their own conclusions."

Tricks may be used not only by individuals but also by groups. Political groups have found tricks to be particularly useful in maintaining power. Such tricks are particularly likely when the political process is understood by only a limited number of group members. Some social scientists (see, for example, Mills, 1950) claim that in today's world of highly specialized scientific knowledge, in which few people know enough about such subjects as politics, economics, and medicine to differentiate between truth and trick, it is easy for professionals to trick people with social legerdemain (sleight-of-hand) and mumbo jumbo. The risks involved are the social responses when such tricks are disclosed, toward both those involved and the profession in general. The disclosure of tricks makes people distrustful of later claims even when they are not tricks. Tricks have both advantages and costs that are weighed by the careful trickster in whatever sphere.

Rhetoric or propaganda is symbolic communication that involves untruths, frequently both evasions and lies, that are intended not only to create a false picture but also to lead hearers to behavior that they would not otherwise engage in. (The term rhetoric can also be applied to oratory in general, in which case it refers to the art of speaking or writing effectively. We are not using the term in this sense.) In the following example we can see the use of rhetoric to convince listeners of the positive aspects of swinging (mate-swapping). The rhetorical nature of Doc's statements is indicated by the researchers' comments based on additional information they were able to obtain about his activities:

Doc: My present wife and I lived together for about a year and have now been married about seven years. And we've been avid nudists before and since our marriage. I think truthfully that probably there are two things, and I'll put them in order, that my wife and I share in common that keeps our marriage together: (1) Sex, we are very compatible, and (2) our love for nudism . . .

Researchers' comments: At this point in time, Doc's and Denise's marriage was anything but together. She had just returned from a six-month vacation with her boyfriend and there had been doubt that she would ever return. In fact, Doc was so certain that she would not return that he had given some of her clothes to Lola, which was a source of conflict between them when Denise returned.

Doc: I think that swinging will destroy a weak relationship, whether it be marriage or whatever. I think that it will strengthen a strong relationship. I think that swinging in many cases will revitalize the marriage as far as your sexual interests and desire [goes]. I think that everything is comparative. I think that in order to know how much you enjoy each other physically or sexually that it is absolutely necessary sometimes to compare. I think that variety truly is the spice of life. And I think we accept this in everything other than sex . . .

Researchers' comments: Doc may or may not have believed this at the time, but in later private statements to me Doc explained that Denise had failed to keep up with other people and had let herself go. That he looked at swinging as a way to get rid of her without telling her flat out to leave. Further, after we'd been studying him for about eight months, Doc fell in love with a beautiful 19-year-old, Darlene. He was terribly possessive of her and jealously guarded his "rights." He would hardly even share her conversation with the young men; he most definitely had no intention of "sharing" her so they could "compare." Doc also gave up his free sex life and played it 100 percent straight. No parties and no cheating. . . .

Doc: Truthfully, I think almost all people would like to be involved. I think that they are prevented from getting involved for a number of reasons: Inhibitions, background, brainwashing, not being able to handle it. Usually, people, as is the custom in society, when they go together, when they fall in love, they do it on a very monogamous basis. They convince each other that you're for me and I'm for you and Holy bonds of matrimony shall never —. Then they go out and cheat on each other . . .

Researchers' comments: As with most swingers, Doc is attacking the traditional form of extramarital sex, cheating. While Doc also attacked cheating in private talks, it was clear that he also took part in it. On one occasion he showed up at my house with two 17-year-olds, whom he had promised to get high-paying jobs in the massage parlors via contacts he knew. It was clear that Denise didn't know about this and he asked me not to tell anyone. On another occasion, I actually took part in a coverup for Doc. He and I were supposed to have gone up to Oceanside to draw some money out of his bank account, while we really had arranged to meet two 21-year-olds down at the nude beach. As with the 17-year-olds, he had promised them a job working in a massage parlor, using the contacts he had made. While the 17-year-olds bought the story and became involved with him doing sex, the 21-year-olds flipped out and demanded to be taken home immediately. They couldn't imagine getting it on with someone the same age as their father.*

Doc was the leader of a group of about twenty swingers who formed the nucleus of swinging parties held by Doc and his wife. These parties also involved newcomers and intermittent partygoers, and Doc's rhetoric was designed at least in part to lead these "uncommitted" people into behavior that they might reject if they knew "the truth" about Doc's activities. Though some joined in without being significantly in-

* This excerpt from Investigative Social Research (*SAGE, Library of Social Research*, Vol. 29) by Jack D. Douglas, Copyright © 1976, pp. 158–160, is reprinted by permission of the Publisher, Sage Publications (Beverly Hills/London).

fluenced by Doc's rhetoric, others seemed to accept the rhetoric and make use of it as explanation for their participation. Such phrases (rhetorical devices) as "the couple that swings together clings together" were used to sway newcomers rather than to express some "eternal truth." Only later did participants see that swinging might have quite different effects on marital cohesion.

Rhetoric is used in a variety of ways in both deviant and nondeviant settings. Whether it is used by an advertiser to sell products, an adult to control a child ("spinach will give you muscles"), or a pimp to add a new girl to his stable, the methods are much the same. Like tricks, rhetoric involves the belief of the one toward whom the technique is directed. Folk sayings warn us of the dangers of rhetoric — "Don't believe everything you hear" — and some burden of guilt is often attached to those who believe too readily and don't seek confirmation elsewhere.

Seduction involves leading another to do something that violates the rules the other holds. The one who is seduced is "led astray." The successful seducer is able to get another to do something that is likely to involve shame or guilt for the one seduced. The task of the seducer is to convince the one to be seduced that there is relatively little risk of shame or guilt and that the benefits and pleasures of violating the rule are worth the risk, *even though that may not be true.* The intent of the seducer is not to change the attitude of the other but to change the behavior in the interests of the seducer. If an individual is convinced of the rightness of the action and is simply trying to get others to see that point, we do not speak of seduction. In seduction the seducer intends to alter the behavior of the other so that the seducer's desires will be met.

The idea of seduction is customarily applied to sexuality, but it occurs in many other circumstances. In our example, Doc could be seen as seducing others into the world of swinging and in particular seducing those he desired as sexual partners. Becker's study of becoming a marijuana user recognizes the role of others in that process; when people are encouraged to smoke marijuana for the purposes of the one who encourages them — to provide support or company, to take advantage in some way of their "drugged" state, or to provide new customers for marijuana sales — we can also properly speak of a seduction process.

Regardless of the goal of seduction, a number of steps appear to be recognizable. The steps we will describe were identified by Douglas and Rasmussen in their study of the nude beach (1977). Although it is a *tentative* formulation, we will draw on it in the remainder of this book as a potentially useful source of explanation. A brief examination of steps in the seduction process will show how a seducee can be led to engage in activities formerly viewed as deviant.

First, the seducer almost always tries to isolate the seducee from the social world in which the rule to be broken has been supported and enforced. The seducee is taken out of social contexts that provide threats of shame for violating the rule. Isolated from negative social prohibitions, the seducee is likely to become open to new experiences and possibilities. In sexual seductions this step may involve a new setting, such as a motel, which does not have the kind of associations that one's parents' living room might have. Religious seducers often establish "retreats" where new recruits are isolated from ties with their former lives (see, for example, Lofland, 1966).

Second, the seducer puts the seducee into a new social context that elicits the kinds of emotions being sought and supports the rationale that has been constructed. The mood for new emotions is set while the cues for old guilts and shames are hidden. "Candlelight and wine" set the mood for a sexual seduction in a way that church music and religious statues might not. Religious seducers may put the seducee in a new context such as a temple that will inspire appropriate religious feelings. Meditation centers along the California coast, overlooking the cliffs and breakers, with the sound of the ocean filling the air, enhance meditation possibilities with seductive qualities that are not so easy to create or sustain in midtown Manhattan.

Third, the seducer provides temptations for the seducee to become deviant, or, better, to *choose* deviance. The sexual seducer may use charm, subtle sexual gestures, more overtly erotic behavior, or any behavior that will sexually arouse the seducee. As the deviant act becomes more tempting, risks are easier to dismiss. Since isolation from other shaming contexts and the presence of emotionally enhancing features of the environment have set the stage, temptation can be more effective. Religious seducers may hold out love as a temptation, an encompassing love that potential recruits have been reluctant to feel in the past.

Fourth, the seducer avoids arousing the seducee's awareness that the new behavior violates the seducee's rules; the seducer will not refer to the topic and may even minimize talk. The model of the seducer as "the strong, silent type" exemplifies this technique. Religious seducers may use a new language so that previous feelings about traditional religion are not aroused. (See, for example, the religious works of L. Ron Hubbard, founder of Scientology.)

Fifth, the seducer moves the seducee along toward the goal of deviance in small steps, one at a time. The seducee can adjust to each level of deviance before moving on to the next.

Sixth, the seducer moves the seducee toward the desired act or state *fluidly* to avoid any break in the "spell" — that is, any decrease in forward movement toward the seducer's goal. Any break may allow the seducee to "stop and think" and thus perhaps to contemplate the earlier rule with its associated guilt and shame.

Seventh, the seducer produces appropriate explanations in support of the proposed deviance. Such explanations are particularly persuasive when they involve a reworking of the seducee's own traditional values. As former social contexts fade and passions rise, such explanations gain in plausibility.

During this process conflict may arise among participants and observers over whether "pure conversion" or "vile seduction" is underway. The question is a difficult one, involving as it does the "real motives" of the seducer/converter, but in everyday life people do concern themselves with just such controversies, and their methods for doing so can instructively be studied by sociologists.

Like tricks and rhetoric, seduction is regarded as involving a certain responsibility on the part of the object of dishonesty, here the seducee. Seducers themselves may argue that the seducee acted "in free will." The degree of responsibility attributed by others to the seducee may well rest on the presumed skill of the seducer, the greater skill being associated with the lesser responsibility.

Until now in this chapter we have been considering dishonesty as an everyday activity engaged in by criminals and noncriminals alike, though we have emphasized the noncriminal and even the nondeviant. In this way we have provided a background against which to see that those who engage in criminal activities do many of the same things that others do when they engage in noncriminal activities. That which is dishonest is not necessarily criminal. Labeling theory argues powerfully that a fundamental difference between criminals and noncriminals is the existence of laws that allow some to be labeled criminal and others not. If all dishonesty were made illegal, we would all be criminals.

In the remainder of this chapter and in the next two we will consider a variety of activities that are labeled criminal and the ways in which they resemble and differ from noncriminal activities. In criminal activities we will encounter the use of the everyday processes of evasions, lies, fronts, tricks, rhetorics, and seductions in forms similar to those used in the everyday life of the noncriminal. We will begin with *property deviance* — rule-breaking behavior related to property. Property deviance carried out by amateurs, to which we turn now, is closer to legal dishonesty than the professional property deviance we consider in Chapter 10, though a common thread runs through all three.

Ambiguities of Property Deviance

Not all dishonesty related to property is deviant, and even less is criminal. Though all societies have extensive rules defining property and establishing who can and cannot use it and in what ways, these rules and their specificity vary greatly from society to society, time to time, and even social group to social group. Only those rules that are also laws define criminals. And only the absence of any rule eliminates deviance.

In societies such as the United States, built over many centuries on the customs and laws of private property rights and obligations, most of the work of police and judicial officials is concerned with property deviance, specifically property crime. Officially reported acts of property deviance, however, are only the tip of a huge iceberg. Various kinds of property deviance, such as vandalism and employee theft, go largely unreported and even undetected, and we need to recognize that such activities are both pervasive and carried out by those who do not end up labeled "criminal." Property deviance by business people, professionals, and officials is very extensive; we will devote an entire chapter to the topic. Every citizen of the United States is affected in some way by property deviance, be it knowingly, as when a purse or bike is stolen, or unknowingly, as when corporations conspire to set prices.

Some excellent social science studies have been made of property deviance, but they are few in comparison to the extensiveness of the phenomenon and the importance the public attaches to it. Part of the reason may be that the amateur property deviant, acting alone, does not seem so clearly a subject for sociological study. Indeed, early sociologists drew on psychological explanations to theorize about such behavior. The recognition by the new perspective of the pervasiveness of social rules and the many faces of dishonesty brings the lone property deviant within the sphere of sociological analysis, for such people can be viewed as breakers of specific rules and their behavior can be analyzed as instances of rule-breaking in general. The lone deviant is a part of the social world and may well engage in evasion, lies, and so forth, in ways that can be compared with those of other members of society. (For a modest study of lone professional criminals see Edwin M. Lemert, "The Behavior of the Systematic Check Forger," 1958.) It may be, of course, that amateur property deviants are not studied widely by sociologists because such deviants are not seen as titillating, romantic, exciting, or strange. It may also be that amateur property deviants are difficult to locate, especially those who are not caught by the police. Whatever the reason, those working within the new perspective are likely to devote more attention in the future to amateur property deviance. In the meantime we will consider what is presently available.

First, however, we need to clarify the idea of property deviance and particularly the fundamental idea of *motivation*. It is commonly assumed, both by people in general and by the police, that property crimes involve *intention* on the part of the criminal. One is presumed to *know* that one is doing something illegal. Such an assumption has pervaded much early work, and great attention has been given to *why* one would commit an illegal act that could lead to imprisonment. Could such an act be rational, or must it be the result of irrational pathology? The new perspective has questioned such an assumption, with results that might appear surprising.

In minor acts of deviance it is common for those involved not to think of their actions as deviant even when they know in general, in the abstract, that what they are doing will be seen that way by officials or others. This account by Douglas illustrates such a situation:

> In the area where I live there are laws against allowing dogs on the beach. I myself have observed numerous people getting tickets from the police for having dogs on the beach, and thus I clearly *know* that such behavior is illegal.
>
> One day I was walking my dog along the beach when I saw police officers moving towards me. It was only as they approached that I realized with shock that I was guilty of what I had seen all of those other people get tickets for. Yet up to the point where the police approached, I had failed to see the "obvious" relation between their own acts and my own. I was simply taking my dog for a walk and we happened to be on the beach.

It is certainly possible for people to *pretend* that they don't know about the rule they are breaking, but it is also possible for people really to be unaware of their rule-breaking even when they know the rule. It is, however, only by examining experience that this point becomes obvious; from the outside it seems irrational and even impossible. The commitment of earlier social scientists to the rationality of human action made the issue of motivation particularly puzzling to them. Only by examining *experience* can we discover that we can both *know* something and not apply it to our own behavior.

There are a wide variety of dishonest and even illegal behaviors that one can engage in without recognizing their deviant or illegal qualities. We can identify three major reasons why such "ignorance" is possible.

First, and most obvious, it is possible that people break even "publicly known" laws because they don't really know what the law forbids in exact detail, and thus they don't "know" the law. For example, many people drive while "legally drunk" without being aware that they have exceeded the legal limit. They might well be surprised or even shocked to be arrested for "drunk driving." It is likely in this case that people informally develop their own social criteria for drunkenness — "when I can't stand up," "when the world goes around," "when my eyesight blurs" — and thus do not see themselves as "drunk" in legal but rather in social terms. The number and the technicality of laws in the United States make it extremely likely that one can break a law without realizing it. Infrequent enforcement of such laws contributes to such a possibility.

Second, people may break laws because "everybody does it." In Boston, traffic rules fall into this category. It is illegal to jaywalk and to double-park, and yet not only are these rules regularly broken but those who are apprehended often respond with outrage rather than guilt. As we shall see below in discussing employee theft, many employees "steal" from their companies but see their actions not as illegal but rather as a "fringe benefit" of their jobs.

Third, people may break laws because they get "swept away" by an activity that becomes deviant or illegal. In such situations people do not start out committing a deviant act but rather get involved in something in which the deviance dimension emerges slowly. This process may take place even in rather serious illegal activities, as the following example demonstrates. Notice that the initial talking and planning here were not really illegal and that the line between legal and illegal was crossed almost imperceptibly:

> We three college students — Mac, Art and Tom — were rooming together while attending V_____ University. On the day of our crime all three of us spent over three hours in the library — really working. That was on Sunday and our crime was committed at 1:30 that night (or rather Monday morning).
>
> The conversation began with a remark about the numerous recent bank failures in the state, probably stimulated by one of us glancing at a map of the state. It then shifted to discussion of a local bank that had closed its doors the day before. Tom, who worked at the postoffice occasionally as special mail clerk, happened to mention that a sack containing a large amount of money had been received at the postoffice that afternoon, consigned to a local bank that feared a run.
>
> The conversation then turned to the careless way in which the money was handled at the office — a plain canvas sack thrown into an open safe. We discussed the ease with which a thief could get into the building and steal the money. Tom drew a plan showing the desk at which the only clerk worked and the location of the only gun in the office. At first the conversation was entirely confined to how easily criminals might manage to steal the money. Somehow it shifted to a personal basis: as to how easily we might get the money. This shift came so naturally that even the next morning we were unable to decide when and by whom the first vital remark had been made.
>
> A possible plan was discussed as to how we might steal the package. Tom could go to the office and gain admittance on the pretense of looking for an important letter. Then Art and I, masked and armed, could rush in, tie Tom and the clerk, and make off with the package. We had lost sight of the fact that the package contained money. We were simply discussing the possibility of playing an exciting prank with no thought of actually committing it. We had played many harmless pranks and had discussed them in much the same way before; but the knowledge that there was danger in this prank made it a subject to linger over. . . .
>
> We found further inaction impossible: we had either to rob the postoffice or go to bed. Tom brought out his two guns; I hunted up a couple of regular plain handkerchiefs, and Art added some rope to the assortment. At the time

we were still individually and collectively playing a game with ourselves. Each of us expected one of the other two to give the thing the horse laugh and suggest going to bed and letting the letters wait till morning. But it seemed that we forgot everything — our position in school, our families and friends, the danger to us and to our folks. Our only thought was to carry out that prank. We all made our preparations more or less mechanically. Our minds were in a daze.

Putting on our regular overcoats and caps, we left the rooms quietly. On the way downtown we passed the night patrolman without any really serious qualms. Tom entered the postoffice as was his usual custom, being a sub-clerk, and Art and I crept up to the rear door. Tom appeared at a window with his hat, a signal that there were no reasons why our plan would not be effective. At the door, in full illumination of a light, we arranged our hand-kerchiefs over our faces and took our guns out of our pockets. We were ready.

"Have you enough guts to go through with this thing?" I asked, turning to Art, who was behind me.

"If you have," he answered.

Frankly I felt that I had gone far enough, but for some unknown reason I did not throw out a remark that would have ended it all then and there. And Art didn't. He later said that he was just too scared to suggest anything. We were both, it seems, in a sort of daze.

Tom opened the door and we followed our plan out to the end. There was no active resistance by the regular night man.

Then after we left the office with thousands of dollars in our hands we did not realize all that it meant. Our first words were not about getting the money. They were about the fact that our prank (and it was still that to us) had been successful. When we reached our rooms, having hidden the money in an abandoned dredger, the seriousness of the thing began to penetrate our minds. For an hour or so we lay quietly and finally settled on a plan that seemed safe for returning the money without making our identity known. Then I went to sleep.*

Though such a story may not be entirely accurate — for it certainly serves to justify behavior in a way that minimizes its deviance — it displays processes that *may* occur when deviant or illegal acts are being constructed.

The movement from nondeviance to deviance and in particular from legal to illegal activity is a subtle and complex one that demonstrates the continuity between the two sides. Even motivation is not sufficient to explain that movement. As we turn now to an examination of illegal activities directed toward property and carried out by amateurs, we must remember how similar such activities are to their nondeviant and legal counterparts.

* Reprinted from *The Gang* by Frederick Thrasher, by permission of The University of Chicago Press. Copyright © 1942.

Amateur Theft Against Business

In Chapter 11 we will consider deviant acts committed by business people against each other or the rest of the public. In this section we deal with theft *from* business carried out by amateurs, both employees and customers. Professional theft is our subject in Chapter 10. The forms of theft dealt with here are extremely common, and they are not always recognized as theft, as "real theft," or even as dishonesty.

EMPLOYEE THEFT

Theft by employees from the companies for which they work is undoubtedly the most pervasive and costly form of property deviance of any kind in the United States. Almost none of it is reported to the police or shows up in the official statistics on crime, in part because it may be too costly for business to do much about it. Employee theft is so common that store budgets may allow for it as part of their operating expenses. In spite of its pervasiveness, there are few good studies of employee theft by social scientists (though see Dalton, 1959; Ditton, 1977; and Altheide, Altheide, Adler and Adler, 1978). Some useful surveys by business security experts consider the problems and methods of employee theft and security responses to it.

Consider the following description of the typical middle-class employee thief and the prevalence of this form of theft:

> Millions of people steal billions of dollars worth of merchandise annually from the businesses and organizations where they work. These are not the "street criminals" whose immoral behavior is presented daily by the news media as a "menace" to society, property, and safety. Nor are they like the wheelers and dealers who pull off lucrative stock frauds, land swindles, bank swindles, or "paper" insurance capers. The people focused on in this essay are predominantly solid, respectable citizens who pay taxes, root for major league stars, believe in the "American way of life" and the virtues of hard work and honesty, and are quickly angered by the thought of welfare chiselers, street hoodlums, and the permissiveness and immorality which they believe is upsetting an established social order. Moreover, few of these people regard themselves as thieves, even though it is estimated that as many as 50 per cent of the nation's work force steals (Lipman, 1973). While no one really knows the dollar amount that is taken in cash and property annually, in 1973 the FBI estimated the value at $15 billion. This figure is even more fascinating when compared to the estimated $1 billion lost to street crime in the same year (Altheide et al., 1978, in Douglas and Johnson, 1978: 90).

With a labor force of roughly 90 million, the FBI estimate of $15 billion a year loss through employee theft means that the average employee would be stealing approximately $175 a year. And those who have direct business experience would probably consider this estimate low.

What do employees steal from their employers and places of employment? Our first idea might be that they steal the company's products: clerks in bookstores steal books, people in jewelry stores steal jewels, and so on. And indeed they do, though businesses do try to control this kind of theft. Raw materials and business supplies and equipment also disappear with some regularity. If one also considers such individually small but collectively large expenses such as private phone calls, private use of company mail, and other such activities, the scope of opportunities for employee theft becomes clear, as does the everyday nature of the activity and its frequent image as "not really theft." (The complexities of employee theft, as well as its difficulty and promise as a research subject, was recognized by Melville Dalton in his classic study, *Men Who Manage,* 1959.)

In employee theft we can see the processes of *self-deception, rhetoric,* and *tricks* operating. Rhetoric can be used to redefine theft as "fringe benefits," "informal compensation," and "privileges." Some of those who engage in such redefinition may also be involved in self-deception, believing their own rhetoric.

One researcher (Anonymous, 1971) found that the television workers he studied distinguished among clearly defined *personal property,* clearly defined *company property,* and *fringe property,* such as damaged goods and surplus goods that could not be used in the business. When such damaged goods are "created" by those who then make off with them, we can see the role of *tricks* in employee theft. For example, employees in supermarkets may be allowed to eat food from damaged packages; such a rule makes it possible for employees themselves to damage packages and then "legitimately" provide themselves with snacks. The way in which such behavior can be institutionalized is portrayed by an experienced cab driver in a novel (N. Waksler, 1972) who informs a new cab driver: "What with your fares, your tips, and your clips, you can make a pretty decent living." The inclusion of "clips" as a routine part of income was reported by Liebow (1967); some employers he studied paid blacks exceedingly low salaries on the grounds that "they will steal from the company anyway," thus encouraging them to steal if they were to make a decent income. Employers who tacitly allow such theft gain power over their employees, because whenever they want to dismiss one they can do so claiming theft.

Rhetoric, tricks, self-deceptions, and employer acquiescence are all important in explaining the prevalence of employee theft as a form of amateur property deviance. When temptation is great and the threat of discovery is small, employee theft is further encouraged. As employees work in a particular place for some time, opportunities and methods become more evident. Employees are the ultimate insiders, those with the very best knowledge of how the company works, how the security force operates, and so on. In fact, the very "best" employee thieves may be those who *are* the security force intended to prevent just such theft. Altheide (1974) has argued that security measures in general have this "ironic" effect (see Matza, 1969, on the nature of irony) of making deviance more possible for those who meet the security requirements and in particular for the security enforcers themselves. Who enforces the law against the enforcers? (One of Altheide's students who had worked as a security officer wrote about just such issues; see Siegel, 1978.)

Extensive rhetorical support exists for such employee theft. Many people in the United States consider cheating large business or government agencies legitimate for a number of reasons. Erwin and Smigel (1970), for example, found a sharp distinction in attitudes toward theft from individuals and small businesses on the one hand and from large businesses, corporations, and governmental agencies on the other. The impersonality of the corporation may put it outside common feelings and ideas of moral responsibility. One may see corporate and bureaucratic organizations as worlds of strangers toward whom one's ideas of morality do not apply. If someone steals your $20 calculator, you may well expect sympathy from others; if an employee of IBM steals one, people are less likely to say "Poor IBM."

Other support for employee theft draws on the widespread feelings of resentment about the power discrepancy between employees on the one hand and managers and employers on the other. (See, for example, Altheide et al., 1978.) Employees may explain theft in terms of feelings that they are being manipulated by the company, that they have been treated unfairly, or that they have been embarrassed or shamed by higher-ups in front of their fellow employees and friends. John Bradford (1976) has argued that scientific managers who formalize, bureaucratize, and speed up work tend to generate great employee resentment and alienation from the organization and thus indirectly encourage employee theft. He discovered many forms of such "theft," including work slowdowns and the secret taking of time off from work while still being paid for it. Alvin Gouldner (1954A) found similar processes in his famous study of a gypsum factory. He also found employee resentment to company procedures for "theft control" by a tightening up of security. Such procedures made it more difficult for workers to take what they saw as legitimate "side payments" or "perquisites" of their jobs, which the British refer to as "perks."

Both employers and security analysts seem to agree that they cannot win the security game, especially because increased security measures seem to increase both resentment and theft, and that the best that can be hoped for is some form of coexistence. The employers most successful at reducing employee theft seem to be those who build personal relations with employees, so that employees develop moral commitments that discourage theft from the company.

Employee theft is a complex social process involving interactions between employers and employees, individuals and organizations, and a variety of perspectives. The line between theft and nontheft is ambiguous and open to varied definition. The very acceptance of employee theft as a "normal" phenomenon makes its status as deviance somewhat ambiguous. Such ambiguity makes it possible for some people to slowly move into rather serious and extensive theft without seeing themselves as thieves until, perhaps, they are well committed to the process. A similar process is involved in customer theft.

CUSTOMER THEFT

Businesses also lose considerable money through theft of merchandise by customers; such theft constitutes the second largest form of property deviance committed against business (employee theft being the first). In Chapter 10 we will consider professional theft by customers; here we are concerned with theft by amateurs. Retail businesses such as department stores generally estimate that from 1 to 2 percent of all their merchandise will disappear because of "shrinkage loss," a category that includes damage and misplacement of articles, employee theft, and both amateur and professional customer theft.

Customer theft — carried out both by actual customers and by those for whom the customer role is a front — is often termed *shoplifting* when carried out by amateurs. It frequently seems motivated by a personal desire for the specific item taken. Amateurs, unlike professionals, seldom sell the goods they take; instead they use them. An informant observed to Waksler as he set out one cold December day in a loose-fitting, many-pocketed coat: "Well, I'm off to do my Christmas stealing." Thus he "purchased" his Christmas gifts for friends and relatives. Teenagers most commonly steal items that other teenagers purchase, such as records and fashionable clothes. The elderly poor are likely to steal food and nonprescription drugs as well as needed articles of clothing. Public "acceptance" of theft by the elderly poor is demonstrated in an instance, reported to Waksler, of a security officer who was removed from his job in a pharmacy *because* he arrested an elderly shoplifter.

Mary Owen Cameron, in the best study of customer theft done to date, *The Booster and the Snitch* (1964), describes the "amateur adult pilferer," typically a woman with a family who does not have enough money to buy both what her family needs and the luxury items that she herself desires:

> Adult women pilferers, generally belonging to families of rather modest income, enter department stores with a strong sense of the limitations of their household budgets. They do not steal merchandise which they can rationalize purchasing: household supplies, husband's clothes, children's wear. But beautiful and luxury goods for their personal use can be purchased legitimately only if some other member of the family is deprived. Although pilferers often have guilt feelings about their thefts, it still seems to them less wrong to steal from a rich store than to take from the family budget. (Cameron, 1964: 159).

Cameron makes clear that such amateurs do not think of themselves as thieves but engage in self-deception, rhetorical devices, and other procedures that make sense out of their behavior for them. In fact, security officers who apprehend them often must work hard to convince them that they are "really" thieves.

Surprisingly many people steal without seeing themselves as thieves. Libraries, for example, consider theft a most serious problem, and yet those who steal books would seldom call themselves thieves. It is claimed that 2 to 30 percent of some library collections disappear every year (Bahr and Bahr, 1979). According to these authors, "Users of the New York Public Library make off with 10 percent of its collection each year." They further write:

> The books most frequently stolen from our shelves [Allentown (Pa.) Public Library] are spiritual self-help books. . . .
> Nationally, about 5 percent of all new books disappear from library shelves within six months of purchase, and the overwhelming majority are fiction.
> When a medical library in Portland, Ore., added an electronic surveillance system, a physician protested . . . that the device was an insult to his honesty and integrity. Yet somebody's integrity was certainly in question: as of its last inventory, the library had lost 6 percent of its collection — 3100 expensive medical books (p. 34).

Of particular importance here is the surprise displayed by those who steal books when they are accused of theft and threatened with prosecution. Clearly they do not view themselves as thieves.

Like many other forms of deviance, shoplifting may be engaged in for the excitement of the act itself. This motive may operate alone or in combination with a desire for the items taken. It may be just such excitement that motivates *kleptomania,* a compulsion to steal that is often cited as a "cause" of customer theft. On the other hand, kleptomania may be, as Bierce suggests in *The Devil's Dictionary* (1967), merely used to describe a rich thief. It may serve as a useful lie for those who are caught shoplifting: "I couldn't help it." "It's kleptomania."

In the forms of illegal dishonesty we have been considering, there is some disagreement over the "wrongness" of the acts. Often employees justify their theft in terms of job conditions or the nature of the companies for which they work. Customer thefts are more often recognized as "wrong," though amateurs may maintain that their acts are not as wrong as "real theft." Some even develop a rhetoric that their theft is "right," given the nature of the institutions from which they steal. Stealing from stores may even be considered by a small number of people as a political act, justified by the "oppressive" nature of those businesses. During the 1960s an informant spoke to Waksler of "liberating a steak" from the grocery store, presumably in response to the store's policy of taking advantage of customers through high prices.

Next we consider acts that are more generally regarded as wrong in terms of moral values prevalent in the United States, though here, too, we will encounter some ambiguity. Slowly we are making our way to what people see as "real" theft, though the line over which one steps is broad and vague.

Amateur Theft Against Business and the Public

In this section we consider the amateur forms of three kinds of illegal dishonesty that involve not only business but the public at large — burglary, mugging, and robbery. Although research data are scanty, we want to indicate what is known about these crimes in their amateur forms so that we can compare them with their professional forms, which we look at in Chapter 10.

BURGLARY

Burglary involves entering the premises of another with the *intent* to steal, even if such theft does not take place. Amateur burglary against both individuals and business, especially breaking and entering homes, businesses, and parked cars, is extremely widespread in the United States and reaches what some view as epidemic proportions in some cities. Its extent and the wide variety of objects stolen makes it unlikely that there are any dominant or common characteristics or motives among all those who engage in this activity. Some criminologists and many members of the public believe that "epidemics" of theft are largely the work of heroin addicts seeking money to purchase illegal heroin, but the evidence for such a claim is not strong. Such theft seems to be a somewhat recent phenomenon, and certainly theft has many other motives. On the other hand, there is some evidence that when heroin is provided through legal means, as in some rehabilitative programs in England, the burglary rate falls.

Unlike employee theft and customer theft, burglary involves a person's illegal presence. Not only does a burglar steal; a burglar breaks property rules by being in a place illegitimately. In fact many of those whose property has been stolen are upset not only by the loss of property but by the fact that a "stranger" has "violated" the place where they live or work. An informant describing a burglary to Waksler spoke with feeling about having her clothes thrown around and torn and her jewelry stolen, but her particular outrage was directed to the fact that the burglar had used her bathroom. Though we can speak of burglary in terms of property loss, the sense of violation that is sometimes associated with it seems to bear some similarities to responses to rape.

Amateur burglaries are committed by a wide variety of people — working alone or together — for a wide range of motives. One explanation for burglary draws on Merton's theory of anomie (see Chapter 2, pp. 45–49), focusing particularly on those who have accepted the success values of the United States but either do not see legitimate means available to them or for some other reason reject legitimate means. These people are what Merton calls "innovators," those who use illegitimate means (burglary) to achieve generally accepted goals (monetary success).

Social science knowledge about amateur burglary is very limited. The topic has for the most part not been studied by intensive field research methods, largely because it is so individualized, varied, and sporadic. We have nonetheless introduced it here because its existence is important to recognize. As we shall see in Chapter 10, professional burglary has been studied to a greater extent. There is some evidence, however, that amateur burglary reflects consumer patterns; burglars are likely to steal popular consumer items that can be readily exchanged for cash. A stolen television set or stereo or bicycle can be sold more easily than a rare painting or a piece of antique furniture; the latter items are generally stolen by professionals who have the connections necessary to unload them. Amateur burglary thus seems to be a way to get money when other means are, for a variety of reasons, seen as restricted or unavailable.

MUGGING

Mugging is a term used informally to describe a particular kind of robbery, either armed or unarmed, directed toward individuals rather than larger groups and businesses and involving physical contact between the participants with at least potential physical harm to the victim. Mugging may be done by either amateurs or professionals, but the low level of skill and knowledge it requires makes it predominantly an amateur activity. Hunt, who has devoted considerable study to the topic, says of mugging:

[The term] has apparently filled a need, becoming the useful generic label for robberies with varied techniques but a single underlying behavioral style — one characterized by desperation, recklessness, impulsivity, a lack of criminal professionalism, and, especially, the use of physical contact often involving violence far in excess of what is needed to obtain the victim's money (Hunt, 1972: 23).

Although the term "mugging" is relatively recent, there is no reason to assume that the practice itself is new. There does, however, seem to be a current trend toward an increase, though this judgment is based on rough estimates rather than on official statistics. Hunt suggests that there were about 60,000 muggings in 1964 and close to 175,000 in 1970, three-fourths occurring in cities (Hunt, 1972: 23).

Mugging, the major form of the "crime in the streets" to which the media, officials, and the public in the United States have increasingly turned their attention, is a source of particular concern to city dwellers. This fear became pronounced in the 1960s and 1970s, reaching almost epidemic proportions in both New York City and Washington, D.C. One observer commented: "The only couple that now walks in Central Park is Bonnie and Clyde." Robert Lejeune and Nicholas Alex have described the general effects of public concern with mugging:

In recent years, one crime has preoccupied the popular mind and the mass media that amplify and shape it. This crime is the mugging. Along with the villain who lurks in hallways, elevators, and streets, the mugging has come to symbolize for many citizens a growing sense that the social order has broken down, or at least has changed beyond recognition. The emergence of the mugger and his victim as new social types or roles, as characters on the urban stage, vividly dramatizes the problem of order to which humans, as members of an organized society, must continually address themselves. . . .

Very likely, both the personal nature of the crime and its increased frequency in recent years have made it the dramatic focus for the fear and anger of urban citizens. But there is more to it than that. Mugging seems to call into question the assumptions that have, heretofore at least, governed the role of the citizen in an urban environment. Because it has shattered the basic frame of everyday life, this disruptive encounter has sociological significance beyond the concern it evokes from many of the potential preys in the "urban jungle." His encounter with the mugger leaves the victim in a position to question his basic assumptions about himself, about others, and about his surroundings (Lejeune and Alex in *Urban Life and Culture*, October 1973: 260–261).

Mugging involves dishonesty in two forms. First, it is the "obviously" dishonest act of taking something that does not belong to one — money or goods that are the property of another. Second, and more fundamental, mugging violates our assumptions about *whom* we can trust. The criminal subcultures and criminal organizations we will examine in

Chapter 10 are to some extent less threatening to social order than muggers, for the former are more identifiable — communities with professional criminals are likely to recognize them as such and to come to terms with them, often by merely steering clear of them. Muggers, on the other hand, could be *anyone,* a perception particularly clear to those walking alone at night in the city. Those who choose to remain at home at night rather than risk being out exemplify this concern that anyone encountered on the street *could be* a mugger.

Severe violence is rare in muggings but every mugging possesses that potential. "Everyday" muggings more frequently succeed on the basis of threats alone with little actual physical contact taking place. Although some muggers may prefer to use violence, some violence in mugging is a response to the actions of victims — either self-defense or panic that is met by violence on the part of the mugger. Mugging seems more likely to be a means rather than a goal. Nonetheless, the very existence of instances where the victim "does nothing" and is still assaulted makes *any* mugging an ambiguous situation for the victim, one in which the behavior of any mugger is uncertain.

Lejeune and Alex (1973) found in their study of 37 mugging victims that for many of them the experience left lasting feelings of fear and anger. Some developed a general anxiety and distrust of public settings. Many victims had not taken seriously the media stories of muggings until they were mugged.

Research on mugging by the interviewing of victims presents particular difficulties, for it is virtually impossible to reconstruct the event. Given the strong feelings activated in a mugging, neither muggers nor victims are likely to be able, even if willing, to reconstruct what happened. Much of such reconstruction is likely to draw on prior common-sense knowledge — "I know what muggings are like so I will 'remember' my experience in those terms" — and thus seems to support such knowledge when in fact it merely draws on it. Even interviews with muggers would present similar problems. Observations of muggings are both unlikely and fraught with ethical problems; sociologists might well find it difficult to stand by and watch muggings instead of intervening. Detailed research on mugging seems to await new and innovative methods.

UNARMED AND ARMED ROBBERY

All robbery involves at least an implicit threat of physical injury — otherwise why would one turn over money or possessions to another? Though mugging emphasizes threat and violence, other forms of robbery minimize them. The robber may say, and mean: "I really don't want to hurt you." Many armed robbers claim that they carry weapons "just in case" and not with any commitment to using them "unless it's really necessary."

There are no studies of amateur robbers as high in quality as the studies of professionals by Letkemann (1973), Cressey (1953), Lemert (1958), and others. The evidence we do have, such as videotapes of bank robberies, suggests that armed robberies are committed predominantly by young men. Professional robbers show contempt for amateurs, particularly for their tendency to become scared and nervous during the robbery and to use "unnecessary force" and violence.

An element in the study of robbery often neglected by social scientists is the *danger* faced by the robbers themselves. Some amateurs may be attracted by such a risk; robbery is indeed a dangerous activity, as evidenced in news reports of shoot-outs in which robbers are injured or killed. One task of professional robbers, as we shall see in the next chapter, is to minimize these risks, whereas amateurs often act in ways that increase the risks.

Some states have established mandatory sentence laws for armed robbery, and some retail stores that are frequently held up post signs on their front doors that say, for example, "If you commit armed robbery, you will go to prison!" We do not know the extent to which such laws reduce amateur robbery or encourage its *unarmed* form. It does seem, however, that at least in the United States unarmed robbery is a dangerous enterprise, especially when many people, store owners in particular, arm themselves for self-protection. In England, where it is less common for the general public, robbers, and even police to possess weapons, unarmed robbery seems more feasible.

At least some of our information about amateur robbers comes from studies of professional robbers, who view amateurs as "bums" or "young punks" (Letkemann, 1973: 23–24). Professionals, however, also may be involved in "teaching" amateurs to become professionals, especially when the two categories have opportunities for frequent interaction, as in prison. Other amateurs may plan the move to professional status without prison experience. One of the respondents in Lonnie Athens's case studies of criminal homicide declared:

> I felt I was a mature man. I was deadly serious, 24 hours during business. I only played when there was no business to take care of. I wanted to be a professional [criminal], not an amateur (Athens, 1974).

Amateur robbery seems to be a somewhat difficult activity to sustain, and we might speculate that there is considerable movement into professional robbery, to less dangerous forms of crime, or even into noncriminal lives and occupations.

In Chapter 10 we consider professional crime and examine professional robbery. In order to appreciate the differences, consider this statement by Ray Johnson. He spent 25 years in San Quentin and other prisons for his criminal activities and is now a social researcher in San Diego studying amateur armed robbery for the 6400 "7-Eleven" stores, which are frequently held up. He advises clients on appropriate behavior when faced with amateur robbers. Such advice is, of course, unnecessary when professional robbers are involved, because their profession requires their "knowing how to act like robbers." Johnson offers this advice:

> [The victim] should try to make the transaction go as quickly and smoothly as if he were selling the guy a shirt. The quicker you get him and you separated, the better it is for everybody — and compliance is the best way.
>
> Try to warn him about anything that might startle him. Often shootings occur when the guy hears someone in the back room and becomes startled. All it takes is a quarter inch of pressure, and off goes the gun.
>
> The most dangerous period often occurs after the guy has got the money and is uncertain what to do with the clerk to increase his chances of getting away. That happened to one of the clerks we trained. The robber stood there with the money in his hand, kind of uncertain. So she said: "The last three times I was robbed, they told me to lie down. Do you want me to lie down?" So the guy said, "Yes, lay down." She did, and he was gone (Johnson, 1978: 52).

Burglary, mugging, and both unarmed and armed robbery appear to be clearly and distinctly dishonest. It is difficult to imagine one engaging in them unwittingly. Yet the three college students who burglarized the postoffice, discussed earlier in this chapter, apparently did not really *intend* their clearly criminal activity. Self-deception is possible even in burglary, mugging, and robbery. Thus, for instance, one may see oneself as an unarmed robber who carries a gun "just for protection" or "just in case" and not as a real part of one's equipment. In a variety of ways one can claim to *not really be* what one appears to be.

One important distinction between amateur and professional criminals may be that amateurs don't see themselves as "really" criminals, even though they may admit, as least to themselves and perhaps to close associates, that they do burglarize or mug or rob. Professional criminals, on the other hand, seem more likely to identify themselves as burglars or thieves or whatever, though many may deny the negative evaluations of such activities by the "straight" world.

The Many Faces of Dishonesty Reconsidered

In this chapter we have moved from simple lying to oneself to armed robbery. We can see the links that all these activities have with *both* honesty and dishonesty; we can also see the links that join the criminal and noncriminal worlds. Divisions are not clear, and boundary lines may be crossed unintentionally or unwittingly. Rhetoric, for example, serves to blur already vague lines and may facilitate both dishonesty and crime by calling them forms of honesty or "not really crime."

We have seen that *dishonesty* is an important aspect of everyday life, facilitating interactions and minimizing conflict. Dishonesty in everyday life may also serve as a bridge from noncriminal to criminal activities, as for example when occasional employee theft turns into systematic theft or burglary. In Chapter 10 we will see that *honesty* is a basic feature of criminal subcultures and criminal organizations, so essential that in its absence such subcultures and organizations cannot exist. We will also see the ways in which evasions, lies, fronts, tricks, rhetorics, and seductions are used by professional criminals in ways similar to their use in noncriminal everyday life and in amateur crime, though to somewhat different purposes. It is important to recognize that while professional criminals use such techniques, they have not *created* them, but simply draw upon and elaborate techniques readily available in everyday life.

It would be far easier for sociologists if dishonesty were always deviant and honesty always nondeviant. They are not, however, and it becomes important for sociologists to recognize the complex relations between honesty and dishonesty, nondeviance and deviance, and noncriminal and criminal acts, and to respect the nature of what is being studied, however much it might differ from common-sense expectations.

10

The Many Faces of Dishonesty: Criminal Subcultures and Criminal Organizations

In Chapter 9 we discussed what is known as *amateur* crime. We now consider *professional* crime; we are concerned with those who in some sense make crime a profession.* As in Chapter 9, we will draw on the new perspective, especially in showing the continuity between criminal activities and everyday noncriminal life.

Crime as a Profession

In 1937 Edwin Sutherland wrote his now-famous study, *The Professional Thief*. Using information provided by his key informant, "Chic," Sutherland compared the life of the "professional thief" to the lives of members of the socially accepted professions and found enough similarities to suggest that certain kinds of crimes as practiced by certain kinds of criminals could be viewed as professions. Sutherland identified significant differences between amateur and professional criminals, differences that sociologists continue to recognize today.

According to Sutherland, professional criminals:

1. Have "a complex of abilities and skills, just as do physicians, lawyers, or bricklayers."

* Those members of socially accepted professions — business executives, doctors, government officials, and so forth — who engage in criminal activities will be considered in Chapter 11.

2. Have a status "based upon . . . technical skill, financial standing, connections, power, dress, manners, and wide knowledge. . . ."
3. Possess "a complex of common and shared feelings and overt acts."
4. Associate with other professional criminals; (see our earlier discussion of *differential association* in Chapter 3, pp. 78–79).
5. Engage in activity that is organized, "in the sense that it is a system in which informal unity and reciprocity may be found . . ." (Sutherland, 1937: 197–219).

Although members of society may be reluctant to view crime as a profession, criminals with the above attributes share sufficient characteristics with the "legitimate" professions to make sociological study of them *as* professionals fruitful. It is with these professional criminals that we are particularly concerned in this chapter.

Criminal Subcultures

Subcultures based on criminal activities are probably about as old as cultures themselves. Pirates have certainly existed almost as long as trade by camel caravans and ship. Myths and stories of Robin Hood in the fourteenth and fifteenth centuries illustrate the operation of a criminal subculture. The novels of Charles Dickens portray such subcultures in great detail. Early social science research, however, drawing on an absolutist perspective, tended to neglect the organized dimension of such subcultures; rather, theories of social disorganization persisted. Sutherland's emphasis on the organized quality of professional crime led to a theoretical breakthrough in sociology, directing sociologists to look for the organized, "normal," everyday features of criminal activities.

Further encouragement along these lines was provided by David Maurer's vivid studies, *The Big Con* (1940) and *Whiz Mob* (1955). The tremendous impact of his work derives both from its quality and from its movement beyond mere transcription of the abundant and colorful memories of ex-thieves to systematic study of day-to-day activities from the perspective of insiders. Only in recent years have studies of comparable value emerged. This new work from such sociologists as Ned Polsky (1967), John Irwin (1970), Werner Einstadter (1969), Neal Shover (1971), Carl Klockars (1974), and (1974) Letkemann (1973) has generally supported many of the findings of Sutherland and Maurer, though some differences have come out (as in Einstadter's study of systematic armed robbers, 1969).

The following statements are now commonly accepted by sociologists as true of criminal subcultures:

1. Those engaged in criminal activities, especially when they are members of criminal subcultures, may share many characteristics with "legitimate" professionals. The comments of Sutherland's informant, "Chic," reveal an organized style of committing crime quite different from that of amateur criminals.

2. Criminal subcultures have existed for centuries, though both their content and their prevalence vary according to time and place. Though he was unusually committed and successful, Chic provided overall an accurate picture of criminal subcultures in his own time, as evidenced by later documentations. Recent evidence also suggests, however, that in Chic's day criminal subcultures had begun to weaken in the increasingly individualistic, complex, and changing United States. John Irwin (1970) has argued that their strength may have always been limited to old ethnic communities of some eastern and midwestern cities and a few other cities such as San Francisco and New Orleans.

3. Criminal subcultures continue to exist in the United States, though their strength and other properties vary from place to place. In general they remain strongest in the East and Midwest and weakest in the South and West. They are also, however, strong in such places as Miami Beach and Las Vegas, resorts where a rich clientele provides valuable resources for many professional criminals.

4. Criminal subcultures differ greatly in the degree to which they fit Sutherland's original model of professional activity. For example, thieves, especially con artists and shoplifters, seem to be both highly professional and highly active in subcultures, burglars somewhat less so, and armed robbers even less. Although Sutherland emphasized the importance for subcultural involvement of a shared social identity as a "professional," Einstadter (1969), Letkemann (1973), and others have found that such an identity may be based on the idea of "career," "occupation," or "job."

Members of criminal subcultures seldom restrict themselves to the practice of a single type of crime; indeed they increasingly come to participate in a variety of criminal activities engaged in or supported by other members of the subculture. Safecrackers, for example, may commit other types of crime, especially those requiring related techniques. (See, for example, Shover, 1971, 1974; for a fictional account of the diverse activities a criminal group may be called upon to engage in, see Donald Westlake's humorous novel, *The Hot Rock*, 1970.) An example of this willingness to change "jobs" is provided by Jerry, the major informant in an extensive study of drug dealing (see Adler, Adler, and Douglas, forthcoming). Jerry moved from shady sales work to marijuana smuggling to check forgery to a business deal that resembled a con to smuggling cocaine and emeralds, and so on. This "adaptability" suggests that criminals such as Jerry are committed not to a particular type of crime or to crime in general but to "hustling."

Self-Definitions of Criminals as Hustlers

Professional or career criminals commonly identify themselves as "hustlers." Not all hustlers, however, see themselves, or are seen by others, as criminals. "Hustler" is a broader category than "criminal" just as "deviance" is a broader category than "crime." Noncriminal hustlers may be involved in activities that are "shady" but not actually illegal.

Hustlers are always on the lookout for an "angle," a way of beating someone else out of money or other valuables. Legal methods may be preferred but illegal strategies often prove more remunerative and are willingly selected. Hustlers are proud of their skills and many of those who make their living without actually breaking the law share their status of "hustler" enthusiastically with those engaged in illegal activities.

The hustler sees the world as a jungle, a scene of continual conflict and combat in which the clever and alert person outwits the "mark."* If we substitute "thug" for "mark," this picture is not unlike that drawn by victims of muggings, by the police, and the public, though the hustler's response to this definition of the situation differs from that made by these others. The theme of the jungle in which the alert "fox" outwits the "cony,"† and the immense sense of pride felt upon victory, is repeated over and over in accounts and memoirs of hustlers:

> Full-time hustlers never can relax to appraise what they are doing and where they are bound. As is the case in any jungle, the hustler's every waking hour is lived with both the practical and subconscious knowledge that if he ever relaxes, if he ever slows down, the other hungry, restless foxes, ferrets, wolves, and vultures out there with him won't hesitate to make him their prey. . . . What I was learning was the hustling society's first rule; that you never trusted anyone outside of your own close-mouthed circle, and that you selected with time and care before you made any intimates even among these (Malcolm X, 1965: 109, 87).
>
> There's a mark born every minute and a con man every hour. The con man is born to take care of the marks. Of course, I am a con man. There really are only two classes of people — marks and con men. I decided early in life that the angle boy gets the worm. I didn't make the rules. I just try to live by them. I'd rather be a con man than a mark.

---

* A *mark* is the object or victim of a confidence artist's game. The term has been extended to the object of any illegal activity.

† A *cony* is a rabbit but the term is used to apply to a mark. See below, pp. 313–314, for a discussion of *cony-catching*.

You know how it goes in this dog-eat-dog world. You got to take the other guy before he takes you. You know, the real sharpies outwit the marks. Of course, it all depends on how you get ahead. My way was no different from, say, a lawyer or businessman. You know, a lawyer has a license to steal (Roebuck, 1964: 241–243).

Hustlers often search for or try to create forms of hustling that, though perhaps deviant, are not criminal. The ideal, as a seventeen-year-old inmate told Douglas at Petersburg Federal Reformatory for Juveniles, is to find a lucrative line of work that other people avoid because it is seen as immoral, but that is not technically illegal. Of course such work is rarely found unless the searcher has some very specialized knowledge or skills. Notice, however, that *legal* hustling is generally chosen not for moral but for practical reasons; *illegal* hustling may bring undesirable reprisals from law enforcers. Some, though not many, hustlers succeed in approaching the ideal. They may engage in activities that, although technically illegal, are subject to little if any enforcement — they may, for example, run massage parlors or clubs that offer nude dancing. Arrests are infrequent, penalties light, and, because of the ambiguity of many laws related to sexual activities, those involved may be able to avoid legal problems by altering conditions slightly.

Hustling provides a bridge between the noncriminal and criminal worlds. A shady operation, for example, can become either criminal or noncriminal simply by changing its emphasis. Hustlers may learn techniques that can be applied in both worlds. Hustling also involves use of the many modes of dishonesty we discussed in the last chapter: evasions, lies, fronts, tricks, rhetorics, and seductions. The very concept of hustling itself may well be useful in self-deception and may be considered a rhetoric used to explain one's activities. Later in this chapter we will look at five forms of professional crime in which these dimensions in varying combinations will appear. First, however, we will consider some of the reasons offered to explain *why* one would choose hustling as a way of life.

Motives of Hustlers and Criminals

Studies of experienced and successful criminals strongly emphasize the "normal" motivations of those studied, in contrast and even outright opposition to psychoanalytic explanations that focus on "abnormality" or "psychopathology." (For a standard and popular study of deviance based on psychoanalytic explanation, see Greenwald, *The Call Girl*, 1958.) Psychoanalysts emphasize "abnormal" motives and tend to see the acts themselves as proof of that abnormality. Sociologists have come to recognize the far more "normal" motives that characterize professional criminals.

There are a number of reasons for the limits of psychoanalytic explanations. First, early psychoanalytic theory embodied an absolutist stance that saw criminals as categorically abnormal. Second, psychiatrists see only a small and nonrepresentative part of the criminal population — those who seek or accept psychiatric "help." Psychoanalytic explanations have been particularly biased by the fact that very few who identify themselves as hustlers or professional criminals will seek or accept such help; they may in fact view themselves as having no problem. It may even be that hustlers and criminals who are "perfectly normal" are those least likely to come to the attention of psychiatrists. Sociologists are not arguing that criminals are all "well adjusted," but rather that their being criminals *in itself is not sufficient evidence of their being "abnormal."*

Beginning with Sutherland (1937), who argued that the professional criminals he studied were motivated by a sense of professional pride, sociologists have come increasingly to focus on "normal" motives for criminal activities. There is a danger, however, that sociologists, by focusing on "normal" motives, will overlook other less "normal" motives that may also be at work. Letkemann, in his study of *Crime as Work* (1973), was able to learn about the complex technical skills involved in the criminal activities of those he studied and the motivation of a "job well done," but his very focus minimized the chances that his respondents would talk about non-work-related motives. This is another form of the danger we discussed in terms of the Chicago school (Chapter 3, pp. 62–64) with its idealization of crime.

Evidence continues to mount, however, in support of the existence of many common motives among criminals and noncriminals. An excerpt from Thomas Plate's journalistic account, *Crime Pays* (1975), displays just this continuity:

> It used to be believed that all criminals were casualties of society, a sort of class of unfortunates. We believed that the underlying causes were such regrettable factors as a deprived childhood, a weak family structure, a lack of religious conviction, a Y gene, the ghetto experience, an early mistake that snowballed into a lifetime of error — and so on. Indeed, in many circles in the United States, these remain the accepted explanations for professional crime.
>
> But, as Harvard professor James Q. Wilson, among others, has pointed out, such easy assumptions about crime have little if any basis in solid fact. There is simply no good reason why crime must be understood as the direct outcome of bad housing, unemployment, ghettos, and so forth.
>
> I would go further. It is my hypothesis that professional crime, as we will define it, is divorced from these factors.

Professional crime is the deliberately illegal pursuit of money along well-defined lines. The cause of *professional* crime is not just the criminal's desire for money, but also the surfeit of it in society. . . .

Professional crime is primarily a money crime. This is its essential character. For the professional criminal — whether white, black or brown, immigrant or native-born, child of middle-class or of poverty — the motive force is business: *green* is beautiful (Plate, 1975: 1–2).

It is clear that Plate sees money as a main motive for professional criminals. His focus is on particularly successful criminals, but we must not underestimate money as at least *one* motive in professional crime, in hustling, and even in amateur crime. When crime stops paying, its practice is drastically reduced.

It is useful to distinguish between motives for *beginning* a criminal activity and motives for *continuing* it. Money may be an important motivation for continuing, but it does not seem a sufficient motive for *choosing* a criminal rather than a noncriminal route to financial success. The risks of choosing a criminal career seem high — possible imprisonment, in some forms of crime a high risk of being killed, and myriad other dangers. Sociological concern with "normal" motives can overlook the basic fact that criminal and noncriminal careers are not *exactly* the same.

Even though the idea that poverty, slums, and unemployment *cause* crime is questionable, such factors may be important for the opportunities that they do or do not provide. They may, for example, provide the "invitation" to crime (see Matza, 1969, and above, Chapter 7, pp. 226–227), opportunities to begin a criminal career that are less accessible to others. Poverty and unemployment may be seen as useful preconditions to a strong desire for money. Daniel Bell (1953) has argued that in some poor urban areas of the United States crime is a "way of life" that enables many to get ahead in life and eventually to succeed when noncriminal routes are seen as unavailable. (Bell's theory is a refinement of Merton's theory of anomie, described in Chapter 2, pp. 45–49.) Plate, however, though he minimizes unduly the importance of such factors as poverty and slums, does provide evidence that many career criminals do have "legitimate opportunities" available to them and choose not to take them. Those who succeed at crime may well have been able to succeed at a somewhat similar noncriminal occupation — locksmith, salesperson, security guard, business executive, are but a few.

In fact, researchers are often struck by the intelligence of the professional criminals they study — an indication perhaps of the initial bias with which those researchers began their studies — and even speculate that those criminals might have more easily succeeded in noncriminal careers. Indeed, Jerry, the key informant in a study of soft drug dealers (Adler, Adler, and Douglas, forthcoming), had already been successful at various legal occupations including real estate sales. He continually abandoned legitimate though long-term opportunities for earning large sums and instead gravitated toward criminal opportunities that would make money more quickly, risking imprisonment, physical injury, or even death.

In many ways Jerry epitomizes the hustler, tempted to "get rich quick" by "taking the big gamble." "The big one" was just around the corner. Few legitimate activities provide such a chance to "get rich quick," though not all illegitimate activities do, either. The *belief* that the illegitimate opportunities will pay off, however, is an important motive for many who begin hustling. Those who succeed are particularly likely to continue; those who fail may continue their pursuit of the success that they know is "just around the corner."

Many criminal activities are seen as promising a "big score" quickly and with the kinds of risks that are exciting enough to increase the appeal. The "quick big score" and the "excitement" are given as motives by well-established professional criminals as well as by those just starting out. Every time a burglar breaks into a house or business there is the chance of being caught or even killed, but there is also the possibility of making "the big score." Every time an armed robber pulls a bank job, the risks of being caught are linked to the excitement of perhaps a "million-dollar haul." The excitement of the crime itself has been recognized by many researchers; Neal Shover has given numerous examples, both from his own studies and those of others, that show just such excitement:

> For instance, if you're punching a safe and you hear that pin hit the back of the safe—*clingggg!* — you know you're home free. If you're peeling it and you see that smoke come out — which is from that fire insulation in there — whenever you pop that door and see that smoke, you know that you've cracked the rivets and it's all yours. And when you pull that safe door open: it is a *charge*.
>
> I think the most safes I ever made was six in one night. But that was four of them in one building, and you just go from safe to safe. But man, it never became less. It's not like fucking, where the first time it's pretty wild, then each time it tapers off; you get part of the same drive, the same action, but it's not like the first. Safes are not like that. Each time it's more so because you figure the odds are more in your favor of it being the big score.*

This statement indicates both the inappropriateness of the psychoanalytic model as a source of explanation of what appear to be such "rational" choices and the weaknesses of a sociological model that makes crime seem "just like" noncrime. Consonant with the new perspective,

---

* From "The Good Burglar" by Neal Shover. Unpublished manuscript, 1974, University of Tennessee. Used by permission of the author.

many researchers are now recognizing the ways in which *criminal motives are both like and unlike noncriminal motives.* Criminals can be seen as both rational *and* as having some reasons that differ from those that predominate in the "straight" world. Furthermore, this view of criminals makes it possible to take seriously the idea of a criminal subculture — not a loose association of personality defectives but a subculture that, like other subcultures, provides support for those engaged in deviant activities.

Although subcultures may not motivate one's beginning of a criminal career, links with other criminal professionals may come to provide important motives for continuing a life of crime. Prison experiences may even solidify such group feelings, both by forging links between beginners and veterans and by providing opportunities, especially for those whose prison record limits their opportunities for legitimate careers. Many experienced criminals claim that at some time they have become "locked into" crime, both because their criminal records restrict their legitimate opportunities and because their success in acquiring "easy money" makes more laborious occupations seem unappealing. In both of these areas, criminal subcultures provide both practical and rhetorical support for members.

Continued research is needed on the reasons why professional criminals begin and continue their activities. The motives of the hustler are worth further consideration; keep them in mind as we examine some detailed instances of professional criminal activities.

Five Examples of Typical Professional Criminal Activities

A wide variety of criminal activities can be considered professional and subculturally based and supported. We have chosen five to focus on: confidence games, shoplifting, pickpocketing, burglary, and robbery. Our consideration of professional shoplifting, burglary, and robbery will allow fruitful comparison with the amateur pursuit of those activities (see Chapter 9). We begin with confidence games because con artists are particularly likely to see themselves as professionals and as sharing similarities with "legitimate" business people and because they make extensive use of everyday practices of dishonesty. We mentioned earlier that con artists, shoplifters, and pickpockets have been found to be most professional and most involved in criminal subcultures, burglars somewhat less so, and robbers even less; in what follows we will see some explanations for such findings.

CON GAMES

Confidence (con) games are practices that involve swindling "marks" or victims out of money, property, or other valuables. The confidence or trust of the mark is gained through rhetoric, staging, and other symbolic techniques that make things appear other than they are. A crucial component is the skill of the con artist. A talented con artist can create a sense of reality that may seduce even the most practical of people. Descriptions of con games often appear quite transparent to those who have never been marks. To counter skepticism, we offer the following fictional account and ask readers to consider how they might have acted in this situation.

For those unfamiliar with mystery stories involving the amateur detectives Pam and Jerry North, Pam's comments may appear disjointed, and in fact they are characteristically so, but they will ultimately become clear and are only momentarily disconcerting. As the scene opens, Pam and Jerry have just finished a game of tennis at a resort where they are staying when they are approached by a man:

> The man approaching had narrow shoulders and a narrow face. . . . He was wearing a dark business suit; his shirt was complete with tie. He even wore a hat . . . He came toward them and said, to two white-clad humans, both of them dripping moderately, "Been having a game?"
> "Yes," Jerry said. "Tennis."
> The man in the business suit saw nothing odd about this answer. Jerry felt he had wasted it.
> "Name of Ashley," the man said.
> "North."
> The man who had the name of Ashley looked away abruptly; looked toward the swimming pool.
> "I'll swear it is," Ashley said. "What do you know?"
> The Norths looked toward the swimming pool. A man was coming down from it, along the path toward the courts. He, also, wore a business suit. He wore a Panama hat. He, too, was a narrow man.
> Ashley looked at Pam North, at Jerry North. He said, in a tone of awe, "Worthington."
> "I'm sorry," Jerry said. "We're both sorry," Pam said, feeling that two could play at this game, also.
> "Down from Hialeah," Ashley said. "What do you know?"
> "I'm afraid — " Jerry North said.
> "*Must* have heard of him," Ashley said. "Everybody's heard of him. Worthington Farms, Kentucky."
> "I'm sorry," Pam North said.
> The man under the Panama advanced toward them.
> "Thoroughbreds," Ashley said. "Derby winner. Triple crown."
> "Oh," Pam said, "you mean he raises horses?"
> Ashley looked at her quickly. He looked away again. He raised his voice slightly. He said, "Mr. Worthington?"
> The man under the Panama said, "Yup."
> "Name of Ashley. Met you at — "
> "Yup. 'Lo, Ashley."

"Mr. North. Mrs. North."

The man under the Panama said, "Ma'am. Sir."

"Down from Hialeah?"

"Yup."

"I wonder if — " Ashley said.

"Thought you might," Worthington said. "Yup. Ladybug in the sixth. Monday. Shoo-in. Short odds. Maybe three to one. Can't have everything. Five lengths, could be. Well, got a plane to catch. Ma'am. Sir. Ashley."

He turned, as if to go away. He did not, Pam thought, turn with any decisiveness.

Ashley looked at Jerry North and raised his eyebrows. Jerry was conscious that he himself blinked slightly.

"If you're going back to Miami," Ashley said, to Worthington, who did not, Pam thought, actually seem to be going any place. "On this filly. I can't get away. Stuck here. Wonder if — "

"You'll talk about it. Gets out and the odds — "

"Mum," Ashley said. "As an oyster, Mr. Worthington. It would be a favor. Isn't often anybody can get the word from a man like you, Mr. Worthington. Is it, Mr. North?"

There was excitement in Ashley's voice. There was even a kind of awe in his voice. Opportunity, his tone said, was not only knocking at the door. It was trying to beat the door down.

"I guess not," Jerry said. There was, somewhere, a light tapping.

"Not much," Ashley said, again to Worthington. "Not enough to hurt the odds. Maybe fifty?"

He reached to his hip pocket, took a wallet out. "If I can feel I've got my own money on her — "

"You'll keep your mouth shut," Worthington said. "Generous of you, suh."

Ashley waited. Worthington considered; his narrow face was all consideration.

"Sort of got me, haven't you?" he said. "Well — all right."

"My friend here, too?"

Ashley indicated Gerald North.

Mr. Worthington sighed heavily, a man trapped by his own inadvertence.

"You're crowding me," he said. "But — yup." He took a small notebook from his pocket. It had a pencil between the leaves.

"Thomas J. Ashley," Ashley said. "I'm staying at the Key Lodge."

"Fifty on the nose," Worthington said. He sighed again. Ashley opened his wallet and gave Worthington a bill. It was a fifty-dollar bill. Worthington looked at Jerry. Jerry felt, momentarily and obscurely, that this had all been decided.

"Gerald — " he began, and Mr. Worthington began to write in his small notebook. And Jerry was aware that his hand was reaching toward Pam's straw handbag, in which, when they are dressed for tennis, all things are carried, including billfolds.

But then Ashley, who was looking toward the hotel, made a small "uh-uhing" sound, and the man named Worthington looked in the same direction, and Pam and Jerry looked.

Paul Grogan, managing director of The Coral Isles, was advancing, under the white plume of his hair — a plume which had become a banner. While he was still many yards away, Mr. Grogan held his right hand out stiffly, the index finger pointing like a gun.

Mr. Worthington did not say anything at all. He began to walk briskly toward the patio, beyond which there was an exit to the street. Mr. Ashley said, "Well . . ." and also went.

"And stay out," Mr. Grogan said, still from a distance, and in what was not quite a shout. "Catch you here once more and . . ."

He did not finish. It was evident that he was not going to catch the Messrs. Worthington and Ashley. Not without running. He did not run. He walked on, still briskly, to the Norths. He said, "That pair of small-time con men. I hope you didn't fall for — "

"Of course not," Pam North said. "We never even thought of it, did we, Jerry?"

Jerry swallowed. Jerry said, "Of course not."

"Ashley," Grogan said. "Not that his name is Ashley, probably. Anyway, he's been at it for years, with one partner and another. Other one's new. Heard somewhere he used to be a lawyer in New York and got in some kind of a jam. Got in jail too, apparently. Anyway — " He shrugged his shoulders, and responsibility for two small-time con men slipped from them.*

Worthington and Ashley used a variety of lies and tricks in this con game, claiming that they were strangers to one another, that one was a horse breeder who would reluctantly place bets, that they would "do a favor" for Jerry North by placing a bet for him, and so forth. Yet the whole process unfolds so smoothly that for many readers it is only Grogan's appearance that signals trouble.

Worthington and Ashley were engaged in a *short con,* a swindle that requires a minimum of staging and special effects and relies largely on a quick pitch to the mark. The *pigeon drop* is one of the classic short con games. It involves convincing a mark that the con artist has found a large sum of money that will be shared with the mark if the mark will put up some money with a third person as a show of good faith. The con artist and the third person then disappear with the mark's money. This "plot outline" sounds obviously phony as we are presenting it, but in the hands of a skillful con artist it can be quite convincing, as is evidenced by the remarkable success it continues to meet with.

The prime task of the con artist, in both the short and long con, is to "convince" the mark that it is possible to "strike it rich" by joining in on the proposed activities. As that moment approaches, the mark is

* Abridged from pages 18–21 in *Murder by the Book* by Frances and Richard Lockridge (J. B. Lippincott Company) copyright © 1963 by Frances and Richard Lockridge. Reprinted by permission of Harper & Row Publishers Inc.

increasingly likely to suspend doubt in the operation and to have confidence in the con artist. What con artists refer to as the "larceny in the heart" of the mark is used both to work the con and to justify it for, as con artists claim, "You can't con an honest man." An important point in the con is the actual transfer of money from mark to con artist; thereafter the task of the con artist is aided by the mark's commitment to the activity and thus the mark is more likely to believe the stories the con artist offers preparatory to abandoning the mark.

A big "virtue" of the con game from the point of view of the con artist is the high probability that marks will not seek police assistance. First, marks often come to realize that they have been "played for suckers," an admission that many are unwilling to make to the police or even to friends and relatives. Second, the activity proposed by the con artist is often either shady or clearly illegal — once again something that one would not bring to the police. The weakness and awkwardness of the mark's position as "victim" is particularly evident in the long con.

The *long or big con* is a more complicated production that may take some time to work, involve a wide variety of criminal accomplices, and entail the construction of *physical fronts* such as phony boxing arenas, phony stock market exchanges, phony Western Union offices, or other structures whose very existence are used to persuade the mark of the "legitimacy" of the undertaking. These physical fronts or *big stores*, as they were called, are no longer used widely; they were very effectively used to establish a legitimate-looking setting for con games. They were carefully built to look real in every detail and contributed to the confidence of the mark in the action being proposed.

The *wire* was one of the classic long cons. The physical fronts constructed for the con included a phony Western Union office and a phony bookie joint (an illegal gambling room for off-track betting on horse races). At the time, race results were reported by Western Union wires (telegrams). The wire con worked by convincing the mark that his new "friends" (the con artists) were able to get race results from the Western Union office before the bookies could. It would therefore be possible to place bets on horses that had already won but about which the bookies did not yet have the information. The mark then was presumably being involved in a scheme to cheat bookies out of money. Con artists seldom directly proposed such a scheme to the marks; they simply staged the operation, letting the mark see them operating — picking up early results at the Western Union office, rushing to the nearby bookie joint, placing their bets amid all the turmoil of the betting scene, and then collecting money. Any mark with a "gambling spirit" was certainly tempted by such a "sure thing," and many were eager to take part. Once the mark was hooked, he would place increasingly large bets until, one of the large bets being in the hands of the bookie, the bookie joint would close suddenly, perhaps through a phony police raid, and the mark would be left with no way of collecting on the bet or recovering the amount bet. Clearly few marks who participated in the wire con rushed off to tell their sad tale to the police.

All con games work on the mark's desire for fast money, and con artists claim that marks deserve what they get. Con artists in particular see a continuity in motives between the noncriminal and the criminal world. The con artist feels superior to the mark, for the mark is merely greedy but the con artist is skilled. The extent of this skill is demonstrated in both the general conceptualization of the con game and the specific techniques involved. David Maurer, in his classic study, *The Big Con* (1940), describes the elements:

> A confidence man prospers only because of the fundamental dishonesty of his victim. In his operations, he must first inspire a firm belief in his own integrity. Second, he brings into play powerful and well-nigh irresistible forces to excite the cupidity of the mark. Then he allows the victim to make large sums of money by means of dealings which are explained to him as being dishonest and hence a "sure thing." As the lust for large and easy profits is fanned into a hot flame, the mark puts all his scruples behind him. He closes out his bank account, liquidates his property, borrows from his friends, embezzles from his employer or his clients. In the mad frenzy of cheating someone else, he is unaware of the fact that he is the real victim, carefully selected and fattened for the kill. Thus arises the trite but nonetheless sage maxim: "You can't cheat an honest man" (p. 13).

Some classic short and long cons are still used successfully, but even with classic forms, con artists customarily find it both more effective and safer to change the specific forms of the cons. As people learn about old cons, new ones are developed. Nowadays long cons deal less with gambling and more with real estate speculation and other activities aligned with the business world. Short cons have changed less and still succeed. The elderly are often viewed as particularly desirable marks.

Con artists are especially skilled in making use of the many faces of dishonesty. Their competence at lies and the construction of fronts is pronounced, and they have developed an impressive rhetoric that justifies their actions — a rhetoric often supported by the marks themselves. The very *dishonesty* of the mark makes the con game possible. Nonetheless, their work demands that con artists be able to *trust* the many others upon whom their work depends.

The *overlap* between deviant and nondeviant worlds (Matza, 1969) is exemplified by the application of con-game terminology to nondeviant everyday activities. In his article "On Cooling the Mark Out: Some Aspects of Adaptation to Failure" (1952), Goffman describes the process used by con artists to "keep the anger of the mark within manageable and sensible proportions. The operator stays behind his team-mates in the capacity of what might be called a cooler and exercises upon the mark the art of consolation. An attempt is made to define the situation for the mark in a way that makes it easy for him to accept the inevitable and quietly go home" (in Rose, 1962: 484). The aim is to prevent the mark's making trouble. Goffman applies the idea of "cooling out" to a variety of everyday situations, such as those in which retail store employees deal with dissatisfied customers, college personnel "ease out" failing students, bosses tell employees that they have been bypassed for promotion, and spouses or lovers terminate relationships. Goffman recognizes the widespread use of this con-game process: "Persons who participate in what is recognized as a confidence game are found in only a few social settings, but persons who have to be cooled out are found in many. Cooling the mark out is one theme in a very basic social story" (p. 486).

SHOPLIFTING AND PICKPOCKETING

In Chapter 9 we considered *amateur* shoplifting; here we look into *professional* shoplifting (the stealing of displayed goods from a store). We also examine pickpocketing (the stealing of goods from a person's pocket or purse without the victim's awareness), which by its nature is a professional rather than an amateur crime. It involves techniques and skills and often the use of accomplices. Mugging and robbery might be viewed as its amateur equivalents, since they involve stealing goods from a person directly, but they differ in that the victim is aware of the theft.

We consider professional shoplifting and pickpocketing together because of the qualities they share: a long history of development and refinement, a complex body of techniques for dealing with victims and obtaining goods, and an involvement with other members of criminal subcultures.

The long history of these activities is exemplified in the following account of pickpocketing in *The Second Part of Cony-Catching*, by Robert Greene,* published in 1592. The language is antiquated; the incident bears many similarities in style and spirit to present practices:

> There walked in the middle walk [central aisle of St. Paul's] a plain country farmer, a man of good wealth, who had a well-lined purse, only barely thrust up in a round slop, which a crew of foists† having perceived, their hearts were set on fire to have it, and every one had a fling at him, but all in vain, for he kept his hand close in his pocket, and his purse fast in his fist like a subtle churl, that either had been forewarned of Paul's, or else had aforetime

* A cony-catcher is literally one who catches rabbits (conies), but the word cony came to be applied to the mark or victim and cony-catcher to the thief.
† A foist is a pickpocket.

smoked some of that faculty. Well, howsoever it was impossible to do any good with him, he was so wary. The foists spying this, strained their wits to the highest string how to compass this bung, yet could not all their politic conceits fetch the farmer over, for jostle him, chat with him, offer to shake him by the hand, all would not serve to get his hand out of his pocket. At last one of the crew, that for his skill might have been doctorate in his mystery, amongst them all chose out a good foist, one of a nimble hand and great agility, and said to the rest thus:

"Masters, it shall not be said such a base peasant shall slip away from such a crew of gentlemen-foists as we are, and not have his purse drawn, and therefore this time I'll play the stall myself, and if I hit him not home, count me for a bungler for ever"; and so left them and went to the farmer and walked directly before him and next him three or four turns. At last, standing still, he cried, "Alas, honest man, help me. I am not well"; and with that sunk down suddenly in a swoon. The poor farmer, seeing a proper young gentleman, as he thought, fall dead afore him, stepped to him, held him in his arms, rubbed him and chafed him.

At this, there gathered a great multitude of people about him, and the whilst the foist drew the farmer's purse and away. By that the other thought the feat was done, he began to come something to himself again, and so half staggering, stumbled out of Paul's, and went after the crew where they had appointed to meet, and there boasted of his wit and experience.

The farmer, little suspecting this villainy, thrust his hand into his pocket and missed his purse, searched for it, but lining and shells and all was gone, which made the countryman in a great maze. . . . (Salgádo, 1972: 217–218).*

Methods of pickpocketing and shoplifting have changed historically in response to a variety of factors and social changes. Different clothing styles and changes in store architecture require modifications in methods of thievery. Further adaptations are induced by protective techniques developed by victims to prevent such activities. Change appears to be a constant and reciprocal process, with both thieves and victims responding to the activities of one another.

The technical complexity of shoplifting and pickpocketing is shown in the professional vocabularies or *argots* that have developed. An argot implies the existence of a body of shared and specialized techniques similar in form to those that characterize legitimate professions; it also suggests the existence of a subculture within which such a vocabulary has meaning. Members of such a subculture speak "their own language." The technical complexities of shoplifting are portrayed with clarity in Mary Owen Cameron's famous study, *The Booster and the Snitch* (1964). She wrote mainly about *snitching* or amateur shoplifting, but she presents useful information about *boosting* or professional shoplifting as well. The following excerpt from her glossary of shoplifting argot indi-

* From *Cony-Catchers and Bawdy Baskets* ed. by Gamini Salgádo. Published by Penguin Books, 1972.

cates just how specialized the "art" is in terms of both the distinctions made and the techniques and aids developed:

Heel: a real "professional" commercial shoplifter.

Booster: any commercial shoplifter or any thief who turns to shoplifting intending to sell the merchandise he steals.

Snitch: thieves' argot for a pilferer.

Clout (verb or noun): to shoplift; one who is engaged in the act of shoplifting.

Bennywork: clouting under the protection of an overcoat.

Pennyweighter: jewel thief.

Skin worker: fur thief.

Crotch worker: a booster who has trained herself to hold merchandise beneath her dress and between her legs and walk out of the store.

Cover, shade, stall (verb or noun): to act as an accomplice to the clout.

Booster skirt or bloomers, pants, coat, apron: garments especially designed to hold stolen merchandise.

Booster box: a garment box or other box designed in advance by the booster to look like a wrapped package but with an opening into which articles may be placed (Cameron, 1964: 43).

While argot may differ from time to time and place to place, the point is that an argot exists. Similarly there is a pickpocketing argot, one version of which has been studied by Maurer (1955).

Both shoplifting and pickpocketing involve technical skills and a knowledge of social contexts, but pickpocketing requires more specific knowledge of victims, since they are *confronted directly.* Shoplifters seek to *avoid* victims. Both activities depend upon secrecy and on such everyday techniques as lies, tricks, and fronts to conceal activities from victims or from any interested others. In addition, pickpocketing involves consideration of modes of confrontation. Maurer notes:

Some Americans [pickpockets] . . . are *front workers* or *front men;* that is, they can and do *work* facing the victim. . . . Most of the European tools,* especially the old-timers, are *front workers,* probably because of the custom, generally more prevalent in Europe than in America, of cutting men's side pants pockets with the opening parallel to and just below the waistband, instead of with the opening following the line of the outside trouser seam, which runs at right angles to the waistband. Thus a European tool will *take* this type of pocket, called a *top britch* or *top bridge,* while facing the victim, and he *takes* it exactly as an American tool would *take* a hip pocket when standing behind the victim. Trousers cut with *top britches,* while worn in this country by a certain class of people, are now not common in standard business suits, but are frequently found in work clothes. European tools, however, often continue to *work* from the front, even after they have been in America for years. Most American tools avoid *working* directly facing the

* A tool is the member of the pickpocket mob who does the actual stealing.

mark by taking *pit scores* or *insiders* from the side, approaching the mark diagonally or at an angle. For working the hip pockets or the side pants pockets, they like to be behind the mark, or slightly to the right or left as the case may be, facing the same way as the mark but well out of his line of vision (Maurer, *Whiz Mob,* p. 70).

In addition to methods of confronting the victim or avoiding such confrontation, there are skills involved in assessing the victim's potential as a mark. As Maurer notes:

> In other words, the tool is a practical psychologist. He listens to conversations in the crowd, and from them pieces together information he can use. He sees every move where money is involved. He notes the build, stance, dress, and manner of everyone he can see. He almost automatically separates local citizens from travelers; if he is in a *road mob,* he will take the travelers by preference (other things being equal) because they are likely to carry more money; if he is a *local* operator, he will want to avoid robbing local residents, since they may upset his arrangements with the police. He knows how to smell an officer of the law; some types he avoids religiously, other types he robs with pleasure. He recognizes other thieves, even though he has never seen them before, with uncanny precision. "Mobs recognize a frame anywhere they see it in a tip. Also, there are damned few who wouldn't recognize each other on sight." He registers any attention whatever from onlookers as he *works.* He knows how to be unobtrusive and almost a nonentity in a crowd or on a street-corner; he also realizes that he must be prepared to melt away into a crowd if he sees anyone who is looking too closely.
>
> He is always alert, always under tension, though of a different kind, even when he is not *working,* for he is well aware that someone may tap him on the shoulder at any moment. Perhaps this perpetual tension is one of the reasons why a very high percentage of pickpockets are narcotic addicts — a higher percentage than has been encountered in any other *racket* (Maurer, *Whiz Mob,* p. 71).*

Like Cameron's material, Maurer's shows the existence of an argot that categorizes salient features of an activity and of the social context in which it takes place. It also indicates the extensive knowledge that pickpockets possess.

Both shoplifters and pickpockets develop a variety of *diversionary tactics* or tricks to conceal their activities by drawing attention elsewhere. Some situations involve ready-made diversions of attention; crowd scenes with lots of noise and attention-getting activities swirling around people are ideal settings for shoplifters and pickpockets. Carnivals and circuses are particularly suitable for pickpocketing because bumping into strangers is a normal occurrence. Where diversions are not "naturally" found, they may be created, especially when shoplifters or pick-

---

* Quotations from David W. Maurer, *Whiz Mob,* copyright © 1964. Reprinted by permission of College and University Press Services Inc.

pockets work in groups, as we saw in the description of cony-catching. One of the group members may be assigned the task of creating a diversion. In shoplifting one of the group members may divert the attention of salespeople or undercover detectives by starting an argument, faking a fainting spell, or in some other way making a scene.

Shoplifting and pickpocketing are by nature *nonviolent;* their success depends on their not even being *noticed.* Both are the polar opposite of mugging, relying on skill instead of force. We should not, however, overestimate the skill involved in shoplifting and pickpocketing; the techniques may require time and training but they can be learned readily enough by most of those who are so inclined. Of particular importance to success is that one learn *patience.* The successful shoplifter or pickpocket is even willing to walk away from a promising score to which considerable time has been devoted, and to start all over again with another, if risks cannot be minimized or if some unforeseen circumstance arises.

Shoplifters and pickpockets customarily work in groups in which each member has an assigned task, as we saw in some of the examples. Criminal subcultures are a fruitful source of group members. Shoplifters also draw on criminal subcultures for resources to convert stolen goods into money. Seldom do professional shoplifters steal goods for their own use; they steal them for conversion into cash. Pickpockets are more likely to steal money and thus avoid the conversion problem, though they may want to convert wristwatches, jewelry, rare coins, or credit cards into cash. This conversion function can be met in a variety of ways, but a particularly useful resource within the criminal subculture is the *fence,* the one whose job is selling stolen goods. As a source of group members and as a resource for converting stolen property into cash, criminal subcultures are vital to shoplifters and pickpockets.

BURGLARY AND ROBBERY

Career burglars and robbers customarily see themselves as professionals, or at least as people with an "occupation" or "trade," and they customarily draw on the criminal subculture for varied goods and services. Even when they work alone, they often make use of fences, lawyers in the employ of members of the criminal subculture, and other resources.

While burglary involves theft from places entered illegally and robbery involves theft directly from people, the two activities share a number of characteristics. Aspiring burglars and robbers both learn their skills and adopt criminal identities primarily from adolescent interactions with professionals who are highly skilled and experienced. Often such interactions take place in prison. Federal prisons, which harbor many skilled thieves, are particularly useful places for inexperienced

thieves seeking knowledge. Admission to prison is not in itself sufficient, however; experienced criminals must be willing to pass on their
knowledge, and they will make choices of "suitable students" among
those who are available. The dangers of a life of crime make trustwor-
thiness and reliability crucial in relations among members of professional crime, so "students" are selected with care. Unreliable prison
associates can get one in trouble both inside prison and outside. New
inmates must prove themselves reliable before they are likely to be
taken on as "students."

Prisons then are useful places for aspiring thieves to make "contacts"
with experienced professionals. Oldtimers can teach a great deal of
"social theory" related to burglary and robbery while in prison (see, for
example, DeBaum, 1950), but they are particularly important also in
providing "hands on" experience once the "students" are released from
prison. It is this "learning by doing" that is fundamental in the process
of becoming a "good" thief.

Burglars and robbers learn many of the same kinds of things, though
some of the specifics differ. Important elements in a thief's education
include learning how to find a good prospect for theft, gather relevant
information, plan the job, and deal with unexpected contingencies in
carrying out the job, such as the police. In this process, the good student develops *larceny sense*. We will consider each of these factors as
they apply to thieves in general and as they differ for burglars and
robbers.

Finding a good prospect for theft is a skill that can be learned both
through personal experience and the teachings of others. The following
statement by a thief suggests some of the issues involved in recognizing
a good prospect:

> An underworld education makes a lot of difference to a man. In every way.
> Say you're a legitimate businessman and you're taking a ride in an automo-
> bile with a man that's a loser, that's been in the rackets for years. Like me.
> We see a group of men walking down an alley in a steady stream. That means
> they're going to a temporary book as the regular book on the main street is
> closed up. But to you, it's just people walking down the alley. And we're
> riding along, I see an attractive young woman stepping out of a big restau-
> rant. It's about one-thirty in the afternoon. She has a thick envelope under
> her arm and she's walking toward the bank. That doesn't mean anything to
> you. But to me it means she's bringing money to the bank, I'm gonna get
> back and check on her, see if she does that every day, it might be worth while
> grabbing. As we ride along for eight or ten blocks, I've seen a half dozen
> things that are not legitimate and you have seen nothing but the ordinary
> street scenes. A man that's a thief, whenever he's moving around, will rec-
> ognize a hundred opportunities to make a dollar.*

* From "Burglary as an Occupation" by Neal Shover. Unpublished Ph.D. dissertation,
University of Illinois, 1971. Reprinted by permission of the author.

While criteria for a "good prospect" will differ depending on whether one is a burglar or robber, having an "eye" for such prospects is an important part of thieving. Robbers commonly identify victims on their own, as did the thief quoted above; burglars may rely also on *tipsters* or *fingermen*, those who gather information on potential burglary sites. Having located a good prospect, thieves next gather relevant information about the circumstances of potential victim or site. Robbers may observe victims for days to discover the pattern of their activities and the most suitable place and procedure for the planned robbery. Burglars similarly will expend a great deal of energy "casing the joint," the place where the burglary is to take place. The knowledge that burglars and robbers gather about the workings of the social world might well make sociologists envious, for "good" thieves will devote enormous attention to detail.

Planning the job involves bringing together equipment, personnel, and other required materials and working out the details of how the actual job will take place. Robbers will plan out ways of *victim manipulation,* since they will be dealing directly with victims, while burglars will focus efforts on *secrecy* and especially on ways of avoiding suspicion. The robber's skills are more *interpersonal* while the burglar's skills are more *technical,* related as they are to the complicated technology of breaking and entering, of spotting and silencing burglary devices, and of removing money from safes and vaults. Both robbery and burglary may involve the thief's physical skills, either as threat in robbery or in performing some of the athletics that may be called for in breaking and entering.

In the actual carrying out of the theft, different contingencies arise in robbery and in burglary. Robbery involves dealing with another person, the victim. Professional robbers develop many skills in this regard, a most important one being *self-presentation.* Such self-presentation is vital *in teaching victims their role as victim.* It might seem that one would know "naturally" how to be a victim, but in fact such is not the case. Most robbery victims do not have previous experience in being robbed. What information they do have is often drawn from the mass media, in which victims are commonly shot or else are heroes, outwitting the robbers and sending them off to prison. Robbers, on the other hand, don't want victims to play either of these roles — they want them to be simple robbery victims and must teach them to be so. Letkemann (1973: 114) documents robbers' knowledge of special ways of dealing with these mass-mediated misunderstandings so as to instantaneously teach people how to be successful robbery victims. Two particular methods are *catching people off guard* and convincing victims quickly that *the robbers are in control and will tell the victims what to do.*

Catching people off guard can be done in a variety of ways. Skilled professionals will look for times when people are least awake, least expecting anything like that to happen, or otherwise unprepared. Some robbers, for example, like to hit banks and other businesses on Monday morning just as they open because people are still groggy from the weekend.

Convincing victims that robbers are in control and will tell the victims what to do can also be accomplished in a variety of ways. An important point to convey to victims is that they will be safe if they do what they are told. Robbers may well find it useful to present themselves as both serious and dangerous even if they don't intend to harm the victims. They must do so in such a way to make their point without causing victims to become hysterical and thus uncontrollable, and thus robbers must be sensitive to the entire social situation as it develops. Most professional robbers want to avoid violence while conveying the impression that they are violent. Professional robbers may well develop excellent acting skills, even modulating their voices to give just the right effect. Some prefer loud voices that sound commanding, while others feel that çalm and low voices sound both more confident and sinister.

Robbers are often quite aware of the image they present and may devote considerable effort to constructing just the right effect. Routine problems arise and routine solutions are found. For example, it is common for bank or business managers to be the only people on the site who know how to open the safe or vault, and thus robbers may construct images that are directed particularly to those managers. Robbers don't want to shoot managers, for then the money is inaccessible, so they develop methods for convincing bank managers that it is wisest to do what the robbers say instead of playing "the hero." One of Letkemann's informants detailed his personal technique for dealing with managers:

> Ah, he will cooperate, because there's two ways of having a manager very easily to cooperate. First of all this guy's in a state of shock. You have hoods on your head, you have a heavy weapon in your hand and you see two or three guys there, swearing language — he knows we're vulgar — he knows — we made him know that we are brutal, subhuman bastards, you know. We project that image to him, you know. And usually they are in a state of shock, but if it's a very cold customer we would say, "Well, listen, you open the door or we shoot the first one!" And one of my partners would grab the — a woman by her hair, you know, and she would scream every time, 'cause it's sorrowful, you know, and then the man he would say, "Well, these damn fucking subhuman bastards, he's going to kill her," you know, and this, you talk two or three times like that and usually he'll go all the way (Letkemann, 1973: 105).

It is to the advantage of robbers to foster this view of themselves as "subhuman bastards" even though they may be both intelligent and gentle when they are not "working."

While burglars make use of quite different skills in planning and executing a job, they too must make wide use of experience and a variety of skills. Furthermore, underlying the work of both burglars and robbers, and what distinguishes professionals from amateurs and good thieves from bad thieves is what Sutherland has called "larceny sense" in the case of the con man, what Maurer called "grifter sense" in the case of pickpockets, and what might be called "rounder sense" in the case of robbers. We will stay with the term *larceny sense* to identify that intuitive or innate quality that makes any professional gifted. Just as one may or may not have "the hands of a surgeon" or "the heart of a warrior," one may or may not have "larceny sense." One can rob or burglarize without it, but if one has it one has an added advantage. "Larceny sense" is drawn on in a variety of circumstances. It may be particularly important in an emotional undertaking such as armed robbery where feelings are strong, speed is vital, and there is little time for the robber to "think things out." Those who respond intuitively in the right way are said to have "larceny sense." They may justify their actions simply by saying, "Things seemed right" or "Things didn't feel right," "It felt wrong."

We have been considering the knowledge that is drawn upon by those who approach thieving as a profession or occupation. It should be clear that much of what they draw upon is everyday knowledge available to everyone. Part of the skill of the professional thief lies in spotting *criminal angles* to everyday realities, criminal possibilities that can be revealed through an understanding of everyday life. Most people in the noncriminal world pass by criminal possibilities daily, *possibilities that are there if one chooses to look for them.* Experienced criminals study and carefully construct the meanings and implications of obvious everyday affairs, actively seeking the criminal possibilities. In this sense they are meticulous researchers with practical goals. (For similar activities by police and by social scientists, see Sacks, 1972.)

We have not distinguished between unarmed and armed professional robbers as we did in considering amateur robbers. Our reason is that robbers themselves do not draw this line carefully. The issue for them is not the *carrying* of a gun but *the reasons for which the gun is used.* Carrying guns is not uncommon among robbers; they may be carried for emergency use or may be used for threats, but professional robbers generally avoid *using* guns wherever possible. Amateurs are far more likely to *use* guns. Professionals attempt to reduce the number of unforeseen possibilities by careful planning and to meet unforeseen possibilities that do arise in other ways.

Learning how to use a gun as a physical object is very easy. Learning how to use a gun as a social symbol that facilitates a robbery without actual shooting is far more difficult. Such learning is available in criminal subcultures, while unaffiliated amateurs must rely on experience alone — an often dangerous method. In fact, amateur criminals of all types are in a sense far more dangerous than professional criminals, because *amateurs may not know what they are doing.*

The distinction between armed and unarmed robbers is more significant to police, lawmakers, and the general public than to robbers themselves. One's identification as an unarmed or armed robber depends heavily on whether one is caught by the police and where a gun is at that time. Someone who is carrying though not using a gun is legally an armed robber, even if the gun is unrelated to the robbery taking place. If a robber forgets a gun at home, that robber becomes unarmed. Since professional robbers avoid gun use, the distinction becomes even less important. The main concern to robbers is that penalties for being caught differ depending on whether one is armed or not, but if one doesn't expect to get caught, the issue is not necessarily of great significance.

Our consideration of five types of professional criminals indicates the ways in which their activities are both similar to and different from the work of "legitimate" professionals. We have also indicated the contributions that criminal subcultures can make to such activities. We are now prepared to consider the extent to which such professional criminal activities are organized.

Organized Crime vs. organized crime

Earlier in this chapter we quoted Sutherland's comment that "Professional theft is organized crime." The phrase "organized crime" has been used widely but in quite different ways. Three meanings of the phrase are particularly prevalent:

1. Some crime, and in particular some amateur crime, is either *unorganized* (without plan or rules) or *disorganized* (inconsistently or ambiguously related to rules). Muggings, for example, may be spur-of-the-moment, *unorganized* activities relying primarily on brawn and surprise. Crimes planned without an eye for contingencies, ineffectively arranged and executed, are *disorganized.* Some amateur crimes, however, and an even larger proportion of professional crimes are planned and executed with care and success, and thus we speak of such crimes as *organized.* The five types of professional crime we have just discussed show these elements of organization, and it is to this property of crime that Sutherland was referring.

2. Some crime is carried out by solitary individuals. Most amateurs and some professional criminals work alone. Some amateurs and many

professionals, however, have ties to other professional criminals as colleagues and associates and thus are a part of a *criminal organization*. Criminal organizations are often referred to as *organized crime*. We are speaking here of more than a criminal subculture that provides resources; we are speaking of a group of individuals with specific roles and tasks. A team of burglars who get information about potential jobs from specific others and who dispose of their goods through long-term arrangements with specific fences might together be viewed as a criminal organization and thus as organized crime. Criminal organization of this type draws heavily on criminal subcultures, though important links may also be forged with the noncriminal world, such as with police, lawyers, and business personnel.

3. When the mass media speak of *Organized Crime*, customarily the term refers to a single criminal organization, nationwide or even worldwide, that is highly structured, hierarchically arranged, and responsible for large amounts of systematic criminal activity. As we shall see below, the very existence of Organized Crime in this sense is open to question.

We will distinguish among these three senses of *organized crime* as follows:

1. Since the crime we are studying in this chapter is professional, we will *assume* that it is also organized in the first sense.
2. We will consider various types of *organized crime* in the second sense, that of criminal organizations established to carry out certain criminal activities.
3. *Organized Crime*, designated by capital letters, will be examined in terms of the evidence for and against its existence as a single national or multinational organization.

Our main interest is in the variety of ways in which crime is organized by criminal organizations, the factors that encourage such organization, and the evidence for and against the existence of an overarching organization or Organized Crime.

Organized crime is a controversial subject among sociologists who study deviance and crime. Disagreement centers on whether there is one giant corporation of crime (Organized Crime) or many smaller organizations that are largely independent of one another and often in direct conflict. No one doubts that there is organized crime in the sense that groups of criminals sometimes work together to accomplish their criminal activities, though the specifics of such organization are not agreed upon by researchers. The big controversy is over the size of such organizations and their centralization in one Crime Monopoly that dictates to lesser subdivisions or, on the contrary, their independent existence as unaffiliated organizations of varying size.

The United States public generally seems to believe that Organized Crime as a formal and centralized organization exists. "The Mafia," "The Cosa Nostra," "The Syndicate," and other names are used to refer to such an organization. Police officials and the media alert the public to the "grave dangers of the spreading tentacles of Organized Crime." Social scientists have been more split in their views. Those who draw heavily on official information, particularly that provided by the police, not surprisingly accept the idea of a Crime Monopoly, a gigantic conspiracy of Organized Crime. The best presentation of this view is probably that of Donald Cressey in his work *Theft of a Nation* (1969), in which he argues that:

> In the United States, criminals have managed to put together an organization which is at once a nationwide illicit cartel and a nationwide confederation . . . (p. 1).
>
> Nowadays, moreover, free enterprise does not exist in the field of illicit services and goods — any "mom and pop" kind of small illicit business soon takes in, voluntarily or involuntarily, a Cosa Nostra man as a partner . . . (p. 74).
>
> [T]he Cosa Nostra organization is so extensive, so powerful, and so central that precise description and control of it would be description of all but a tiny part of all organized crime . . . (p. 109).

Organized Crime is seen as a massive, nationwide, possibly worldwide, corporate organization with thoroughgoing vertical and horizontal integration of members, a *formal organization* and *bureaucracy* in the full sociological sense. The picture is much like the one shown in the early television series "The Untouchables."

Other sociologists, particularly those studying deviance, drawing on different evidence, have come to a somewhat different conclusion, though even these have some large disagreements. Generally, however, they have argued that the official view of Organized Crime, accepted uncritically by many social scientists, is in fact a modern conspiracy theory propagated by officials. They argue that official police information on Organized Crime is highly invalid and unreliable for many reasons, the primary one being that both police and criminals may gain from public belief in Organized Crime. Such a belief, true or not, can be used by police to get increased funds and power and by criminals to increase the threats they pose. Some sociologists therefore argue that extensive observational studies of criminal activities are necessary to understand criminal organization in general and to establish the actual existence of Organized Crime. They note that the few studies of this kind that have been done all indicate the existence of many small, independent, and often warring criminal organizations. The evidence for the existence of unaffiliated criminal organizations is strong; evidence for Organized Crime is weak.

The largest criminal organizations identified by direct observational studies were those in some large eastern cities, especially New York City, and some midwestern cities, notably Chicago, in the 1920s during Prohibition. It is certainly possible that these large organizations, heavily Italian, served as the basis of an *idea of Organized Crime* that persisted after the demise of the organizations themselves. Even the centralization of these organizations in their heyday may have been overemphasized, for while there is evidence of cooperation as in the notorious Appalachia meeting, there is also evidence of warfare between rival factions and repeated series of "gangland slayings."

It is often claimed that Organized Crime is heavily involved in the distribution of illegal drugs. Adler, Adler, and Douglas (forthcoming) found no identifiable Mafia or Cosa Nostra members directly involved in high-level soft-drug dealing in Southern California. All the top-level organizations Douglas knew about directly, and the lower levels as well, were independent of any larger organization, being directed instead by independent entrepreneurs.

Though Douglas did not find evidence of Organized Crime, the study did discover the details of criminal organization for the groups studied. Top-level organizations were found to be tightly organized internally but to experience a high turnover in personnel. There were occasional friendly or business relations between such organizations, and they participated in occasional large social gatherings, but there was no evidence of any central coordination among the top-level organizations and certainly no central authority structure.

It might at first seem that what organization does exist in the sphere of professional crime is largely a result of the nature of the task at hand — a way of carrying out the activity more efficiently — but Douglas's study of soft-drug dealing suggests that much of the existing organization *has come about in direct response to law-enforcement pressures.* In the beginning of the booming soft-drug traffic in the early and mid-1960s there was a large trade in small amounts of soft drugs across the United States border with Mexico. As government pressure against such drugs increased, individuals developed more sophisticated methods of concealing and smuggling drugs. "Project Cooperation," launched in the United States and Mexico against smuggling in the late 1960s, spurred a shift by smugglers from land transportation (relatively inexpensive and readily available) to air and sea (more expensive and generally requiring more planning). Each leap toward stricter law enforcement boosted the amount of money, resources, technical knowledge, and "staff" organization necessary to get drugs from their point of origin to the hands of buyers.

While evidence here is based on soft-drug dealing, and we lack extensive data on other spheres of criminal activity, there seems sufficient reason to hypothesize that *degrees and types of law-enforcement pressure are dominant factors in determining degrees and types of organization of criminal activities.* It seems likely, for example, that if government pressures had not become intense, soft-drug dealing would still be an unorganized, largely situational activity carried out by "mom and pop" entrepreneurs. Government pressures seem, however, to have driven small-time operators out of business; they have been the ones most likely to be arrested or otherwise stopped. Affiliation with a large organization often appears the only way of continuing with criminal activities. Only well-organized, rational, technically proficient, cautious, and highly capitalized groups seem to be able to meet the contingencies presented by strong government pressure directed against their activities.

Other participant observation studies of drug dealing have arrived at similar conclusions. While Jerry Kamstra's direct observation of Mexican smuggling, *Weed* (1974), was limited in time and scope, it has the advantage of looking at the whole smuggling world from South of the Border. His picture accords with the one presented above:

> Many of the changes wrought by our cooperation between the Mexican and American governments (Operation Intercept) made the marijuana industry stronger, however. Whereas before it had been an industry composed of many separate operators, including innumerable fly-by-night newcomers, now the amateurs were sifted out. For the professional smugglers, it was a simple matter of survival — organize and help one another, as the Mexican and American governments were doing, or perish (Kamstra, 1974: 72).

We do not argue that law-enforcement pressure is the only factor in the movement toward increasing organization of criminal activities. The benefits of organization that operate in the noncriminal world operate in the criminal world as well. We do say, however, that law-enforcement pressure ironically (as noted by Matza, 1969) *rewards* greater criminal organization. The unorganized, disorganized, and amateur are most likely to be driven out of business by such pressure. Other factors at work include individual leadership ability — indeed, some criminal organizations may be largely developed by an individual with expertise in creating and sustaining an organization — and the nature of the criminal activity. Some activities are greatly enhanced by criminal organizations (con games, professional shoplifting, and smuggling of bulky substances such as marijuana), while others seem to operate successfully as lone or situational activities (smuggling of cocaine and other easily concealed substances, pickpocketing, and some burglary).

Although studies of soft-drug dealing by Douglas and others have found no evidence of Organized Crime, studies of heroin dealing have led to somewhat different findings. Most studies and analyses agree that the heroin distribution system involves highly organized and capitalized smugglers and importers at the top level of organization and unorganized independent dealers at the street levels. Even Cressey, who sees top-level management as part of Organized Crime, recognizes the lack of organization at the street level. Whether or not top-level management of heroin distribution is affiliated with top-level management in other criminal activities — and evidence is inconclusive — sociological evidence indicates clearly that lower-level dealers are not part of such a "conspiracy." In fact, it would be tremendously risky for top-level management to forge strong ties with the lower echelons, which are most subject to arrest. The immunity of top-level management is often provided by its *loose* ties with street dealers.

Evidence for a multiplicity of top-level organizations rather than a single "Syndicate" is provided by some of the popular studies of heroin dealing as well. Plate (1975) concluded from his sources in professional crime that any unity that existed in the past was disrupted by heavy law-enforcement pressures beginning in 1972. He argues that a number of high-level arrests fragmented top-level smuggling, so that there is even less coordination among top-level organizations than in the past (see, especially, pp. 109–110). Some excellent investigative accounts claim, however, that top-level heroin trade is practically a monopolistic enterprise run by the "Mafia." It may be that Organized Crime has existed but has become increasingly fragmented. The picture is certainly not a clear one, and continued research seems in order.

We are led to conclude from existing data that there are many criminal organizations, some quite large, but that relations among them are infrequent, weak or nonexistent. Such activities as gambling, loan-sharking, prostitution, and professional violence ("enforcement"), often attributed to a single "Syndicate," in fact seem to be subject to varying degrees of organization, and there is little evidence that these activities are "overseen" by a single organization. Both gambling and loan-sharking give rise to rather extensive and complex organizations, though relatively independent gambling rings and loan-shark operations do exist. Organization seems to be a method for more efficiently carrying out activities and responding to enforcement pressure rather than a result of "Syndicate" supervision. In prostitution, where organization may be less necessary for efficiency and where law enforcement is sporadic, we find a range from lone streetwalkers to large and highly organized prostitution rings. Those who engage in professional violence ("enforcers") do exist, but what little systematic evidence we have suggests that they are often loners rather than members of criminal organizations, hired when work is available.

In the absence of concrete evidence to either confirm or deny that Organized Crime exists, we suspect that those who argue for its existence, particularly law-enforcement officials and criminals themselves, have practical reasons for their proclamations. Our concern is that sociologists avoid accepting self-serving proclamations as statements of fact. Whether or not Organized Crime exists, the *idea* of Organized Crime seems to be a potentially fruitful topic for sociological study.

The Many Faces of Dishonesty and the New Perspective

In this chapter we have considered professional and organized crime and criminal subcultures. In doing so we have drawn on the new perspective in a number of ways. Examining how professional criminals construct their activities as *professions* (or occupations or jobs), we have recognized the ordinary, everyday, "normal," nondeviant character of their activities while not denying that they are illegal and in that respect different. Our image of the "hustler" has highlighted how the criminal world both resembles and differs from the "straight" world. We have recognized the expertise and technical abilities as well as social skills that underlie many professional criminal activities, skills that seem far beyond the capacities of the "psychopaths" and "sociopaths" of earlier theories. Our consideration of five different types of crime reveals a wide variety of *organized* activities. Many of the skills are similar to or even exactly like those of the "straight" world. And yet we have recognized that entering a criminal rather than a noncriminal profession is a fundamental *choice* that has grave implications for those who make it. We have seen, too, how earlier subcultural theories of deviance can be modified to consider criminal subcultures not as *causes* of crime but as *resources* upon which criminals can draw in the conduct of their criminal activities. In discussing Organized Crime we have seen how sociologists' constructions of meanings can be even more problematic than members' constructions. We have emphasized that group members' constructions may be variously motivated and cannot necessarily be taken as evidence for the *existence* of a phenomenon.

The dependence of the new perspective on data gathered from actors themselves presents increasing problems as we move to forms of crime that are socially viewed as more serious. Some studies have been done of robbers, burglars, and fences, but the forms of crime that are most highly organized — hard-drug dealing, gambling and loan-sharking — or most negatively sanctioned by the public — professional violence — present sociologists with formidable obstacles to the acquisition of experiential data. We have indicated the problems of accepting "talk about" these phenomena as valid description, since that talk itself is social behavior, may be used for a variety of purposes, and thus cannot be accepted as a reflection of what really goes on. Although we have speculated on the basis of existing data, there is no substitute for observations of participants acting in their social worlds.

11

The Many Faces of Dishonesty: White-Collar and Official Deviance

The "criminal" is commonly associated in the public imagination with activities such as violence, burglary, robbery, mugging, and "organized crime." Illegal activities engaged in by legitimate professionals and business people (those in the white-collar occupations) and by officials responsible for lawmaking and law enforcement (government officials and the police) are often regarded as "not really criminal" and their perpetrators as "not really criminals" and as "not criminal types." The small number of early social science studies done of these activities tended to assume this public view. Some sociologists, however, and in particular those who adopt the new perspective, recognize that such a distinction may derive more from moral considerations than analytic distinctions. As we consider white-collar and official deviance, we suggest the many similarities of such deviance to other deviant activities and to everyday dishonesty. We will also see, however, the many resources that white-collar and official deviants have for concealing their deviance and for avoiding the labels "deviant" and "criminal" — resources perhaps not so readily available to other kinds of deviants.

Defining White-Collar and Official Deviance

Both white-collar and official deviance tend to be interwoven in many ways with legitimate, legal activities. We must therefore devote some attention to the nature of those activities with which we will be concerned in this chapter. Since there are some unique issues that arise in relation to official deviance, we will consider it separately after we have looked at white-collar deviance.

WHITE-COLLAR DEVIANCE

Crime reported in official statistics is largely lower-class crime, which serves as the basis for the public image of the criminal. White-collar crime is far less "visible," seldom making its way into crime statistics, and consequently contributes little to the public image of crime. To the extent that crime and criminals have been conceptualized largely in terms of lower-class acts and members, that conceptualization tends to apply with difficulty or not at all to many middle- and upper-class criminal activities. For both the public and early social scientists, *crime* has been equated with *lower-class crime.*

Edwin Sutherland (1940, 1949) was largely responsible for directing the attention of social scientists to what he named "white-collar crime." His concern was with certain kinds of crimes found predominantly among middle- and upper-class people — those who are (1) socially most respected, (2) best off financially, and (3) most powerful. The extent of such crimes, though often ignored or minimized, is substantial. Sutherland calculated, for example, that in 1938 the six top criminals on the FBI's most-wanted list took in $130,000 from burglaries and robberies while the "white-collar criminal" Ivan Kreuger swindled some $25,000,000 from stock investors.

In recent years in the United States there has been a surge of public concern and even outrage over disclosures of the existence of many forms of business, professional, and official deviance. The public outcry against everything from price fixing by businesses to "drug pushing" by pharmaceutical companies has even begun to move government officials to change their enforcement priorities. The Justice Department has increased its investigations and prosecutions of antitrust violations, and even the FBI is reconsidering its overwhelming concentration on such "cops-and-robbers" crimes as bank robbery. In 1979 the director of the FBI, William H. Webster, noted these changes in an interview:

Judge Webster, in view of the tight budget President Carter is proposing for the FBI as well as for most of the rest of the federal government, what are the bureau's priorities?

Our top-priority programs are white-collar crime, organized crime and, of course, foreign counterintelligence. Coming hard on those would be things like civil rights, general property crimes, personal crimes and antitrust.

About 18 percent of our resources in the field are currently directed against white-collar crime, and about the same for organized crime.

Where are you concentrating your efforts against white-collar crime?

I'd say that government frauds, public corruption and major bank-embezzlement cases constitute our prime targets. Fraud in government programs is a cause of major efforts. We already have 41 indictments in the General Services Administration investigation. The Small Business Administration investigation is now off the ground.

These efforts are going to require a great deal of cooperation with other government agencies and with the inspectors general being appointed in a number of agencies.*

In 1980 the FBI unveiled a series of "sting operations" (secret investigations in which agents pose as criminals to discover criminals) directed against business people and officials, including members of Congress.

Prompted by public exposés and stories as well as by a new theoretical perspective that questions absolutism and strives to see through public fronts, some sociologists have recently become more concerned with white-collar crime *as a form of deviance.* They regard it as being fully as deviant as other kinds of crime and as displaying similarities as well as differences. By taking a broad look at the world of deviance as a whole and by developing appropriate research methods, sociologists have begun to discover vast worlds of white-collar deviance. Increasingly they have focused their research and analysis on professional, business, and official deviance. In doing so they have recognized the limits to some of the earlier theories of deviance. For example, Merton's general theory of deviance, which argued that those who value success but do not have access to legitimate means of achieving it may choose illegitimate means, cannot adequately account for criminal negligence committed by a well-paid doctor, the acceptance of stolen goods by the head of the local bar association, the violation of antitrust laws by the vice-president of a huge corporation, the illegal dumping of 200 pounds of mercury a day into a public river by a giant corporation, or the failure over several years to report any income at all by the president of one of the largest multinational corporations.

Because many earlier theories of deviance do not adequately explain white-collar crime and deviance, their adequacy in explaining lower-class crime and deviance also becomes questionable. Many earlier theories may contain a bias, defining criminality *in terms of* lower-class behavior rather than in terms of the nature of crime itself, thus failing to recognize the existence of professional, business, and official crime *as crime.* Yet only by applying the same criteria to all crime and all deviance, regardless of the class membership of those who engage in such activities, will we come to understand the phenomena themselves.

The study of professional, business, and official deviance has presented problems to social scientists. Of particular difficulty has been

* From *U.S. News and World Report,* January 29, 1979, page 52. Copyright © 1979 by U.S. News and World Report.

value neutrality (see Chapter 1, pp. 15–18) — the conducting of studies that neither support nor discredit those being investigated. The deviance of politicians, business executives, professionals, and government officials is hotly debated among the general public, legislators, lawyers, and social scientists, and political passions are high. These passions make it particularly difficult for social scientists or anyone else to analyze white-collar deviance in a value-neutral fashion. Analysts who focus on the labeling process when discussing armed robbery may suddenly turn into ferocious labelers when considering business people, politicians, or doctors. The quiet and rational professor who analyzes gang violence and gang rape in terms of subcultural values may become a stern preacher of absolute values and morality when discussing "blood-sucking doctors," "tax-evading business people," or "crooked politicians." Particularly striking is the apparent self-deception involved, the unwillingness to recognize that agreed-upon criteria for analyzing deviance were developed to apply to *all deviance*. While in studying lower-class deviance sociologists are more subject to overappreciation and normalization of deviant activities, in studying white-collar deviance and crime they seem more likely to err through underappreciation and moral stigmatization. If we appear to be too appreciative or accepting of white-collar deviance in these pages, readers should keep in mind our goal of explaining such behavior *in its own terms* and suspending our own moral evaluations.

We have referred to *white-collar* and *lower-class* crime and deviance in this section in contexts here that should make their meaning evident, but it may be useful to articulate the ideas embodied in these terms. The issue of class has plagued the study of deviance. We have sought to distinguish between *class* and *crime*, using the terms white-collar and lower-class to apply to *types of activities and not necessarily to class membership*. Lower-class crimes are those which customarily appear in official statistics and which are frequently *attributed to* members of the lower class, but members of any class can commit such crimes. Anyone can engage in burglary or robbery, as, for example, the Patty Hearst case suggests. White-collar crimes, on the other hand, are customarily carried out by members of the middle and upper class because they are generally the only ones with the resources to commit them. Few members of the lower class, for example, are in a position to engage in price-fixing, stock swindles, or medical malpractice. Though there is a relationship between the kinds of crimes one is likely to commit and the class to which one belongs, the relationship is not one of necessity, and class membership alone will not *determine* the kind of crime one will commit. Class provides one with certain kinds of opportunities, but the choice of crime one makes ultimately depends on a wide variety of factors.

OFFICIAL DEVIANCE

In many respects a type of white-collar deviance, official deviance has some unique features that necessitate its separate consideration here. Official deviance is not the term commonly used in everyday discussions; people more usually speak of "corruption," "graft," "payoff," "political ripoff," "usurpations of power," and "abuses of power." The diversity in terms and in the ways they are used have caused semantic and practical confusions in both public discussions and scholarly analyses. (For examples of the problems in defining "corruption," see Brooks, 1910; James Scott, 1972, especially pp. 3–6; and Heidenheimer, 1970, especially pp. 3–9.)

To clarify our own use of terms, we begin with the idea of *officials*. By officials we mean *those who have the legal function of making, changing, abolishing, and enforcing laws.* Much of what we say here will apply to all rule-makers and rule-enforcers, especially as they use their power in what may be viewed as deviant ways, but our focus will be on lawmakers and law enforcers as legitimate public functionaries legally entrusted with their tasks. Officials, then, for our purposes, include those who make and enforce laws on the federal, state, and local levels. Our particular interest will be in members of Congress and the police. Analysis of official deviance involves detailed understanding of nondeviant official political structures, our focus on the United States lets you draw on your own understanding of those structures.

What, then, is official *deviance?* As recognized by Robert Brooks (1910) and elaborated on by later political scientists such as Heidenheimer (1970), terms such as "corruption" have fundamentally problematic meanings, closely paralleling those of such terms as "immorality" or "deviance." The public often labels political actions "corrupt" according to absolutist criteria, assuming that everyone would come to similar conclusions. In fact, there are great disagreements over what is moral and immoral, corrupt and not corrupt, in political action. What one individual views as a "payoff" another may view as a "contribution." Determinations of official deviance such as corruption or graft are at least as situational as determinations of any other kind of deviance.

At the most general level we will define *official deviance* as *acts judged to involve abuses of public power for private ends.* (This is a modification of Scott's definition of official corruption, 1972: 5.) We will also draw on Max Weber's view of *power* as *the ability to carry out one's wishes even in the face of opposition* (Weber, 1958). Official deviance is then *the use of publicly authorized power to overcome the opposition of others in order to satisfy personal ends.* While there are a wide variety of forms of official deviance, two major types can be distinguished: *usurpations of power*, or use of power for nonmonetary ends, and *graft,* or use of power for monetary ends.

Usurpations of power take a variety of forms and involve a wide range of potential personal gains. Most usurpations of power, like most forms of graft, are small, ambiguous, and controversial, and their status as deviance or illegality is often difficult to determine. The most frequent claims that power has been abused for nonmonetary reasons appear in allegations of *police brutality* — usually, that "more force than necessary" was used by police and against others: suspects, convicted criminals, or even the general public. Suggested motives for such "excessive" force include "police mentality," racism, a "macho" ethic, and psychopathology; sometimes motives are not considered but the claim is simply of "excessive" force. Police often disagree with others' claims, arguing that "outsiders" do not know what is necessary for them to carry out their job. Police may view what others term "brutality" as an important "tool" for doing their job; the observational studies of police activities by Reiss (1968) and Westley (in Henslin, 1976) provide valuable insights into police explanations.

Other usurpations of power can be seen in the sphere of traffic violations. While police cruisers and cars bearing official license plates may well park illegally for legitimate reasons — one does not expect a police cruiser to circle the block looking for a metered parking space while a bank robbery is in progress — there is reason to suspect that the government vehicle double-parked in front of the bakery or coffee shop may not be on official business.

Many abuses of power, though irritating at times to those involved, are of minor importance to the public in general. Some may even claim that such acts are not really "abuses of power" but simply "fringe benefits" of the job. (The reasoning here parallels that offered for employee theft, discussed in Chapter 9, pp. 287–288.) Even instances of police brutality may be overlooked or supported by members of the public. Readers should be able to provide both their own examples of such "abuses" of power and their own responses to such acts.

Official graft is the use of official powers for individual financial gain. Some forms of official graft are illegal; others, while legal, are publicly denounced. We will consider both forms as deviant, the one breaking laws, the other nonlegal social rules.

Graft is illegal when it involves the violation of laws defining the remuneration of officials. Bribes are a form of graft and may be relatively unambiguous in nature, as when a drunk driver stopped on the highway gives money to a police officer, does not receive a ticket, and proceeds down the highway. While the police officer in such a situation can be legally charged with illegal behavior, we should also recognize the deviance of the drunk driver in offering a bribe, for that too is an illegal activity. To avoid such illegality some drivers keep a $10 or $20 bill together with their license, handing over both to any police officer who stops them. If the officer takes the money and does not give a ticket, the bribe works; if the officer questions the presence of the money, the driver can simply claim that its presence doesn't mean anything. Although bribes involve the abuse of power, they also may involve cooperation and even inducement by the one who is doing the bribing. Another clear example of bribery is the common practice of payment by building owners to inspectors so that violations of the building code will go "unnoticed." In this instance, too, one can see both parties "benefiting," but the abuse of power for personal gain is straightforward.

Other forms of illegal graft are far more ambiguous. Indeed ambiguity may be fostered by those involved in the practice. The process of "laundering" money, brought to public attention in the Watergate investigations, involves passing money through various bank accounts and individuals so that its illegal origins are obscured. The use of dummy corporations, fronts, and false financial statements can also be used to further confuse the matter. While the motive for such actions is financial, such money is often used by politicians to obtain and keep office and thus obtain and keep power. Money in this case serves as a means as well as an end, with graft being a way of obtaining both money and power.

Illegal graft, and in fact official deviance in general, is often extremely difficult to prove legally, though publicity may label officials as rule-breakers or offenders of public morality. Walter Lippmann wrote that very few cases of "real" corruption can be legally proven:

> The prosecuting agencies, when spasmodically they set to work, can deal only with the crudely overt features of political corruption. Anyone who has observed closely a prosecutor's office on the trail of a political ring knows how enormous is the gap between scandalous political conduct and specifically indictable offenses; in my time I have seen case after case of politicians who could not be indicted, or, if indicted, convicted, though they were guilty as Satan, because the development of conclusive legal proof was lacking (Lippmann, 1930).

Given the illegality of graft, it is no surprise that enterprising officials have developed a variety of techniques for benefiting financially without *directly* engaging in illegal activities. Consider the politician who helps a developer get official approval for a plan for a building, a shopping center, or even a whole area of the city. No money or other financial benefits need be given to the politician, but at some later date the politician may be "sold" for almost nothing a valuable piece of property. Or perhaps the politician simply receives inside information about developments worth investing in. Are these instances of graft? Are they simply "favors"? Illegality is virtually impossible to prove in such instances, and yet readers may well feel that some violation of legal or moral rules has taken place.

Instances of legal or "honest" graft add to the problems of defining official deviance. The distinction between kinds of graft was eloquently made by George Washington Plunkitt, a key figure in the Tammany Hall scandals:

> Everybody is talkin' these days about Tammany men growin' rich on graft, but nobody thinks of drawin' the distinction between honest graft and dishonest graft. There's all the difference in the world between the two. Yes, many of our men have grown rich in politics. I have myself. I've made a big fortune out of the game, and I'm gettin' richer every day, but I've not gone in for dishonest graft — blackmailin' gamblers, saloon-keepers, disorderly people, etc. — and neither has any of the men who have made big fortunes in politics.
>
> There's an honest graft, and I'm an example of how it works. I might sum up the whole thing by sayin': "I seen my opportunities and I took 'em."
>
> Just let me explain by examples. My party's in power in the city, and it's goin' to undertake a lot of public improvements. Well, I'm tipped off, say, that they're going to lay out a new park at a certain place.
>
> I see my opportunity and I take it. I go to that place and I buy up all the land I can in the neighborhood. Then the board of this or that makes its plan public, and there is a rush to get my land, which nobody cared particular for before.
>
> Ain't it perfectly honest to charge a good price and make a profit on my investment and foresight? Of course, it is. Well, that's honest graft (Riordan, 1963).

Even if an official violates a law with the intention of serving the public interest, such intention is always problematic. When the *consequences* of the act are judged to serve the public interest, the public is customarily more willing to accept the argument that such interest was intended. Controversy over whether John F. Kennedy ordered or countenanced the assassination of leaders in Cuba and Vietnam came *after* the failure of his policies toward those nations; if his policies had succeeded, at least some people might have been willing to "not know" about such possible activities.

OFFICIAL DEVIANCE AS DANGER AND THREAT

The main difference between official deviance and other forms of deviance is that officials are publicly charged with making and enforcing rules and possess legitimate access to the power necessary for their task. The illegitimate use of power by those with legitimate access to it presents a unique threat to society. Such a dilemma was recognized during the Watergate controversy, when there was talk of physically removing Richard Nixon from the White House if he would not leave voluntarily. It was argued that Nixon's command of the Armed Forces might make such a task impossible. Such speculation indicates the dangers of deviance by those with legitimate access to power.

Official deviance differs in a second way from other forms of deviance, for government serves as a model for other social patterns. Henry Steele Commager described this model and the unique threat posed by official deviance:

> Government, as Justice Louis D. Brandeis observed half a century ago, "is the potent, the omnipresent teacher. For good or for ill, it teaches the whole people by its example." If government tries to solve its problems by resort to large-scale violence, its citizens will assume that violence is the normal way to solve problems. If government itself violates the law, it brings the law into contempt, and breeds anarchy. If government masks its operations, foreign and domestic, in a cloak of secrecy, it encourages the creation of a closed, not an open, society. If government shows itself impatient with due process, it must expect that its people will come to scorn the slow procedures of orderly debate and negotiation and turn to the easy solutions of force. If government embraces the principle that the end justifies the means, it radiates approval of a doctrine so odious that it will in the end destroy the whole of society. If government shows, by its habitual conduct, that it rejects the claims of freedom and of justice, freedom and justice will cease to be the ends of our society (1970).

Official deviance, then, can serve as a model for other forms of deviance. The pardon of Nixon was seen by many observers as an acceptance of official deviance and led to the argument that other, nonofficial "criminals" ought also to be pardoned.

While all the other forms of deviance we consider in this book can be viewed in terms of rule-followers and rule-breakers and of labelers and the labeled, official deviance leads us to a consideration of *the deviance of the labelers themselves,* those whose official role in society involves labeling others. Official labelers have at their command the legitimate use of power and even violence. It is their *legitimate access to power and violence* that makes their deviance such a danger and a threat — for who is to police the police?

Professional, Business, and Official Subcultures and Deviance

In Chapter 3 (pp. 77–78 and 90) we discussed membership in a subculture as an explanation of deviance. Such membership was not, we concluded, *sufficient* to explain deviant activities but it did help to explain how *opportunities* might become available. The concept of subculture can be applied to a wide range of groups, including those based on social class, ethnicity, religion, race, and criminal activities. Customarily, however, the concept has been applied to lower-class groups; seldom are middle- and upper-class groups considered in subcultural terms. We will now consider professionals, business people, and officials as subcultural members, remarking on the similarities to and differences from subcultures as they are usually conceptualized.

Let us first review the characteristics of subcultures that we identified in Chapter 3. We said that the term subculture is currently applied to social groups with these characteristics:

1. They are *identifiable* parts of the larger society, different in some but not all aspects from the larger society.
2. As a part of that society, they are subject to at least some of its rules and laws.
3. As groups with identifiable differences from the larger society, they have their own conduct norms for members.
4. They are functioning unities — that is, for at least some purposes they are capable of acting as a whole.
5. They are conscious of themselves as units in some way separate from the broader society.

In what ways can different professions, different businesses, and different official agencies be viewed as subcultures?

All professions and many businesses and official agencies share among themselves some identity by which they can distinguish themselves from the larger society. Some professions can draw upon a long history. Doctors, for example, identify Hippocrates, a Greek of the fifth century B.C., as the founder of their "art." The practice of medicine has changed greatly since that time, yet there has been a significant continuity as well. Doctors commonly recognize both the ancient status and the importance of their profession. Such is true also of many groups of business people. Varied businesses also have their long and rich histories, and business people are often convinced that what they are doing — banking, manufacturing, trade — is vital in the world. Business people may look at themselves as the creators of the modern world — the entrepreneurs who create and build, develop and expand human potentials. Thomas Burns, former vice president of International Telephone and Telegraph (ITT), went so far as to observe: "It is natural for patriotism to shift from the countries to the corporations" (Burns, 1974: 244).

When groups have a strong sense of their own identity and the importance of their activities, members will develop conduct norms for participants and they will at times act together as a whole in relation to other groups and to the larger society. Some of these conduct norms may violate the rules of outsiders, a violation that insiders, like all subcultural members, may justify by claiming that outsiders do not really "understand" the activities of the subculture.

We have noted that subcultures are subject in some ways to the rules and laws of the larger society. This characteristic is especially apparent when we consider lower-class subcultures and in particular lower-class criminal subcultures. The situation is somewhat different for professional, business, and official subcultures. While they, too, are subject to the rules and laws of the larger society, *because of their social position their rule-breaking may be excused or even supported and they are frequently in positions of power that make it possible for them to change rules.*

Regarding the social toleration or even acceptance of professional, business, and official rule-breaking, one need only consider the great doctors who violated the social rules and even laws of their societies to create new knowledge and find new ways of solving medical problems. Many share the conviction that the early doctors who secretly dissected cadavers to discover how the body worked — against all laws and ideas of right conduct in their day — were right and their official enforcers and regulators wrong. As Durkheim said long ago, the great creators are almost always violators of the old rules — deviants — and creators of new rules that lead to social change. Pasteur, Freud, and many others stand as heroes both to professional subcultures and to the public at large. Rule-breaking on the part of professional, business, and official subculture members, however, *does not necessarily lead to such breakthroughs;* it may instead be self-serving or even negligent. Nonetheless, subcultural and public support of the "heroic" view of rule-breaking can provide subculture members with a freedom and flexibility that members of lower-class subcultures do not enjoy.

This idea of heroic or "good" deviance, coupled with the power of these subcultures, makes it extremely difficult for any outside groups, and notably government bureaucracies, to police them. Although *all* subcultures claim some independence from the rules of the broader society, professional, business, and official subcultures seem to have sufficient power to enforce such claims in a variety of circumstances. Professionals in particular — doctors, lawyers, sociologists, psychologists, and in fact all professionals — customarily insist that they alone truly understand the complexities of their disciplines and thus they alone can make decisions about how they "ought" to act. When outsiders try to "meddle," as subcultures view it, in their activities, subcultural members generally respond by becoming better organized, more distinct from the broader society, and more demanding of internal loyalty. All subcultures attempt to respond in this way; professional, business, and official subcultures are more likely to have the power and resources to do so successfully.

In terms of the five characteristics of subcultures listed earlier, it would seem that we can legitimately speak of professional, business, and official subcultures. Such subcultures do differ from lower-class subcultures in power, resources, public tolerance of rule-breaking, and ability to influence rule-making. Nonetheless, the similarities are sufficient to warrant the use of subcultural explanations in making sense of professional, business, and official deviance. Failure to invoke such explanations in the past seems attributable more to bias and a desire to see such activities as "different" than to any inapplicability of subcultural theory itself.

Explaining Professional, Business, and Official Deviance

From the point of view of the new perspective, one serious limit of earlier theories of deviance was their image of deviants, and of criminals in particular, as *different in kind* from nondeviants. Theories of psychopathic and sociopathic personalities are the clearest examples of such distinctions, but all earlier theories seem to have drawn some line between "us" and "them." One consequence was a failure even *to recognize the existence of* professional, business, and official deviance, for those people were viewed by theorists as "us," the nondeviants. Existing theories were not seen to apply to "us." The new perspective, on the other hand, recognizes certain fundamental aspects of human action that characterize both deviant and nondeviant, criminal and noncriminal behavior. Professional, business, and official deviance can be seen as simply other instances of the many faces of dishonesty. From this perspective we expect to find that white-collar deviants share many motives with others — criminals, deviants, and those who are "merely" dishonest in their everyday lives.

What are the motives behind professional, business, and official deviance? When such deviance is recognized by the public — often only as a consequence of a major scandal — a common-sense explanation often offered is *greed*. It is claimed that "people are never satisfied," "people can never get enough," and thus "the rich get richer and the poor get poorer." While certainly we do not want to discount greed as a motive, it does not seem sufficient to explain the many varieties of white-collar deviance and the many instances where those involved do not "make money" by their actions. Furthermore, since greed can be viewed as a motive for any money-making activities, legal or illegal, deviant or nondeviant, it does not seem to add greatly to our understanding. In what follows we will consider other motives that seem to explain white-collar deviance more fully.

THE HUSTLER MOTIVE

Hustlers, as we saw in Chapter 10, are always on the lookout for an "angle," a way of successfully beating someone else out of money or anything else that is valued; they see the world as a jungle in which the smart operator outwits the "mark." Many professionals, officials, and business people, and particularly those who start their own businesses or are involved in selling, not uncommonly see themselves as hustlers and see hustling as the only way to "make it." While members of white-collar subcultures may be more reluctant to break laws — although we do not have the evidence to confirm such an idea — many do seem ready enough to engage in activities that are shady or defined by the public at large as in some way unethical, particularly when they can thereby further the legitimate business activities in which they are engaged.

The hustler motive, which is particularly evident in lower-class professional crime, may well be equally important in the business world in general, both deviant and nondeviant. Some observers have suggested that it is strongly supported by cultural values. Let us look more closely at this idea.

CULTURAL VALUES FAVORING WHITE-COLLAR DISHONESTY AND DEVIANCE

Some sociologists have referred to the United States as a "criminogenic society" whose basic values and structures inevitably produce certain types of crimes, including business and professional crimes. A few sociologists drawing on conflict theory (such as Quinney, 1974) have attributed all crime in the United States to the capitalism that characterizes the economy. Critics of such theories say that white-collar deviance also exists in fiercely anticapitalistic societies such as the Soviet Union (see Smith, 1976).

Other sociologists have recognized the existence of two value systems in the United States culture: one involves beliefs and practices that are viewed as morally good, such as justice, fairness, democracy, equality, and honesty; and one relates more directly to practical day-to-day activities. Sykes and Matza (1957) have referred to the latter as a system of *subterranean values* — values which are hidden and private but which guide action. We have chosen instead to refer to *practical values*, because values that have been termed subterranean have turned out to be openly acknowledged rather than concealed. Practical values involve such activities and beliefs as "smart dealing" and "there's a sucker born every minute." Practical values involve activities that may not be defined as "good" but rather as "sensible." "Taking advantage of a sucker" may not be viewed as "morally good" but often is viewed as a sensible practical activity. These practical values seem to support business and professional deviance and even illegality. If, for example, an item is mistakenly overpriced and nonetheless sells, a salesperson who points out the error to the customer might well be viewed as either deviant or "crazy." Those who attempt to be scrupulously fair in filling out their income tax returns are more often labeled "fools" than "good."

Many business enterprises in the United States operate by deceiving the public in some way. The public, however, is commonly viewed as the blameworthy party. Values placed on individualism, private initiative, and competition often outweigh those of honesty and fairness in business dealings. Competition and the value placed on winning can also serve as an impetus to shady if not illegal activities. The concern for free speech may override efforts to stop fraudulent advertising. The incompatibility between moral and practical values as well as the everyday dishonesty counseled by some of these practical values provide a background against which business deviance can take place.

Edwin Schur has presented one of the most balanced arguments linking values and crime in the United States. Rejecting the more extreme statements about a "criminogenic society," he offers substantial evidence that basic values and patterns of behavior indirectly encourage white-collar deviance and make it difficult to prevent:

> Sociologists are reluctant to accept the idea that a society's major values or dominant characteristics "cause" crime. Because of their very dominance or socially approved nature, these elements also underlie a great deal of acceptable, sometimes highly desired behavior. And in either case, to consider them as major causal factors is difficult — because of the many other factors and processes intervening "between" the values and the acts. In any case, reference to such values clearly will not enable us to predict which individuals will commit crimes and which won't, since the very same values promote both law violation and law-abidingness. At the same time, we can hardly ignore the fact that the general quality of American life significantly shapes and colors crime problems. . . . The inclination to try to "take advantage of" the other party is, in a sense, built into the structure of social relations in our kind of social order; it is precisely for this reason that the so-called formal mechanisms of social control, including law, must play such an important role in modern society. . . . [I]t is difficult not to conclude that American society has embraced an ideology of what might be termed capitalism with a vengeance — a reverence for the values of individualism, competition, and profit of such intensity as to provide incentives to crime that go well beyond a level that must be considered inevitable in a modern complex society, even a basically capitalist one (Schur, 1965).

Schur argues, not that either capitalism or the culture of the United States *causes* crime, but that certain values and certain social arrangements make certain kinds of crime both possible and "understandable." Competition seems to be a particularly important factor: to the extent that success through competition is more highly rewarded than honesty and fairness in competition, the existence of dishonesty and unfairness will not be a surprise.

SHARED MOTIVES IN WHITE-COLLAR AND LOWER-CLASS DEVIANCE

Besides the hustler motive and the cultural values that support, encourage, or at least facilitate white-collar deviance and crime, we also have some evidence that many of the motives that characterize lower-class deviance and crime, both amateur and professional, also lie behind white-collar deviance and crime. Although we lack extensive sociological studies, we do have illustrative evidence of the kinds of motives that can lead to white-collar deviance. One such example — a case of fraud described by Blundell (1976) — provides rich data on this topic.*

Equity Funding was a conglomerate that grew rapidly during the 1960s and early 1970s. Though it was involved in many lines of business, it specialized in mutual funds and then increasingly in insurance. Apparently a fabulously profitable growth company, it turned out to be fraud. Our interest here is in the motives of those involved.

Comments by the perpetrators reveal all the elements we have seen in both amateur and professional dishonesty and crime: seductions, self-deceptions, excitement and risk, ambition for success, fears of punishment, being trapped into deviance, and so on. The fraud was allegedly begun by the president of the corporation, Stanley Goldblum, and its chairman, Michael Riordan, shortly after the company went public. They started with a small fraud, one that did not look significant at the time to the few people who knew about it, and thus they stepped over what Matza (1969) calls the "invitational edge."

The first fraud was a bit of book manipulation, initiated by Goldblum and carried out by the treasurer of the corporation, Jerome Evans. Evans may not even have viewed his initial act as fraudulent but simply as a little irregular. Once begun, the procedure escalated. There is no reason to assume that the initial act was motivated by any desire to perpetrate the massive fraud that resulted; rather, as in so many other instances of becoming deviant, the initial somewhat ambiguous act required for its concealment greater and greater deviance that in time was quite obviously fraud to all participants. There seemed, however, no way to stop the fraud other than by admitting it, a step that quite obviously did not appeal to those involved.

---

* The following data on Equity Funding are all drawn from Blundell (1976) and all references are to that source.

Although we do not know Goldblum's motives for beginning the fraud, at least one of his motives for continuing it was to conceal what had already been done. Additional evidence suggests that others became involved in the fraud little by little, seduced, deceiving themselves, and swept away by the excitement of the activity.

The process began with Goldblum's asking Evans, the treasurer, to enter as income money that had not yet come in but that would be arriving soon. In what follows we can see how, step by step, Evans became deviant:

> Evans posted phony figures in the books at the end of 1964 and waited for the cash to come in. It didn't. Evans asked about it, and Goldblum assured him it was coming; meanwhile, there were even more "give up" commissions for Evans to put on the books for the first quarter. Reluctantly, Evans did so. Strand after fine strand, for quarter after quarter, the web was cast over Evans until, in time, he found he could not resist at all. By now he knew there were no real commissions coming; Goldblum knew he knew, and the pretense was dropped. Year after year, Evans doctored the books at Goldblum's order. The president no longer even bothered to give Evans a commission figure — just an earnings-per-share target that Evans was to meet. The arithmetic was up to Evans. . . .
>
> The treatment of Evans by Goldblum; the encouragement to do what seemed at first a little thing, for a plausible reason; then the request to do it again and yet again, until finally there was no excuse, just an assumption that the subordinate was now firmly enmeshed in the conspiracy, run through the Equity Funding tale. "Nothing was ever laid out completely to me," says Larry Collins, a former officer jailed for his part. "It all evolved in little bits and pieces, gradually; it took a long time before it finally hit you that you were committing a crime. 'Don't worry,' they said. That's what they *always* said at Equity Funding. 'Don't worry' " (pp. 49–50).

While the step-by-step path to deviance is often traveled, it is certainly not the only path. Evans may have been seduced and then trapped, but at least one of those involved in the fraud appears to have become involved knowingly and willingly from the very beginning: Alan Green, a 24-year-old computer programmer:

> "My first reaction was surprise but not shock," Green admits. "I thought to myself, 'Far out! This is really something.' And I was flattered that I was being asked in. Lewis said that he and Evans specifically were trying to become more important within the company, and the way they were doing it was to build up the size of EFLIC. 'We're on a power trip,' he said."
>
> Green himself was on no power trip. He considered corporate life a hideous bore and he rejected its values. He was little interested in money; his payoff for joining the fraud was a raise that amounted to a grand total of $600 before he quit to roam about the country in a van. The only thing that person-

ally interested him in the fraud was an opportunity to do computer programming. He thought that might be intellectually stimulating (pp. 70–71).

It seems clear that those who became involved in this fraud did so for reasons quite like those motivating other amateur and professional criminals.

Few among the executive staff of the company, according to Blundell (pp. 53, 78) did in fact *choose* nondeviance. One who did, John Templeton, involved in internal auditing for the company, recognized right away that something was wrong with the figures. Eventually he resigned, though not without much deliberation.

Goldblum's interactions with others might fruitfully be considered in terms of the seduction process we described earlier (pp. 279–281). He seems to have chosen his seducees carefully and was known as a good psychologist who understood people and how to manipulate them. A key to his success seems to have been his appeal to young people with little business experience. An important conspirator, Fred Levin, had been made president of a subsidiary company when he was barely past thirty. He had strong personal ties to Goldblum. Had he opposed the seduction, he would have been betraying this personal tie.

Most of those involved in the Equity Funding fraud got very little money out of it. What they did get was pride in their own and their company's success as well as a sense of excitement. As one of them said, "I did it for the jollies." Seldom did they think of their activities as "criminal." Once they did so, for most of them it seemed "too late" and they were "trapped."

From this example we can see the complexity of motives as well as their similarities across kinds of deviance and crime. We can also see the uses that can be made of honesty, loyalty, authority, and group solidarity in creating and sustaining deviance. Blundell concluded:

> . . . there is a lesson. Corporations can and do create a moral tone that powerfully influences the thinking, conduct, values and even the personalities of the people who work for them. This tone is set by the men who run the company, and their corruption can quickly corrupt all else. A startling thing about Equity Funding is how rarely one finds, in a cast of characters big enough to make a war movie, a man who said, "No, I won't do that. It's wrong." As for the majority who were sucked in and drowned, their motives were many and mixed. The important thing is that the fraud unerringly pressed upon their weaknesses, some of which they were unaware of at the time, and quickly overthrew them almost before they realized what had happened (p. 46).*

* Quotations from *Swindled* ed. by Donald Moffitt (Princeton, N.J., Dow Jones Copyright © 1976). Pages 49, 50, 70, 71. Reprinted with permission of Dow Jones, Princeton, N.J. Copyright © 1976.

The case of Equity Funding is just one example and on the basis of it we cannot make any extensive claims about white-collar crime. The importance of the example lies in the motives that it does disclose — motives that bear many similarities to those of other deviants. Detailed sociological study of white-collar crime is likely to uncover many such similarities. The case of Equity Funding shows the promise of such analysis.

Since white-collar deviance is not well documented by sociological research, we do not know its extent, its nature, its cost to the public, or the scope of the forms in which it appears. It is quite clear, however, that white-collar deviance *does* exist, appears in a wide variety of forms, and shares at least some characteristics with other forms of deviance and crime. To sociologists who would study it, it presents problems — its complexity, the expertise often needed to understand its workings, the difficulties of sustaining value neutrality in research, and its power to keep out outsiders. No sociology of deviance can, however, be complete without taking white-collar deviance into account, for it is full-fledged deviance on a par with any other form.

Many factors in United States society facilitate and even encourage white-collar deviance and, in particular, official deviance. One such factor is the existence of bureaucracies, which we discuss next.

Bureaucracies and Official Deviance

Some social scientists maintain that official deviance is a relatively recent phenomenon. James Scott (1972), among others, argues that earlier forms of government, especially monarchy, did not clearly distinguish between *the private* and *the public,* and thus the idea of using public office for private gain would not even make sense. In fact, some monarchies do distinguish between *private* and *public,* as in the English distinction between the "king's two bodies," an idea well developed in English law by the seventeenth century.

Rather than seeing official deviance as a *recent* phenomenon, it seems historically more accurate to see it as a *bureaucratic* phenomenon. Even in ancient societies, those which were most *bureaucratized* — such as Egypt, Babylonia, Rome, Persia, China, the Byzantine Empire, and the Ottoman Empire — showed most concern with and evidence of official deviance. Probably the most complex and stringent system of controls ever applied to official deviance was found in the Confucian system of traditional China.

The general rule seems to be: *wherever bureaucratic forms of government exist, there will be specific rules governing the use of government resources for personal ends.* In order to understand this principle we must first be clear about the nature of bureaucracy. A bureaucracy is a way of structuring social arrangements that involves: (1) a hierarchical arrangement of jobs in which those below are responsible to those above, (2) rational assignment of jobs, (3) arrangement of tasks according to rational principles, (4) formal rules and routines, and (5) accounting procedures. The pervasiveness of bureaucratic procedures in the United States today and in much of Western society may blind us to the fact that other, nonbureaucratic types of social arrangements are even possible: A monarchy is not bureaucratic but monarchical; one is a queen not because of one's expertise but because of one's ancestry and sex. Tribal societies where the chief holds that position through inheritance or through physical power are not bureaucratic. Nuclear families in the United States are nonbureaucratic arrangements: one does not ask who in the unit is most qualified to be "mother"; the job goes to the one of the proper age, sex, and relationship to other members.

Why should there be a link between bureaucracy and official deviance? S. N. Eisenstadt has argued (in *The Political Systems of Empires: The Rise and Fall of the Historical Bureaucratic Societies,* 1963) that wherever bureaucratic forms of government are used, there is a strong tendency for officials to feel that their official powers entitle them to personal privileges. Specifically, they tend to increasingly use official powers for private gains, thus becoming official deviants. Eisenstadt documents this link, but we still need to consider why it exists. The answer may lie in the nature of bureaucracy itself and in particular its hierarchical arrangement, with those above having "special privileges" that those below do not have. Thus, for example, secretaries commonly have one hour for lunch and may be reprimanded or penalized for taking even an extra five minutes, while executives have no such restrictions. Factory workers may have to punch a time clock, and they may have their wages docked for being even a minute late, while factory owners customarily have far more leeway in arriving at and departing from work. Readers can certainly provide myriad examples of their own. However, bureaucracies also *restrict* special privileges, and here we see the source of official deviance. The line between "rights" of a job or position and "abuses" of that position is difficult to draw. The ambiguity of the idea of "special privileges" makes drawing that line even more difficult. *The bureaucratic response is to make rules.* And, as we have already seen in our discussion of labeling theory, the more rules there are, the more rulebreakers. Practices that in monarchies or tribal governments might go unnoticed come to be prohibited in bureaucracies. There is no reason to believe that the actual practices differ; what does differ is the degree to which such practices are identified, labeled, and dealt with as instances of deviance.

MAKING, FOLLOWING, AND BREAKING RULES
IN OFFICIAL BUREAUCRACIES

In earlier discussions we have seen that those who are labeled deviant are themselves seldom involved in the making of the rules in terms of which they are so labeled. The only exception was in the case of professional and business deviance, where we saw professionals and business people attempting to use their power to affect the rules that applied to them. When we consider official deviance, however, we see that those who make the rules prohibiting certain forms of deviance *are themselves the ones who might be engaging in just those activities.* While bureaucratic governments are customarily very concerned with limiting official deviance, their procedures for doing so depend heavily on those who are potential deviants.

Officials who are to be regulated by rules concerning official deviance are themselves the ones who devise the rules, interpret them legally, and use power to enforce them. Of course there are different groups and levels of officials, especially in a complex and pluralistic system of government like that of the United States. Indeed, the United States government structure, on the federal, state, and local levels, involves a complex system of checks and balances to guard against officials' power to legislate away their own deviance. At the federal government level there is a tripartite separation of powers that presumably sets one group of officials to watch the others: the judiciary watches the executive and legislative bodies; the executive watches the judiciary and legislative; and the legislative watches the judiciary and the executive.

Even in the face of such checks and balances, however, rule-makers and enforcers can use loopholes in laws aimed at controlling them and can find ways of avoiding the enforcement of rules against them. For example, United States citizens have attempted to prevent special-interest groups from gaining "undue" influence over politicians. Layers upon layers of laws have been drawn up to control the financial contributions that special-interest groups can make to politicians. While these attempts at control have been going on at least since the Progressive Era, there remain enormous loopholes that have allowed *expansion* of such contributions through political action committees ("pacs"), which funnel huge sums to politicians from business and labor organizations and other special-interest groups.

One outcome of such reform acts has been to put established incumbent politicians at a great advantage over newer politicians seeking election, an outcome that may or may not have surprised the incumbents who passed the laws. While newcomers seeking election have found their campaign contributions limited by the new laws and thus their campaigning activities curtailed, incumbents, under similar campaign restraints, have been able to use their powers of office to get free media news coverage, their franking (free mailing) privileges to mail out messages to all voters in their districts, and their established powers to help and harm businesses and other special-interest groups and to induce those groups to contribute to them through political action committees. As Eugene McCarthy, among others, has forcefully argued, newcomers seeking election are now denied the one major resource they had been able to use before the "reforms" — the use of extensive campaign contributions for advertising that could compete with the news coverage readily available to incumbents. Therefore, while restrictions on campaign contributions may limit the influence that special-interest groups can thereby exert, these restrictions also deny resources to newcomers seeking election and give a decided advantage to incumbents who have access to a wide range of legal activities. It thus turns out that those who make the laws (incumbents) are less restricted by such laws than are "outsiders" (newcomers).

While reform acts have eliminated or limited certain kinds of political activities, they have also been circumvented in a variety of creative ways. One reason that politicians increasingly have called upon actors and singers for assistance is that their services do not come under the constraints placed on campaign contributions. *The Wall Street Journal* observed:

> It's happening again. Presidential candidates are falling all over themselves trying to line up political support from American country singers and rock stars because the singers can stage benefit concerts for their chosen candidates and raise huge sums of money free of the personal contribution limits of the campaign finance laws. When will our system be free of this irrationality in the distribution of political resources? When will we be liberated from this concentration of political power in the hands of The Few?
>
> If we're going to have the contribution limits, the benefit concerts should quite clearly be subject to them. If we don't have the courage for this reform, surely we can at least take steps to equalize the talent so it won't distract attention from the merits of the contest. Perhaps a lottery, so that George Bush would have equal chance with Jimmy Carter to get the services of The Eagles. Maybe a football-draft-style system, with the candidate lowest in the polls winning the big-draw talents like Linda Ronstadt. If the American people have to be protected from manipulation by other concentrations of wealth and power, what's so sacred about this one? (December 5, 1979)*

While *The Journal* seems to deny the possibility that celebrities themselves may be politically motivated — so that, for example, Jane Fonda might not want to use her talents to publicize Ronald Reagan's campaign — it does recognize that those who already have political power are well situated to draw on celebrity support and that political un-knowns are at a disadvantage.

An important factor in government officials' relations to the laws they make and on occasion break or bypass is the degree to which they can legally gain by their official activities. If officials gain greatly from the legal functioning of the government, they are less likely to violate laws. The traditional Prussian bureaucracy was famous for its incorruptibility. As James Scott (1972) has argued, a partial explanation is that the Prus-sian state was explicitly aimed at advancing the interests of the landed nobility and those identified with their interests — categories from which official bureaucrats were recruited. For those officials, to identify with the state interests was also to identify with their own interests.

In speaking of personal gain through official positions we are not referring solely to financial gain. The Prussian bureaucracy, the British civil service of the nineteenth and twentieth centuries, and the United States federal civil service of the twentieth century have shared the public ideologies and moral stances of their governments and have thus found it in their own ideological and moral interests to support those governments. This high degree of personal identification with the gov-ernment is customarily accompanied by an intense degree of self-policing, ultimately the most effective system of policing officials or anyone else. Honor and pride in doing one's official duty provide an important hedge against official deviance.

When personal identification with government weakens and when officials no longer see their private gain as synonymous with official rule-following or nondeviance — as happened among middle-class civil servants in the United States in the face of increased taxation and infla-tion and other events of the 1960s — increased attention to private gain *instead of* official rule-following emerges as a possibility. Under such conditions rule-violations may become increasingly justified as "getting my due," "watching out for number one," "playing it smart," and "playing politics." The literature documenting just such a process is huge. (For examples see Douglas and Johnson, 1977B.)

To sum up our discussion of official deviance, we have emphasized the complexity of a situation in which those who make the laws are either the same people or closely associated with those people who break the laws; the tendency of bureaucracies to make rules and rules and more rules further complicates the issue. A consideration of this situation has disclosed that the most effective controls on official devi-ance are not rules and the punishment of rule-breakers but rather offi-cials' perceptions of rule-following *as in their own personal interests*. The implications of this finding for deviance of all kinds are intriguing and worthy of readers' consideration.

Police Deviance

So far in this chapter we have focused on the official deviance of law *makers*. In this section we consider the deviance of those whose task is to enforce existing laws, the law *enforcers*.

A popular common-sense and social science explanation of police deviance is the "bad-apple theory," which emphasizes individual guilt and responsibility. For example, when one or more police officers are found guilty of burglary, taking bribes, brutality, or any other form of illegal activity, the chief of police, incumbent political officials, and others may call them "bad apples," the claim being that every police force will have some "bad apples" and it is they who are responsible for illegality and deviance. Such claims deny the possibility that there may be something about the police force itself, the political administration, or the demands of the job that facilitate or even encourage such acts.

In fact, however, there turn out to be certain very clear patterns of police deviance, suggesting that more is involved than individual "wickedness." While such regularities may emerge in response to a variety of conditions, such as the existence of "bad apples," once such patterns are established they become independent forces, affecting subsequent responses to situations.

Police departments of the big cities of the northeastern and midwestern United States have had a great deal of "corruption" since their establishment in the nineteenth century. At that time the police became very important clients of political machines and benefited greatly from supporting and aiding the machines. The lucrative police retirement systems and widespread opportunities to become involved in extensive systems of "graft" that began then have continued to the present day. While New York City provides a somewhat extreme example, as it has since the heyday of the Tammany Hall machine, the detailed revelations of the Knapp Commission make clear the extent of possible police deviance. We present this material in some detail because of the scope of the police deviance it identifies and the care with which the evidence was gathered. The Knapp Commission Report (1972) states:

> We found corruption to be widespread. It took various forms depending upon the activity involved, appearing at its most sophisticated among plainclothesmen assigned to enforcing gambling laws. In the five plainclothes divisions where our investigations were concentrated we found a strikingly standardized pattern of corruption. Plainclothesmen, participating in what is known in police parlance as a "pad," collected regular bi-weekly or monthly payments amounting to as much as $3,500 from each of the gambling establishments in the area under their jurisdiction, and divided the take in equal shares. The monthly share per man (called the "nut") ranged from $300 and

$400 in midtown Manhattan to $1,500 in Harlem. When supervisors were involved they received a share and a half. A newly assigned plainclothesman was not entitled to his share for about two months, while he was checked out for reliability, but the earnings lost by the delay were made up to him in the form of two months' severance pay when he left the division.

Evidence before us led us to the conclusion that the same pattern existed in the remaining divisions which we did not investigate in depth. This conclusion was confirmed by events occurring before and after the period of our investigation. Prior to the Commission's existence, exposures by former plainclothesman Frank Serpico had led to indictments or departmental charges against nineteen plainclothesmen in a Bronx division for involvement in a pad where the nut was $800. After our public hearings had been completed, an investigation conducted by the Kings County District Attorney and the Department's Internal Affairs Division — which investigation neither the Commission nor its staff had even known about — resulted in indictments and charges against thirty-seven Brooklyn plainclothesmen who had participated in a pad with a nut of $1,200. The manner of operation of the pad involved in each of these situations was in every detail identical to that described at the Commission hearings, and in each almost every plainclothesman in the division, including supervisory lieutenants, was implicated.

Corruption in narcotics enforcement lacked the organization of the gambling pads, but individual payments — known as "scores" — were commonly received and could be staggering in amount. Our investigation, a concurrent probe by the State Investigation Commission and prosecutions by Federal and local authorities all revealed a pattern whereby corrupt officers customarily collected scores in substantial amounts from narcotics violators. These scores were either kept by the individual officer or shared with a partner and, perhaps, a superior officer. They ranged from minor shakedowns to payments of many thousands of dollars, the largest narcotics payoff uncovered in our investigation having been $80,000. According to information developed by the S.I.C. and in recent Federal investigations, the size of this score was by no means unique.

Corruption among detectives assigned to general investigative duties also took the form of shakedowns of individual targets of opportunity. Although these scores were not in the huge amounts found in narcotics, they not infrequently came to several thousand dollars.

Uniformed patrolmen assigned to street duties were not found to receive money on nearly so grand or organized a scale, but the large number of small payments they received present an equally serious if less dramatic problem. Uniformed patrolmen, particularly those assigned to radio patrol cars, participated in gambling pads more modest in size than those received by plainclothes units and received regular payments from construction sites, bars, grocery stores and other business establishments. These payments were usually made on a regular basis to sector car patrolmen and on a haphazard basis to others. While individual payments to uniformed men were small, mostly under $20, they were often so numerous as to add substantially to a patrolman's income. Other less regular payments to uniformed patrolmen included those made by after-hours bars, bottle clubs, tow trucks, motorists, cab drivers, parking lots, prostitutes and defendants wanting to fix their cases in court. Another practice found to be widespread was the payment of gratuities by policemen to other policemen to expedite normal police procedures or to gain favorable assignments.

Sergeants and lieutenants who were so inclined participated in the same kind of corruption as the men they supervised. In addition, some sergeants had their own pads from which patrolmen were excluded.

Although the Commission was unable to develop hard evidence establishing that officers above the rank of lieutenant received payoffs, considerable circumstantial evidence and some testimony so indicated. Most often when a superior officer is corrupt, he uses a patrolman as his "bagman" who collects for him and keeps a percentage of the take. Because the bagman may keep money for himself, although he claims to be collecting for his superior, it is extremely difficult to determine with any accuracy when the superior actually is involved (1972).

(See also Peter Maas, *Serpico*, 1973, and, for a novelistic account that compares the deviance of a police officer and a priest, see John Gregory Dunne, *True Confessions*, 1977.)

It seems clear, both from the Knapp Commission findings and those of other investigators, that within police subcultures such practices are difficult to define as deviant, given their widespread existence and their acceptability to those who practice them. In the face of such extensive official illegality, carefully structured by those involved, the "bad-apple" theory seems to have little explanatory power. The real problem is in understanding how such practices can be viewed as so nondeviant by police and so deviant by "outsiders." The discrepancy between insiders' and outsiders' views is as wide as we can find in any sphere of deviant activity.

An important factor in understanding such widespread police deviance seems to be the presence or absence of a history of political machines. In most large cities of the South and West, with no history of political machines, such pervasive corruption, especially graft, is largely absent. Certainly in those cities there are instances of police deviance, which are periodically brought to public notice, but there does not seem to be the pervasive, departmentwide, historical patterning that characterizes police departments in those cities that had powerful political machines. Evidence suggests that political machines were important in *starting* regularized police deviance, systematizing and rewarding it, and thus making possible the development of a *deviant police subculture*. This subculture standardized deviant behavior, established rules for it, set controls to what deviance was "acceptable" and how it was to be engaged in, and thus made it possible for the subculture to continue even if the political machine weakened or disappeared. This deviant police subculture is particularly important in socializing new recruits, teaching them to "go along with the system," not to "rat" on fellow officers, and to accept the system or even actively participate in it. Active participation is viewed by members of the subculture as "playing it smart."

While deviant police subcultures based on graft and personal financial gain are characteristic only of certain cities, other forms of deviant police subcultures seem to exist in almost all big police departments in the United States and Britain and in federal enforcement agencies as well. Such patterns may be typical of police departments throughout the world, but there are few studies of this topic outside of the United States and Britain. Peter Manning (1975, 1977) has argued that two aspects of police work are particularly important in the development of deviant police subcultures: *impossible public mandates* and *job stress.*

Impossible public mandates are public expectations of police duties that for a variety of reasons police cannot meet. For example, police are expected to control crime while *simultaneously* respecting individual liberties. While theoretical distinctions between these two activities may seem clear and straightforward, practical distinctions in any particular case may be far more difficult to make. Critics of the police often suggest that police either "coddle criminals" or "take advantage of law-abiding citizens," and in fact there may be instances of just that, but the point here is that even those police who *try* to both control crime and respect individual liberties may find that in any given situation they *cannot* do both.

Public mandates may also be rendered impossible by the tremendous regional, local, and interdepartmental conflicts among different enforcement agencies. Federal agencies such as the FBI and the Treasury Department may work against each other, perhaps because each wants credit for any "busts," or because each sees its own concerns as most important, or even because general feelings of interagency rivalry have been developed and institutionalized. Police attempting to control drugs and vice, for example, might well find that federal agencies so restrain them that such control is virtually impossible.

Deviant police subcultures may arise to resolve just the kind of problems we have been discussing. While the police as individuals may develop their own solutions, the development of a deviant police subculture provides a routinized set of ways to respond to regularly occurring events that do not seem resolvable in nondeviant terms. Two deviant activities seem particularly important features of deviant police subcultures: (1) police violation of laws, especially laws of evidence and laws protecting individual rights, in order to enforce other laws, and (2) deceptive self-presentation. Police may, for example, present themselves before the public as in control of all crime and ceaselessly at work seeking criminals. While deceptive self-presentation may be useful in assuaging the public in the face of that public's impossible mandates, such deception may also be used by police to draw attention away from such activities as sleeping on the job, on-the-job drinking, and doing personal errands on working time (see Altheide and Johnson, 1979). Manipulation of official statistics may also be used in the service of deceptive self-presentation, both by individuals and by departments and agencies as a whole.

Sociologists who are familiar with the day-to-day workings of police departments have generally concluded that not only is the whole criminal justice system held together in important ways by the use of deception and official deviance but also that *without massive social change involving the social structure, values, practices, and expectations it could not be otherwise.* If the entire police system were forced to operate strictly in accordance with existing laws, it would grind to a halt. There are now in the United States so many laws and such pervasive violations of some of them that apprehension of all lawbreakers would overwhelm police, prosecutors, courts, and detention facilities. Readers might usefully consider the consequences of arresting *all* who use drugs, including marijuana; all fornicators, those who have sexual relations with anyone other than their spouses; all illegal gamblers; and all employee thieves. Then add all the other lawbreakers we have considered in the pages of this book.

How are police expected to act toward all these lawbreakers? Public guidelines are ambiguous at best. Often the public asks for "equal justice" while at the same time expecting police to enforce laws against "other people." In the face of such a dilemma, a deviant police subculture provides police with an answer, a way of coming to terms with the situation, generally through some form of *compromise justice*. Compromise justice is a mechanism constructed by members of the criminal justice system to fit laws to concrete situational realities. It involves funneling criminals or presumed criminals in at the lowest appropriate level of the criminal justice system. Police may make on-the-street determinations of innocence or guilt, lawyers may plea-bargain, accused criminals may plead guilty to lesser charges and avoid trial, and through a variety of other techniques compromises can be made with the justice system. (See Skolnick, 1966; and Abraham Blumberg, 1967.)

While deviant police subcultures may emerge as a way of coming to terms with *impossible public mandates*, they may also come into being as a resource for meeting the *job stress* of police. A significant number of police either drink (both on and off the job), use drugs (sometimes obtained from supplies they or other officers have seized), draw on the services of prostitutes, or in other ways use resources available to them as ways of responding to or avoiding job pressures and as "rights" justified by subcultural rules. Although there is a police saying that "A smart cop is never cold, wet, or hungry," indeed police work asks just that of the police, that they be willing, if necessary, to be cold, wet, and hungry. Deviant "rights" may be viewed by police as the consequent "rewards." Police who draw upon such deviant resources as drugs and prostitutes are not unlike employee thieves; the major difference is in the kind of "goods" available to each.

While deviant police subcultures are widespread, we must be aware that not all police *engage in* deviant activities. The vast proportion, however, either condone it for others or at least "look the other way." Serpico (Maas, 1973), the police officer who brought police deviance to public attention through his complaints to public officials and his book, is clearly deviant in terms of the deviant police subculture. The Knapp Commission found a wide range of individual activities, ranging from steadfast refusal to be involved in graft to those whose deviant activities ranged far and wide. The Commission Report describes this range:

> Of course, not all policemen are corrupt. If we are to exclude such petty infractions as free meals, an appreciable number do not engage in any corrupt activities. Yet, with extremely rare exceptions, even those who themselves engage in no corrupt activities are involved in corruption in the sense that they take no steps to prevent what they know or suspect to be going on about them.
>
> Corruption, although widespread, is by no means uniform in degree. Corrupt policemen have been described as falling into two basic categories: "meat-eaters" and "grass-eaters." As the names might suggest, the meat-eaters are those policemen who, like Patrolman William Phillips who testified at our hearings, aggressively misuse their police powers for personal gain. The grass-eaters simply accept the payoffs that the happenstances of police work throw their way. Although the meat-eaters get the huge payoffs that make the headlines, they represent a small percentage of all corrupt policemen. The truth is, the vast majority of policemen on the take don't deal in huge amounts of graft.
>
> And yet, grass-eaters are the heart of the problem. Their great numbers tend to make corruption "respectable." They also tend to encourage the code of silence that brands anyone who exposes corruption a traitor. At the time our investigation began, any policeman violating the code did so at his peril. The result was described in our interim report: "The rookie who comes into the Department is faced with the situation where it is easier for him to become corrupt than to remain honest" (1972).

Our consideration of police deviance has rejected the individualistic explanation of police deviance — the "bad-apple" theory — and has indicated that a significant proportion of police deviance and a significant factor in the emergence and continuation of deviant police subcultures is a response to the very ambiguities of police work. Other motives for deviant behavior — the hustler motive, espousal of different values, and different definitions of situations, to name but a few — may well add to an explanation of police deviance; we are suggesting, however, that a fundamental explanatory factor is the very nature of police work, and in particular impossible public mandates. We have noted that the discrepancy between insiders' and outsiders' views of police work is as wide as we can find in any sphere of deviant activity. It seems that outsiders hold expectations that are virtually impossible for insiders to meet. The regularity and patterned nature of police deviance suggests that it serves important functions for police that nondeviant behavior cannot. The discrepancy also suggests that impracticable public expectations have undermined public control of the police. Even practicable expectations often meet police resistance, because public expectations in general have come to be seen by police as unrealizable. Police deviance thus can be seen as a response, a way of coming to terms with the world. Failure to recognize the *social* sources of police deviance leaves incomplete any explanation of that deviance.

Concluding Note on White-Collar and Official Deviance

In this chapter we have applied to white-collar deviance the same analytic concepts we have applied to other forms of deviance. The image of the "hustler," drawn from a consideration of professional criminals, seems appropriate to the motives and methods of some participants in white-collar deviance. A recognition of professional, business, and official subcultures suggests another commonality between lower-class and white-collar deviance.

What also emerges, however, is a recognition of the differences between white-collar and lower-class deviance. Of particular significance, white-collar deviants have access to power, resources, public tolerance of their acts, and to procedures that influence rule-making — access that is generally unavailable to lower-class deviants. Those who can make rules are clearly in positions to label their own activities as nondeviant.

We have also seen that particular problems arise with official deviance, where those involved in making and enforcing laws are in advantageous positions to subvert those laws or to design them in terms of their own personal interests. In considering police deviance we have seen also that such manipulation of rules by rule-enforcers may be a response to impossible public mandates.

The new perspective has directed us to consider white-collar and official deviance on a par with other types of deviant activities. If theories of deviance are to be accurate, they must apply equally to all instances of deviance and not "respect" class lines. A consideration of white-collar deviance also may provide us with new theoretical ideas and concepts that can be applied to the explanation of lower-class deviance. Seldom are power or access to lawmaking and law-enforcing procedures emphasized in studies of lower-class crime (though see Cicourel, 1968, whose ethnomethodological work recognizes such factors); they emerge clearly in studies of white-collar crime and might fruitfully be used in the sociological study of deviance. Considering deviance *as a social phenomenon* and recognizing variations based on the characteristics of the data rather than on preconceptions and biases characterize the sociological study of deviance from the new perspective.

12

Cognitive Deviance

Thus far in Part II we have focused on activities that at least some people judge to be wrong, bad, evil, sick, immoral, perverted, rule-breaking, or lawbreaking (illegal), and thus deviant.* We have directed our attention particularly to *acts,* things that people *do.* Homosexuality, rape, assault, drug-taking, theft, and deceit are all *behaviors.* We have discussed the ways in which those behaviors are defined, conceptualized, explained, and justified by those who engage in them and thus have dealt with *thoughts about acts* as well as the acts themselves. We have seen that deviants and nondeviants may have very different ideas about the acts at issue — not only whether they are right or wrong but also what they *are.* Is homosexuality a "perversion" or simply a "pleasurable sexual preference"? Is drug-taking an "escape from reality" or a "means of expanding consciousness"? Is employee theft "stealing" or a "fringe benefit"? These questions, and the many that could be asked of all the forms of deviance we have considered, relate to *thoughts* about the acts themselves.

Our concern in this chapter is with thoughts and ideas about the nature of the world and how it works. For data we will draw heavily on a variety of belief systems that might loosely be termed "religious." Such systems illustrate the idea of cognitive deviance with particular clarity. Cognitive deviance has a far broader range of applicability, however, which we will address later.

---

* Jacque Lynn Foltyn, University of California at San Diego, gathered the data for this chapter, wrote drafts of the material, and collaborated with the authors in the development of theories and ideas. Foltyn has done extensive work in the sociology of religion, especially in the areas of cults and new religions.

This chapter displays more clearly than any other in this book the application of the new perspective to the sociology of deviance, for the very idea of cognitive deviance emerges from the new perspective. Some of the topics we consider are customarily dealt . . . not by the sociology of deviance but by the sociology of religion, the sociology of social movements, psychology, psychiatry, and parapsychology. Our considerations here illustrate the ways in which the new perspective can serve as a bridge between different substantive areas of sociology and psychology.

The formulations in this chapter are new and are offered as tentative. We think that the idea of cognitive deviance holds great promise for helping us to understand varied forms of deviance and the responses made to it. Here we suggest the lines along which investigation might proceed, but we recognize the need for detailed research on the topics we discuss; firm formulations must await such work.

First we will examine the concept of *cognitive deviance* and then consider a variety of examples.

Nature of Cognitive Deviance

The word *cognition* refers to the process and products of knowing. The *products* are thoughts and ideas that derive from what one knows. What we *know* is fundamental to all our other ideas — beliefs, disbeliefs, guesses, suspicions, judgments, and so forth. For centuries philosophers have been concerned with cognition and have devoted extensive study to the nature of knowledge (epistemology) and the nature of reality (ontology).

Sociological concern with cognition is more recent. Absolutism virtually precludes such concern, for absolutism assumes that knowledge is absolute. There are tentative considerations of cognition in the later work of Durkheim (see especially *The Elementary Forms of the Religious Life,* 1912), and Karl Marx (see above, Chapter 2, pp. 55–56) recognized that those in different positions in the social world "know" different things. Only with Karl Mannheim (1929), however, did sociologists begin to devote serious attention to the *social* aspects of knowledge and only with the development of the new perspective, and in particular the publication of Berger and Luckmann's *The Social Construction of Reality* (1966), have sociologists come to recognize the pervasive social relativity of knowledge.

The idea of *cognitive deviance* is new in the vocabulary of sociologists. Peter Berger used the term "cognitive minorities," and that concept was adopted and developed by William M. Newman in his theoretical study of minority groups in the United States. According to Newman, three

Figure 12.1
Three Types of Minority Groups: Physical, Cognitive, and Behavioral

Type	Variance from social archetypes and/or norms in terms of	Some examples in the U.S.
Physical	Appearance	Blacks, the handicapped, the aged, Asians
Cognitive	Beliefs	Jews, Irish Catholics, various religious sects, social communes
Behavioral	Conduct	Homosexuals

Source: Newman, 1973: 35.

kinds of minority groups can be identified, as listed in Figure 12.1. Of cognitive minorities Newman says:

Groups that differ from the social norms in terms of political, religious, and social doctrines may all be viewed as cognitive minorities. While sociologists have traditionally studied the experiences of various ethnic Catholics and Jews in America's Protestant-dominated society, there are a wide variety of smaller religious groups that may appropriately be viewed as cognitive minorities. At different points in American history one might include among such groups the Society of Brothers, the Amana Community, Seventh Day Adventists, Christian Scientists, Theosophists, Buddhists, Quakers, Muslims, and Black Muslims — to mention but a few of the wide variety of smaller religious groups in the United States. In the realm of political groups, the history of the Communist party in the United States is an interesting case study in the movement of a group from minority to deviant status (Howe and Coser 1957). The Communist party was not originally a secret organization in this country. Once the host society began to view this new political philosophy as a threat, the party was driven underground through the Palmer Raids in the 1920s and subsequent anti-Communist legislation. In addition, many of the "hippie communes" formed in the late 1960s and early 1970s may be viewed as cognitive minorities that differ from the norms of the society in terms of social philosophy.

The distinction between behavioral and cognitive minorities is perhaps a difficult one to illustrate in many instances. After all, patterns of social conduct are ways of acting out ideas, while ideas are essentially reflections about human action. Yet in this dialectic between thought and action there are situations in which differences in conduct are much more important for group relationships than cognitive differences. Homosexuals are disvalued in society, not because of what they think, but because of what they do. This minority group also represents an interesting reversal of the deviant-minority transition just discussed. Unlike the Communist party, which began as a minority group and is now legally defined as a deviant group, homosexuals have been in the process of moving from a deviant position to a minority position in society. There is even an Episcopal congregation of homosexuals in one West Coast community. The movement of groups between these two statuses, deviant and minority, should provide another important area for future research. Not only is this area important for understanding group relationships, but it could also provide additional information about the overall process of social change and changing social values (pp. 37–38).*

The very idea of *cognitive* deviance reveals that social rules apply not only to how one behaves but also to *how and what one thinks.* At first it might seem virtually impossible to identify cognitive deviance, since thoughts are invisible and remain private unless we choose to disclose them. In fact, sometimes we can identify cognitive deviance only when those with "deviant" ideas choose to express them. At other times cognitive deviance may be identified through the use of everyday inferences: if one is identified as a member of a group that is judged to hold deviant ideas, one can by inference be said to hold such ideas oneself. Some cognitive deviants then choose to disclose their deviance, others are labeled deviant solely on the basis of what labelers infer that they think, and yet others are "secret cognitive deviants," whose deviance is known only to themselves.

While the term cognitive deviance is not widely used either within sociology or outside of it, the issues to which it refers have increasingly drawn both sociological and public attention. Social conflicts over what is real, true, and known have increased rapidly in recent years. Traditional "knowledge" about sanity and insanity, for example, has been strongly challenged by new ideas, both within social science and in public forums. In varied ways Perry in *The Far Side of Madness* (1974), Szasz in *The Myth of Mental Illness* (1961), Laing in *The Divided Self* (1965), and Foucault in *Madness and Civilization* (1965) have been concerned with cognitive deviance — whether it is labeled madness, mental illness, insanity, or something else. The view of this phenomenon as cognitive deviance allows its investigation in social rather than psychological, psychiatric, biological, or medical terms. These and other thinkers have disclosed the basic ambiguity of such ideas as sanity and insanity, which has led to a questioning of their reality. Focusing on the experiences of those labeled and the activities of labelers, they have provided important data for reconceptualizing madness as cognitive deviance. Since our concern is with the broad topic of cognitive deviance, we will not expand on the instance of mental illness, but we think that its formulation in these terms is a fruitful line of future inquiry.

At first it might appear to readers that social rules governing thought

* Table and quotation from *American Pluralism: A Study of Minority Groups and Social Theory* by William M. Newman. Copyright © 1973 by William M. Newman. Reprinted by permission of Harper & Row Publishers, Inc.

are an unwarranted and almost outrageous infringement on privacy, but in fact social rules concerning what is true, what is real, what is known, and how one thinks are of primary importance to social groups and to society as a whole. Rules of reason, of logic, of science and technology, and of everyday, practical common sense are the moral foundations of social life. Violations of basic rules of cognition are generally believed by members of groups to be socially threatening. Extreme cognitive deviance may even be viewed as threatening to all social order or as leading to universal chaos. Galileo (1564–1642), for example, was coerced into denying his scientific finding that the earth revolved around the sun because members of the Catholic clergy saw it as threatening the entire Christian view of the world. Only the seriousness of the perceived threat can make sense out of the extremity of the reaction to Galileo's ideas. Violation of basic rules of cognition can also be interpersonally threatening. When others claim to "know" what you take to be false, frustrating arguments and impotent rage are common.

In view of the fundamental importance of knowledge for social action, it is little wonder that conflicts over what is true are so bitter and often so violent. Religious wars are a prime example, with each side convinced of the truth of its own position. What emerges as truth in such conflicts is established not on the basis of truth itself but rather on the basis of who has the power to decide what truth is. Conflicts between capitalism and communism often display just such bitterness and violence.

In what follows we will consider a variety of different belief systems that are in some way viewed as deviant. Throughout this discussion readers may find it useful to consider their own ideas of knowledge and truth and their own responses to ideas that deviate from theirs.

Flying Saucers

Are flying saucers real? Clearly this question cannot be answered sociologically. What we can do as sociologists, however, is consider the ways in which those who answer "yes" to the question are viewed as cognitive deviants by those who answer "no." The following account by Jack Douglas is a useful starting point:

> Some years ago my mother was visiting us in Los Angeles. We went to dinner with her at the home of one of her sisters. After dinner, as we were sitting watching the distant mountains dim in the setting sunlight, my aunt said casually, "We often watch the saucers take off over the mountains at night." We said nothing in response, though I vaguely remember muttering in slight surprise, "Ahh-h. . . ." But we had no sooner gotten into our car and driven away when my mother burst out laughing, "God, she's really gone nuts this time!"

Douglas's mother clearly viewed the aunt as a cognitive deviant, and many members of the United States public would agree. Such people "know" that flying saucers are unreal and that accounts of sightings are "untrue." Those who believe in flying saucers may be labeled insane, crazy, nuts, weird, wacky, unbalanced, and so on.

There are also, however, many individuals and organized groups in the United States who "know" that flying saucers are real. Outsiders might say that such people "believe in" flying saucers, but insiders are far more likely to claim that they "know." Many people take the existence of flying saucers as fact and govern their actions accordingly. (For one of many accounts that take flying saucers as real, see John Fuller, *The Interrupted Journey*, 1967).

In the United States and in much of Western society, *physical* evidence is generally accepted as legitimate, though even physical evidence can be interpreted to fit with what is already known. If one sees what "appears to be" a flying saucer, one's explanation will in all likelihood draw on one's previous beliefs. Those who "believe in" Western science may be satisfied with an explanation that what they saw was really swamp gas, while those who already "believe in" flying saucers may use what they see as confirmation of their ideas. A main difference between those who do and do not accept flying saucers as real is in the grounds used to establish such reality. While some people base their belief in the existence of flying saucers on what they take to be sufficient physical evidence, derived either from personal experience or from "expert" knowledge about UFOs, many others do so on the basis of nonphysical evidence. They may cite a "feeling" that such phenomena "must" be real, that some form of life "must" exist on other planets, and that flying saucers are thus expectable and reasonable.

Some theorists, drawing on psychological explanations, have attempted to attribute belief in flying saucers to a deep need on the part of believers for a *savior myth* to replace Christian savior myths and to come to terms with everyday problems. This explanation *assumes* that flying saucers are unreal by scientific rules of evidence and that the scientific rules are the right ones. Yet how do psychiatrists, psychologists, sociologists, or any social scientists know better than anyone else whether flying saucers are real? Berger and Luckmann (1966) emphasize the importance of sociologists' *studying* the social world and not making claims about its reality. In the remainder of this chapter our concern will be with what people *take to be real* and the implications of divergent views about what exactly is real. Against the background of a consideration of flying saucers, we can now consider the nature of *occult beliefs* in general and then examine some of these belief systems or *alternative realities* in greater detail.

Nature, Extent, and Revival of the Occult

The word *occult* suggests that which is secret, hidden, and mysterious; in general it refers to a conception of reality as governed by supernatural forces. We are using it here in contrast to *scientific,* a conception of reality as governed by orderly natural forces that are available to investigation through the five senses. Occult and scientific explanations differ in what each takes to be real, true, and known. In many ways people in the United States take for granted the scientific view of reality, accepting it as "normal" and "self-evidently" true. The many varieties of occult belief offer other views that are judged deviant by those who hold to scientific conceptions; for many, the very term *occult* has negative connotations.

In the eighteenth and early nineteenth centuries, during the Enlightenment and the Industrial Revolution, it was expected that occult beliefs would disappear in the face of science, since science was "obviously" a more satisfactory system of explanation. Much of the occult was stigmatized by scientific rationality as irrational, false, even mad. The stigmatization did not entirely eradicate the occult but did move it out of public sight. Many social analysts thought the occult had been publicly laid to rest and might someday disappear permanently even from its private refuges. Contrary to such expectations, the past few decades have seen a tremendous revival of interest in the occult, as evidenced by television shows and movies; occult journals, magazines and books; a rapid growth of occult stores, mail order houses, workshops, and educational facilities; and an increased demand for the services of such practitioners as fortune tellers and psychics.

Opinion polls in recent years have indicated that the United States public takes the occult far more seriously than might be imagined, given the public acceptance of scientific explanations. A significant number of people claim to have had occult experiences. An even larger proportion claims belief in occult phenomena, as indicated by the Gallup Poll summarized in Figure 12.2.

A variety of reasons have been offered for increasing interest in the occult. Some social scientists (such as Truzzi, 1973) see such interest as a form of entertainment. In a society that demystifies the world with scientific rationality many occult phenomena are regarded as exciting, mysterious, sensational, fantastic, and different. Books, television series and specials, and movies that deal with the occult, and such activities as seances, fortune telling, and use of the Ouija board may be rich sources of entertainment for many. Entertainment, however, if it helps explain people's *participation* in such activities, does not sufficiently ex-

Figure 12.2

Gallup Poll (1978) on Occult Phenomena	
Phenomenon	*Percentage of population that believes in the phenomenon*
UFO's[a]	57%
Angels	54
ESP[b]	51
Devils	39
Astrology	29
Ghosts	11
Witches	10

[a] Unidentified flying objects.
[b] Extrasensory perception.

Source: Reprinted by permission of the Gallup Poll.

plain their *belief* in them. One does not customarily believe in something merely because it is entertaining. It appears that entertainment may initiate a process that brings other factors into play. Thus, for example, some people who have begun using the Ouija board "for fun" have come to take it very seriously and to both trust and fear its powers. We do not have sufficient evidence to explain exactly how this process works or what additional factors may be involved.

Perhaps the acceptance of occult beliefs may be more satisfactorily explained as a response to *scientific absolutism.* In its ideal or "storybook" form, Mitroff (1974), writes, science is concerned with truth of all kinds wherever it may be found and however disconcerting or strange it may be; in practice, however, science is in many ways a belief system resembling religious belief systems. Scientists, like human beings in general, not infrequently reject those ideas that do not fit with what they already "know" and may be less critical of "acceptable" than "unacceptable" ideas. (For a detailed account of this process, see Ian Mitroff, *The Subjective Side of Science,* 1974.) The perceived unwillingness of scientists to take seriously concerns that some people have — flying saucers, acupuncture, chiropractic, astrology, or ghosts — supports the existence of independent systems for explaining such phenomena. Instances where scientists have turned out to be "wrong" or where there is evidence that their judgments are guided by nonscientific politics or religion, have further undermined acceptance of science as "the only explanation."

Acceptance of the occult is not for the most part either an acceptance of *all* occult phenomena or a rejection of all science. Rather, belief is often highly situational and subject to much ambivalence. Those who accept one occult phenomenon may not accept another. Those who accept flying saucers as real may not "believe in" astrology. On the other hand, those who do not "believe in" astrology may nonetheless be moved to caution or optimism by their daily horoscope. While fortune cookies may not be "believed," seldom are they ignored or entirely discounted. So-called rational people will often restrict or modify their behavior to appease some unknown force that might deal them bad luck if they crack a mirror, open an umbrella in the house, or refuse to throw spilled salt over their shoulder. Even scientists may avoid walking under a ladder, may be sure to knock on wood to forestall evil, or in other ways may avoid "taking chances." Such practices indicate a willingness to entertain possibilities that lie outside the "natural" world of science.

The occult then may be seen as an alternative to science or at least to scientific absolutism. It may also serve as a resource when science fails to provide "suitable" explanations. With the decline of the traditional Judeo-Christian religions, many people no longer believe that they can call on any outside agency of intervention for assistance or comfort. Trying to find a suitable faculty within oneself or in another dimension is understandable when many individuals feel that they are little more than pawns within the larger culture. The widespread interest in occult phenomena suggests that a rationalized society may leave unsatisfied many individual needs, especially in regard to feelings of security and self-determination. Interest in the occult may thus be a kind of rejection of the values of a rationalized existence. While some may find occult explanations useful and satisfactory, others may reject them as deviant.

We now turn our attention to a particular occult phenomenon, astrology. We consider the ideas about reality, truth, and knowledge that underlie its practice. Then we examine "new religions" as a somewhat different example of cognitive deviance.

Astrology

On any morning, newspaper readers throughout the United States can be found consulting their daily horoscopes with varying degrees of interest and seriousness. Virtually every daily paper features the horoscope. While we are not claiming that all who read their horoscopes are "believers," the appearance of such an item as standard, "normal" newspaper fare suggests that astrology has a public existence. More serious interest in astrology is indicated by the wide variety of books and magazines reporting on the topic and by the ready availability of astrologers for those who wish to consult them. The 1979 edition of the *Bell System Yellow Pages* for Boston has twenty-four entries under "Astrologers."

Astrologers provide advice on nearly everything. One can obtain information on astrological dieting, sex, or birth control as well as general direction for one's life. Elaborate computer systems provide detailed horoscopes, and simple computers are available in public places such as restaurants, airline terminals, and supermarkets. Zodiac T-shirts, bumper stickers, and jewelry are readily obtainable. In some circles it is not uncommon for those meeting for the first time to inquire into one another's signs, and the behavior of others may be explained in terms such as "Well, she's a Leo, you know, so that's why she acts like that." Astrologers are likely to make headlines when they predict earthquakes and other natural disasters, the outcomes of political events, and the futures of celebrities. While many of those who "follow" astrology may do so because they find it entertaining, amusing, or interesting, others find it a valid system that can provide knowledge about the course of future events and explanations for why people are the way they are and do what they do.

Astrology is occult, as we are using the term, since it views reality as operating through supernatural forces, forces different from those recognized by Western science. According to astrology, celestial bodies influence terrestrial affairs, both in the physical and the human sphere. Knowledge of the operation of such bodies and their effects makes it possible to explain the past and to predict the future. Both human temperament and human destiny are seen as dependent upon the zodiac or sun sign under which one is born. Thus Capricorns are tenacious, Leos are proud, and so on.

An individual's zodiac sign is calculated from information about the position of the sun in relation to the stars and planets at the exact time and place of birth. The term *zodiac* applies to twelve astrological constellations and the animals that symbolize them. According to astrology, the heavens are divided into twelve constellations, sectors, or "Houses" that correspond to particular celestial configurations resulting from the rotation of the earth. The influence of a "House" on a person depends upon the position of the celestial bodies within it as the "House" is about to rise in the eastern skies. Each "House" influences some aspect of life, such as marriage, friendship, enmity, or health. Each planet is believed to have its own particular qualities: Venus governs love; Mars, impatience; Mercury, deceit. When the moon or sun occupies the ascending House, there are more specific powers. Unusual celestial events such as comets and eclipses of the sun and moon are particularly significant influences.

Knowledge of astrology by those who accept it can be used to reduce uncertainty in life and to make decisions about actions to be undertaken. Vacations, travel, business deals, affairs of the heart, social activities, and the entire range of human activities may be planned in accordance with astrological predictions. Nowhere in Western science is such advice readily available.

The Chaldeans of Babylonia devised the first known system of astrology around 3000 B.C., drawing on their observations of such astronomical phenomena as shooting stars, comets, solar and lunar eclipses, and the effects of the moon on tides. Religion, astronomy, and astrology were interwoven in their system. The motions of the planets and stars were taken to be symbolic communications from the gods about the fate of individuals and nations. Through observations of the regularity of the motions of celestial bodies, the Chaldeans worked out mathematical conceptions that became the basis of subsequent astrological and astronomical studies.

From Babylonia, astrology spread to and became popular in ancient China, India, Egypt, and Greece. By the fourth century B.C. the Greeks had adapted astrology to fit their polytheistic religion and their developing science of astronomy. Like astronomy and Aristotelian physics, astrology was viewed as a science. Romans of the Roman Empire adopted astrology along with many other ideas from Greece. The Roman emperors relied heavily on astrology. Marcus Aurelius, for example, planned his battles in accordance with the stars. Another Roman emperor, Titus, believed strongly in his horoscope; he died, apparently in good health, on the day his astrologer predicted. With the decline of the Roman Empire, astrology declined; Christian scholars rediscovered it in the Middle Ages.

The changing position of astrology in Christianity demonstrates how an accepted belief can become a deviant one and how a deviant practice can later return to legitimacy. Early Christian theologians tried to modify astrology in order to reconcile it with the teachings of the Catholic Church. St. Augustine, Bishop of Hippo and head of the Eastern part of the Roman Catholic Church around A.D. 400, led the first real assault against astrology, thus labeling it deviant in terms of Catholic theology. The dominance of the Catholic Church in Europe in subsequent centuries sustained the deviant status of astrology. By the beginning of the thirteenth century, however, the Church was becoming less dogmatic and more secular; astrology reappeared. Crusaders returning from the Holy Land, where they had learned about astrology from the Arabs, helped popularize it. St. Thomas Aquinas, a Catholic intellectual of the thirteenth century, was able to reconcile Church doctrine with the theories of astrology, and astrology once again became nondeviant. The Vatican even employed astrologers to advise the Pope.

During the Renaissance, when rational thinking and science were being established as the criteria for knowledge and when occult explanations were falling into disfavor, belief in astrology, oddly enough, was unparalleled. Virtually everyone accepted the truth of astrology. The fact that the much-admired ancient Greeks had held it in high esteem contributed to its popularity. In the spirit of the Renaissance, astrology came under close scientific scrutiny in an attempt to calculate horoscopes more accurately. Under such scrutiny astrology fell into disfavor and was disassociated from astronomy, which came into ascendance. The astronomical computations of the Polish astronomer Copernicus and the telescopes of Galileo, by demonstrating that the earth is not the center of the universe, undermined astrological theory. Astronomy became an exact science and astrology was stigmatized, particularly by scientists, as "false."

Earlier we suggested some reasons for today's reappearance of occult concerns. As sociologists we take no stand on the "truth" of astrology, but we do recognize the importance of the stands that others take, and there are many who are dismayed at the reappearance of astrology, both for what it indicates and what it might lead to. Modern scientists are among those concerned by the growing acceptance of occult phenomena in general and of astrology in particular. Some have collectively stigmatized astrologers as fakes and charlatans and labeled their practices simply magic and superstition. Scientists have declared that astrology is a waste of time, money, and effort and proclaimed that it had no relation to the events of the physical world.

Scientific objections to astrology are many. It is claimed that astrology cannot explain why the moment of one's birth is so important. Why not, for example, the moment of conception? Other objections refer to the different fates that may befall people who have the same horoscope, even exactly the same date and time of birth. Astrology's failure to answer such objections *to the satisfaction of scientists* has led scientists to discount astrology.

With science as a dominant explanatory force in present-day Western society, it is not surprising that an explanatory system not based on that science would be denounced. The very existence of astrology is a threat to science because it offers an alternative; presumably if science were as complete a system as believers think it is, no alternative would be necessary. Scientists who speak out against astrology seem to view it not only as wrong but also as bad or evil, and clearly as cognitive deviance. Such reactions by scientists suggest that science possesses absolutist qualities. Like religion, science, too, is a belief system that is viewed by many believers as the *only* source of truth.

The labeling of astrology as false, even insane, has not, however, led to astrology's demise. In fact such labeling has frequently spurred astrologers to new efforts to establish the legitimacy of their system. New scientific insights have been adopted and reworked by astrology, and new findings that might undermine astrology are being used to reinforce it. While Copernicus' discovery that the sun, not the earth, was the center of the solar system might have devastated astrology, in fact astrology was able to adjust. When three new planets were identified in the solar system — Neptune, Uranus, and Pluto — astrologers responded that they had always expected new planets would be found. The innate rhythms of plants and animals or "biological clocks" discovered by biologists in the 1920s and 1930s were used by astrologists as proof of astrology. Time studies of biorhythms are now being similarly used by astrologers as substantiation of their system.

Astrologers claim, generally quite rightly, that their critics seldom know much in detail about astrology but reject it out of hand. When Sir Isaac Newton was ridiculed by British astronomer Edmund Halley for believing in astrology, Newton retorted: "Sir, I have studied the subject, you have not." Indeed astrology has not been subjected to extensive systematic study by many scientists.

Psychology also has challenged the validity of astrology by labeling it a "delusional system." The claim is that astrology is a way of denying responsibility for one's own actions by attributing them to outside forces. Evidence can be provided to show that interest in astrology and the occult in general often increases greatly in times of economic and political upheaval or instability. Astrology was popular, for example, in Rome during the devastating Punic Wars, in the United States after the Civil War and after World War I, and in Nazi Germany. During World War II, Hitler and Goebbels encouraged astrologers to make favorable predictions about the outcome of the war for propaganda purposes. Opponents of astrology see it as an "unrealistic" solution to problems in times of crisis and as a support for "irrational" and "illogical" thought. They *assume* that astrology is wrong and science is right.

Absolute proof is unlikely to emerge for either the system of astrology or that of science. *Ultimately both rest on belief.* Each accuses the other of discounting data, slanting arguments, and being unwilling to take the other seriously. The bitterness of some of the clashes suggests that each is seriously threatening the beliefs of the other. Science now seems to have the power to label astrology as *cognitive deviance* in a way that is publicly significant, but the rise of occult concerns in general and astrology in particular threatens such power by providing alternative belief systems to that of science.

New Religions as Cognitive Deviance

The term *occult,* which we have defined as a conception of reality as governed by supernatural forces, can be applied to religion, but there are some important differences between the occult and religion. The major difference was identified by anthropologist Bronislaw Malinowski in *Magic, Science, and Religion* (1948; see also Homans, 1941).

According to Malinowski magic, or what we are terming the occult, has practical goals, providing the basis for decision-making in everyday life. The occult tells one what to do in the face of dilemmas. Religion, on the other hand, involves a relationship to the supernatural, which may provide practical guidance but is essentially directed to proper behavior in terms of the supernatural, such as worship or respect for the sacred. (See Durkheim, *The Elementary Forms of the Religious Life*, 1912.) While both the occult and religion are concerned with supernatural forces and their effects on everyday life, the occult focuses on everyday life while religion focuses on the nature of supernatural forces themselves.

Belief in the occult can be labeled cognitive deviance; religion, with its emphasis on the nature of the supernatural, is even more subject to such labeling. Throughout history a wide variety of religions have been stigmatized because of the beliefs espoused by followers. Traditional, established religions have customarily stigmatized new ones, the latter threatening the claims to absolute truth of the former. The power of traditional religions and the strong commitment of the followers of new religions have made for long and bitter struggles.

Which religions are likely to be viewed as instances of cognitive deviance? Any *new* religion seems to be subject to such a label, applied by traditional religions or by other traditional belief systems. Controversies over religious beliefs have been among the most heated, intense, and longest lasting in history. They have inspired massive immigrations, stimulated nation building, and led to huge losses of life and property. History abounds with examples of religious conflict, with each party convinced of the truth of its beliefs and the "proper" relation to the supernatural. Moses led followers of the new religion of Judaism to Canaan, the promised land, and away from the persecution of the Egyptian followers of another and long-established religion. The new religion of Protestantism met with the Inquisition, conducted by the Catholic Church as a way of seeking out, making penitent, or destroying heretics. The Inquisition, which lasted in Spain from 1480 to 1834, indicates the strength and determination of all the involved parties. (For a biased but intriguing novelistic account of this period, see Charles Maturin, *Melmoth the Wanderer*, 1820.)

The struggle between new and old religions may be the major source of conflict between groups or may be combined with other motives. Besides religious differences, there were a variety of political and economic reasons for the attempted German extermination of the Jews. When cultural differences accompany religious ones, it is not always possible to determine which factor predominates in conflicts. In Northern Ireland today, religious conflict and other factors are inextricably intertwined. Religious differences may be both reasons for conflict and symbols of other kinds of differences. Religious controversy can last for hundreds of years and may be closely tied with nationalism and political movements. Even where conflicts are described by participants in religious terms there may well be other factors involved.

Sociologists have been interested in studying religion since the days of Auguste Comte, the founder of sociology. Many of the major sociological theorists devoted extensive attention to religion. (See, for example, Durkheim, *The Elementary Forms of the Religious Life*, 1912; Weber, *The Protestant Ethic and the Spirit of Capitalism*, 1905; and, for current examples, Berger, *A Rumor of Angels*, 1969, and *The Sacred Canopy*, 1967.) Early theorists focused on religion as a "system sustainer, system integrator and people pleaser" (Gerlach, 1977), but such functions make sense only in terms of traditional and established religions; new religions tend to be system disruptors, system challengers, and even sources of individual confusion. While traditional religions support and uphold societal values and social conventions, new religions often challenge both traditional religions and society as a whole, which is why they arouse severely repressive responses. Such cognitive deviance is viewed as a threat to the established social order.

As we consider some of the ways in which new religions are viewed by established religions and by other institutions in society, we should remind ourselves that today's established or traditional religions were all at one time *new* and were objects of some of the same kinds of attack that they now make upon others.

The general populace at large as well as followers of traditional religions often view new religions with skepticism, disgust, or even fear, regarding them as havens for the "deprived, disorganized, devitalized, or defective" (Gerlach, 1906). Such new religions may be referred to, both by people in general and by sociologists in particular, as "sects" or "cults" to distinguish them from "Churches" or "real" religion. (Sociological usage derives from Troeltsch, 1956.) A Church is an institution whose members follow a traditional, established religion that is accepted as legitimate by the society in which it exists. Membership in a Church is customarily based upon birth. The Church itself is characterized by its large size and hierarchical organization as well as its existence for generations. In contrast, a sect or cult is a smaller organization, customarily established during the lifetime of its members, which involves their intense participation. Judaism, Christianity, Buddhism, and Islam all began as innovative sects or cults, labeled as deviant by established religions of the time. What is a Church in one society, for example Zen Buddhism in Japan, may be a cult or sect in another, as is Zen Buddhism in the United States.

The terms Church, sect, and cult refer not only to structural differences such as size and organization but also to the relation of these organizations to other societal organizations. The terms also include, at least implicitly, a moral judgment that one is superior to another. Church members may view sect members as crazy or deluded, while sect members may view Church members as not "really" devoted to religion and not actively involved in it.

If traditional religions are viewed as upholding the values of a society and maintaining social conventions, new religions, with different values and conventions, constitute a challenge and are likely to be responded to as deviant. Social scientists have often adopted the perspective of the established society and have supposed, for this reason, that new religions provide alternatives for "misfits" who do not blend in with the rest of society.

Social science explanations of new religious movements have, in the past, directed particular attention to two questions: (1) why do new religious movements arise? and (2) why do people join such movements? (Hine, 1977). A number of explanations of why religious movements arise have been derived from structural analysis (Level II) and have attributed cause to "rapid cultural change, social disorganization; dislocation of values, etc." (Hine, 1977: 646). Level VI explanations based on individual psychology have claimed that such movements are joined by individuals with "maladjustments, pathologies, emotional inadequacies or specific personality attributes which predispose" (*ibid.*) them to seek religious solutions to private problems. Hine designates three models used by social scientists to study social movements in general and religious movements in particular: *the disorganization model* (Linton, 1943; Wallace, 1956; Barber, 1941); *the deprivation model* (Toch, 1965; Aberle, 1965; Yinger, 1957); and the *deviant or defective individual model* (Catton, 1957; Brown and Lowe, 1951). We have discussed these kinds of theories earlier. They claim that new religions attract persons who for reasons of socioeconomic deprivation or disorganization or for reasons of some personality defect cling to anything novel because they cannot adjust to their lives. The extensive media attention given to such new religions as the "Moonies" and the People's Temple often includes explanations of this kind.

There are various reasons for people's joining a new religion. Social science explanations that focus on "social problems" or "individual pathology" appear to *assume* that the religion joined is *wrong* and such a wrong decision requires explanation. Seldom are "social problems" or "individual pathology" used to explain membership in traditional, established religions, except by some members of new religions. Such analysis discounts the possibility that new religions might be attractive to "normal" people and that people might join for reasons other than pathology, disorganization, or deprivation.

Recently these kinds of explanations of new religions have been criticized (Glock, 1964; Hine, 1977; Gerlach, 1968, 1977; Straus, 1976, 1979;

Richardson, 1977, 1979). The following description captures the spirit of the new perspective:

> The prototype is of the *Seeker,* and the watchword of the new view is *autonomy.* The person is no longer an object being pushed around by unseen forces . . . but is instead a *subject* exercising volition at every turn. . . . He is not "brainwashed" or under "mind control," but is *negotiating* a workable arrangement with those who would seek his *allegiance* . . . (Richardson, 1979: 16–17).

This new perspective recognizes that new religions may come into existence for a variety of reasons and may have many attractions for their followers.

In his study of the Pentecostal Movement in the United States, Gerlach (1977) found new members to be rather "typical" Americans, middle-class and apparently well satisfied with their lives *until* they joined the new religion. His findings are similar to those of Weber, who argued in *The Protestant Ethic and the Spirit of Capitalism* (1905) that new religious belief systems (his example was Protestantism right after the Reformation) could be of fundamental importance in bringing about social change. Weber claimed that such Protestant virtues as working hard, deferring gratification, saving money, and actively participating in the everyday world supported capitalism in a way that the traditional Catholic other-worldly focus could not. Weber saw the social innovation that often takes place in new religions as crucial to social change and believed it responsible for the rationalization of Western civilization.

The current decline of traditional religions seems to be related to the rise of science and technology and the establishment of "rationalism." The rise of new religions, on the other hand, like the rise of the occult, seems to be related to criticisms of science, technology, and rationalism. Some of these new religions have come under heavy criticism. Battles have been particularly severe and objections strong with regard to the followers of the Reverend Sun Yung Moon (the "Moonies"), of the Hare Krishna movement, of the Reverend Jim Jones (The People's Temple), and of Scientology. Opposition is clear in the title of a *Reader's Digest* article, "Scientology: Anatomy of a Frightening Cult" (May 1980). Many opponents of these new religions have accused their leaders of kidnapping, brainwashing, and in other ways making captives of their converts. Such criticism of new religions is not new; for example, W. J. Schnell's *Thirty Years a Watch Tower Slave* (1956) chronicles the experiences of a Jehovah's Witness who saw himself a captive of the religion. Immense cognitive differences can be seen between those who view followers of such religions as captives and those who view them as enlightened followers of newly disclosed truth. Holders of such opposed views often enter conflicts with one another. On one side are customarily ranged nonbelievers, relatives of believers, and "deprogrammers" as well as disillusioned former believers; on the other side are believers, civil libertarians, and others who recognize the problematic status of any new religion.

Certainly all new religions do not encounter violent resistance and antagonism, but seldom do new religions arise without any resistance, because their very existence is a challenge to accepted rules of cognition. The number of new religions currently on the scene all over the world, and particularly in the United States, is a measure of the degree to which traditional religious views are under assault.

One important aspect of new religions, much more important than for those involved with the occult, is the uniting of believers in a subculture. New religions commonly ask for extensive participation of new members. When such participation is organized into a subculture, participants receive extensive support from one another for their beliefs and develop rhetorics for meeting the objections of nonbelievers. Without such subcultural support, as is more commonly true of followers of the occult, individuals are more on their own and may be "seduced" away from their cognitive deviance. The importance of such support can be seen in the current movement toward developing subcultures among those concerned with the occult (Jorgenson, 1978). Such subcultures accept the general notion that ideas and practices that lack legitimacy in the broader society are worthy of further consideration. For followers both of the occult and of new religions such subcultural support provides members with reinforcement of their own beliefs and techniques for discounting nonbelievers.

In order to better understand cognitive deviance as it exists in the everyday world we turn now to a case study of a new religion. We have intentionally chosen a case involving intense feelings and great conflict, because it illustrates the extremes possible in cognitive deviance, the power of responses to such deviance, and the difficulties of understanding extremely different cognitive views of the world.

THE PEOPLE'S TEMPLE

On November 18, 1978, more than 900 members of a cult originating in California and living in Guyana drank Kool-Aid laced with cyanide in the largest mass incident of suicide and murder in recent times. Some members willingly drank the liquid as a means of departing from this world and entering the next; others went along with differing degrees of reluctance. The event made newspaper headlines for weeks and evoked public horror, amazement, titillation, and concern. The behavior itself was certainly viewed as deviant by many, but our concern here is with the ideas that supported it — ideas that in some respects appear to be instances of cognitive deviance.

The People's Temple began as a San Francisco-based new religion, led by the Reverend Jim Jones. Its avowed purpose was to help the poor, and recruits were drawn from those with experiences of racial inequality, rapid social mobility, loneliness, and unfulfilled personal and social goals (Braungart, 1979). Once established, this new religion grew rapidly in the face of varied public response. Some politicians and social leaders applauded the group's efforts to help the poor, while other leaders expressed concern over its "fringe religion" appearance and what they judged its "deprived, depraved" membership. Responses to those who joined the Temple were similar to those we have discussed earlier toward joiners of any new religion. Followers were seen as seeking an escape from the larger society, and their membership was viewed as a "crutch" by both the general populace and many social scientists. Members' claims that they joined to seek personal change and societal transformation were customarily denied by outsiders.

The People's Temple mixed political with religious activity, combining a neo-Marxist ideology with Christian piety (Braungart, 1979). Like other utopian groups, the Temple criticized the existing structure and values of society and conceived "of the future in terms of socially transcendent ideals" (Braungart, 1979: 2). Seeking socialism, equality, and a new communal order, Temple members renounced their worldly possessions and devoted themselves and their resources to "the cause."

Like other new religions, the People's Temple was inspired, begun, led, and sustained by a *charismatic* leader, one whose personal qualities were taken as providing legitimation and justification for power and authority. The Reverend Jim Jones was seen by members as possessing extraordinary personal powers. Strong, forceful, and spellbinding, he was accorded respect and granted power by his followers.

Maintaining power can present certain problems for any leader. When that power is based on tradition (the way things have always been) or on rational-legal principles (as when police are legally granted certain kinds of power), it is customarily easier to sustain than when it is based on the far more ambiguous quality of charisma. These aspects of power, first characterized sociologically by Max Weber, were used by D. P. Johnson in analyzing the People's Temple ("Dilemmas of Charismatic Leadership: The Case of the People's Temple," 1979; for a quite different analysis of a charismatic religious leader, see Freud, *Moses and Monotheism*, 1939.) Johnson focused on two of the many strategies that Jones developed in order to sustain his power in the group: demands for absolute loyalty from members and increasing isolation of group members from the broader society.

Jones's increasing demands for group loyalty paralleled the organizational growth of the Temple. With growth came increasing heterogeneity of the membership, a condition that can decrease the loyalty that a leader has come to expect. Varied views are potential sources of challenge to group ideas and ideals. Jones responded to, or perhaps even anticipated, such a threat by isolating the Temple from the rest of society, eventually moving a large number of his followers to Guyana in South America, where the community of Jonestown was founded. While this exodus was explained as a response to persecution, its effect was to unite members in their cognitive deviance, as well as to protect Jones's power by eliminating outside challenges. The isolation of Jonestown made members almost exclusively dependent on one another for their physical and emotional well-being.

Isolation, paradoxically, presents problems for charismatic leaders and leaders of cults in general, because one important basis for solidarity — intolerance of and persecution by the broader society — is removed. Once the move to Guyana was made, Jones changed his methods of group control in order to maintain his power. His demands for continual expressions of loyalty from members increased and he imposed strict subordination rituals on members. He required that certain sexual acts be performed and demanded that his followers engage in practice drills for mass suicide. As members questioned Jones's indoctrination and intimidation practices, he increased his demands for loyalty and subordination. The final demand, followed by many and forced on others, was the mass death in the face of what members defined as a threat to the continuance of the People's Temple.

The People's Temple violated in many ways rules and values accepted and taken for granted in United States society and publicly acknowledged as legitimate. The Temple violated basic democratic values, offering instead a kind of communalism that seems to have been required even of reluctant members. Indications that some members were held in Jonestown against their will suggest another violation of United States values concerning freedom of choice and movement. Those who believed in the People's Temple and its tenets, including its commitment to suicide in the face of threats, seem clearly definable according to United States standards as cognitive deviants. The rules and practices with which Jones forced nonbelievers to participate as well and denied them opportunities to leave provide additional evidence of cognitive deviance.

In the attempt to understand the People's Temple, various explanations have been offered, most of them focusing on the Reverend Jim Jones as mad, evil, manipulative, and power-hungry, a person who coerced his members for his own good and his own glorification. Such interpretations deny the possibility that Jones was responding to his own peculiar religious vision and in particular question his honesty. If he is viewed as dishonest, we might reexamine the "seduction process" we discussed in Chapter 9 (pp. 279–281) and consider the ways in which Jones "seduced" members. This model seems to fit quite well the practices of the People's Temple. The implication is, however, that the seducer *does not believe* in the claims being made. How is such a judgment to be made sociologically? We now turn to consider this troublesome question.

Fakes and True Believers

In Chapter 9 we considered self-deception and deception of others. We noted the ultimate impossibility of "knowing" the mind of another and thus the impossibility that either people in general or sociologists in particular could "know" whether one was being honest or dishonest, truthful or deceitful. Such determinations are ultimately inferential. In this section we distinguish between *fakes*, those who admit to not believing in what they are saying and doing, and *true believers*, those who claim to believe in what they are saying and doing. Those engaged in self-deception seem to fall somewhere between. Our concern here is with the kinds of evidence used to distinguish between fakes and true believers in the realms of the occult and of new religions.

Many people discount the possibility of the very existence of true believers in the occult and new religions, viewing all their followers as deluded and all their leaders as either deluded or fakes. Astrologers, palm readers, Tarot card readers, "cult" leaders, and others are said to be lying about having secret powers in order to make money, to achieve power over the "gullible," or to gain personally in some other way.

Leaders and participants in occult activities and new religions also recognize the existence of fakes but claim that there are also true believers. Those who see themselves as true believers are perhaps even more antagonistic toward fakes than are nonbelievers, because true believers feel threatened by fakes. Fakes injure the reputation of true believers and can be cited as evidence by those claiming that they are *all* fakes. Fakes destroy credibility in both the occult and new religions. Furthermore, as we discussed in Chapter 9, some degree of honesty is necessary for all social groups that intend to endure, and fakes betray the honesty that insiders expect of other insiders.

As might be imagined, both outsiders and insiders encounter some difficulty distinguishing fakes from true believers. Some occult "purists" insist that a fundamental way to determine whether one is a fraud is whether or not that person charges a fee for services or otherwise "collects" money. With such a stringent criterion one would clearly identify many frauds. Jorgenson (1978: 17–18) found a less re-

Figure 12.3

Mexican farmer J. Carmen Garcia, shown holding one of his five-foot collard greens, has astounded scientists by growing giant vegetables, including 60-pound cabbages and 10-pound onions. He says he got the secret from a man who learned it while a prisoner of aliens from space who live underground and eat giant vegetables. Garcia has given the secret to the Rosicrucians, a mysterious society in San Jose, Calif. that specializes in secrets.

Source: Boston Globe, June 1, 1980.

strictive criterion: that fees charged or money collected fall within some agreed-upon limit, and that other parts of a loose "code of ethics" be followed. Many other criteria can be used, but none so far created is foolproof.

Fakes are particularly likely to make use of occult or religious claims because the criteria for truth in these areas are so ambiguous and vague. While con games of this sort — and fakes in fact are con artists — do seem to require some skill, many fakes succeed in giving an appearance of legitimacy and may be readily accepted both as true believers and as possessors of extraordinary powers. The practices of fakes range from being virtually indistinguishable from those of true believers — except to the most knowledgeable of insiders — to being "obviously" fake to any but the most gullible.

Fakes depend upon gaining the confidence of potential followers and, especially in the sphere of the occult, the use of tricks: words, acts, or devices designed to deceive. Expert tricksters do not need to lie, brag, or evade; they simple set up a situation so that clients will draw erroneous inferences. Psychics customarily give clients information about their lives, and tricksters extract information from clients to be used later as a display of psychic abilities. The kinds of questions we are raising here are: when a fortune teller looks into a crystal ball, is anything there to be seen? Do some people see nothing and lie while others do indeed see something? Are all who claim to see something lying? Clearly such are not sociological questions. Sociological evidence strongly supports the existence of fakes, since some of their modes of operation are known, but there is also evidence that some persons see themselves as true believers (see, for example, Festinger, et al., *When Prophecy Fails*, 1956.)

It is easy to trick others into thinking that you can read their minds. Little experience is necessary, though professional fakes may have polished their act to an art. A *stock spiel* or psychological reading consisting of highly general statements that in some sense can apply to anyone may be used for all clients. A stock spiel that has had a remarkable success rate among both men and women is quoted below. Readers might consider how well it would apply to them if told by the "proper" person under the "proper" conditions.

> Some of your aspirations tend to be pretty unrealistic. At times you are extroverted, affable, sociable, while at other times you are introverted, wary and reserved. You have found it unwise to be too frank in revealing yourself to others. You pride yourself on being an independent thinker and do not accept others' opinions without satisfactory proof. You prefer a certain amount of change and variety, and become dissatisfied when hemmed in by restrictions and limitations. At times you have serious doubts as to whether you have made the right decision or done the right thing. Disciplined and controlled on the outside, you tend to be worrisome and insecure on the inside.
>
> Your sexual adjustment has presented some problems for you. While you have some personality weaknesses, you are generally able to compensate for them. You have a great deal of unused capacity which you have not turned to your advantage. You have a tendency to be critical of yourself. You have a strong need for other people to like you and for them to admire you (Snyder and Shenkel, 1975).

This spiel has been used in social science studies of the processes involved in fortune telling. When subjects are told that the spiel is actually an accurate description constructed just for them, half have believed the sketch to be a perfect personality fit. Similar findings have occurred over a 30-year period. A clever reader will have a battery of stock spiels for different categories of people — young unmarried people, the newly divorced, the lovesick, the elderly — which may be adapted to the perceived situation.

Another device used by fakes is a *cold reading*, done on the basis of information "gleaned," as Goffman terms it (1959: 2–6), from the client. Cold readers use clues in a way that would make Sherlock Holmes proud. They may begin with stock spiels but modify them on the basis of what they can learn about the particular client. They may draw on public directories or other public information about clients or have accomplices examine clients' personal belongings left in closets or cloak rooms. More frequently cold readers depend on the information available before them on the person of the client. The client is sized up and carefully studied. Age and physical features are noted — eyes, weight, build. How are the hands used? Are they held down in a constrained way? Do they gesture excitedly? Are nails manicured or bitten down? How does the client use the eyes? Is eye contact sustained or avoided? Close attention is paid to the style, appearance, cleanliness, and quality of the client's clothing. Clothing, manner of speech, grammar, and vocabulary may be useful guides to socioeconomic status. (For these and further details, see Hyman, 1977.)

After making an initial assessment, cold readers begin to test it by speaking in general terms of a variety of subjects and carefully watching the client's response. Does the client avoid eye contact, stiffen, or appear troubled when certain topics are introduced? Readers generally assume that clients come to them with some particular problem, and they use a range of clues to determine what the problem might be. More than anything else cold readers are good listeners. It is not unusual in a cold reading for the client to do 75 percent of the talking, in all likelihood without realizing it (Hyman, 1977, p. 29). Clients may give readers many details about their lives and then be amazed when readers seem to know so much about them.

Cold readings are customarily enhanced by the use of props to set the stage. Crystal balls, Tarot cards, and other "mechanisms" may be used both to give legitimacy to the front and to provide stalls for readers while they are thinking and assembling the information they have gathered. A confident delivery and the enlistment of clients as active participants help establish the legitimacy of what is going on.

Successful cold readers, like successful con artists, armed robbers, and others whose deviance involves knowledge of others, have extensive practical understanding of the very social behavior that sociologists study. Cold readers may in fact make use of polls, studies, and statistics and will "play the probabilities" when deciding on an approach to take to a client. To be on the safe side, however, they may also profess a modesty in their own talents and, in addition, emphasize that the client must cooperate for the reading to work. Failure or mistakes can thus be alibied if they do occur (Hyman, p. 77). Cold readers may also flatter clients and, as Hyman notes,

> tell him what he wants to hear. He wants to hear about himself. So tell him about himself. But not what you know to be true about him. Oh, No! Never tell him the truth. Rather, tell him *what he would like to be true about himself!* (Hyman, 1977: 18).

Stock spiels, cold readings, "tricks," and fakery in general are most successful with those who, for a variety of reasons, *want to believe* — those who want what the occult practice or new religion is offering. Like marks in con games, clients of these fakes may participate actively in their own deception. They may ignore happenings that would be dead giveaways to a skeptic. Thus, as in all seduction processes, the success of fakes involves some degree of deception on the part of both the seducer and the seducee.

The charge of fraud is directed not only toward occult practices but toward new religions as well. Many and varied religious leaders have been called fakes, seekers merely of power or money. Among those so accused have been the Reverend Jim Jones of the People's Temple, Daddy Grace, Amy Semple MacPherson and her Church of the Four-Square Bible, and Mary Baker Eddy when she began the Christian Science religion, which now spans the world.

The task of distinguishing fakes from true believers is complicated by the fact that those who view themselves as true believers may view other practitioners, whether competitors or not, as fakes. Claims and counterclaims abound. (For an illustration in the field of natural health practices, see Roth, *Health Purifiers and their Enemies,* 1977.) The motives for labeling another a fake may be to emphasize the legitimacy of one's own practices and beliefs, to discredit a competitor, or to indicate that one believes in only some occult or religious practices but not all. Astrologers, for example, may discount the possibility of flying saucers, and members of the People's Temple may see snake-handling cults (as described by Weston La Barre, *They Shall Take up Serpents,* 1962) as "crazy."

Another complication arises when fakes *become* true believers. Cold readers may come to believe that they "really are" psychic and can really divine the future. Positive feedback from clients may convince fakes that they had deceived themselves in thinking that they were "making it up" when in fact they had psychic powers that they hadn't recognized.

Both occult and religious phenomena are ultimately beyond either proof or disproof. Either the phenomena are not capable of being studied scientifically, or those concerned reject the scientific method of establishing proof. While earlier absolutist sociologists as well as some of today's sociologists have not felt it inappropriate to decide on the truth or falsity of the beliefs of others, the new perspective sees such judgments as lying outside sociologists' expertise. Within the new perspective, attention is focused on people's acts and words. How people distinguish between true and false, real and unreal, or fakes and true believers emerges as an important sociological topic. Studies can be done of those who call themselves true believers and are so viewed by others, those who call themselves fakes but are viewed as true believers by others, and so forth through the varied alternatives and combinations. Study of the rules of evidence used by those who make such distinctions can also be instructive. In this way sociologists explore people's practices without interjecting their own values. Ultimately it is immaterial to sociology whether or not flying saucers exist.

Cognitive Deviance and the Sociological Enterprise

A consideration of cognitive deviance leads to two important insights for sociology as a whole and for the sociological study of deviance in particular: (1) There are social rules governing thoughts as well as actions, and (2) Determining the validity of thoughts, ideas, and beliefs is a social process that sociologists can investigate, but they cannot themselves make such a determination. Both of these insights are consonant with the new perspective. The first displays the pervasiveness of the social world; the second directs sociologists to participants' experiences.

In this chapter we have focused on ideas, beliefs, and thought systems that are viewed as deviant. We have seen that the occult and new religions are frequently labeled as cognitive deviance. When new religions are able to grow old, they are likely to become nondeviant in the public eye, and may themselves label others as cognitive deviants. In identifying cognitive deviance, scientists have played an important role, labeling those whose ideas differ from those accepted by science. Doctors who discount faith healing, biologists who reject the efficacy of Vitamin C in curing colds, psychiatrists who view homosexuality as maladjustment, and sociologists who seek to explain "cults" but not "churches" are all involved in labeling certain beliefs as deviant. All these sciences, however, were themselves at one time viewed as forms of cognitive deviance. Believers in the occult, new religions, and other "different" belief systems customarily oppose and challenge the scientific view, for they "know" that they possess the truth.

While the existence of fakes complicates the identification of true believers — for they are not always so readily distinguishable — it is clear that indeed people believe quite different things. Furthermore, such beliefs can be labeled cognitive deviance, for they violate rules of *what one is expected to believe and not believe, to take as true and as false.*

Our subject in this chapter has been those whose deviance is primarily that of belief. However, if we return briefly to the other kinds of deviance we have been considering in this book, we can see elements of cognitive deviance there as well. In Chapter 6 we saw the ways in which some people provide alternative explanations for their deviant sexual practices. Such explanations for homosexuality in particular are gaining greater public acceptance. In the rather recent past, homosexuals' explanations of their behavior were denied legitimacy by many, including social scientists, being taken instead as excuses, mere rhetoric, or indications of self-deception. As evidence mounted that homosexuals really "believed" what they were saying, their ideas moved to being cognitive deviance. Today they are moving toward cognitive nondeviance. Even the conservative popular columnist Ann Landers has changed her tune about homosexuals' being "perverted."

Differing views of drugs can also be considered in terms of cognitive deviance. There is little agreement on such issues as what drugs do to the body, whether they are addictive, what kinds of experience they provide, and so on. Customarily those on different sides of the issue believe they possess the truth and that opponents are either deluded or lying in order to protect their own interests.

Throughout Part II we have seen examples of cognitive deviance in the explanations deviants offer for their behavior. Not all deviants, however, are cognitive deviants. Only those who offer alternative explanations for their activities, ideas that differ from those accepted by those doing the labeling, can be seen as cognitive deviants. Other deviants, particularly fakes and con artists, only pretend to believe and thus only *appear to be* cognitive deviants. Once they are recognized as con artists or fakes, they may be labeled as deviants but their status as cognitive deviants disappears. Other deviants break rules they nonetheless believe in: some acts of violence and some amateur crime fall into this category. Such deviants may feel that they are justified in their behavior by their special circumstances but do not challenge accepted ideas of reality or truth.

In the last chapter we argued that official deviance presents serious threats to society. Cognitive deviance is equally if not more threatening, for it challenges ideas about truth and reality. Durkheim recognized the importance to societies and social groups of a "collective consciousness," a shared conception of the social world. Cognitive deviance undermines such a conception. Consider the following hypothetical situation: A hospital. Medical personnel with their beliefs in science. A Jehovah's Witness medically requiring a blood transfusion but refusing it as contrary to God's will. A person with cancer refusing chemotherapy and asking for Laetrile. A Christian Scientist with a broken ankle refusing aid and praying to be healed. An acupuncturist and a chiropractor arriving to treat patients. A person selling copper bracelets to cure arthritis. A priest. How would such a hospital function? Could a hospital allow all such activities? If only some, how would such decisions be made? Readers might consider who they would allow to stay, and the reasons they would use in making such decisions.

Such are the problems presented by cognitive deviance. One solution is to declare one or a few beliefs and practices legitimate and to outlaw the others as cognitive deviance. The greater the power available to the labelers, the more effective labeling will be. Nonetheless, cognitive deviance continues to appear. Sometimes, as in new religions that survive, what begins as cognitive deviance becomes nondeviant; sometimes, as with Galileo's heretical idea that the earth was not the center of the universe, it replaces formerly legitimate ideas; sometimes, as with astrology, it vacillates between deviant and nondeviant status; and sometimes it just dies out and disappears altogether.

Against such a background, it is not unreasonable to recommend that sociologists take seriously the various belief systems that proponents offer, accept the possibility of alternative world views, and study the processes by which such beliefs are developed, sustained, and challenged — without deciding who possesses the truth. One can never be sure whether today's cognitive deviance will be tomorrow's great truth or utter foolishness.

Conclusion

Deviance is any thought, feeling, or action that members of a social group judge to be a violation of their values or rules.

We have come quite a distance since we first encountered this definition in Chapter 1. We said we wanted to leave the definition of deviance open to avoid excluding phenomena that might prove to be important. We then proceeded to examine a wide variety of explanations of deviance and many kinds of phenomena that could be judged deviant in some way. It should now be clear that our choice of definition emerges out of labeling theory and out of Becker's statement: "Deviance is not a quality that lies in behavior itself, but in the interaction between the person who commits an act and those who respond to it" (1963: 14). Such a choice clearly directs us to sociology, for we are viewing deviance as the outcome of *social* behavior that takes place in a *social* context. We have repeatedly criticized the theories that seek to locate deviance elsewhere, whether in individual personality, the physical organism, or the world beyond individuals.

It should also be clear that our definition of deviance emerges from the new perspective that we have detailed and used throughout this book. This new perspective recognizes that there are many views about what social rules are and what behavior constitutes following them. The new perspective seeks to understand both social rules and deviance from them from a multiplicity of perspectives. It advocates value neutrality, for the suspending of evaluation makes visible to us the many ways in which people act in the world and the many explanations they offer for their actions.

Value neutrality may leave some readers feeling frustrated, since it offends their personal convictions that some things are "really" wrong or bad or evil. Our position in this book, however, is that judgments of good and bad are not a part of *sociological explanation* and interfere with that explanation. Only by suspending our judgment have we been able to see deviance from both the viewpoint of deviants themselves and that of those who judge them deviant. Moral judgment is part of social life, but in order to study it we must stand aside from it. Sociologists' attempts to determine what is good and bad may be, as Berger and Luckmann say of sociologists' efforts to determine what is true, "somewhat like trying to push a bus in which one is riding" (1966: 13). Readers may have taken a variety of stances toward the deviance we have examined, as the authors themselves do, finding some of it good, some bad, some worth pursuing, and some to be avoided at all costs. Such responses, however, are not a part of *doing* sociology; *they are not sociological but simply social,* part of the social world itself.

Throughout this book we have sought to engage readers in the process of doing sociology. We have devoted considerable attention to what sociologists have done, how they have developed theories, the sources of their ideas, how they responded to the works of others, and how in general they *acted* as sociologists. We see sociology not as detached and isolated from the world it studies, but rather as closely tied to that world. The sociological dilemma is to find ways to respect the experiences of those being studied while remaining sufficiently detached to avoid seduction by them. Phenomenology in particular provides guidelines for coming to terms with this dilemma, demonstrating the possibility of studying the social world while respecting its integrity.

By emphasizing the difficulties involved in sociological explanation and the many criticisms that can be directed to the work of earlier theorists, we have highlighted both the importance of common-sense explanations in the world of everyday life and their inadmissibility as sociological explanation. Of the latter we ask that it go beyond common-sense explanations to an understanding of social behavior for its own sake and in its own terms. We have criticized some theorists for their failure to recognize the common-sense aspects of their own theorizing and for their taking for granted much that we feel can be questioned and subjected to sociological scrutiny. We do not minimize the importance of common-sense explanations, but we have noted that they are designed to help people engage in practical activities rather than to gain understanding for its own sake. We see being members of social worlds and studying those social worlds as quite different enterprises, both important but not interchangeable.

Readers might find it useful to review briefly Figure 2.1 (p. 32–33) and to consider the many explanations we have considered in these pages. The new perspective depends heavily on the work of earlier theorists, integrating their important insights, modifying some of their ideas, and even benefiting from what we now view as their errors and failings. We see the new perspective itself as simply another step toward the understanding of deviance as a social phenomenon, subject to whatever modification and change may promise further insights. We expect that as the new perspective is increasingly applied to the sociological study of deviance, we will come to understand deviance more fully while also modifying and refining the new perspective.

In this book we have been unable to consider all types of deviance. In fact no treatment of deviance can be exhaustive, since deviance emerges through social relations and is constantly coming into and going out of existence. We hope that those varieties we have considered can serve as models for studying other forms. We encourage readers to use these ideas in their own examination of the deviance they encounter in everyday life, whether their involvement be as participants, onlookers, condemners, or labelers. Consideration of *who* calls *what* deviant and *why* is crucial.

We urge further research from the new perspective. Chapter 12, "Cognitive Deviance," in particular opens up a new area for sociological investigation, that of deviant *ideas*. Whereas earlier studies of deviance focused on activities, the new perspective helps us to recognize that there are social rules for thinking — rules whose violation can be considered deviance. The idea of cognitive deviance directs us to new data that promise to be a fruitful source of sociological understanding. For future research we particularly encourage attention to the cognitive elements in *all* forms of deviance.

We want to reemphasize the new perspective as *emerging* and *tentative*. Its continued development rests on continued empirical investigation. Understanding the nature of deviance as an element in the social world requires that we pay careful attention to that world in all its detail and fullness. Continued efforts will be required to come to terms with its ambiguity, its multiple perspectives, and its problematic character — both for participants and for those who study it.

A fundamental feature of deviance revealed by the use of the new perspective and holding promise of enhancing our understanding is the continuity between deviance and nondeviance. We see deviance as an aspect of everyday life, and we see that people learn to engage in deviance by participating in everyday social groups. In this sense we see deviance as a normal, everyday, ordinary activity — as are responses to deviance. Similar processes underlie being deviant and responding to deviants; in doing the one it is possible to learn how to do the other. By recognizing the ordinary nature of deviance, we see that in studying deviance we are not studying "them," people of a different kind with special characteristics or acted upon by a different kind of fate; we are studying "us," for all of us are in some ways deviant. We can gain understanding of deviance by examining and learning from our own experiences. Even the forms of deviance that one finds most offensive or even abhorrent can to some degree be understood on the basis of one's own experiences. Even the most extreme forms of deviance can to some degree be, as Matza says, *appreciated,* though such appreciation involves neither condoning nor engaging in such activities. Value neutrality makes such appreciation possible, for it allows us to understand without requiring that we either approve or disapprove in moral terms.

Our goal as sociologists, then, is to figure out how the social world works. We encounter particular problems as we try to understand the familiar, the taken-for-granted, the everyday social world of common sense. The understanding we achieve may not be as neat, clear-cut, and unambiguous as we might like, and our findings may not always fit with what we want, expect, or hopefully anticipate. Nonetheless, we must take information as it comes to us and understand it as it presents itself, for we want to understand what is, not see only what we think ought to be. We have attempted in this book to contribute toward such understanding, and we look forward to the work of others in continuing to advance our knowledge of deviance and of the social world.

Bibliography

Some of these materials were first published in another language, some many years ago, and others have appeared in a number of editions. We have included the *first* publishing date here and in the text, and additional information, such as English editions or more recent publications, where possible.

Abell, George O. and Bennett Greenspan. "The Moon and the Maternity Ward." *The Skeptical Inquirer: The Zetetic Journal of the Paranormal* 3: 4 (Summer 1979), 17–25.

Aberle, D. F. "A Note on Relative Deprivation as Applied to Millenarian and other Cult Movements," in W. A. Lessa and E. Z. Vogt, eds., *Reader in Comparative Religion*. New York: Harper and Row, 1965.

Achilles, Nancy. "The Development of the Homosexual Bar as an Institution," in Gagnon and Simon (1967).

Adler, Freda. *Sisters in Crime: The Rise of the New Female Criminal*. New York: McGraw-Hill, 1975.

Adler, Patricia A. and Peter Adler. "Tinydopers: A Case Study of Deviant Socialization." *Journal of Symbolic Interaction* 1: 2 (Spring 1978), 90–105.

———, Peter Adler, and Jack D. Douglas. "Drug Dealing." Forthcoming.

Alexander, Franz and William Healy. *The Roots of Crime*. New York: Alfred A. Knopf, 1935.

——— and Hugo Staub. *The Criminal, the Judge, and the Public*. New York: Collier Books, 1962.

Alexander, Yonah. *International Terrorism*. New York: Praeger, 1976.

Allport, Gordon W. *Becoming*. New Haven: Yale University Press, 1955.

Altheide, David. *Creating Reality*. Beverly Hills, Calif.: Sage, 1977.

———. "The Paradox of Security." *Urban Life and Culture* (1974).

——— and P. Adler. "Employee Theft," in Douglas and Johnson (1978).

——— and John Johnson. *Bureaucratic Propaganda*. Boston: Allyn and Bacon, 1979.

Amir, Menachem. *Patterns of Forcible Rape*. Chicago: University of Chicago Press, 1971.

Anderson, Nels. *The Hobo: The Sociology of the Homeless Man*. Chicago: Phoenix Books, 1961. First published in 1923.

Anonymous. "Criminal Deviancy in a Small Business," in H. Taylor Buckner, *Deviance, Reality and Change*. New York: Random House, 1971.

Ardrey, Robert. *African Genesis*. New York: Atheneum, 1961.

Arnold, David O., ed. *The Sociology of Subcultures*. The Glendessary Press, 1970.

Asch, Solomon E. *Social Psychology*. New York: Prentice-Hall, 1952.

Athens, Lonnie H. "The Self and the Violent Criminal Act." *Urban Life and Culture* 4 (April 1974), 98–112.

Baechler, Jean. *Suicides*. New York: Basic Books, 1979.

Bahr, Robert and Alice Harrison Bahr. "Throwing the Book at Library Thieves." *Parade* (April 8, 1979), 31, 34.

Barber, Bernard. "Acculturation and Messianic Movements." *American Sociological Review* 6 (October 1941).

Bayet, Albert. *Le Suicide et la Morale*. Paris: Felix Alcan, 1922.

Becker, Howard S. "Labeling Theory Reconsidered," in Becker (1973), pp. 177–208.

———, ed. *The Other Side: Perspectives on Deviance*. New York: Free Press, 1964.

———. *Outsiders: Studies in the Sociology of Deviance*. New York: Free Press, 1963, rev. ed., 1973.

———. "Whose Side Are We On?" *Social Problems* 14 (1967), 239–247, and reprinted in Douglas (1970A).

———, Blanche Geer, Everett Hughes, and Anselm Strauss. *Boys in White*. Chicago: University of Chicago Press, 1961.

Bell, Daniel. "Crime as an American Way of Life." *Antioch Review* 13: 8 (1953), 131–153.

Berger, Peter L. *A Rumor of Angels*. Garden City, N.Y.: Doubleday, 1969.

———. *The Sacred Canopy: Elements of a Sociological Theory of Religion*. Garden City, N.Y.: Doubleday, 1967.

——— and Thomas Luckmann. *The Social Construction of Reality*. Garden City, N.Y.: Doubleday, 1966.

Berk, Richard A. *Collective Behavior*. Dubuque, Iowa: William C. Brown, 1974.

Bieber, Irving. *Homosexuality: A Psychoanalytic Study of Male Homosexuals*. New York: Basic Books, 1962.

Bierce, Ambrose. *The Enlarged Devil's Dictonary by Ambrose Bierce*. Compiled and edited by Ernest J. Hopkins. Garden City, N.Y.: Doubleday, 1967.

Bittner, Egon. "The Police on Skid-Row: A Study of Peace Keeping." *American Sociological Review* 32 (1967), 699–715.

Blanck, Gertrude and Rubin. *Ego Psychology: Theory and Practice*. New York: Columbia University Press, 1974.

Blumberg, Abraham S. *Criminal Justice*. Chicago: Quadrangle Books, 1967.

———, ed. *Current Perspectives on Criminal Behavior*. New York: Alfred A. Knopf, 1974.

Blumer, Herbert. "Society as Symbolic Interaction," in Rose (1962) and reprinted in Blumer (1969).

———. "Sociological Implications of the Thought of George Herbert Mead." *American Journal of Sociology* 71 (1966), 174 and reprinted in Blumer (1969).

———. *Symbolic Interactionism: Perspective and Method*. Englewood Cliffs, N.J.: Prentice-Hall, 1969.

Blundell, William E. "Equity Funding: 'I Did It for the Jollies,' " in Moffitt (1976).

Bond, Rene and Winston Hill. "Interview with a Pornographic Film Star," in Goode (1974).

Bordua, David, ed. *The Police.* New York: Wiley, 1967.

Boyle, Jack. *Boston Blackie.* The Gregg Press Mystery Series, Otto Penzler, ed. New York: Gregg Press, 1979. First published in 1919.

Braungart, R. G., J. P. Hunt, and M. M. Braungart. "The Social Origins of the People's Temple Cult." Paper presented to the meetings of the Southern Sociological Society, Atlanta, Ga. (April 1979).

Bredemeier, Harry C. and Richard M. Stephenson. *The Analysis of Social Systems.* New York: Holt, Rinehart and Winston, 1962.

Brill, A. A., ed. *The Basic Writings of Sigmund Freud.* Modern Library.

Brooks, Robert C. *Corruption in American Politics and Life.* New York: Dodd, Mead, 1910.

Brown, Daniel G. and Warner L. Lowe. "Religious Beliefs and Personality Characteristics of College Students." *Journal of Social Psychology* (February 1951), 103–129.

Brown, Roger. *Social Psychology.* New York: Free Press, 1965.

Brownmiller, Susan. *Against Our Will: Men, Women, and Rape.* New York: Simon & Schuster, 1975.

Bryan, James H. "Apprenticeships in Prostitution." *Social Problems* 12: 3 (Winter 1965), 278–297 and reprinted in Gagnon and Simon (1967).

Bullough, Vern L. *Sexual Variance in Society and History.* Chicago: University of Chicago Press, 1976.

Burns, Thomas S. *Tales of ITT.* Boston: Houghton Mifflin, 1974.

Cameron, Mary Owen. *The Booster and the Snitch.* New York: Free Press, 1964.

Cameron, Norman. *Personality Development and Psychopathology: A Dynamic Approach.* Boston: Houghton Mifflin, 1963.

Catton, William R., Jr. "What Kind of People Does a Religious Cult Attract?" *American Sociological Review* 22 (October 1957), 561–566.

Cavan, Ruth S. *Suicide.* Chicago: University of Chicago Press, 1928.

Cavendish, Richard. *The Powers of Evil.* London: Routledge & Kegan Paul, 1975.

Chambliss, William. *Crime and the Legal Process.* New York: McGraw-Hill, 1969.

Cicourel, Aaron V. *The Social Organization of Juvenile Justice.* New York: John Wiley, 1968.

Clinard, Marshall B. *Anomie and Deviant Behavior.* London: Collier-Macmillan, 1964.

——. *The Black Market: A Study in White-Collar Crime.* Rinehart, 1952.

—— and Richard Quinney. *Criminal Behavior Systems,* 2nd ed. New York: Holt, Rinehart and Winston, 1973.

Cloward, Richard A. and Lloyd E. Ohlin. *Delinquency and Opportunity.* New York: Free Press, 1960.

Cohen, Albert K. *Delinquent Boys: The Culture of the Gang.* New York: Free Press, 1955.

Collins, Randall and Michael Makowsky. *The Discovery of Society,* 2nd ed. rev. New York: Random House, 1978.

Commager, Henry Steele. "Is Freedom Dying in America?" *Look* (July 14, 1970).

Commission on Obscenity and Pornography. *Report.* New York: Random House, 1970.

Cooley, Charles Horton. *Human Nature and Social Order.* New York: Charles Scribner's Sons, 1902.

——. *Social Organization.* New York: Charles Scribner's Sons, 1909.

Coser, Lewis A. "Presidential Address: Two Methods in Search of a Substance." *American Sociological Review* 40: 6 (December 1975), 691–700.

Cressey, Donald R. "Application and Verification of the Differential Association Theory." *Journal of Criminal Law, Criminology, and Police Science* 43 (May-June 1952), 43–52.

———. "Changing Criminals: The Application of the Theory of Differential Association." *American Journal of Sociology* 61 (1955), 116–120.

———. *Other People's Money.* New York: Macmillan, 1953.

———, ed. *The Prison: Studies in Institutional Organization and Change.* New York: Holt, Rinehart & Winston, 1961.

———. "Role Theory, Differential Association and Compulsive Crimes," in Rose (1962).

———. *Theft of a Nation.* New York: Harper & Row, 1969.

Cressey, Paul G. *The Taxi-Dance Hall: A Sociological Study in Commercialized Recreation and City Life.* Chicago: University of Chicago Press, 1932.

———. *Bloody Harlan.* 1955.

Crichton, Michael. *The Great Train Robbery.* New York: Alfred A. Knopf, 1975.

Currie, Elliott P. "Crimes without Criminals: Witchcraft and Its Control in Renaissance Europe." *Law and Society Review* 3 (August 1968), 7–32.

Dalph, Edward W. *The Silent Community: Public Homosexual Encounters.* Beverly Hills, Calif.: Sage, 1979.

Dalton, Melville. *Men Who Manage.* New York: Wiley, 1959.

Daniels, Arlene Kaplan. "The Social Construction of Military Psychiatric Diagnoses," in Dreitzel (1970).

Davenport, William. "Sexual Patterns and Their Regulation in a Society of the South Pacific," in J. A. Beach, ed., *Sex and Behavior.* New York: Wiley, 1965.

Davis, Fred. "Deviance Disavowal: The Management of Strained Interaction by the Visibly Handicapped." *Social Problems* 9 (Fall 1962), 120–132 and reprinted in Becker (1964).

Davis, Kingsley. "Illegitimacy and the Social Structure." *American Journal of Sociology* 45 (Sept. 1939).

———. "Prostitution" in Robert Merton and Robert Nisbet, eds. *Contemporary Social Problems.* New York: Harcourt, Brace and World, 1962.

DeBaum, Everett. "The Heist: The Theory and Practice of Armed Robbery." *Harpers* 200 (February 1950), 69–77.

de Grazia, Sebastian. *The Political Community.* Chicago: University of Chicago Press, 1948.

de Sade, Marquis (Donatien Alphonse François Sade). *Justine or the Misfortunes of Virtue.* New York: Capricorn Books, 1966. First published in French in 1791.

———. *The 120 Days of Sodom.* New York: Grove Press, 1966.

Deutscher, Irwin. *What We Say/What We Do.* Glenview, Ill.: Scott, Foresman, 1973.

Dexter, Lewis Anthony. "On the Politics and Sociology of Stupidity in our Society," in Becker (1964).

Dickson, Donald T. "Bureaucracy and Morality: An Organizational Perspective on a Moral Crusade." *Social Problems* 16 (1968), 143–156.

Ditton, Jason. "Perks, Pilferage, and the Fiddle." *Theory and Society* 4 (1977), 39–71.

Dostoyevsky, Fyodor. *Notes from the Underground,* in *Three Short Novels of Dostoyevsky.* Garden City, N.Y.: Doubleday, 1960. First published in Russian in 1864.

Douglas, Dorothy. "Managing Fronts in Observing Deviance," in Jack D. Douglas, ed. *Research on Deviance.* New York: Random House, 1972.

———. "The Novitiate: Socialization into a Deviant Sex Role." Unpublished manuscript (March 1969).

Douglas, Jack D. *American Social Order: Social Rules in a Pluralistic Society.* New York: Free Press, 1971A.
———. *Creative Deviance and Social Change.* Forthcoming.
———. *Crime and Justice in American Society.* New York: Bobbs-Merrill, 1971B.
———, ed. *Deviance and Respectability.* New York: Basic Books, 1970A.
———. *Investigative Social Research.* Beverly Hills, Calif.: Sage, 1976.
———. *The Relevance of Sociology.* New York: Appleton-Century-Crofts, 1970B.
———, ed. *Research on Deviance.* New York: Random House, 1972.
———. *The Social Meanings of Suicide.* Princeton: Princeton University Press, 1967.
——— et al. *Introduction to Sociology.* New York: Free Press, 1973.
——— and John M. Johnson, eds. *Business and Professional Deviance.* Philadelphia: Lippincott, 1978.
———, eds. *Existential Sociology.* Cambridge, Eng.: Cambridge University Press, 1977A.
———, eds. *Official Deviance.* Philadelphia: Lippincott, 1977B.
Douglas, Jack D. and Paul K. Rasmussen with Carol Ann Flanagan. *The Nude Beach.* Beverly Hills, Calif.: Sage, 1977.
Douglas, Mary. *Natural Symbols: Explorations in Cosmology.* New York: Random House, 1970, 1973.
Drapkin, Israel and Emilio Viano, eds. *Victimology: A New Focus.* Lexington, Mass.: Lexington Books, 1974.
Dreitzel, Hans Peter, ed. *Recent Sociology No. 2: Patterns of Communicative Behavior.* New York: Macmillan, 1970.
Dunne, John Gregory. *True Confessions.* New York: Dutton, 1977.
Durkheim, Emile. *The Division of Labor in Society.* New York: Free Press, 1964. First published in French in 1893.
———. *The Elementary Forms of the Religious Life.* New York: Collier Books, 1961. First published in French in 1912.
———. *The Rules of Sociological Method.* New York: Free Press, 1964. First published in French in 1895.
———. *Suicide: A Study in Sociology.* Glencoe, Ill.: Free Press, 1951. First published in French in 1897.
Duster, Troy. *The Legislation of Morality.* New York: Free Press, 1970.
Edgerton, Robert B. *Deviance: A Cross-Cultural Perspective.* Menlo Park, Ill.: Cummings, 1976.
Einstadter, Warner. "The Social Organization of Armed Robbery." *Social Problems* 17 (1969), 64–83.
Eisenstadt, S. N. *From Generation to Generation.* New York: Free Press, 1965.
———. *The Political Systems of Empires: The Rise and Fall of the Historical Bureaucratic Societies.* New York: Free Press, 1963.
Emerson, Robert. *Judging Delinquents.* Chicago: Aldine, 1969.
Erikson, Kai T. *Wayward Puritans.* New York: Wiley, 1966.
Esquirol. *Des Maladies Mentales.* Paris, 1838.
Farberow, Norman L., ed. *Taboo Topics.* New York: Atherton, 1963.
——— and Edwin S. Shneidman. *The Cry for Help.* New York: McGraw-Hill, 1961.
Faris, Robert E. L. *Chicago Sociology: 1920–1932.* San Francisco: Chandler, 1967.
———. *Social Disorganization.* New York: Ronald Press, 1955.
——— and H. Warren Dunham. *Mental Disorders in Urban Areas.* Chicago: University of Chicago Press, 1939.
Festinger, Leon, Henry W. Riecken, and Stanley Schachter. *When Prophecy Fails.* Minneapolis: University of Minnesota Press, 1956.

Fisher, Charles S. "Observing a Crowd: The Structure and Description of Protest Demonstrations," in Douglas (1972).

Ford, Clellan and Frank Beach. *Patterns of Sexual Behavior*. New York: Harper & Row, 1951.

Foucault, Michel. *The History of Sexuality. Volume I. An Introduction*. New York: Vintage Books, 1980.

———. *Madness and Civilization*. Pantheon Books, 1965.

Frank, Lawrence K. "Social Problems." *American Journal of Sociology* 30 (1925), 462–473.

Freud, Sigmund. *The Basic Writings of Sigmund Freud*. A. A. Brill, ed. Modern Library.

———. *Civilization and Its Discontents*. New York: W. W. Norton, 1961. First published in German in 1930.

———. *The Complete Introductory Lectures on Psychoanalysis*. James Strachey, trans. and ed. New York: W. W. Norton, 1966. First published in German in 1933.

———. *The Interpretation of Dreams*. New York: Avon Books, 1965. First published in German in 1900.

———. *Moses and Monotheism*. New York: Vintage Books, 1955. First published in German in 1939.

———. *Three Contributions to the Theory of Sex*. New York: E. P. Dutton, 1962. First published in German in 1905.

———. *Totem and Taboo*. New York: Norton, 1952. First published in German in 1918.

Fuller, John G. *The Interrupted Journey: Two Lost Hours "Aboard a Flying Saucer."* New York: Dell, 1967.

Gagnon, John H. and William Simon, eds. *Sexual Deviance*. New York: Harper & Row, 1967.

Gamson, William A. *Power and Discontent*. Homewood, Ill.: Dorsey Press, 1968.

Gans, Herbert. *The Urban Villagers: Group and Class in the Life of Italian-Americans*. New York: Free Press, 1962.

Garfinkel, Harold. *Studies in Ethnomethodology*. Englewood Cliffs, N.J.: Prentice-Hall, 1967.

Gerlach, L. P. "Five Factors Crucial to the Growth and Spread of Modern Religious Movements." *Journal for the Scientific Study of Religion* 7 (1968), 23–40.

———. "Pentacostalism: Revolution or Counter-Revolution?" in Zaretscky and Leone (1977).

Giallombardo, Rose. *Society of Women*. New York: John Wiley and Sons, 1966.

Gibbs, Jack P. and Walter T. Martin. "A Theory of Status Integration and Its Relationship to Suicide." *American Journal of Sociology* 23 (1958), 140–147.

Giddens, Anthony. Excerpts from address to American Sociological Association, 1975. *Phenomenological Sociology Newsletter* 4: 2 (Feb. 1976), 5–8.

Glock, C. Y. "The Role of Deprivation in the Origin and Evolution of Religious Groups," in R. Lee and M. W. Marty, eds. *Religion and Social Conflict*. New York: Oxford University Press, 1964.

Glueck, Sheldon and Eleanor T. Glueck. *Delinquents in the Making*. New York: Harper, 1952.

———. *Unraveling Juvenile Delinquency*. New York: Commonwealth Fund, 1950.

Goffman, Erving. *Asylums*. Garden City, N.Y.: Doubleday, 1961.

———. *Behavior in Public Places*. New York: Free Press, 1963A.

———. *Interaction Ritual*. Garden City, N.Y.: Doubleday, 1967.

———. "On Cooling the Mark Out: Some Aspects of Adaptation to Failure."

Psychiatry: Journal for the Study of Interpersonal Relations 15: 4 (November 1952), 451–463 and reprinted in Rose (1962).

——. *The Presentation of Self in Everyday Life.* Garden City, N.Y.: Doubleday, 1959.

——. *Stigma.* Englewood Cliffs, N.J.: Prentice-Hall, 1963B.

Gold, Martin. "Suicide, Homicide, and the Socialization of Aggression." *American Journal of Sociology* 63 (1958), 651–661.

Goodall, Jane van Lawick. *In the Shadow of Man.* New York: Dell, 1971.

——. *My Friends the Wild Chimpanzees.* Washington, D.C.: National Geographic Society, 1967.

Goode, Erich. "The Criminology of Drugs and Drug Use," in Blumberg (1974).

——. *The Marijuana Smokers.* New York: Basic Books, 1970.

——. *Sexual Deviance.* New York: Marrow, 1974.

Gordon, Milton M. *Assimilation in American Life.* New York: Oxford University Press, 1964.

——."Assimilation in American Life: Theory and Reality." *Daedalus* 90: 2 (Spring 1961), 263–285.

Gouldner, Alvin. "The Myth of a Value-Free Sociology," in Douglas (1970A).

——. *Patterns of Industrial Bureaucracy.* Glencoe, Ill.: Free Press, 1954A.

——. *Wildcat Strike.* Yellow Springs, Ohio: Antioch, 1954B.

Greene, Robert. See Salgãdo.

Greenwald, Harold. *The Call Girl.* New York: Ballantine Books, 1958.

Greisman, Harvey. *Social Meanings of Terrorism: Verification, Violence and Social Control.* Unpublished manuscript.

Guenther, Anthony L. *Criminal Behavior and Social Systems,* 2nd ed. Chicago: Rand McNally, 1976.

Gurr, Ted Robert. *Why Men Rebel.* Princeton, N.J.: Princeton University Press, 1970.

Gusfield, Joseph R. "Moral Passage: The Symbolic Process in Public Designations of Deviance." *Social Problems* 15 (Fall 1967), 175–188.

Hakeem, Michael. "A Critique of the Psychiatric Approach," in Joseph Roucek, ed., *Juvenile Delinquency.* New York: Philosophical Library, 1958, pp. 79–112.

Halbwachs, Maurice. *The Causes of Suicide.* New York: Free Press, 1978. First published in French in 1930.

Hall, Calvin S. and Gardner Lindzey. *Theories of Personality.* New York: Wiley, 1957.

Hammond, Phillip E., ed. *Sociologists at Work.* Garden City, N.Y.: Doubleday, 1967.

Hartshorne, Hugh and Mark May. *Studies in Deceit.* New York: Macmillan, 1928.

Heidenheimer, Arnold J., ed. *Political Corruption.* New York: Holt, Rinehart and Winston, 1970.

Henry, Andrew F. and James F. Short, Jr. *Suicide and Homicide.* Glencoe, Ill.: Free Press, 1954.

Henslin, James M. "Trust and the Cab Driver," in James M. Henslin, ed., *Down to Earth Sociology,* 2nd ed. New York: Free Press, 1976.

Hill, Richard J. and Kathleen Stones Crittenden, eds. *Proceedings of the Purdue Symposium on Ethnomethodology.* Lafayette, Ind.: Purdue University Press, 1968.

Hine, V. H. "The Deprivation and Disorganization Theories of Social Movements," in Zaretscky and Leone (1977).

Hirschi, Travis and Hannan Selvin. *The Causes of Delinquency.* Berkeley: University of California Press, 1969.

Hite, Shere. *The Hite Report: A Nationwide Study of Female Sexuality.* New York:

Macmillan, 1976.

Hitler, Adolf. *Mein Kampf.* Boston: Houghton Mifflin, 1943.

Hochschild, Arlie Russell. "The Sociology of Feeling and Emotion: Selected Possibilities," in Millman and Kanter (1975).

Hollander, Xaviera. *The Happy Hooker.* New York: Dell, 1972.

Hollingshead, August B. and Frederick B. Redlich. "Social Stratification and Psychiatric Disorders." *American Sociological Review* (April 1953), 163–169.

———. "Social Stratification and Schizophrenia." *American Sociological Review* (June 1954), 302–306.

———. *Social Class and Mental Illness.* New York: Wiley, 1958.

Homans, George C. "Anxiety and Ritual: The Theories of Malinowski and Radcliffe-Brown." *American Anthropologist* 43 (April-June 1941), 164–172.

Hooker, Evelyn. "The Homosexual Community," in *Perspectives in Psychopathology.* New York: Oxford University Press, 1965 and reprinted in Gagnon and Simon (1967).

———. "Male Homosexuals and Their Worlds," in J. Marmor, ed., *Sexual Inversion: The Multiple Roots of Homosexuality.* New York: Basic Books, 1965.

Hooton, Earnest Albert. *The American Criminal.* New York: Greenwood, 1939.

Hubbard, L. Ron. *Dianetics.* Arizona: Hubbard Dianetics Research Foundation, 1955.

Hughes, Everett C. "Dilemmas and Contradictions of Status." *American Journal of Sociology* 50 (1945), 353–359.

———. *French Canada in Transition.* Chicago, Ill.: University of Chicago Press, 1943.

Hughes, Helen MacGill. *Delinquents and Criminals.* Boston: Holbrook, 1970.

———. "Robert E. Park," in *The Encyclopedia of the Social Sciences.* New York: Crowell-Collier, 1968.

Humphreys, Laud. *Out of the Closets: The Sociology of Homosexual Liberation.* Englewood Cliffs, N.J.: Prentice-Hall, 1972.

———. *Tearoom Trade.* Chicago: Aldine, 1970.

Hunt, Morton. *The Affair.* New York: New American Library, 1973.

———. *The Mugging.* New York: Signet Books, 1972.

Husserl, Edmund. *The Idea of Phenomenology.* The Hague: Martinus Nijhoff, 1964. Lectures delivered in 1907.

———. *Ideas: General Introduction to Pure Phenomenology.* New York: Collier Books, 1962. First published in German in 1913.

Ichheiser, Gustav. *Appearances and Realities: Misunderstanding in Human Relations.* San Francisco: Jossey-Bass, 1970.

Irwin, John. *The Felon.* Englewood Cliffs, N.J.: Prentice-Hall, 1970.

——— and Donald R. Cressey, "Thieves, Convicts, and the Inmate Culture," in Arnold (1970).

Jackman, Norman, Richard O'Toole, and Gilbert Geiss. "The Self-Image of the Prostitute." *The Sociological Quarterly* 4 (1963), 150–161 and reprinted in Gagnon and Simon (1967).

Jacobs, Jane. *The Death and Life of Great American Cities.* New York: Vintage Books, 1963.

Johnson, Ann D. *The Value of Truth and Trust: The Story of Cochise.* San Diego: Value Communications, 1977.

Johnson, D. P. "Dilemmas of Charismatic Leadership: The Case of the People's Temple." Presented at the meetings of the Southern Sociological Society, Atlanta, Georgia (April 1979).

Johnson, John M. *Doing Field Work.* New York: Free Press, 1974.

Johnson, Ray D. Interviewed in *U.S. News and World Report* (July 17, 1978).

Jorgenson, D. L. "The Esoteric Community in the Valley of the Sun: An Ethnographic Study of Social Structure and Organization." Paper presented at the meetings of the American Sociological Association. San Francisco (September 1978).

Kamstra, Jerry. *Weed*. New York: Harper & Row, 1974.

Kassenbaum, Gene and Daril Ward. *Prison Treatment and Parole Survival*. New York: Wiley, 1971.

Keniston, Kenneth. *The Uncommitted*. New York: Harcourt, Brace & World, 1965.

Kiefer, Otto. *Sexual Life in Ancient Rome*. London: Abbey Library, 1934.

Kinsey, Alfred C. et al. *Sexual Behavior in the Human Male*. Philadelphia: W. B. Saunders, 1948.

———. *Sexual Behavior in the Human Female*. Philadelphia: W. B. Saunders, 1953.

Kitsuse, John I. "Societal Reaction to Deviant Behavior." *Social Problems* 9 (Fall 1962), 247–256 and reprinted in Becker (1964).

Klockars, Carl B. *The Professional Fence*. New York: Free Press, 1974.

———. "White Collar Crime," in Sagarin and Montanine (1977).

Kluckhohn, Clyde. *Culture*. Cambridge: Harvard University Press, 1971.

———, ed. *Culture and Behavior: Collected Essays*. New York: Free Press, 1962.

——— and Henry A. Murray, with the assistance of David M. Schneider, eds. *Personality in Nature, Society and Culture*. New York: Knopf, 1948.

Knapp Commission. *Report on Police Corruption*. New York: George Braziller, 1972.

Kobrin, Solomon. "The Conflict of Values in Delinquency Areas. *American Sociological Review* 16 (1951), 653–661.

Kohak, Erazim V. *Idea and Experience: Edmund Husserl's Project of Phenomenology in Ideas I*. Chicago: University of Chicago Press, 1978.

Kohlberg, Lawrence. "Moral Education in the Schools: A Developmental View." *The School Review* 74: 1 (Spring 1966).

——— and Rochelle Mayer. "Development as the Aim of Education." *Harvard Educational Review* 42: 4 (November 1972), 449–496.

Krafft-Ebing, Richard von. *Psychopathia Sexualis*. New York: Bantam Books, 1965. First published in 1886.

La Barre, Weston. *They Shall Take up Serpents*. Minneapolis: University of Minnesota Press, 1962.

Laing, R. D. *The Divided Self: An Existential Study in Sanity and Madness*. Baltimore: Penguin Books, 1965.

Lander, Bernard. *Towards an Understanding of Juvenile Delinquency*. New York: Columbia University Press, 1954.

Lang, Kurt and Gladys E. Lang. *Collective Dynamics*. New York: Crowell, 1961.

Laqueur, Walter. *Terrorism*. Boston: Little, Brown, 1977.

Le Bon, Gustave. *The Crowd*. New York: Viking, 1960. First published in French in 1895.

Lecky, W. E. M. *A History of European Morals from Augustus to Charlemagne*. New York: Braziller, 1955.

Lejeune, Robert and Nicholas Alex. "On Being Mugged." *Urban Life and Culture* 3 (October 1973), 259–287.

Lemert, Edwin M. "The Behavior of the Systematic Check Forger." *Social Problems* 6 (1958), 141–149 and reprinted in Becker (1964).

———. *Human Deviance, Social Problems, and Social Control*. Englewood Cliffs, N.J.: Prentice-Hall, 1967.

———. "Paranoia and the Dynamics of Exclusion." *Sociometry* 25 (1962), 2–20.

————. *Social Pathology.* New York: McGraw-Hill, 1951.

Letkemann, Peter. *Crime as Work.* Englewood Cliffs, N.J.: Prentice-Hall, 1973.

Levy, Gerald E. *Ghetto School.* Indianapolis, Ind.: Western (Bobbs-Merrill), 1970.

Leznoff, Maurice and William A. Westley. "The Homosexual Community." *Social Problems* 3: 4 (April 1956), 257–263 and reprinted in Gagnon and Simon (1967).

Lichtheim, George. *Marxism: An Historical and Critical Study.* New York: Praeger, 1965.

Liebow, Elliot. *Tally's Corner: A Study of Negro Streetcorner Men.* Boston: Little, Brown, 1967.

Lind, Andrew W. *Island Community: A Study of Ecological Succession in Hawaii.* Chicago: University of Chicago Press, 1938.

Lindesmith, Alfred R. *The Addict and the Law.* Bloomington: Indiana University Press, 1965.

————. *Addiction and the Opiates.* Chicago: Aldine, 1968. A revised edition of *Opiate Addiction,* first published in 1947.

Lindner, Robert. *Rebel Without a Cause.* New York: Grune and Stratton, 1944.

Linton, Ralph. "Nativistic Movements." *American Anthropologist* 45 (1943), 230–240.

————. *The Study of Man.* New York: Appleton-Century-Crofts, 1936.

Lippmann, Walter. "A Theory About Corruption." *Vanity Fair* 35: 3 (November 1930).

Lockridge, Frances and Richard. *Murder by the Book.* Philadelphia and New York: Lippincott, 1963.

Loevinger, Jane. *Ego Development: Conceptions and Theories.* San Francisco: Jossey-Bass, 1976.

Lofland, John. *Doing Social Life.* New York: Wiley, 1976.

————. *Doomsday Cult: A Study of Conversion, Proselytization and Maintenance of Faith.* Englewood Cliffs, N.J.: Prentice-Hall, 1966.

———— and Rodney Stark. "Becoming a World-Saver: A Theory of Conversion to a Deviant Perspective." *American Sociological Revew* 30 (December 1965), 862–875.

Lombroso, Cesare. *Crime: Its Causes and Remedies.* Boston, 1911. First published in Italian.

Lorenz, Konrad. *On Aggression.* New York: Bantam Books, 1966.

Lyman, Stanford M. and Marvin B. Scott. *The Drama of Social Reality.* New York: Oxford University Press, 1975.

————. *A Sociology of the Absurd.* Pacific Palisades, Calif.: Goodyear, 1970.

————. See also Scott and Lyman.

Maas, Peter. *Serpico.* New York: Bantam Books, 1973.

McCord, William and Joan McCord. *Psychopathy and Delinquency.* New York: Grune, 1956.

McDougall, William. *An Introduction to Social Psychology,* 11th ed. Boston: Luce, 1916.

Machiavelli, Niccolo. *The Prince.* Published with *The Discourses* by Modern Library. New York, 1950. Written in 1513.

McHugh, Peter. "A Common-Sense Perception of Deviance," in Douglas (1970A) and Dreitzel (1970).

Malcolm X. *The Autobiography of Malcolm X.* New York: Grove, 1965.

Malinowski, Bronislaw. *Magic, Science and Religion and Other Essays.* New York: Free Press, 1948. Contains essays published between 1916 and 1941.

————. *Sex and Repression in Savage Society.* Cleveland: World, 1955. First published in 1927.

Mannheim, Karl. *Ideology and Utopia.* New York: Harcourt, Brace & World, 1936. First published in German in 1929.

Manning, Peter K. "Deviance and Dogma." *British Journal of Criminology* 15 (1975), 1–20.

———. *Police Work.* Cambridge: Massachusetts Institute of Technology Press, 1977.

Marshall, Donald S. and Robert C. Suggs, eds. *Human Sexual Behavior.* Englewood Cliffs, N.J.: Prentice-Hall, 1971.

Marx, Karl. *Capital: A Critical Analysis of Capitalist Production.* Vol. I. Frederick Engels, ed. New York: International Publishers, 1967. First published in German in 1867.

———. *The Economic and Philosophic Manuscripts of 1844.* New York: International Publishers, 1964. First published in German in 1932.

——— and Frederick Engels. *The Communist Manifesto (Manifesto of the Communist Party).* New York: International Publishers, 1948. First published in 1848.

Masters, William H. and Virginia E. Johnson. *Human Sexual Response.* Boston: Little, Brown, 1966.

Maturin, Charles Robert. *Melmoth the Wanderer.* Lincoln: University of Nebraska Press, 1961. Transcription of the 1820 edition.

Matza, David. *Becoming Deviant.* Englewood Cliffs, N.J.: Prentice-Hall, 1969.

———. *Delinquency and Drift.* New York: Wiley, 1964.

Maurer, David W. *The Big Con,* rev. ed. New York: Signet, 1962. First published in 1940.

———. *Whiz Mob.* New Haven; College and University Press, 1964. First published in 1955.

Mead, George Herbert. *Mind, Self, and Society.* C. W. Morris, ed. Chicago: University of Chicago Press, 1934.

George Herbert Mead on Social Psychology. Anselm Strauss, ed. Chicago: University of Chicago Press, 1956.

Merton, Robert K. *Social Theory and Social Structure.* Glencoe, Ill.: Free Press, 1949. Revised edition, 1957. Reprinted in 1963.

Messinger, Sheldon L., Harold Sampson, and Robert D. Towne. "Life as Theater: Some Notes on the Dramaturgic Approach to Social Reality." *Sociometry* 25 (1962), 98–110.

Methvin, Eugene H. "Scientology: Anatomy of a Frightening Cult." *Reader's Digest* 116: 697 (May 1980), 86–91.

Meynell, Hugo. "Philosophy and Schizophrenia." *Journal of the British Society for Phenomenology* 10: 2 (May 1971), 17–30.

Miller, Walter B. "American Youth Gangs: Past and Present," in Blumberg (1974).

———. "Lower Class Culture as a Generating Milieu of Gang Delinquency." *Journal of Social Issues* 14: 3 (1958), 5–19 and reprinted in Arnold (1970).

———. "Violent Crimes in City Gangs." *The Annals of the American Academy of Political and Social Science* 364 (March 1966), 97–112.

Millman, Marcia and Rosabeth Moss Kanter. *Another Voice: Feminist Perspectives on Social Life and Social Science.* New York: Anchor Books, 1975.

Mills, C. Wright. "The Professional Ideology of Social Pathologists." *American Journal of Sociology* 49 (1942), 165–180.

———. *The Sociological Imagination.* New York: Oxford University Press, 1950.

Mishima, Yukio. *Sun and Steel: Personal Reflections on Art and Action.* Tokyo, Japan: Kodansha International, 1970.

Mitford, A. B. *Tales of Old Japan.* Rutland, Vt. & Tokyo, Japan: Charles E. Tuttle.

Mitroff, Ian I. *The Subjective Side of Science: A Philosophical Inquiry into the Psychology of the Apollo Moon Scientists.* Amsterdam: Elsevier, 1974.

Moffitt, Donald, ed. *Swindled!* Princeton, N.J.: Dow Jones Books, 1976.

Money, John and Anke Ehrhardt. *Man and Woman, Boy and Girl.* Baltimore, Md.: Johns Hopkins University Press, 1972.

Morris, Monica B. *An Excursion into Creative Sociology.* Oxford: Basil Blackwell, 1977.

Morselli, Enrico. *Suicide: An Essay on Comparative Moral Statistics.* New York: D. Appleton, 1882.

Musto, David F. *The American Disease.* New Haven: Yale University Press, 1973.

Nader, Ralph. *Unsafe at Any Speed.* New York: Grossman, 1965.

National Commission on the Causes and Prevention of Violence, 13 vols. *Staff Report.* Washington, D.C.: U.S. Government Printing Office, 1969.

National Commission on Marihuana and Drug Abuse. *Marihuana.* Washington, D.C.: U.S. Government Printing Office, 1972.

Newman, William M. *American Pluralism: A Study of Minority Groups and Social Theory.* New York: Harper & Row, 1973.

Nitobe, Inazo. *Bushido: The Soul of Japan.* Rutland, Vt. & Tokyo, Japan: Charles E. Tuttle, 1969.

Ortega y Gasset. *The Revolt of the Masses.* London: Allen and Unwin, 1961.

Palmer, Stuart. *The Violent Society.* New Haven, Conn.: College and University Press, 1972.

Park, Robert E. *The Crowd and the Public.* Chicago: University of Chicago Press, 1972. First published in 1904.

——— and Ernest W. Burgess. *Introduction to the Science of Sociology.* Chicago: University of Chicago Press, 1921.

Parsons, Talcott. *The Social System.* New York: Free Press, 1964. First published in 1951.

Perry, John Weir. *The Far Side of Madness.* Englewood Cliffs, N.J.: Prentice-Hall, 1974.

Piaget, Jean. *The Moral Judgment of the Child.* New York: Harcourt, Brace, 1932.

Plate, Thomas. *Crime Pays.* New York: Ballantine, 1975.

Polsky, Ned. *Hustlers, Beats, and Others.* Chicago: Aldine, 1967.

Ponse, Barbara. "The Meaning World of Lesbians." Unpublished manuscript, 1974.

Pope, Whitney. *Durkheim's Suicide.* Chicago: University of Chicago Press, 1976.

Psathas, George, ed. *Phenomenological Sociology: Issues and Applications.* New York: Wiley, 1973.

Queen, Stuart A. "The Ecological Study of Mental Disorders." *American Sociological Review* 5 (April 1940), 201–209.

Quinney, Richard. "Crime Control in Capitalist Society," in C. Reasons, ed., *The Criminologist: Crime and the Criminal.* Pacific Palisades, Calif.: Goodyear, 1974.

———. *The Social Reality of Crime.* Boston: Little, Brown, 1970.

——— and John Wildeman. *The Problem of Crime.* New York: Harper & Row, 1977.

Rabin, Arthur. "Psychopathic (Sociopathic) Personalities," in Hans Toch, ed., *Legal and Criminal Psychology.* New York: Holt, Rinehart and Winston, 1961.

Rader, Dotson. *I Ain't Marchin' Anymore.* New York: Random House, 1969.

Rasmussen, Paul. *Massage Parlors.* Unpublished Ph.D. dissertation, University of California, San Diego, 1979.

——— and Lauren Kuhn. "Massage Parlors." *Journal of Urban Life and Culture* (November 1976).

Ray, Marsh B. "The Cycle of Abstinence and Relapse Among Heroin Addicts." *Social Problems* 9 (1961), 132–140 and reprinted in Becker (1964).

Reage, Pauline. *The Story of O.* New York: Ballantine Books, 1965. First published in French in 1954.

Reckless, Walter C. *The Crime Problem.* New York: Appleton-Century-Crofts, 1961.

Reik, Theodore. *Compulsion to Confess.* New York: Farrar, Straus, & Cudahy, 1959.

Reiss, Albert J., Jr. "Police Brutality—Answers to Key Questions." *Trans-Action* 5 (July-August 1968), 10–19.

———. "The Social Integration of Queers and Peers." *Social Problems* 9 (Fall 1961), 102–120.

Richardson, J. T., ed. *Conversion Careers: In and Out of New Religions.* Beverly Hills, Calif.: Sage, 1977.

———. "A New Pardigm for Conversion Research." Paper presented at meetings of the International Society for Political Psychology (1979).

Riesman, David, with Nathan Glazer and Reuel Denny. *The Lonely Crowd.* New Haven: Yale University Press, 1950.

Riordan, William L. *Plunkitt of Tammany Hall.* New York: Dalton, 1963.

Rock, Paul. *The Making of Symbolic Interactionism.* London: Macmillan, 1979.

Roebuck, Julian. "The 'Short Con' Man." *Crime and Delinquency* (July 1964).

Rogers, Joseph W. *Why Are You Not a Criminal?* Englewood Cliffs, N.J.: Prentice-Hall, 1977.

Rogow, Arnold A. and Harold D. Lasswell. *Power, Corruption, and Rectitude.* Englewood Cliffs, N.J.: Prentice-Hall, 1963.

Rose, Arnold M., ed. *Human Behavior and Social Processes: An Interactionist Approach.* Boston: Houghton Mifflin, 1962.

Rosenberg, Bernard, Israel Gerber, and F. William Howton. *Mass Society in Crisis.* New York: Macmillan, 1971.

Roth, Julius A. with the collaboration of Richard R. Hanson. *Health Purifiers and their Enemies.* New York: Prodist, 1977.

Rubington, Earl and Martin S. Weinberg. *Deviance: The Interactionist Perspective.* New York: Macmillan, 1968.

Rude, George. *The Crowd in History.* New York: Wiley, 1964.

Sacks, Harvey. "Notes on Police Assessment of Moral Character," in David Sudnow, ed. *Studies in Social Interaction.* New York: Free Press, 1972.

Sagarin, Edward. *Deviants and Deviance.* New York: Praeger, 1975.

———. *Odd Man in: Societies of Deviants in America.* Chicago: Quadrangle Books, 1969.

Salgãdo, Gamini, ed. *Cony-Catchers and Bawdy Baskets: An Anthology of Elizabethan Low Life.* Harmondsworth, England: Penguin Books, 1972.

Sanders, William B. *Detective Work.* New York: Free Press, 1977.

———. *Rape and Women's Identity.* Beverly Hills, Calif.: Sage, 1980.

Sartre, Jean Paul. *Being and Nothingness.* New York: Philosophical Library, 1956.

———. *Nausea.* New York: New Directions, 1964. First published in French in 1938.

———. *No Exit.* New York: Knopf, 1954. First published in French in 1946.

Schafer, Stephen. *The Victim and His Criminal: A Study in Functional Responsibility.* New York: Random House, 1968.

Schmidt, Calvin F. *Suicides in Seattle.* Seattle, Wash.: University of Washington Press, 1928.

Schnell, W. J. *Thirty Years a Watch Tower Slave.* Grand Rapids, Mich.: Baker Book House, 1956.

Schreiber, Jan. *The Ultimate Weapon: Terrorists & World Order.* New York: Morrow, 1978.

Schur, Edwin M. *Crimes Without Victims: Deviant Behavior and Public Policy.* Englewood Cliffs, N.J.: Prentice-Hall, 1965.

———. *Labeling Deviant Behavior.* New York: Harper & Row, 1971.

———. *Our Criminal Society.* Englewood Cliffs, N.J.: Prentice-Hall, 1969.

Schutz, Alfred. *Collected Papers,* 3 vols. The Hague: Martinus Nijhoff, 1967A, 1964, 1966.

———. *The Phenomenology of the Social World.* Northwestern University Press, 1967B. First published in 1932.

Scott, James C. *Comparative Political Corruption.* Englewood Cliffs, N.J.: Prentice-Hall, 1972.

Scott, Marvin B. and Stanford M. Lyman, "Accounts." *American Sociological Review* 33 (February 1968), 46–61 and reprinted in Lyman and Scott (1970).

Scott, Robert A. "A Proposed Framework for Analyzing Deviance as a Property of Social Order," in Scott and Douglas (1972).

——— and Jack D. Douglas, eds. *Theoretical Perspectives on Deviance.* New York: Basic Books, 1972.

Sellin, Thorsten. *Culture Conflict and Crime.* New York: Social Science Research Council, Bulletin 41, 1938.

Shapiro, Laura. "The Womanly Art of Self Defense." *Real Paper* 2: 10 (March 7, 1973), 6, 8.

Shaw, Clifford R. and Henry D. McKay. *Juvenile Delinquency and Urban Areas.* Chicago: University of Chicago Press, 1942.

Sherif, Muzafer. *The Psychology of Social Norms.* New York: Harper and Brothers, 1936.

Shibutani, Tamotsu, ed. *Human Nature and Collective Behavior.* Englewood Cliffs, N.J.: Prentice-Hall, 1970.

———. *Improvised News: A Sociological Study of Rumor.* Indianapolis, Ind.: Bobbs-Merrill, 1966.

———. *Society and Personality: An Interactionist Approach to Social Psychology.* Englewood Cliffs, N.J.: Prentice-Hall, 1961.

Short, James F., Jr. and Fred L. Strodtbeck. *Group Process and Gang Delinquency.* Chicago: University of Chicago Press, 1965.

Shover, Neal. "Burglary as an Occupation." Unpublished Ph.D. dissertation, University of Illinois, 1971.

———. "The Good Burglar." 1974. Unpublished manuscript.

———. "Structures and Careers in Burglary." *Journal of Criminal Law, Criminology & Police Science* 63 (1972), 540–549.

Siegel, Gene C. "Cashing in on Crime: A Study of the Burglar Alarm Business," in John Johnson and Jack D. Douglas, eds., *Crime at the Top.* Philadelphia: Lippincott, 1978.

Silver, Allan. "The Demand for Order in Civil Society," in Bordua (1967).

Simmel, Georg. "The Sociology of Sociability." *American Journal of Sociology* 3 (November 1949), 254–261.

The Sociology of Georg Simmel. Kurt H. Wolff, trans. and ed. New York: Free Press, 1950.

Simon, William and John H. Gagnon. "The Lesbians: A Preliminary Overview," in Gagnon and Simon (1967).

Skolnick, Jerome H. *Justice Without Trial.* New York: Wiley, 1966.

Smelser, Neil J. *The Theory of Collective Behavior.* New York: Free Press, 1963.

Smith, Hedrick. *The Russians.* New York: Ballantine, 1976.

Sorokin, Pitirim. *Contemporary Sociological Theories.* New York: Harper & Brothers, 1928.

Spergel, Irving. *Racketville, Slumtown, Haulburg: An Exploratory Study of Delinquent Subcultures.* Chicago: University of Chicago Press, 1973.

Srole, Leo. *Mental Health in the Metropolis: The Midtown Manhattan Study.* New York: McGraw-Hill, 1962.

Stoddart, Kenneth. "Pinched: Notes on the Ethnographer's Location of Argot," in Turner (1974).

Stone, Lawrence. *The Family, Sex and Marriage in England, 1500–1800.* New York: Harper & Row, 1977.

Straus, R. A. "Becoming an Insider: Toward a Subject-Centered Analysis of Participation in Cults and Other Contemporary Social Worlds." Unpublished manuscript, 1979.

———, "Changing Oneself: Seekers and the Creative Transformation of Life Experience," in Lofland (1976).

Sullivan, Harry Stack. *Collected Works.* New York: W. W. Norton, 1953–1964.

Sumner, William Graham. *Folkways: A Study of the Sociological Importance of Usages, Manners, Customs, Mores, and Morals.* New York: Mentor. First published in 1906.

Sutherland, Edwin H. "The Diffusion of Sexual Psychopath Laws." *American Journal of Sociology* 56 (September 1950), 142–148.

———. *Principles of Criminology.* Philadelphia: Lippincott, 1924, 1934, 1939.

———. *The Professional Thief.* Chicago: University of Chicago Press, 1937.

———. *White-Collar Crime.* New York: Holt, Rinehart & Winston, 1949.

———. "White Collar Criminality." *American Sociological Review* 5 (1940), 1–12.

Suttles, Gerald D. *The Social Order of the Slum.* Chicago: University of Chicago Press, 1968.

Sykes, Gresham M. and Thomas E. Drabek. *Law and the Lawless: A Reader in Criminology.* New York: Random House, 1969.

——— and David Matza. "Techniques of Neutralization: A Theory of Delinquency." *American Sociological Review* 22: 5 (October 1957), 664–670.

Szasz, Thomas S. *The Manufacture of Madness.* New York: Harper & Row, 1970.

———. *The Myth of Mental Illness.* New York: Harper & Row: 1961.

Tagiurri, Renato and Luigi Petrullo. *Person Perception and Interpersonal Behavior.* Stanford, Calif.: Stanford University Press, 1958.

Talese, Gay. *Thy Neighbor's Wife.* Garden City, N.Y.: Doubleday, 1980.

Tannenbaum, Frank. *Crime and the Community.* New York: Columbia University Press, 1938.

Taylor, Ian, Paul Walton, and Jock Young. *The New Criminology for a Social Theory of Deviance.* London: Routledge and Kegan Paul, 1973.

Terman, Lewis M. "Psychological Factors in Marital Happiness." *Psychological Bulletin* 36 (1939), 191–203.

Thibaut, J. W. and H. H. Kelley. *The Social Psychology of Groups.* New York: Wiley, 1959.

Thomas. W. I. *The Unadjusted Girl.* Boston: Criminal Science Monograph No. 4, 1923.

——— and Florian Znaniecki. *The Polish Peasant in Europe and America.* Chicago: University of Chicago Press, 1923.

Thompson, Hunter S. *Hell's Angels: The Strange and Terrible Saga of the Outlaw Motorcycle Gangs.* New York: Random House, 1966.

Thrasher, Frederick. *The Gang.* Chicago: University of Chicago Press, 1927, 1942.

Tilly, Charles, Louise Tilly, and Richard Tilly. *The Rebellious Century 1830–1930.* Cambridge: Harvard University Press, 1975.

Timberlake, James H. *Prohibition and the Progressive Movement 1900–1920.* Cambridge: Harvard University Press, 1963.

Timm, Joan Thrower. "Group Care of Children and the Development of Moral Judgment." *Child Welfare* 59: 6 (June 1980), 323–333.

———. "Moral Development in Literature, Drama, and Poetry." Unpublished manuscript, 1978.

Tiryakian, Edward A. *Sociologism and Existentialism: Two Perspectives on the Individual and Society.* Englewood Cliffs, N.J.: Prentice-Hall, 1962.

Toch, H. *The Social Psychology of Social Movements.* Indianapolis, Ind.: Bobbs-Merrill, 1965.

Troeltsch, Ernst. *Protestantism and Progress: A Historical Study of the Relation of Protestantism to the Modern World.* New York: G. P. Putnam's Sons, 1912. First published in 1906.

Truzzi, Marcello. *The Humanities as Sociology.* Columbus, O.: Merrill, 1973.

Turner, Ralph H. "Value Conflict in Social Disorganization." *Sociology and Social Research* 38 (May-June 1954), 301–308.

——— and Lewis M. Killian.*Collective Behavior.* Englewood Cliffs, N.J.: Prentice-Hall, 1972.

Turner, Roy, ed. *Ethnomethodology: Selected Readings.* Harmondsworth, England: Penguin, 1974.

U.S. News and World Report. Interview with William H. Webster. (January 29, 1979), 52.

van Lawick-Goodall, Jane. See Goodall, Jane.

Varni, Charles A. "An Exploratory Study of Spouse-Swapping." *Pacific Sociological Review* 15 (1972), 507–522.

Wagner, Helmut. "An Anti-Ethnomethodological Address." *Phenomenological Sociology Newsletter* 4: 2 (February 1976), 3–5.

Waksler, Norman. Untitled novel, 1972.

Walker, Edward L. and Roger W. Heyns. *An Anatomy for Conformity.* Englewood Cliffs, N.J.: Prentice-Hall, 1962.

Wallace, Anthony F. C. "Revitalization Movements." *American Anthropologist* 58 (April 1956), 264–281.

Wallace, Samuel E. *Skid Row as a Way of Life.* Totowa, N.J.: Bedminster Press, 1965.

Warren, Carol A. B. *Identity and Community in the Gay World.* New York: Wiley, 1974.

——— and John M. Johnson. "A Critique of Labeling Theory from the Phenomenological Perspective," in Scott and Douglas (1972).

——— and Barbara Ponse. "The Existential Self in the Gay World," in Douglas and Johnson (1977A).

Weber, Max. *The Protestant Ethic and the Spirit of Capitalism.* New York: Charles Scribner's Sons, 1958. First published in German in 1904–1905.

From Max Weber: Essays in Sociology, trans. and ed. by H. H. Gerth and C. Wright Mills. New York: Oxford University Press, 1958.

Weinberg, Martin S. "The Nudist Management of Respectability," in Douglas (1970A).

——— and A. P. Bell. *Homosexuality: An Annotated Bibliography.* New York: Harper & Row, 1972.

——— and Colin J. Williams. *Male Homosexuals.* New York: Penguin, 1975.

Westermarck, Edward. *The Origin and Development of the Moral Ideas.* London: Macmillan, 1912.

Westlake, Donald E. *The Hot Rock.* New York: Simon and Schuster, 1970.

Westley, William A. "Violence and the Police," in Henslin (1976).

Whyte, William Foote. *Street Corner Society*. Chicago: University of Chicago Press, 1955. First published in 1943.

———. "A Slum Sex Code." *American Journal of Sociology* 49 (July 1943).

Wieder, D. Lawrence. *Language and Social Reality: The Case of Telling the Convict Code*. The Hague: Mouton, 1974.

———. "Telling the Code," in Turner (1974). (Excerpt from Wieder, 1974).

Wilson, Edward O. *Sociobiology: The New Synthesis*. Cambridge, Mass. and London, England: Belknap Press, Harvard University Press, 1975.

Wirth, Louis. *The Ghetto*. Chicago: University of Chicago Press, 1928.

———. "Urbanism as a Way of Life." *American Journal of Sociology* 44: 10 (July 1938), 1–24.

Wiseman, Jacqueline P. *Stations of the Lost*. Englewood Cliffs, N.J.: Prentice-Hall, 1970.

Wolfgang, Marvin and Franco Ferracuti. *The Subculture of Violence*. London: Tavistock, 1967.

Wolfgang, Marvin E., Leonard Savitz, and Norman Johnson, eds., *The Sociology of Crime and Delinquency:* New York: Wiley, 1962.

Wright, Sam. *Crowds and Riots*. Beverly Hills, Calif.: Sage, 1978.

Wrong, Dennis H. "The Oversocialized Conception of Man in Modern Sociology." *American Sociological Review* 26: 2 (April 1961), 183–193.

Yablonsky, Lewis. *The Violent Gang*. New York: Macmillan, 1962.

Yinger, J. M. *Religion, Society and the Individual*. New York: Macmillan, 1957.

Zaretscky, Irving I. and Mark P. Leone, eds. *Religious Movements in Contemporary America*. Princeton, N.J.: Princeton University Press, 1977.

Zimmerman, Donald H. "Record-keeping and the Intake Process in a Public Welfare Agency," in Stanton Wheeler, ed. *On Record*. New York: Russell Sage Foundation, 1969A.

———. "Tasks and Troubles: The Practical Bases of Work Activities in a Public Assistance Organization," in Donald Hanson, ed., *Explorations in Sociology and Counseling*. Boston: Houghton Mifflin, 1969B.

Zola, Irving Kenneth. "Observations on Gambling in a Lower-Class Setting," in Becker (1964.)

Index